Shaping Ceremony

Publication of this book has been aided by grants from
the von Bothmer Publication Fund of the Archaeological
Institute of America, the Center for Humanities of the
University of Rhode Island, and the Warren G. Moon
Endowment of the University of Wisconsin Press.

Shaping Ceremony
Monumental Steps and Greek Architecture

Mary B. Hollinshead

THE UNIVERSITY OF WISCONSIN PRESS

The University of Wisconsin Press
1930 Monroe Street, 3rd Floor
Madison, Wisconsin 53711-2059
uwpress.wisc.edu

3 Henrietta Street, Covent Garden
London WC2E 8LU, United Kingdom
eurospanbookstore.com

Copyright © 2015
The Board of Regents of the University of Wisconsin System
All rights reserved. Except in the case of brief quotations embedded in critical articles and reviews, no part of this publication may be reproduced, stored in a retrieval system, transmitted in any format or by any means—digital, electronic, mechanical, photocopying, recording, or otherwise—or conveyed via the Internet or a website without written permission of the University of Wisconsin Press. Rights inquiries should be directed to rights@uwpress.wisc.edu.

Library of Congress Cataloging-in-Publication Data

Hollinshead, Mary Brooks Berg, author.
Shaping ceremony : monumental steps and Greek architecture / Mary B. Hollinshead.
    pages cm — (Wisconsin studies in classics)
  Includes bibliographical references and index.
  ISBN 978-0-299-30110-1 (cloth : alk. paper)—ISBN 978-0-299-30113-2 (e-book)
  1. Stairs—Greece. 2. Monuments—Greece. 3. Architecture, Greek. I. Title. II. Series: Wisconsin studies in classics.
NA278.S75H65 2015
721'.8320938—dc23
2014007280

Contents

List of Illustrations vii
Preface xi

INTRODUCTION 3

PART I Studying Steps

CHAPTER 1 Biomechanics 19

CHAPTER 2 Theoretical Observations 25

CHAPTER 3 Social Effects and Political Consequences 29

PART II Evidence of Steps over Time

CHAPTER 4 Early Steps

Dreros, Perachora, Eleusis, Lindos, Athens (ramp), Corinth (ramp), Aegina (ramp), Selinus (Temple M) 35

CHAPTER 5 Steps in the Fifth Century

Selinus, Alipheira, Oropos, Latmos, Argive Heraion, Athens: Acropolis (Propylaia, Parthenon, Erechtheion), Agora 41

CHAPTER 6 Steps in the Fourth Century

Perachora, Lato, Olympia, Mount Lykaion, Lykosoura, Labraunda, Amyzon, Halikarnassos 51

CHAPTER 7 Steps in the Third Century

Rhodes City, Lindos, Kameiros, Athens (Kolonos Agoraios), Amphipolis, Morgantina, Argos (Aspis), Thasos, Pergamon (sanctuary of Demeter), Corinth (sanctuary of Demeter and Kore) 61

CHAPTER 8 Steps in the Second Century

Kos, Knidos, Pisidia: Adada, Kapikaya, Sagalassos 72

CONCLUSION 81

APPENDIX Hellenistic Italy

Sulmo, Gabii, Pietrabbondante, Praeneste, Tivoli 89

Catalogue of Sites 97
Plates 107
Notes 173
Bibliography 197
Index 229

Illustrations

FIGURES

Map of the Aegean region 2
Map of Italy 2
Fragment of a dinos by Sophilos 10
Detail of "Tyrrhenian" amphora 11
Corinthian krater depicting the delegation to Troy 12
Detail of Corinthian krater depicting the delegation to Troy 12
Pseudo-Panathenaic amphora 13
Detail of pseudo-Panathenaic amphora 14
Detail of steps, pseudo-Panathenaic amphora 14
Figure on steps: walking, standing, sitting 22
Black-figure band cup with procession 30
Shoes 0.27 m long, with metric scale 107

PLATES

1a. Adada, steps facing the "agora" 108
1b. Adada, profile of steps facing the "agora" 108
2a. Aegina, plan of the sanctuary of Zeus 109
2b. Aegina, ramp to the sanctuary of Zeus 109
3a. Alipheira, plan of the sanctuary of Athena 110
3b. Alipheira, steps to the sanctuary of Athena 110
4a. Amphipolis, plan of the gymnasium complex 111
4b. Amphipolis, steps to the gymnasium 111
5. Amyzon, plan of the sanctuary 112
6a. Argive Heraion, plan of the Middle Terrace and retaining walls 113
6b. Argive Heraion, steps south and east of the South Stoa, up to the Middle Terrace 113
7a. Argos, Aspis, plan of the sanctuary 114
7b. Argos, Aspis, general view of the altar and steps from the west 115
7c. Argos, Aspis, steps and altar from the south 115
8a. Athens, Acropolis, plan with ramp 116
8b. Athens, Acropolis, sixth-century ramp from the north 116
9a. Athens, Acropolis, plan of the predecessor to the Propylaia 117
9b. Athens, Acropolis, reconstruction drawing of the predecessor to the Propylaia 117
10a. Athens, Acropolis, plan of the steps west of the Parthenon 118
10b. Athens, Acropolis, section drawing of the steps west of the Parthenon 118
10c. Athens, Acropolis, steps west of the Parthenon from the north 119
11a. Athens, Acropolis, Erechtheion, actual state plan 120
11b. Athens, Acropolis, Erechtheion, restored plan of the fifth century B.C. 120
11c. Athens, Acropolis, Erechtheion, North Court from the east 121
12a. Athens, Agora, plan of structures on the west side, with benches 122

12b. Athens, Agora, benches on the west side below the Hephaisteion 122
13. Athens, Agora, plan in the Hellenistic period, with steps to Kolonos Agoraios 123
14a. Corinth, Temple Hill and the Sacred Spring, plan 124
14b. Corinth, general view of the ramp and temple from the southeast 124
14c. Corinth, ramp to the temple from the southeast 125
14d. Corinth, the Sacred Spring from the north 125
15a. Corinth, plan of the sanctuary of Demeter and Kore, 400 B.C. 126
15b. Corinth, plan of the sanctuary of Demeter and Kore, 275 B.C. 126
15c. Corinth, sanctuary of Demeter and Kore from the northwest 127
16a. Didyma, Sanctuary of Apollo, plan with spectator steps 128
16b. Didyma, upper edge of spectator steps and temple from the southeast 129
16c. Didyma, spectator steps from the west 129
17a. Dreros, plan of the "agora" 130
17b. Dreros, steps facing the "agora" from the west 131
18a. Eleusis, plan of sixth-century structures 132
18b. Eleusis, the sixth-century grandstand 132
19. Halikarnassos, plan of the Maussolleion 133
20a. Kameiros, plan of the lower sector of town 134
20b. Kameiros, "agora," steps, and precinct from the south 134
21. Kapikaya, grandstand steps from the north 135
22a. Knidos, plan of the sanctuary of Apollo 136
22b. Knidos, model of the sanctuary of Apollo 136
22c. Knidos, spectator steps and altar from the southeast 137
22d. Knidos, spectator steps from the east 137

23a. Kos, plan of the sanctuary of Asklepios 138
23b. Kos, reconstruction drawing of the sanctuary of Asklepios 139
23c. Kos, steps to the Upper Terrace before restoration 139
24a. Labraunda, plan of the sanctuary 140
24b. Labraunda, Great Stairway from the southeast 140
25a. Latmos, distant view of "agora" 141
25b. Latmos, steps along the "agora" 141
26a. Lato, plan of the "agora" and temple area 142
26b. Lato, steps to the prytaneion 143
26c. Lato, theatral steps below the temple 143
27a. Lindos, plan of the sixth-century steps 144
27b. Lindos, sixth-century steps as excavated 144
27c. Lindos, plan of the sanctuary of Athena in the third century and later 145
27d. Lindos, third-century steps before restoration 145
27e. Lindos, model of the sanctuary of Athena 146
28a. Lykosoura, plan of the sanctuary 147
28b. Lykosoura, steps and south side of the temple from the east 147
29a. Morgantina, plan of the agora 148
29a. Morgantina, agora steps from the east 149
30a. Mount Lykaion, steps from the west before excavation 150
30b. Mount Lykaion, excavated steps from the northeast 150
30c. Mount Lykaion, plan of the steps 150
31a. Olympia, plan of the northern sector of the sanctuary of Zeus 151
31b. Olympia, model of the north side of the sanctuary of Zeus 152
31c. Olympia, steps along the north side of the sanctuary of Zeus, from the east 153
32a. Oropos, Amphiaraion, plan of the temple and altar area 154
32b. Oropos, Amphiaraion, steps facing the altar 155

Illustrations

33a. Perachora, plan of the sanctuary of Hera, lower and upper sectors   156
33b. Perachora, aerial photo of the sanctuary, lower and upper sectors, from the west   157
33c. Perachora, steps by the altar from the southwest   158
33d. Perachora, tumbled steps in the upper sanctuary from the south   158
34a. Pergamon, plan of the sanctuary of Demeter   159
34b. Pergamon, sanctuary of Demeter from the east   159
35. Rhodes City, plan of the sanctuary of Apollo   160
36a. Sagalassos, plan of the temple area   161
36b. Sagalassos, reconstruction drawing   162
36c. Sagalassos, profile of the steps from the east   162
37a. Selinus, reconstruction drawing of Temple M   163
37b. Selinus, steps and base of Temple M from the southeast   163
38a. Selinus, plan of the acropolis   164
38b. Selinus, aerial view of the acropolis from the northeast   164
38c. Selinus, acropolis, stepped retaining wall from the southeast   165
39. Thasos, plan of the Herakleion   166
40a. Gabii, plan of the sanctuary of Juno   167
40b. Gabii, reconstruction drawing of the sanctuary of Juno   167
41a. Pietrabbondante, plan of the sanctuary   168
41b. Pietrabbondante, sanctuary from behind the temple, from the northwest   168
42. Praeneste, aerial view of the sanctuary of Fortuna from the west   169
43a. Sulmo, plan of the sanctuary of Hercules   170
43b. Sulmo, sanctuary of Hercules: terrace and steps to the shrine from the south   170
44a. Tivoli, plan of the sanctuary of Hercules   171
44b. Tivoli, model of the sanctuary of Hercules   171

Preface

Investigating change in Greek monumental architecture led me to steps. Although I started from the formalist observation that steps link terraces to form architectural complexes, I soon realized how much steps reveal about human use. Most fundamentally, steps provide direct evidence of where and how people placed their bodies, allowing us to reconstruct individuals' posture, then behavior, then group activities, and even to extrapolate political maneuvering in the distant past. Instead of the bird's eye view of the formalist, I have adopted a ground-level perspective, working from the actions of participants to larger issues of how broad steps express and direct human activities.

Over the long years of producing this book, I have encountered surprising numbers of friends, colleagues, acquaintances, and strangers who confess to an interest in steps. I suspect their interest stems from their somatic experience with stairs and steps, and also their perception of how places are defined by pathways and framing. Colleagues who are scholars of ancient Greece have indulged my fascination with monumental steps as a personal idiosyncrasy; the study of Greek architecture after all can focus on such singular accomplishments as temples and theaters, stoas and tombs. However, the value of steps lies in their lack of single focus, in their connectivity, linking structures and spaces of the built environment. As overt expressions of people's practices, monumental steps also offer specific information that helps describe the interaction between human behavior and built form in the ancient Greek world.

I have visited every site discussed here, so as to view and use these various built forms. I have ascended, descended, and sat on nearly every example of steps, unless prevented by fencing (Gabii) or reburial (Amphipolis, Kolonos Agoraios in Athens). I took many of the photographs, most of which include a pair of shoes 0.27 m long, as an informal scale and a reminder that people once walked, stood, or sat on them (see p. 107). Visualizing topography from two-dimensional images is a challenge. Although the illustrations of sites are grouped separately at the back of the book, plans and photographs are paired for each site so as to provide maximum clarity. As for transliterating Greek names of people, places, and structures, I have elected to use the hellenized version (Mausolos not Mausolus, Kos not Cos) unless a term is commonly used in its Latin form (such as "acropolis" or "Corinth"). All dates are B.C., unless specified otherwise.

Topographical research requires travel to sites. I am grateful to those who supported the journeys that led to this book. The Graham Foundation for Advanced Studies in the Fine Arts and the National Endowment for the Humanities provided crucial funding, and the Center for the Humanities at the University of Rhode Island has supported my work at several critical times, as has the

Preface

University of Rhode Island Foundation. The Archaeological Institute of America's von Bothmer Fund contributed a subvention grant for drawing plans. In the course of my research I have benefited from the hospitality and the facilities of the American School of Classical Studies at Athens (with special help from Bob Bridges) and the American Research Institute in Turkey at Ankara. At the University of Rhode Island, Dean Winifred Brownell has encouraged my work, and members of the Department of Art and Art History, especially Wendy Roworth, Ron Onorato, Barbara Pagh, and Bob Dilworth, have actively supported me and this project.

Several colleagues deserve golden crowns for their efforts on my behalf. David Scahill drove to sites large and small in western Turkey with a woman he had never met, talking architecture and pedagogy all the while. When the manuscript was mostly complete, the late Miranda Marvin provided an astute, precise, and generous critique with her lovely mix of intelligence and exuberance. In preparing plans and images for publication, I have benefited beyond measure from the expertise and engagement of Cornelie Piok Zanon and Linda Mugica. Cornelie drew many of the plans, bringing the knowledge of a scholar, the hand of an architect, and the generosity of a friend to the task of making sites with steps legible. Curator of Visual Resources at the University of Rhode Island Linda Mugica prepared all the images for publication with a professional skill and personal enthusiasm that turned a challenging process into gratifying collaboration. Each of these colleagues has been an essential and substantial contributor—they are the unsung heroes of this book.

This project has shifted shape over time, reflecting my own changing ideas and experiences. An array of friends learned much more about ancient architecture than they ever imagined. Gina Borromeo has contributed enthusiasm and support over many years, as have Bonna Wescoat, the late Rebecca Molholt, Anne Weis, Bridget Buxton, Angela Murock Hussein, Betsy Charnecki, Paula Foresman, Glynnis Kennon, Wendy Oliver, Joyce Barrett, and countless others. Along the way, the kindness of professional colleagues has come as grace notes in the solitary slogging of the scholar. I appreciate timely assistance from Nancy Bookidis, Karen Bouchard, Clemency Coggins, Cecile Colonna, Sherry Fox, Hans Rupprecht Goette, Heather Grossman, Markos Katsianis, Wolfgang Radt, Thangam Ravindranathan, Andrew Reinhard, and David Romano, as well as many scholars who graciously granted permission to reproduce images: Martin Almagro-Gorbea, Marc P. Anderson, Hansgeorg Bankel, Malcolm Bell III, Kalliopi Christophi, Alexandra Christopoulou and George Kakavas, Rosanna DiPinto and Antonio Paolucci, Emanuele Greco, Carlo Fulvio Giuliani, Maria Cristina Guidotti and Andrea Pessina, Samantha Henneberry, Lars Karlsson, Adriano LaRegina, Kalliopi Lazarides and Tatiana Poulou, Evi Lempidaki, Douglas McCarthy, Anneliese Peschlow, Christopher Pfaff, Laura Pompeo, Bodil Bundgaard Rasmussen, David Gilman Romano, Ulrich Sinn, Larissa Skurka, Olga Tabolacci, Marc Waelkens, and Zoubida Zerkane.

I am grateful to Mark Stansbury-O'Donnell, Adam Mehring, Raphael Kadushin, Matthew Cosby, and Carla Marolt at the University of Wisconsin Press, who have been exceptionally responsive and helpful. Jane Barry's diplomatic, expert copyediting has enhanced the text and its coherence. The reviewers for the Press offered productive comments that improved my work in ways that I have been happy to incorporate into the book.

My parents, C. John and Elizabeth B. Berg, did not live to see the end of the book, but they gave

Preface

me a lifetime of care and encouragement. I have loved sharing this project with my three daughters, Cary Hollinshead-Strick, Sarah Hollinshead Sigman, and Jane Hollinshead (Barbera), each a participant in travel, research, and writing. The person who has walked with me every step of this route is Bill Hollinshead, whose challenging edits, steadfast patience, and lasting love have enriched this book, and my life. *Shaping Ceremony* is dedicated to him.

Shaping Ceremony

Map of the Aegean region. (Drawn by C. Piok Zanon)

Map of Italy. (Drawn by C. Piok Zanon)

Introduction

Steps make uneven terrain convenient for humans. They are pathways and destinations for climbing and descending, for sitting and standing. As pathways, steps create processional routes toward and within cities and sanctuaries; as destinations, they serve as grandstands for viewing and participating in communal events. Some steps imply movement, while others suggest static behavior. In fact, the dimensions of steps express a direct relation to body posture, so that we can often tell whether their users were sitting, standing, or walking. By examining monumental steps in ancient Greek architecture, we can derive behavior from architectural form, and trace interactions between human activities and the built environment.

Broad steps intended for public use are rarely considered as significant architectural components, yet they gave shape to challenging slopes, framed ceremonies, and defined nearby structures. (My focus is on independent sets of steps and does not include those that are part of structures such as temples, altars, or stoas.) This book is about monumental steps of stone, built to be permanent. Lost, large-scale stepped structures in wood are attested, as discussed below, but this study is limited to extant remains. Monumentality indicates a size larger than needed for essential function; for steps, monumentality means primarily breadth, since it can be adjusted without changing the end points or height. Despite the widespread assumption that monumentality embodies political dominance, I contend that the intentionally grand, broad steps of the ancient Greek world more often expressed behaviors and attitudes that were fundamentally communal in nature.[1]

Most examples of ancient Greek monumental steps are found in sanctuaries, where they provide tangible evidence of how participants experienced sacred spaces and what they did at festivals. Whether by directing access to places and structures or by framing special locations, steps articulate secular and sacred practices. Broad monumental steps accommodate throngs of people and convey an image of large-scale participation even when empty. Together with historical information from inscriptions and texts, the archaeological evidence of broad steps bears witness to the importance of specific sanctuaries and their large festivals in sustaining social stability and promoting political viability in the ancient Greek world. Over time, the expanding use of monumental steps can be tied to events and strategies, such as compensating for urban displacement (*metoikesis*) or public expression of beneficence (euergetism). In this book I discuss steps at specific sites in the Classical world and their implication for ceremonies, social patterns, and political relations, as well as architectural form.

Introduction

In formal terms, it is breadth rather than length that creates the perception of size because extended horizontal lines perpendicular to the slope in which they are set emphasize the intentional, constructed character of steps. Such breadth suggests a public role. When they are present in repeated rows, the added vertical repetition of broad steps creates visual emphasis and potential for architectural display, as well as the capacity for large numbers of people. The form of monumental steps embodies order, and the scale implies capacity for crowds. Combined, they project authority.

Since steps served to link and frame spaces and structures, examining their evolving role at sanctuary sites over several centuries allows us to document the processes by which large architectural complexes came into existence, integrating multiple structures into coherent compositions. Originally, steps were functional single components, with little apparent symbolic value. However, their proximity to sacred structures (temples, altars) in consecrated precincts, and the need to serve large numbers of worshippers at festivals, promoted their monumental treatment in terms of material, scale, and placement. Once built in such permanent form, steps then embodied the size and grandeur of the events for which they were constructed. Their increasing use reflects both expanded celebrations and expanded awareness of the power and symbolism of architecture itself. A formal path controls and directs the behavior of visitors to a site, and offers opportunities to affect their experience through the placement of structures, as seen in the locations of the various *androns* at Labraunda in Asia Minor, whose fine marble façades faced the processional way. Steps as grandstands adjacent to altars or ceremonial loci provide a spatial accentuation that adds intensity to performance.[2] While steps obtain most of their meaning from their relationships to other components of the built environment, the combined objectives of controlling access and framing spaces promoted symmetry in Greek sanctuary design, extending the principle from individual structures and terraces to entire sanctuaries.

The first goal of this book is to draw attention to steps as components of monumental construction at Greek sites as early as the sixth century. Sites considered to fall within the Greek cultural sphere extend beyond the Greek mainland and islands of the Aegean to include western Asia Minor and south Italy and Sicily. In addition to documenting the number and nature of monumental steps, close critical reading of the respective sites offers an assessment of how broad steps may have functioned in their physical, social, and historical contexts. I also address important issues of scale, ranging from a single person on a slope to the collective experience of sacrificial rites and festivals to political uses of architectural patronage. Surveying specific examples of broad steps from the sixth to the second century reveals growing Greek appreciation for the power of populous celebration as displayed in architecture.

The chronological organization of this book is intended to reveal phases of development at particular sites and to highlight larger social and political trends as reflected in architecture. Because the labels "Archaic," "Classical," and "Hellenistic" trigger aesthetic notions of relative quality or at least expectations about appearance, this book is structured by century. Historically, 480 B.C. was a critical date in Athens, but less significant elsewhere. Without denying Alexander's influence, the historical demarcation of 323 B.C. as a watershed creates an artificial interruption that makes it more difficult to see continuities during the fourth century, and between the fourth and third centuries. Organization by century is equally arbitrary but less likely to foster preconceptions. Readers will find

Introduction

the traditional terms "Archaic," "Classical," and "Hellenistic" here, but I have exercised care in using them. This framework does not presuppose a linear progression but allows for comparisons among contemporary sites together with changes over time. The enduring construction of monumental stone structures requires us to interpret their uses and meanings with attention to their extended uselives, beyond the era of their construction.[3] For example, steps commissioned to demonstrate the generosity, virtue, and authority of a particular patron, such as Hieron II at Morgantina, served public gatherings for centuries past the patron's demise. After displaying an individual's power, the steps later embodied communal activity. I consider sequential changes within sites, as well as among cities and sanctuaries. Sites such as Lindos, Kos, or Morgantina, at which we can observe the addition or enlargement of steps during the active life of the site, furnish valuable evidence of the dramatic effects brought about by incremental modifications. While the form of steps is utilitarian enough (and the slope often specific enough) to circumscribe the range of their uses, their role in a social system can change over time.[4]

Tradition is the result of repetition over time. Since Greek architecture is characterized by the consistent representation of many components, it is not surprising that ancient Greek buildings are usually treated as a set of typologies of form. Most conspicuously, we identify systems of structure and ornament as orders or subsets of them, such as categories of capitals or moldings.[5] Likewise, buildings such as temples and theaters, or separate structures such as altars and tombs, have been analyzed primarily as individual types.[6] While such a strategy facilitates comparisons across time and space, Zedeño has observed, "typologies . . . rarely convey the historical depth and conceptual wealth encoded in behavioral transformations of place."[7] Although my subject is an architectural form, an obvious typological category, my concern is less the morphological taxonomy of steps per se than their social aspects and their role in architectural contexts.

A central challenge to anyone studying early steps is to shed the experience and attendant assumptions of later architectural history. The Romans' extensive use of monumental steps has led some to associate the form with centralized political authority, leading to the corollary supposition that Greek architecture lacked monumental steps until Hellenistic kings built them as flamboyant structures to assert their rule.[8] In fact, they appear much earlier, and careful scrutiny of pre-Roman monumental steps reveals a more complex picture that requires attention to what took place on steps: to festivals and ceremonies, their participants and patrons.

PREVIOUS SCHOLARSHIP

Monumental steps draw little attention in most discussions of ancient Greek architecture.[9] Because they serve as both a distinct form and a connective component within an architectural assemblage, typological analysis cannot offer an adequate explanation. Thomas Becker's comprehensive *Griechische Stufenanlagen* is richly informative but hews to a taxonomic model.[10] Inge Nielsen's wide-ranging *Cultic Theaters and Ritual Drama* is informed by her hypothesis of function, from which she derives the "cultic theater" as a building type.[11] My study overlaps both Becker's and Nielsen's but focuses more on architectural, social, and historical contexts. Among typologies, studies of theaters and assembly places by W. A. MacDonald, Dilke, Ginouvès, and Kolb contain valuable information about stepped structures, as do more recent studies by R. Frederiksen on theaters as

Introduction

well as M.-H. Hansen and T. Fischer-Hansen on political assembly-places.[12] Early studies on spatial relationships among structures in Greek sanctuaries by Scranton, P. W. Lehmann, Martiensen, Doxiadis, and Bergquist present a more integrated view of architecture than the typological approach, yet these formal analyses leave the sanctuaries without human participants.[13]

On the other hand, research focused on the practices of ritual, relying on images, votive objects, inscriptions, and literary testimonia, has provided extensive documentation of human behavior and commentary on performance, but rarely includes much about architectural setting, with the exception of the Athenian Acropolis.[14] That situation has begun to change. To be sure, studies of many individual sites incorporate all available information. Hölscher's parsing of the multiple spatial networks (religious, ritual, monumental, competitive, political) in simultaneous operation at Olympia offers an especially effective mode of discussing patterns of sanctuary use at a single site.[15] M. Scott's analysis of the placement of dedications identifies meaning in spatial relationships within the sanctuaries at Delphi and Olympia, and his recent *Space and Society in the Greek and Roman Worlds* takes a more comprehensive view of his theme.[16] Dickenson and van Nijf's *Public Space in the Post-Classical City* includes Williamson's article on Karian sanctuaries as public spaces, as well as articles on Hellenistic and Roman urban space.[17] Studies under the rubric of Ritual Dynamics have contributed extensive comparanda across many cultures and time periods, with valuable analyses of ancient ritual; articles on Greek ritual and space by Mylonopoulos incorporate physical evidence that includes architecture, even stairways.[18] McMahon has applied many of the same sources and approaches used in this book in her study of the Neo-Assyrian palace at Khorsabad.[19] Papers in Wescoat and Ousterhout's *Architecture of the Sacred* explore intersections of space, ritual, and experience in ancient and medieval times.[20] Accounts and analyses of processions by Connor, Sourvinou-Inwood, Chaniotis, and Graf have drawn on written and archaeological evidence in reconstructing spatial aspects of ritual practice, and studies of pilgrimage and ritual (including theater) increasingly situate behavior in specific settings.[21] Moser and Feldman's *Locating the Sacred* includes studies of societies of various times and places focused on the "emplacement" of ritual.[22] On a broader scale, studies of sanctuaries in their landscape settings, such as those by Jost, Cole, and Alcock and Osborne, not only locate behaviors and beliefs within sanctuary space, but also seek meaning in natural and built environments.[23] De Polignac's general concept of extraurban sanctuaries as territorial outposts for *poleis* has generated years of lively exchange on the relations among sanctuaries, geography, poleis, and politics. His subsequent revisions, emphasizing the role of extraurban sanctuaries as loci for mediation and competition, come closer to my understanding of sanctuaries, which has benefited from subsequent scholarship.[24] This book thus expands the scope of traditional architectural history and shares with modern scholarship a more spatially situated, historically contextual view of structures and behavior.

I aim to focus primarily on settings for ritual and ceremony, using methodology described by P. Wilson: "Interpretation arrives at an apprehension of . . . complexity through a 'bottom-up' approach, from the evidence for material conditions."[25] Close scrutiny of sites with broad steps shows how monumental steps prescribed people's body posture, position, and movement, even as they linked and framed structures and spaces to create integrated architectural complexes. The Greeks' increasing recognition of the power of the constructed environment (beyond the obvious prestige

Introduction

and authority of a single building, such as a temple) led to enhancements, expansion, and emulation at several sanctuaries. The first part of this book presents physical, theoretical, and contextual approaches to studying steps. Specific sites that I use to demonstrate my argument are discussed more fully in part II. Beginning with the biomechanics of the human body on a slope, I use measurements of broad steps as indicators of their function: as retaining walls, routes of access, or grandstands. Theoretical observations about architecture and behavior, the focus of chapter 2, are followed in chapter 3 by a generalized account of festival activities in a sanctuary setting, with attention to how worshippers behaved on steps and some political consequences of well-attended festivals. The chapters of part II, organized by century, present detailed analyses of particular sites across the Greek world (the Greek mainland, Aegean islands, western Asia Minor, south Italy, and Sicily) and document the increasing use of monumental steps over time. The size and importance of sites vary widely, as does available contextual information from objects, inscriptions, and historical records. In each chapter, I emphasize a few key sites so as to develop themes and comparisons; the order is admittedly idiosyncratic. An appendix presents second-century sites in central Italy that appear to emulate contemporary sites in the Greek world and so are often labeled "Hellenistic." I include the Italian sites in the Conclusion for the sake of a more complete discussion. Finally, a catalogue provides additional factual information, plans, and bibliography for each site.

I have omitted a few sites, and I have undoubtedly overlooked others. The rock-cut steps adjacent to the Telesterion at Eleusis are striking examples of monumental steps but are probably Roman (Hadrianic?) in date.[26] At the Greek colony of Cyrene in modern Libya, excavators noted a long, broad stairway about 14 m wide and 150 m long leading to the extramural sanctuary of Demeter and Kore. A date for these steps has not been determined, because they have never been systematically excavated or recorded, and the site has been inaccessible for further inspection.[27] Other monumental steps, at Sia in Pisidia (southwest Asia Minor), are also unexplored and datable to either Hellenistic or Roman times.[28]

BUILDINGS THAT INCORPORATE STEPS

Although my focus is on independent monumental steps and how they served to enhance or link nearby buildings or features, broad steps were incorporated into the design of some freestanding individual structures so conspicuously as to claim our attention. Not surprisingly, broad steps embedded in a single structure generate many of the same visual effects and practical uses, so that within buildings they were used as platforms (roughly equivalent to retaining walls), as routes of access, and as facilities for viewing. Becker included ranks of steps across the façades of temples in Sicily and western Asia Minor in his corpus of monumental steps, and he also discussed large stepped altars.[29] Facing each other across the location of ritual enactment, both stepped components contributed formal coherence to the temple-altar complex while providing places for viewing and performing sacrifice. On the other hand, Nielsen sought to isolate an independent type of building centered on theatral steps.[30] Acknowledging the importance of these earlier studies and the relevance of the material they present to my topic, I have nevertheless chosen to focus on monumental steps that were constructed independent of other buildings so as to emphasize their several functions and their role in public activities.

Introduction

Elevation by means of a platform is a structurally simple way to isolate and so draw attention to a structure. Multi-stepped bases gave visibility and distinction to monumental tombs in Asia Minor and points east, as discussed below (pp. 36–37). While most mainland temples sat on platforms of three steps, the grand Ionic temples of Asia Minor and Doric temples of all sizes in Magna Graecia were often set on higher bases with more steps. The repeated long horizontal lines of temples' platforms, together with their elevation, differentiate these buildings from others and designate them as special structures while creating a sense of emphatic placement on the land. The great temple of Apollo at Didyma (begun in the late fourth–early third century and never completed) encompasses an architectural topography in and of itself. Set on a 3.15 m high base of seven tall steps 0.45 m high (with a central rank of steps half that high for human ascent), the enormous temple articulates an internal vertical drop of nearly 5 m with a 15.24 m wide monumental staircase along the east end of the open-air cella facing the naiskos, probably the seat of the oracle, which housed a sacred spring.[31] This rank of broad steps formed a substantial retaining wall, made necessary by the discrepancy between the ground level of the sacred spring in the naiskos and the elevated platform that proclaimed the temple's prestige. Direct passage from the colonnade to the cella courtyard was diverted by an impassably high "threshold" in the two-columned chamber at the back of the deep pronaos, so that visitors could reach the inner courtyard only by means of vaulted passages from either side of the pronaos to the ground level of the interior.[32] Because inscriptions from the temple specify that the inner chamber was an *adyton*, reserved for priests, it seems more likely that these grand interior steps served groups of attendants at oracular ceremonies instead of throngs of worshippers.[33]

The strong horizontal lines of stepped monumental altars undoubtedly found a visual correspondence in the stepped platforms of temples, often aligned facing them. Within such altars, broad steps served as routes of access to an open court (perhaps for burnt sacrifices and ashes) or to an offering table at the level of the topmost step.[34] The second-century Great Altar at Pergamon represents the most flamboyant example of this use of broad steps, but grand altars with monumental steps are attested from the sixth century on (e.g., the Rhoikos altar at Samos, Cape Monodendri) and throughout the history of Greek architecture, as seen in altars at, for example, Priene, Tenos, and Magnesia.[35] Altars with enough steps to ascend to a distinctive height seem to recapitulate, in an abstract and symbolic way, the elevation of sacred places in a natural terrain. They also allowed more participants to see, hear, and smell the ritual taking place at the altar.[36]

The role of steps in viewing from above, as embodied in the Greek theater, bouleuterion, and other assembly halls, presents challenges for our definitions. The specialized Telesterion at Eleusis incorporated steps for viewing rites within the building (as well as outside it; see below, pp. 38 and 100 as early as the later sixth century; the configuration persisted through multiple modifications of the building. The varying dimensions of the steps over time, from 0.27 m high and 0.30–0.31 m wide (Peisistratid) to 0.40–0.45 m wide (Kimonian) to 0.60–0.72 m wide (Periklean) might suggest a change in practice from standing to sitting, but they may simply reflect rebuilding on a progressively more generous scale.[37] From the fifth century on, facilities for dramatic performance that we define as self-contained theaters were constructed in stone, and their form became more standardized over time.[38] Hansen and Fischer-Hansen have shown that comparable processes of regularization occurred in facilities such as bouleuteria and ekklesiasteria, used for other public gatherings in the late Classical and Hellenistic periods.[39]

Introduction

The present study includes steps that are "theatral" in the sense of enhancing users' seeing and hearing, but are not encased within a clearly defined theater or assembly building. Such distinctions are not difficult when perimeter walls enclose stepped seats, but less formal boundaries sometimes obscure the difference between monumental steps of a theatral nature and what we have come to consider a standard type of building (e.g., steps for ekklesiasteria, or assembly buildings).[40] Niceties of labeling and typology such as these have significant consequences. By excluding assembly-places built to house political bodies, for example, I have concentrated my attention primarily (but not exclusively) on sanctuaries, especially those of the fourth century and later. Maintaining this focus on evidence for monumental steps as independent but interactive components of architectural settings, however, brings useful insights into how festivals took place in a variety of sanctuaries.

EVIDENCE FOR OTHER STEPS: *IKRIA* AND IMAGES ON VASES

This book is about extant examples of monumental steps, but it is worth noting whatever information remains about steps no longer preserved and steps depicted on vases. Based on accounts in written testimonia and careful excavation, archaeologists have identified ancient post-holes that may indicate the placement of stepped wooden bleachers (*ikria*) at Athens, Metapontum, and Corinth. Images on black- and red-figure vases of the sixth and fifth centuries show grandstands in use, with people perched on stepped structures. Without assuming a photographic role of precise representation for painted images, we can nevertheless imagine spectators' actions and glean some information from these vases.

Several ancient authors (all late in date) mention *ikria* in reference to structures in the Athenian Agora. The term refers most specifically to upright wooden posts, as described by Hesychius (probably fifth century A.D.): "[The stands] were upright timbers, with planks attached to them like steps; on these planks the audience sat, before the theatre was built."[41] The meaning of the term was apparently often broadened to encompass wooden benches or bleachers, as well as scaffolding or platforms.[42] Other authors, perhaps derived from the same source, also identify *ikria* in the Agora as predecessors to the theater of Dionysos; these texts have provoked extensive debate about the evolution of the theater cavea, a topic beyond the scope of this study.[43] These testimonia also report that *ikria* were used for sitting and standing, and that they collapsed on at least two occasions in the fifth century B.C.[44] A passage in Aristophanes' *Thesmophorizusai* (v. 395) of 411 B.C. refers to men coming home "ἀπὸ τῶν ἰκρίων" ("from the bleachers"), used metonymically for the wooden benches of the theater.[45]

In the Athenian Agora, holes for wooden posts have been found along either side of the Panathenaic Way, and additional examples have been identified in the Kerameikos near the Dipylon Gate.[46] These post-holes suggest that a grandstand-like structure had been set up along the processional way, comparable to the bleachers we erect along a modern parade route. Taking into account information from Pollux (7.125), who describes *ikriopoioi* as those who build *ikria* around the Agora, and Athenaeus (4.167), who mentions them setting up *ikria* along the route of the Panathenaic procession, we can reasonably assume that temporary wooden structures with stepped benches for spectators to either sit or stand on were set up periodically for a variety of events, from performances to processions.[47] Excavations at Metapontum in southern Italy have revealed traces of what may have been *ikria*. A well-defined stratum of carbonized wood dating to the late seventh century

Introduction

Fragment of a dinos by Sophilos, Athens NM 15499. (Courtesy of the National Archaeological Museum, Athens; photograph by G. Patrikianos)

was identified below the orchestra of the later ekklesiasterion, a large circular structure superseded by a theater in the fourth century.[48] Given the continuity of use demonstrated by the sequence of the two later structures, we assume that the earliest remains had a comparable function and so represent the residue of wooden stands for communal viewing or gathering. Cuttings and curbstones of the fourth century at Corinth have been interpreted as installations for wooden bleachers, providing a later example of such facilities.[49] This evidence, and that from Metapontum, suggests that wooden viewing stands were used from an early date, and in more locations than Athens.[50]

Among the four black-figure vases (or vase fragments) with images of grandstands, the best known is a fragment of an Athenian dinos signed by Sophilos and dated to 570 B.C.[51] The upper of the two friezes shows the funerary games for Patroklos, as in *Iliad* Book 23. Two pairs of horses gallop to the right, with reins to chariots now broken off on the left edge. Facing the horses, on a much smaller scale, is a stepped structure with ten men, all but two with beards, watching the chariot race. Three of the spectators extend their arms in excited gestures; one appears to brandish a long rod (a spear?). Additional stepped seats face the right, where five figures face another part of the race, or else another scene of heroic contest. There were presumably at least six more figures, if the missing part of the structure and the distribution of its occupants was comparable to that preserved facing left. The men are all seated except for a beardless youth at the top step, whose torso faces right even as he turns his head back to watch the chariots. While many scholars have assumed that

Introduction

this eight-stepped structure represents *ikria*, it is rendered in solid black, which could represent either stone or wood.[52]

Two other scenes of chariot races also include ranks of spectators seated on tiered structures. A panel on the shoulder of an Attic "Tyrrhenian" amphora in Florence depicts six men, one above and behind another, seated on an elevated structure as they watch a violent chariot race to the left, with a horse on the ground and a man being trampled.[53] Among the observers, the second man from the bottom is actually standing on the ground, and a small figure sits behind and between the third and fourth figures from the bottom. The four lowest figures each extend an arm in response to the action before them. They sit on a rounded mound depicted in alternating squares of dark and light, like a checkerboard. While this pattern may indicate blocks of stone, it might also represent a cross-section of a wooden structure.[54] On a Corinthian column krater from the Astarita collection now in the Vatican, with a scene of the delegation of Menelaus, Odysseus, and Talthybios to Troy, the material of construction is more specific.[55] Each of the Greeks is shown seated on a separate tier of a stepped structure, evidently built of stone blocks whose regular courses and offset vertical joints are made clear by dark lines against the white paint of the structure. As we consider appropriate proportions for steps, it is worth noting that the lowest-ranking Achaean, the herald Talthybios, is shown with his knees slightly raised as he occupies the bottom step, which is only half the height of the other two steps.

A pseudo-Panathenaic amphora of ca. 540 B.C., from Kameiros Rhodes, now in Paris, depicts four male spectators on a stepped structure cheering on a variety of festive figures, including a flute-player, a smaller hoplite with two shields perched on two overlapping horses, a rider on the horse in the foreground, a smaller man wielding a pickaxe, and a smaller man climbing a pole.[56] Three levels of seating are shown, each treated differently: the lowest is painted black, while the next is white and the topmost is reserved. Two bearded men are seated, one on the first (lowest)

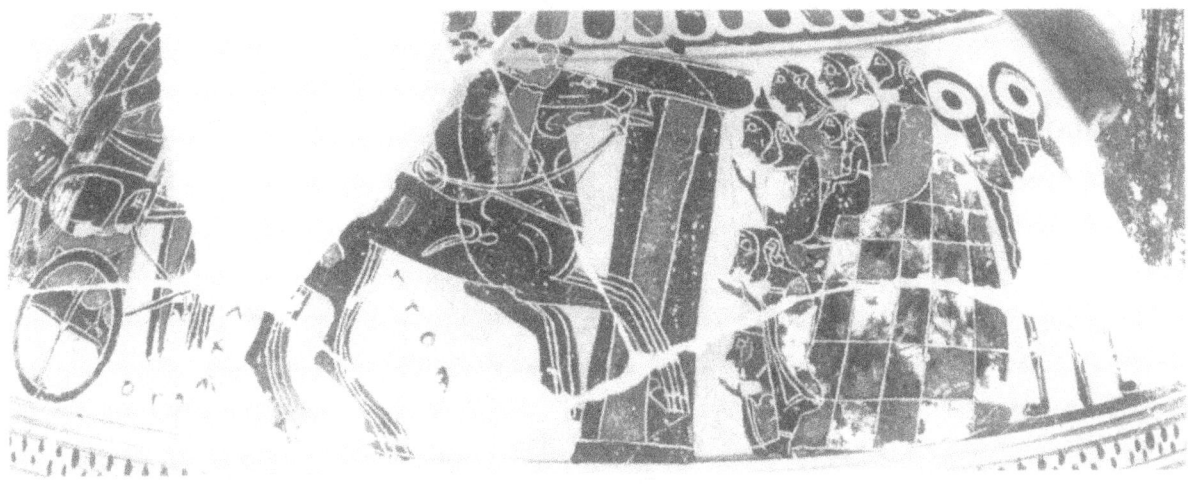

Detail of "Tyrrhenian" amphora, Florence 3773. (Courtesy of the Soprintendenza per i Beni Archeologici della Toscana-Firenze)

Corinthian krater depicting the delegation to Troy, Vatican Astarita 565. (Courtesy of the Vatican Museum)

Detail of Corinthian krater. (Courtesy of the Vatican Museum)

Introduction

Pseudo-Panathenaic amphora, Paris, Cabinet des Médailles 243. (Courtesy of the Bibliothèque Nationale de France)

and one on the third (uppermost) step, facing the activities to the right. On the second step a third bearded man sits perpendicular to the others, his body facing the viewer, while his head and right arm both turn to the right, celebrating the action. The fourth figure, a naked beardless boy, stands on the topmost step behind the seated man, gesturing toward the scene on the right, like the others. Recalling the beardless figure atop the grandstand on the fragment by Sophilos, we can speculate

Detail of pseudo-Panathenaic amphora, Paris, Cabinet des Médailles 243. (Courtesy of the Bibliothèque Nationale de France)

Detail of steps, pseudo-Panathenaic amphora, Paris, Cabinet des Médailles 243. (Courtesy of the Bibliothèque Nationale de France)

Introduction

that standing room at the top may have represented a cheap spot for agile spectators of lower status in antiquity, as it does today. The spectators' enthusiasm is expressed by their outstretched arms and the unusually specific inscription, "good for the tumbler" (κάλος τοῖ κυβιστητῶι), presumably the hoplite, the object of every figure's gaze.[57] The airborne hoplite and the inscription suggest that the scene depicts a contest similar to the *apobatai*, in which riders leaped on and off moving chariots.[58] The figure wielding the pickaxe may be breaking up the ground for a softer landing, as seen in images of jumping; however, his tool is shorter and thicker than other picks, and he looks like a terrestrial counterpart to the man on the pole.[59] Both are naked and smaller in scale than the other figures, and both are working, perhaps together. While the man on the pole could be an athlete, it is more likely that he is a worker, erecting *ikria* in both the literal and extended meanings, as upright posts for the attachment of bleachers, creating seating for the festivities. Neils has offered the equally attractive explanation that they are installing a springboard-like apparatus for the jumping contest, as seen on a red-figure skyphos from the Noble collection, now in Tampa.[60] Both workers look toward the hoplite; the vertical post supported by a diagonal brace provides a visual bracket opposite the men cheering from the steps. While we cannot expect to recreate structures from these painted images, the figures' attitudes and gestures on several vases remind us of the enthusiasm and energy of a crowd closely gathered on steps as we consider the extant physical remains of grandstands.

Before we examine the actual evidence of monumental steps at sites from the sixth through the second century, it is useful to establish a framework for analysis. Since a central theme of this book is the interaction of people and the structures they build, the logical first stage of studying steps is to assess how humans use steps, based on the function of a human body on a stepped incline. A brief discussion of theoretical perspectives relevant to architecture, agency, and ritual broadens the scope of the study, and a third section explores steps' role in generating the kind of social energy suggested by the images on these vases. After exploring these themes in part I, we apply them to the interpretation of the respective sites in part II.

PART I

Studying Steps

CHAPTER 1

Biomechanics

Beyond the basic functions of stabilizing an incline or providing passage up and down a slope, ancient builders had considerable discretion in organizing their steps: not only the number of steps to include between two points, but also the dimensions of riser (vertical face) and tread (horizontal surface). The pitch, or angle of incline, of the terrain was a key factor. The pitch of steps is the relation of riser height to tread width, usually expressed as a ratio or a percentage. It can also be expressed in degrees, measuring the angle between the horizontal and the slope of a rank of steps. While we expect uniformity of pitch in modern construction, the pitch of several examples discussed below (e.g., the Argive Heraion) changes with the changing slope of the land beneath. Slope is the equivalent of pitch, used in reference to landforms.

Builders were also constrained by the scale and capabilities of the human body, although even those limitations could be disregarded in the face of overriding aesthetic principles or cultural conventions. In large temples such as the Parthenon, the canon of setting the Greek temple on a platform of three steps whose size was dictated by the dimensions of the temple meant that the three enormous steps of the temple crepidoma (over 0.50 m high and 0.71 m deep for the Parthenon) maintain the proper design and proportions for a temple, but are useless for human worshippers. Humans could ascend to the stylobate only by way of a flight of smaller steps created by inserting intermediate blocks into the large steps in the middle of the east and west façades. The intermediate blocks form steps with a riser of 0.234 m and a tread of 0.254 m, much friendlier for human use.[1]

Determining the best form for steps involves human anatomy, absolute figures, ratios and proportions, cultural variables, and context. The mean height of men in the Classical and Hellenistic periods has been estimated at 1.705–1.719 m, about 2 percent shorter than the comparable estimate for modern American males (1.742 m).[2] This difference is not so large that we should expect a significant discrepancy in the design of steps on the basis of physical capability. At least as early as Vitruvius in the first century B.C., architectural critics proposed ideal measurements for steps.[3] Vitruvius favored a height of ¾–⅚ of a Roman foot (equivalent to 0.296 m) for ascending, with treads 1½ Roman feet wide, an approximate 1:2 ratio.[4] Those dimensions convert to steps 0.22 m high and 0.44 m wide. In the fifteenth century Leon Battista Alberti prescribed optimal dimensions for steps based on his (inaccurate) observations of the ones in ancient Greek and Roman monuments. Andrea Palladio in the sixteenth century and Vincent Scamozzi in the seventeenth each offered formulae for the dimensions of steps along with recommendations for the design of staircases.[5] Most significant is the formula generated in the seventeenth century by François Blondel, director of the French Royal Academy of Architecture, in his *Cours d'architecture* of 1675–83. Blondel was the first theorist known to have explicitly tied the dimensions of steps to the gait of humans. Converting Blondel's unit of measure to its modern equivalent, the formula reads: 2 × (riser height) + (tread width) = 64.77 cm (25.5 inches), a rule that has been perpetuated by its inclusion in the building codes of several European nations.[6] Since Blondel, others have proposed different formulae and varying desirable measurements. Templer's studies of stairs and their use led to a recommendation of risers from 11.70 to 18.29 cm (4.6–7.2 inches) with treads from 27.90 to 35.60 cm (11.0–14.0 inches) or more.[7] *Architectural Graphic Standards*, the widely used handbook for designers and builders in the United States, lists 0.15–0.18 m (6.0–7.0 inches) as optimum stair height, with a pitch of 30–35 degrees.[8] Current U.S. government regulations allow for variability in "rise/tread combinations" but require a pitch within a 30 to 50 degree range.[9]

Humans walk down steps with a different gait from the one they use ascending, intuitively seeking to keep more of the foot in contact with the tread so as to counteract forward momentum and the downward force of gravity. Consequently, adequate breadth of tread is essential for safe and secure descent.[10] Templer's optimal measurements, based on biomechanical studies combined with epidemiological data about falls and hazards, reflect his primary values of energy efficiency and safety. However, biomechanical analyses must also take contextual information into account. The landscape designer Frederick Law Olmsted, who studied people's preferences for different dimensions of steps, observed the variability of individuals and even of a single individual's experience of steps at given moments.[11] His study preceded by a generation the broader 1934 essay of French sociologist Marcel Mauss, who noted the influence of cultural expectations and behaviors on posture and gait.[12] In assessing the dimensions of ancient steps, it is important to recognize that factors other than safety and efficiency may have taken precedence, such as cost, the constraints of available space, and a variety of cultural factors. Within the limits of human capability, modern assumptions as to what is convenient, comfortable, and appropriate may not have dominated design in antiquity.

The ratio of riser to tread affects the way in which effort is expended ascending and descending. Steep steps, with relatively high risers, up to an overall pitch of 45 degrees, have relatively low *total* energy cost; however, the *rate* of energy expenditure is high, so that such steps make greater demands on the body at a given moment than those that are less steep.[13] In actual practice, the requirement for such an intensive effort, however brief, excludes people who are less physically able, and so limits the steps' use. Studies of modern users reveal a general preference for a sustained rate of physical effort, such as that required by a gentler gradient over a longer distance, as opposed to a lower total energy cost, as required by steeper, shorter steps.[14] However, both contingent and cultural factors undoubtedly affected the proportions as well as the absolute dimensions. Those who live in places with irregular topography and without modern conveyance are—and presumably were—more accepting of steeper, more challenging ascents and descents. The limitations of the human body still apply, but ancient users are likely to have tolerated a greater range of dimensions and proportions of steps than Templer assumes today.

Ramps are more economical of human energy than steps, but only up to a pitch of about 20 degrees (1:2.7), beyond which stairs are more energy-efficient for humans. This figure derives from

Biomechanics

the human ankle's maximum angle of flexion, so that ascending a ramp steeper than 20 degrees distorts the normal gait; likewise, descending a slope steeper than 50 degrees (1:0.8) exceeds the ankle's maximum downward flexion.[15] Of course, ramps also facilitate access for wheeled vehicles and quadrupeds for sacrifice, such as cattle, sheep, and oxen, for whom descent was not an issue. Ramps accommodate crowds more efficiently than steps, since individuals need not check their footing so precisely as they do on steps, and there is more flexibility in placing bodies. A significant drawback to ramps is space, since their gradual path requires approximately five times the area of stairs in achieving a comparable elevation.[16] Several examples of broad ramps (e.g., at Corinth, Athens, Aegina, Selinus), some with periodic steps, are included in this study, as their function and effect are closely comparable to those of monumental steps. The main route up to the Athenian Acropolis was a stepped path that must have begun 80 m west of the Acropolis so as to accommodate its moderate slope as it ascended to the height of the Propylaia.[17] In this case, the stepped ramp ameliorated the steep pitch of the land, presumably to accommodate the vehicles and animals of the Panathenaic procession. The extended broad path with continuous sloping surface punctuated at intervals by small risers must itself have conveyed the idea of a parade, even when empty. In use, the distance between steps would foster a slow and stately rhythm of ascent, promoting behavior and attitudes suitable for ceremonial events.[18]

While fixed measurements in general reflect the capabilities of the human body, the ratio of vertical to horizontal can suggest the primary use of steps or stairs. The dimensions of steps in this study range from risers 0.14–0.50 m in height, and treads 0.20–0.78 m wide. Combining biomechanical studies of the use of steps with contextual information at each site allows us to reconstruct how people experienced, physically and cognitively, each set of steps, leading to an interpretation of their function. Based on criteria of use, we can identify three broad categories of ancient monumental steps: they served as retaining walls, as routes of access, or as facilities for viewing.[19] These are, of course, arbitrary divisions; many broad steps had more than one function.

Steps with treads too narrow for a human foot, often with risers too high for a comfortable human stride, were built as graduated retaining walls. With no expectation of traffic up and down, there was no need to accommodate human size and capability. This design developed from the practical reality that a wall that recedes progressively from a broad base is more effective at supporting the stresses of a slope than a strictly vertical wall face. In earthquake-prone regions such as Greece, Asia Minor, and Italy, a stepped wall should be able to absorb minor displacements with less loss of structural integrity or aesthetic effect than a vertical construction. Temple C (like Temples A, D, and others) on the acropolis of Selinus is set on a dramatic terrace at least 9.8 m high with a stepped base of twenty-three (or more) courses, none recessed far enough to accommodate a foot. The narrow steps of the graduated wall for the modest fifth-century B.C. temple of Artemis at Brauron serve the secondary purpose of displaying votive stelai, a function also attested for the stepped wall below the west end of the Parthenon and elsewhere.[20]

Steps as a route of access facilitate people's movement up and down sloping terrain. For this use, absolute measurements and relative proportions are crucial, as is consistency; unexpected change in either dimensions or proportions of risers and treads mid-staircase interrupts the rhythm of bodily motion, requiring unforeseen adjustments that can lead to falls.[21] At Labraunda and Kos, discrete

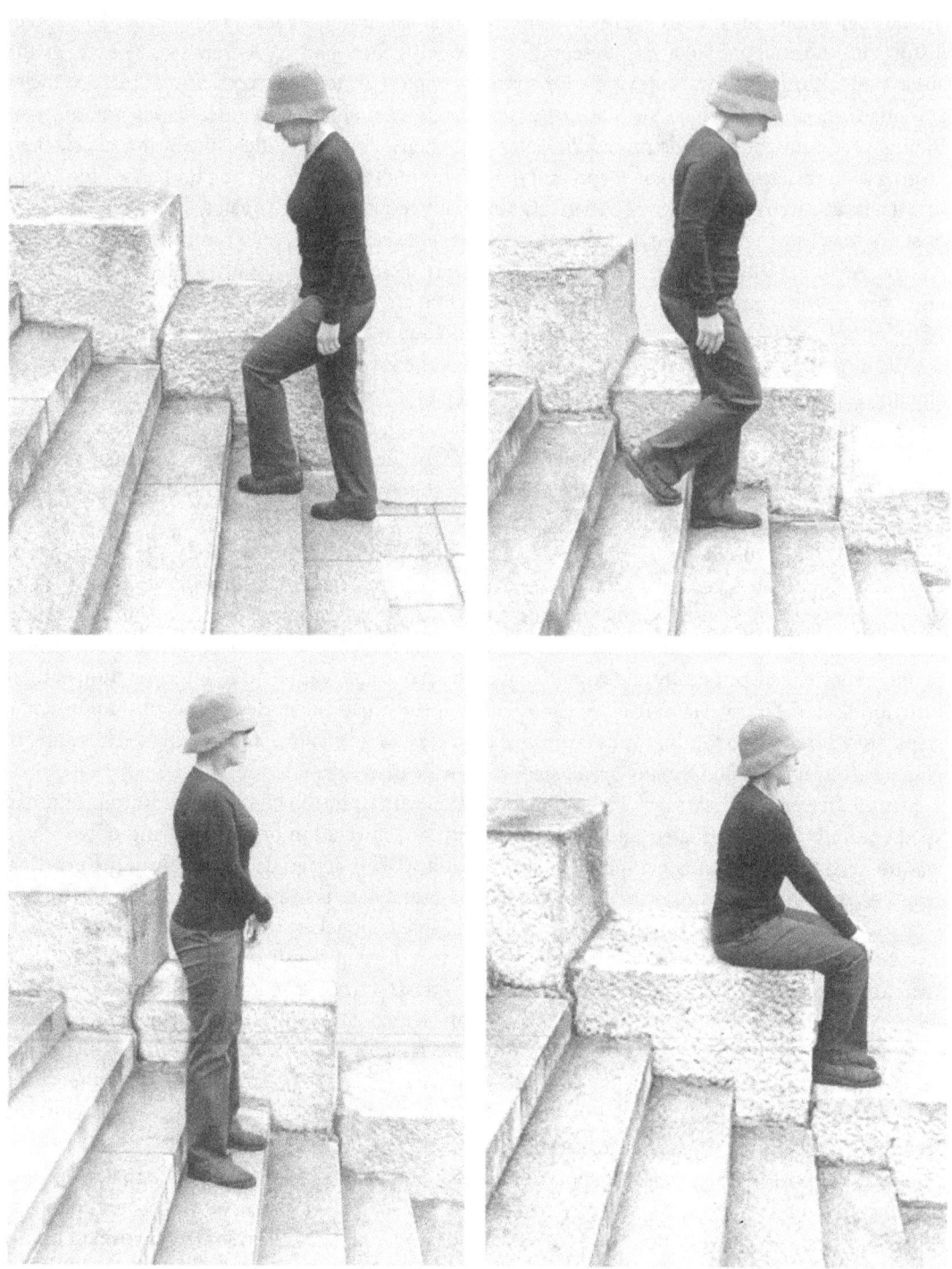

Figure on steps 0.15 m (ca. 6 in) high, 0.305 m (1 ft) deep. (Photos by W. Hollinshead)

Biomechanics

flights of broad steps link separate terraces. Although not strictly aligned (at Labraunda they are at right angles, but adjacent), these steps not only provide access to and from terraces, but through their comparable scale and presentation, convey the message that they are implicitly connected segments of the primary route.

Monumental steps with risers too tall for the human stride and treads at least wide enough for a human foot served as installations for viewing, or theatral steps. A fourth-century B.C. inscription from the Amphiaraion at Oropos refers to the "theater by the altar" (τὸ θέατρον τὸ κατὰ τὸ[μ] βωμόν) at a site where built steps flank the area of the altar.[22] There is significant variation in the vertical dimension of steps used as seats. Examples of optimal heights for seating in *Architectural Graphic Standards* range from 14.4 to 19.0 inches (0.365–0.483 m).[23] Based on biomechanical information and personal observation, it seems reasonable to postulate that steps taller than 0.30 m were used for viewing. This assumption is supported by evidence from sites such as the sanctuary of Demeter at Pergamon, where a stretch of broad steps 0.373 m high and 0.390 m wide is crossed by flights of smaller steps that were clearly designed for greater ease of access, an arrangement seen in the staircases dividing the cavea of nearly every Greek theater into *kerkides*, or wedge-shaped segments.[24]

Steps for observing need not mean seated viewers. The tread of the steps in the agora at Lato, also subdivided by smaller stairways, would be quite narrow for sitting, even allowing for smaller bodies in antiquity and perhaps a tolerance for closer proximity to others.[25] The long stepped retaining wall supporting the treasury terrace at Olympia may also have served as a grandstand for watching races and athletic contests; if so, the spectators stood, as the 0.25 m width of the treads is barely sufficient for a person's foot, and certainly inadequate for seating.[26] These steps could also afford access to and from the terrace, even though their proportions are very awkward and ill suited for ease of movement. Olympia's steps thus could serve all three of the essential functions we have defined for monumental steps, which attests to the ingenuity of their design. As we have seen, evidence for grandstands and their use—textual references to wooden stands (*ikria*) and images of grandstands on Athenian black-figure vases of the sixth century B.C. that depict men sitting or standing on stepped structures—confirms that stepped structures were used for viewing from either a standing or a seated position. This information complements our interpretation of steps' function based on absolute measurements and relative proportions as related to the biomechanics of human movement. At each site, the actual arrangement of steps and contextual information about nearby structures and spaces also provide crucial insight into their primary role.

Ascertaining the customary posture of users can aid in interpreting the function of stepped structures, but caution is in order. Intuitively, we assume that gatherings of longer duration require seats, while briefer events, more directed than discursive, would entail standing room.[27] Passages from Homer, Thucydides, Xenophon, and Cicero (among many) mentioning political assemblies of seated participants have been cited as evidence that steps on which viewers sat were likely to be used for political proceedings, and that facilities with standing room must then have been intended for religious ceremonies.[28] While such behavior may have been true in general, it is inappropriately reductionist to equate sitting with secular political gatherings and standing with religious rituals. Most fundamentally, such interpretations assume a clear separation of sacred and secular that does not apply to antiquity.²⁹ Is feasting on sacrificial meat a religious act? Is a horse race that is part of funerary games sacred or secular? The distinction between sacred and secular existed, but within and around sanctuaries categorizing the nature of activities is often arbitrary and disregards the variety of meanings attached to ancient practices. Interpretations of function by posture also imply that built structures served only one or the other realm. Textual evidence that the ekklesia of some poleis met in theaters reveals greater flexibility of function than modern scholars assume for ancient structures, and ritual activities, both sacred and secular, took place in theaters as well.³⁰ Even within the demarcated limits of a sanctuary, varying degrees of cultic importance were associated with different locations. The continuity and overlap of sacred and secular, together with the documented variety of building use, make assigning specific activities to particular postures unreliable. More factors than we know could have affected whether people sat or stood on steps.

CHAPTER 2

Theoretical Observations

A focus on sanctuaries means attention to rituals and practices, as well as their settings in sacred precincts. This chapter expands the scope of discussion and seeks critical awareness by exploring theoretical perspectives on place-making through architecture as activated by human use, on power expressed in built forms, on the complexity of agency, and on the variability of ritual. It introduces principles derived from anthropological and social theory that will later be woven into our analysis and interpretation of particular sites and their structures.[1]

Any study that includes topography needs to address the concept of place. Place is a socially constructed entity, a subset of space. Architecture is a mechanism for translating space into place by giving articulation to activities. The relationship between space, considered undifferentiated and abstract, and place, considered defined and particular, is an ancient and ongoing philosophical question that is beyond the scope of this study. The Euclidean or Cartesian approach is based on the idea that people appropriate place as a segment of a larger abstract entity called space.[2] On the other hand, proponents of the phenomenological approach believe that human perception based on lived experience generates a sense of place prior to that of space.[3] Societal processes and historical circumstances have a pervasive effect on the perception, cognition, and actions that define place.[4] Humans often designate that a place has special meaning by physically marking or altering their environment. Building broad steps is one strategy for establishing—or intensifying—a sense of place, whether by mediating between exigencies of terrain and architectural structures, by introducing movement, or by defining boundaries and focal areas.[5] As we consider broad steps from the sixth through the second century B.C., the shift from building individual structures in a sanctuary to greater attention to group design suggests a shift from a more phenomenological attitude about place-making toward a more Cartesian concept of space that can be configured to create place. These developments can be understood through a close look at the specific context of each site.

Combining architectural and social history, this study explains changes in built form as related to changes in people's activities and vice versa. Architecture is not a fixed background for events but an expression of human behavior and values in an ongoing process of negotiation. Practice theory offers a useful construct for explaining ancient architecture, as it emphasizes the dynamic interaction between humans (whether individuals, groups, or societies) and the settings they build.[6] Practice theory incorporates Pierre Bourdieu's concept of *habitus*, the conscious and unconscious ways an individual acts, including routine motions and movements of the body as well as those required for carrying out operations within a specific field of endeavor. Building on Bourdieu, Anthony Giddens' theory of "structuration" describes the properties of social systems as both the means and the outcomes of practices they organize, patterns that are innate to an individual or group, and renewed by equivalent conduct repeated over time.[7] Conceived and constructed according to societal patterns of behavior, architecture both expresses the activities and values of those patterns and shapes human conduct in space and time. Steps were built in sanctuaries to support processions to sacrifice and to promote group viewing of ritual, actions that in turn were made permanent in the stone features of the steps.[8] Built structures achieve meaning when they are used. Keith Basso refers to the "interanimation" between structures and their users' conduct, a process by which each activates the other.[9] Edward Casey notes the importance of motion in this process: "the crucial interaction between body, place and *motion* . . . part of the power of place, its very dynamism, is found in its encouragement of motion in its midst."[10] The underlying, essentially diagonal form of steps itself suggests movement; even in their theatral function, steps incorporate bodies in motion on a slope, adding vitality as well as formal framing to a specific location. We shall see that the *pompe*, or procession to sacrifice, brought the energy of performance to routes of access culminating and concentrating around the altar.

Even when we can infer behavior from architectural form, however, the challenge is to understand meaning. While the appeal of studying steps is that we can ascertain where and how people moved, where and how they placed their bodies, we remain ignorant of their perceptions and cognition.[11] Perception and cognition, after all, are based on experience, itself rooted in culture and circumstance. Casey comments, "Even the most primordial level of perceiving is inlaid with cultural categories in the form of differential patterns of recognition, ways of organizing the perceptual field and acting in it, and manners of designating and naming items in this field."[12] Our best hope for fashioning interpretations of meaning lies in describing behavior at sites with comparable configurations, together with comparable contextual information, both material and written.

One strategy for assessing the values given to objects and structures is to describe their performance characteristics: the traits of design, construction, and spatial arrangement that generate and reinforce social behaviors and interactions.[13] For example, monumental size and permanent stone construction are traits that project identity and status, for those who build such structures and for those who use them, while also codifying patterns of conduct. They represent symbolic capital, recognizable as an expression of wealth and prestige in a society.[14] The marble paving of the North Court of the Erechtheion proclaims that it was a spot for important activities, closely tied to the fine marble building beside it. The large rank of steps by the "agora" at Lato, presumably where a civic group met, becomes the tangible expression of that activity, perhaps participatory governance. The performance characteristics of access, restriction, and capacity reveal differential power relationships. Michel Foucault and others envisioned architecture, especially large symbolic structures, as primarily expressive of power based on exclusion and selectivity.[15] Foucault's concept of spatial segmentation—that is, physically separating different human activities in order to control them—applies to monumental steps insofar as they create pathways and regularize circulation within a site, thus directing how individuals and groups experience that set of structures: in what order, from what angle, at what distance.[16] Steps as grandstands help establish specified loci for ritual and

Theoretical Observations

prescribe the size of the crowd afforded optimal viewing and hearing; the upper theatral areas at the sanctuary of Demeter and Kore at Corinth, for instance, could hold fewer than 100 observers, while the seats above the altar of Apollo at Knidos had places for 300 or more. Nevertheless, in architecture and as a general principle, power is not only control, but also capability, sometimes expressed as "power over" and "power to."[17] This distinction holds special importance in discussing physically open, less restrictive forms such as broad steps, as opposed to buildings and closed structures. At many sites considered here, the grand scale and evident capacity of monumental steps convey the power to accommodate or even foster social activity for large numbers of people. Whether full of festive crowds or unoccupied, these steps represent intentional and symbolic displays of large-scale participation, the power of inclusion rather than exclusion.

Monumental structures do not simply occur in public settings; they are commissioned, designed, funded, and constructed before being used. Each of these processes requires an intentional act carried out by an agent, whether an individual or a group. Theories of agency explain how variability and change occur in a system of social practices: how some entity manipulates the collective *habitus*. The concept of agency offers a means of expression for motivation, initiative, creativity, and resistance insofar as these factors represent the ability to effect change.[18] There is little consensus as to what constitutes an agent: the term may refer to an individual, a group of people, a technology, an object, or many variations thereof.[19] Because archaeology's task is to explain the occurrence and character of material remains, interpretations of agency must be contextual, based on inscriptions, historical accounts, and movable finds, as well as the form and placement of built structures.[20] When we examine change in one kind of material culture—architecture—through the expanded use of monumental steps, issues of agency involve patronage or commissioning of specific structures and the difficult question of influence.

Patronage exercised by a political authority, sanctuary overseers, or some other powerful entity, such as a benefactor, is a conspicuous form of agency that we encounter at sites such as Labraunda and Morgantina. Even when inscriptions or written sources supply names of donors, or historical circumstances suggest individual sources for new public structures, the exercise of authority often entails a more complex concept of agency, with multiple actors. At a site such as Lindos on Rhodes, which had broad steps leading to the temple of Athena from the sixth century, worshippers must have processed up to the temple for many generations. When renovations in the early third century changed the path of the parade, who authorized the revisions? Was the route changed simply as a result of architectural redesign? There is insufficient evidence to answer that question at present. During the third and second centuries, written records of royal euergetism (beneficence), such as at Kos, represent only a partial record of financial transactions, with funds from several sources administered by sanctuary officials. When ranks of steps line agora-like spaces at sites in non-Greek Pisidia in southwest Asia Minor, agency and its relation to the *habitus* and operations of the residents' society are far from clear. Influence in architecture can sometimes be traced to individual or political agency, but it is usually a murky subject. The notion of influence itself has been challenged as implying a hierarchy of cultural authority; terms such as "emulation" and "appropriation" impart greater initiative to those who adopt practices or styles established elsewhere. Broad parallels of form are rarely sufficient grounds to postulate influence, given the many challenges of monumental stone construction. The third-century steps and Upper Stoa at Lindos on Rhodes have been compared to the Propylaia of the Athenian Acropolis, and those in the sanctuary of Asklepios on Kos have been compared to Hatshepsut's funerary complex at Deir el-Bahri in Egypt. Second-century sanctuaries in central Italy evidently emulate Hellenistic examples in Greece and Asia Minor. In each case, we must ask what agent (or mechanisms of agency) could have transmitted and expressed such influence, if any, in monumental architecture, and by what means?

Agency is about change, a process that is often considered the opposite of ritual, which is by definition a repeated behavior.[21] Indeed, monumental architecture and religious ritual are often considered fixed, permanent, and unvarying. However, Catherine Bell comments that "formality, fixity, and repetition are not intrinsic qualities of ritual so much as they are a frequent, but not universal strategy for producing ritualized acts."[22] The premise of this book, that there is an ongoing interaction between people and the structures they build, assumes a capability for change within that relationship. Scholars have paid increasing attention to variability and change in ritual in ancient Greek and other societies, and I describe changes in architecture at many sites in part II.[23] Most of the sites presented here are sanctuaries, places for ritual that were shaped by religious enactment, and that gave built form to these ceremonies. However effectively structures and behavior reinforced each other in processions, sacrifices, and feasting in Greek sanctuaries, each festival was a performance, with variables of timing, movement, and spatial arrangement; participating individuals and groups, all with different roles, added potential for deviation from rigid routine as well. Kreinath has categorized types of change in ritual, arguing that rituals are best understood as "forms of discourse and social action."[24] Internal changes within a performance, in the *praxis* of ritual, tend to fall into his category of modifications, which nevertheless may have lasting effects. External change, often socio-political, can result in larger-scale transformations of ritual, such as transferring it to a different location or adding deities.[25] Archaeological evidence supports these concepts. Differing types and frequency of small finds at several sites, including the sanctuary of Demeter and Kore at Corinth, indicate changes in patterns of votive practices.[26] More easily identifiable in the archaeological record, larger-scale transformations include changes in location (resisted by residents of Lykosoura) and dramatic escalation of the scale of both cult activities and facilities for them (as at, e.g., Labraunda and Kos).[27] In arranging part II by century, I aim to draw attention to the long lives of sanctuaries, bearing in mind the limitations of our ability to reconstruct the fine points of time in antiquity, and to explain, as far as possible, changes in the dynamic dialogue of architecture and ritual.

CHAPTER 3

Social Effects and Political Consequences

Shared experience confers authority on ritual. Monumental steps that served as pathways and as grandstands in sanctuaries did not constitute the architectural statement of a temple or the ritual focus of an altar, but they promoted participatory behavior around the central act of sacrifice. Broad steps formed routes for the *pompe*, or procession, escorting the sacrificial animal to the altar, where it was ritually slain and its flesh was cooked and distributed to the attending worshippers. Procession, slaughter and butchering, engaged observation, and shared feasting together constitute a kind of cultural performance, to which dramatic and athletic contests could also be added.[1] The social ties and solidarity of festivals also presented opportunities for political manipulation.

These behaviors—crowds moving, then gathering to engage with the enactment of ritual—created the energy subsequently reinforced by feasting and contests. Every *pompe* was an occasion for display, with officials, musicians, and bearers of baskets, trays, vessels, branches, fillets, and objects specific to the cult, all arrayed in special clothing and finery of many sorts.[2] The Panathenaic procession is the best-known representation of a grand *pompe*, epitomized in the Parthenon frieze.[3] On a sixth-century black-figure band cup, a distillation of a *pompe*, perhaps the Panathenaia, portrays the lower part of Athena with a female (a priestess?) clasping the hand of a bearded male over a flaming altar, followed by a *kanephoros*, three sacrificial victims-to-be (heifer, sow, and ewe) accompanied by five attendants, two *aulos*-players, one *kithara*-player, three robed male worshippers, three hoplites with helmets and shields marching with an unarmed worshipper, and a young man on horseback.[4] The extraordinarily flamboyant procession of Ptolemy Philadelphos in Alexandria in 275/4 B.C., described in (second-hand) detail in Athenaeus' *Deipnosophistai*, was an expanded and politicized version of a *pompe*.[5] A second-century B.C. civic decree from Magnesia on the Maeander specifies the organization of the procession in honor of Zeus Sosipolis in the sanctuary of Artemis Leukophryne:

> the stephanephoros in office together with the male priest and the female priest of Artemis Leukophryne shall ever after lead the procession in the month of Artemision on the twelfth day, and sacrifice the designated bull; that in the procession shall also be the council of elders, the priests, the magistrates, . . . the ephebes, the youths, the boys, the victors in the Leukophryne games, and the victors in the other

Black-figure band cup with procession. (Private collection)

crown-bearing games. The stephanephoros in leading the procession shall carry images of all twelve gods attired as beautifully as possible . . . and shall also provide music, a shawm-player, a pan-pipe player and a lyre-player.[6]

Such festive participatory parades were common practices at Greek sanctuaries, consistent in concept, but variable according to the particular cult and custom; specifications for participation varied as to, for example, gender, age, and social status.[7] Universally, the *pompe* gathered diverse members of one or more communities in various groupings out of their daily routine into festive motion together toward the altar. The performative nature of the *pompe*, as wave upon wave of worshippers walked alongside the prospective victims—oxen, cattle, sheep, goats, pigs—brought a tide of energy and anticipation, anxiety and suspense, to the impending sacrifice. Broad steps that define the way to the altar constitute the formal articulation of this behavior and give it permanent expression. Tilley observed that architecture involves deliberate creation and definition of space, not only somatic and perceptual space, but also existential space, "in a constant process of production and reproduction through the movements and activities of members of a group."[8] In giving form to the existential space of the *pompe*, monumental steps concentrated, shaped, and intensified the

Social Effects and Political Consequences

somatic and sensory effects of processing—motion, proximity, sounds, smells—for participants and observers.

The route of access (space) prescribed by a built path also affected the sequence of perceptions (time) experienced by worshippers. De Certeau described walking as the continuous creation of place in the course of establishing relationships with surrounding spaces and structures.[9] The broad paved way from Mylasa to Labraunda designates desired behavior by promoting passage to the sanctuary. Sourvinou-Inwood proposed a ritual route taking in significant topographical locations for the *pompe* of the City Dionysia in Athens.[10] Yet we have noted the change at Lindos, when third-century renovations redirected the established route of access, suggesting that display and movement—and destination—were more important than a fixed or traditional route within that particular temenos.[11]

The scene on the band cup and the inscription from Magnesia remind us that musicians accompanied the *pompe*. The three instruments mentioned—*syrinx*, *aulos*, and *kithara*—would indicate a gala procession; however, even small *pompai* had music, characteristically performed on the pipe, or *aulos*.[12] Inscriptions from fourth-century Eretria and second-century Kos stipulate that the musicians chosen to accompany competitions at the festival (after the sacrifice) were also to play in the *pompe*.[13] The *prosodion*, a choral lyric sung for the procession, often reinforced the celebratory solidarity of the *pompe*, and sung hymns or paeans were customarily part of the sacrificial ceremony.[14] Stepped structures that framed the space around altars would have captured sounds and rhythms in the open air, offering enhanced acoustics as well as improved viewing.[15] If the procession itself embodies a collective gift of the marchers to the deity, then grandstands articulated a coherent image and gave shape to the idea of ceremony as *agalma*, or gift.[16] Indeed, "observing" Greek sacrifice is best understood more as an engaged and psychologically active participation that involved singing, hearing, smelling, and touching than the passive spectatorship implied by terms such as "viewing" and "watching." Just as music transcends limits of space and structure, so the experience of *pompe* and sacrifice would have engulfed onlookers in the event.[17] Catherine Bell comments that "the ritual-like nature of performative activities appears to lie in the multifaceted sensory experience, in the framing that creates a sense of condensed totality, and in the ability to shape people's experience and cognitive ordering of the world."[18] Building broad steps confers monumentality on communal practice, whether that practice consists of intensifying sacrificial ritual or assembling for civic governance. The visual display of large, regular, built forms reinforces shared behaviors, affirming their value and assuring their permanence.

A periodic event drawing large numbers of people to a comprehensive experience that embodies solemn meaning and generates social energy holds great potential for political leverage. De Polignac and others have cited the mediating role of gatherings and competitions in extraurban sanctuaries in the process of polis formation.[19] In subsequent centuries, the social integration and group affirmation promoted by ceremonies and festivals in sanctuaries served to mitigate political tensions and upheavals.[20] At several sites considered here, I believe, the construction of monumental steps (as part of a larger building program) constitutes tangible evidence of increased attention to communal celebrations so as to compensate for political disruption. Even when it was voluntary, urban relocation or displacement (*metoikesis*), sometimes in the form of moving multiple smaller communities to create a single larger one (*synoikism*), would be quite literally unsettling.[21] The architectural expansion and refurbishing of the sanctuary of Hera at Argos may result from Argos' enforced synoikism of the nearby towns of Mycenae, Tiryns, and Nauplion in the mid-fifth century. The spoils of conquest were apparently used mainly for the sanctuary, supporting the cultural behaviors and connections of the uprooted residents of vacated towns.[22] Voluntary defensive synoikism in the fourth century at Megalopolis apparently stimulated construction (including steps for group participation) in established cult centers at Lykosoura and Mount Lykaion, while small "doublet" shrines in the new city reminded residents of their shared heritage and experience at those major extraurban sites.[23] I propose that in fourth-century Karia, when Mausolos transferred the capital from Mylasa to Halikarnassos, he also enlarged the celebration of Zeus and facilities for it at the nearby sanctuary of Labraunda. The 15 km stone-paved processional way from Mylasa to Labraunda, continued by a broad stepped pathway within the sanctuary, demonstrates Mausolus' intent to temper Mylasa's political loss with a major investment in promoting attractive cultural practices.[24]

These sanctuaries that underwent improvements, including monumental steps, can be linked to historical occurrences of *metoikesis*, attesting to strategies for preserving social stability through enhanced religious celebrations. The steps that may have been auxiliary manifestations of festival proceedings, intended as a setting for events, themselves give formal expression to the location and scope of celebration, and so represent communal authority. Their construction resulted as much from the behaviors of display—processions, sacrifices—enacted in festivals and celebrations as from the visual effect of the steps themselves. As we turn to examine particular examples of steps, we will consider sites that are little known and those that are very familiar, yet whose steps are rarely noted. In each case, biomechanical, theoretical, and political perspectives aid in interpreting the relations between society and structures, between time-limited activities and their lasting stone settings.

PART II

Evidence of Steps over Time

CHAPTER 4

Early Steps

We scarcely need to seek origins in other cultures for the use of broad public steps. They constitute a commonsense solution to everyday problems in construction, from stabilizing a slope to creating a path to accommodating observers. Their occurrence at Greek sites from the sixth century coincides with early examples of large-scale stone architecture, when Greek temples and sanctuaries were given new monumental appearance. Parallels of form have led scholars to seek continuity with steps built in the Aegean Bronze Age or to find prototypes among steps of several cultures of Asia Minor in the ninth through sixth centuries. There is no reason to believe that the "theatral areas" associated with the second-millennium Minoan court complexes at Phaistos and Knossos and at Gournia had any relationship to later monumental steps.[1] The proportions and configuration of the Minoan steps differ from later examples, and there is no evidence that other Minoan architectural forms affected the later Greek tradition. A series of seven steps at Amnisos atop a base of a much larger, longer Minoan wall were previously considered the earliest examples of monumental steps in the Greek world, with possible ties to Minoan predecessors; however, they have recently been redated to the late second century B.C.[2] Schäfer denies any influence from Minoan theatral areas in the stepped form while nevertheless recognizing that the site may have had a numinous aura, retained over generations, leading to its reuse for sacrifice to Zeus Thenatas.[3] The practical advantage of reusing existing architecture as a solid base most likely affected the placement of new structures as well.

As early as the ninth century, monumental steps occur at Phrygian sites in Asia Minor, and large tombs on stepped bases have been attributed to a combination of Lydian, Ionian, and Persian traits. Whether and how these architectural strategies may have affected Greek architectural concepts are open questions. Historically and archaeologically, there is reason to postulate an exchange of ideas, both technical and aesthetic, among the several cultures present in Asia Minor, but a specific eastern ancestry for Greek steps is hard to recognize among the surviving monuments. At the Phrygian capital of Gordion, a grand fifteen-step staircase over 8 m wide was constructed (not cut from rock), leading up from the north to the terrace where a large building stood, consisting of eight rectangular structures side by side. The steps had traces of a pebbled ramp leading up to them and so appear to have been part of a formal path, yet the topmost step leads directly into the face of the end wall of the contemporary Terrace Building.[4] Passage continued along narrower returns perpendicular to the top three steps. Although the ramp in its present circumstances promotes an impression of upward directionality, in antiquity these steps may have focused down, furnishing a grandstand

Evidence of Steps over Time

for viewing whatever took place in the open area to their west; the short returns flanking the three topmost steps contribute a theatral aspect to the steps. Ongoing research suggests that there may have been another, contemporary broad stairway leading up to the terrace from the area in front of the Gate Complex in the southeast.[5] Both sets of steps predate the destruction by fire of Gordion, recently redated to ca. 800 B.C., and they were not used thereafter.[6] Steps cut from bedrock occur often in a variety of Phrygian structures, notably the recurrent configuration of rock-cut steps up to a throne-like platform sometimes called an "altar," and steps are well attested as a design motif in Phrygian architecture of the seventh and sixth centuries.[7] Nevertheless, the built steps at Gordion went out of use early, and they are unlikely to represent precedents for broad steps in Greek architecture.

A hilltop site of the sixth century at Alazeytin, east of ancient Halikarnassos, had a small open area, flanked by steps on two opposite sides, that was considered a public agora-like space.[8] Facing sets of downward-sloping bench-like steps ca. 0.30 m high and 0.60 m deep led Radt to interpret them as a place of communal assembly to share in a viewed experience, whatever its nature.[9] This site has been interpreted as characteristic of the Leleges, whose identity is not at all clear. They may have been early Karians, or "Leleges" may have been simply a Greek term for early non-Greek peoples; many questions remain in interpreting sites attributed to them.[10]

Several monumental tombs with stepped platforms have been characterized as Lydian, Ionian, and Persian hybrids. There was exchange of architectural expertise among these and other groups in Asia Minor and the Near East, but present evidence does not provide a complete picture of how the relationships operated.[11] (Having excluded Greek structures that incorporate steps from this study, I have nevertheless included these monumental tombs as potential sources of stepped forms known to Greeks.) Most familiar is the sixth-century B.C. tomb attributed to the Persian king Cyrus the Great at Pasargadae, set on two successive sets of three steps. This monument has been interpreted as Lydian, Ionian, Anatolian, and Iranian, yet Stronach notes "the uncertain origins of the stepped plinth," acknowledging the possibility that the stepped concept could hark back to Mesopotamian ziggurats or Median stepped altars and temples.[12] The sixth-century Pyramid Tomb at Sardis in Lydia has been restored by analogy with the Tomb of Cyrus as a rectangular tomb chamber on a square base of six equal steps.[13] A large tomb at Taş Kule in Phokaia was entirely carved out of an outcropping of rock. Atop a rectangular (8.8 by 6.2 m) base 2.7 m high, four steps articulate the transition to a smaller square upper storey, whose roof may have been stepped as well.[14] Cahill finds the closest parallels for this enigmatic monument in the Tomb of Cyrus and the Pyramid Tomb, leading him to assign it a date in the sixth or early fifth century.[15] Continuing investigations of pre-Persian sites in Karia have also revealed the use of the stepped podium in grand tombs for emphasis and display.[16]

Stepped bases for tall tombs persisted in western Asia Minor; of special interest is the range of eight monumental steps carved into bedrock below the fourth-century heroon at Limyra.[17] With no provision for human access to these steps, it is clear that they were added solely for visual effect, whether to increase the sense of height when seen from afar or to suggest a route of access, or both. The main approach to the heroon is from the east, and the steps are on the south, where they are

Early Steps

visible from a great distance because of their placement in the landscape. These various funerary monuments with stepped bases or approaches in western Asia Minor gave stepped designs visibility in large public structures. The individual patrons, groups of stoneworkers, and cultures—Phrygian, Lydian, Ionian, Karian, Persian—represent complex and variable interactions. These tombs are neither pre-Greek nor non-Greek, nor entirely Greek. Incorporated into these single structures, stepped bases add both elevation and formal repetition that intensify the tombs' expressions of status and authority. However, since monumental steps appear in individual buildings and in group design at Greek sites as early as the sixth century, direct influence from cultures in Asia Minor seems improbable.

Along with temples, altars, terraces, and stoas, broad steps can be included among the formal elements of sanctuary design, demonstrating that throngs of people participated in gatherings, processions, and ceremonies at several sites across the Greek world. Monumental steps datable to the sixth century B.C. can be identified at Dreros on Crete, on the Greek mainland at Perachora and Eleusis, at Lindos on Rhodes, and at Selinus in Sicily. In addition, broad ramps, some with steps, at Athens, Corinth, and Aegina played equivalent roles in comparable forms.

By the late sixth century, Dreros (Plate 17) on Crete had a stretch of seven steps extending ca. 23 m with short returns at both ends that bracket a level "agora" across a shallow saddle.[18] These steps stabilize the saddle, to which they run perpendicular, and give definition to a broad ca. 30 by 40 m space at their foot. Only three/four steps are now extant, except in the southwest corner of the "agora." Measuring 0.21 m high and 0.35 m wide, they are low enough to give access in the southwest corner to the eighth-century temple a short distance above.[19] In addition, they probably afforded viewing for whatever took place in the open space, although this is a contested issue. This configuration, and the discovery nearby of several inscriptions with fragments of legal texts, have been taken to imply that spectators participated in a political process (hence the label "agora"); nevertheless, evidence remains scant as to the nature of the activities and events that took place.[20] I. Nielsen interprets this configuration as a *theatron* for cultic performances and observes that the modest width of the steps indicates that onlookers stood. The 0.21 m (average) height of the steps, suitable for ascent and descent, but low for seating, supports her hypothesis about posture. On the other hand, it is best to avoid the assumption that seated spectators indicate a civic or political gathering, whereas standing ones mark a religious occurrence.[21] As a retaining wall across the saddle, access to the temple, and grandstand, the steps of Dreros served all three functions of monumental steps, demonstrating efficient and economical planning.

On the Greek mainland, a major building project in the harbor precinct at Perachora (Plate 33) resulted in the construction of a new temple, a new altar, and an adjacent rank of at least seven steps in the last quarter of the sixth century.[22] Reaching a breadth of ca.12 m, the steps have an average height of 0.23–0.24 m. Stabilizing the steep hillside, they also provided access to a route to the Middle Terrace above and east of this sanctuary, as well as a facility for observers to view rituals at and around the altar. They are too low to be comfortable for seated onlookers.[23] The rank of steps begins hard up against the base of the altar—indeed, Ionic columns added to the altar in the fourth century encroach on the lower steps, which were cut away to make room for them. Space was tight.

However, the grandstand of stone steps was well situated for a close view of sacrificial rituals at the altar, and for viewing any festivities that may have occurred in the limited space between temple and altar, on the shore, or on the water if such activities ever took place within the well-defined enclosure of the harbor.[24]

Another rank of steps, dating to the beginning of the sixth century, was built outside the perimeter wall of the sacred precinct at Eleusis (Plate 18). This freestanding "stepped podium," over 8.4 m long, faced onto an open court. Traces of a contemporary altar nearby suggest that this was a location for specific open-air rites. With risers averaging 0.20 m, and treads ranging from 0.41 m (lowest step) to 0.58 m (uppermost step), the three steps gave formal definition to the act of viewing events and ceremonies in the open court, perhaps auxiliary performances for those en route to the Telesterion and its Mysteries.[25]

Steps dated to the sixth century at the sanctuary of Athena at Lindos (Plate 27a–b) on Rhodes were clearly intended to create a pathway up rough, sloping terrain to the temple, situated in isolation atop a dramatic cliff. Later third- and second-century modifications of this approach represent spectacular displays of monumental steps, but even the early path showed grand intentions. Remains of twenty-three low steps, over 7 m wide, were identified beneath the third-century Propylaia, or Upper Stoa. Low walls lined the pathway along both edges. Of varying dimensions, the steps were generally low, with signs of wear indicating extensive use on the surface of their stones.[26] Without doubt such a structure improved passage to the temple, and its breadth implies that significant numbers of people ascended in a procession celebrating the goddess. The scale and capacity of an extended broad route of access would have contributed a sense of the "power to"—of potential—for large numbers of participants. Visually, the formal, constructed rhythm of these steps would have enhanced the presence of the temple, which was unusually small, presumably because of the limitations of its location at the very top of the acropolis.

Comparable monumental passageways in the form of ramps served as routes of approach to the Athenian Acropolis, to the sanctuary around the temple of Apollo at Corinth, to the sanctuary of Zeus Hellanios on Aegina, and to the acropolis of Selinus. At Athens (Plate 8), the path and slope of the sixth-century ramp can be discerned from the extant north sidewall of polygonal masonry, allowing one to estimate its width as ca. 11 m and its length as ca. 80 m.[27] Since none of its upper surface has been preserved, we do not know whether it was stepped or paved. Its exceptional breadth is closely comparable in construction and dimensions to segments of the Panathenaic Way identified in the Agora, representing the grand scale of the Panathenaic procession.[28] At Corinth (Plate 14a–c, a steep ramp leads up the southeast side of the hill on which the sixth-century temple of Apollo is situated. The ramp was at least 7.45 m wide, paved with large blocks, and punctuated by low (0.07–0.14 m) steps at intervals of 0.33–0.41 m. Its pitch varies, reflecting that of the underlying terrain. Near the crest of the hill, the pitch is steep enough that the steps are necessary for human ascent and especially descent. Later interventions—quarrying at the top and construction of the Northwest Shops (fourth century) at the bottom—have made it difficult to assess how this impressive passage related to adjacent structures at either end.[29]

A monumental ramp of similar scale dated to the late sixth century led up to a terrace of the

Early Steps

sanctuary of Zeus Hellanios on Aegina (Plate 2), across the Saronic Gulf from Athens.[30] The sloping pavement of large blocks, 7.20 m wide and preserved to a length of approximately 18.0 m, is interspersed with six steps whose height now varies from 0.16 m to 0.26 m, spaced at regular intervals of ca. 3 meters. This paved way led to a sequence of two terraces (later consolidated into a single large terrace for a Π-shaped Hellenistic stoa), and it originally extended further uphill, as there are remains of an ancient passage to a sanctuary with an altar and a small shrine on the mountain top directly above. (A Byzantine chapel above the head of the ramp now blocks the passage.) Goette has proposed that the lower complex is a Pompeion-like facility for gathering prior to processing up to the summit of the mountain, and for banqueting after sacrifice.[31] Stone paving, especially on this scale, was unusual at this early date, but cuttings nearby indicate that the stone was extracted on site. Paving both stabilized the sloping ramp and established its monumental aspect.[32] The combination of broad ramp and massive flanking terrace walls demonstrates a desire to create a substantial and conspicuous setting for festivals and their attendant activities.

Pompeo's reexamination and reconstruction of Temple M and associated structures at Selinus (Plate 37) has shed light on a sixth-century (570–560 B.C.) site with a remarkable sense of monumentality. North of the sanctuary of Malophoros on the hillside above the Selinus River, the mid-sixth-century oikos-type temple was set 5.8 m above a paved court with a 17 m long altar. Here and elsewhere, paving defines and monumentalizes a horizontal area. Connecting the temple and the altar terrace were steps 24 m wide. They may have been flanked by retaining walls of larger steps on either side, north and south.[33] Although their poor state of preservation makes reconstruction uncertain (their precise dimensions and whether there was an intermediate landing or platform are unknown), the steps evidently stabilized the slope and gave access to and from temple and altar. The steps may have also served as viewing facilities for rites at the altar, since some extant blocks of the lowest steps have cuttings with traces of lead, to hold metal posts for railings.[34] Together, the temple, steps, and altar terrace constitute an architecturally integrated complex. Elevation, symmetry, and frontality emphasize the temple, yet the width of the paved altar terrace and steps balances that small shrine with near equivalence. The breadth and repetition of the steps contributes a grand formality by creating an interlocked system of key religious loci. On the other hand, the movement implicit in steps brings a dynamic tension to the arrangement of parts, as we imagine humans moving upward to visit the temple and turning downward to observe activities at the altar, linking the built structures through their activities. In addition to its internal coherence and symmetry, the complex of Temple M was apparently aligned with the urban grid of the Manuzza sector of the acropolis of Selinus across the river valley, demonstrating an unexpected sophistication in urban planning.[35] Pompeo speculated that a processional way might have extended north from the coast up the river valley, linking the temple at Triolo North (possibly dedicated to Hera), the temple of Malophoros, that of Zeus Meilichios, and Temple M (possibly dedicated to Herakles).[36]

Broad steps appear as an architectural component in the early generations of monumental stone architecture, meeting practical needs while adding formal order to their sites. Monumental steps datable to the sixth century at Greek sites appear to have developed independent of Bronze Age or eastern models, whether Phrygian, Lydian, Ionian, Karian, or Persian. Contemporary with the

Evidence of Steps over Time

emergence of other large scale-stone structures, broad steps at Dreros, Perachora, and Selinus all serve as retaining walls and often have at least one other use, as a route of access or theatral facility by an open space with or without an altar. The stepped pathway at Lindos and those at Athens, Corinth, and Aegina demonstrate that grand approaches are seen in Greek architecture from early times, undoubtedly to accommodate processions and festivities such as the ones depicted in contemporary Athenian vase painting.

CHAPTER 5

Steps in the Fifth Century

Energetic building in the fifth century asserted the existence and authority of the polis and of sanctuaries through monumental architecture. At Selinus and Argos, stepped retaining walls established strong platforms for temples, while remote Alipheira and cosmopolitan Corinth have remains of ceremonial steps affording access to sacred loci. Stepped structures at the Argive Heraion, in Corinth's sanctuary of Demeter and Kore, and on the Acropolis and in the Agora of Athens demonstrate not only their several practical uses but also their ability to bring coherence to architectural ensembles. Beginning with early to mid-fifth-century examples of each category of stepped walls, routes of access, and grandstands, we then consider more complex sites with several different uses of steps.

By the first quarter of the fifth century, Selinus (Plate 38) in southwest Sicily had undergone a massive remaking of the east side of the acropolis, expanding and stabilizing the space east of Temple C. The new terrace was supported by a retaining wall at least 9.8 m high, perhaps taller.[1] Stepped on both sides from a base 17 m wide, holding a huge deposit of sandy fill, the wall's face was visible only on the east, as the west was buried by the filling in of the terrace. The massive east face of twenty-three steps 0.42–0.45 m high, offset ca. 0.20 m, extends 75 m north-south, then turns northwest at a 51 degree angle and continues, with a slight shift to the west, another 50 m.[2] A new altar was constructed in the expanded terrace created by this retaining wall, and three supplementary steps were added below the original six steps across the façade of Temple C to accommodate the lowered ground level.[3] In the course of the fifth century, additional reconstruction in the northeast sector of the terrace included a stepped ramp 2.4 m wide giving direct access to the terrace from the main street to its north. This stepped gradient, even wider in the initial version, was built over in Punic times with twenty-one steps.[4] Selinus' enormous retaining wall is even today an impressive sight. Although the primary reason for its construction must have been to support the refurbishing of the temple and altar on the terrace, this imposing *analemma* (retaining wall) contributes grand scale, elevation, and a message of man-made order that asserted the wealth and power of Selinus.

On a far smaller scale, the temple of Athena in the remote Arkadian polis of Alipheira (Plate 3) was constructed at the beginning of the fifth century high on a hillside, set in a temenos on a terrace with a stepped retaining wall in its northeast corner.[5] Perpendicular to the façade of the temple, steps 9 m wide buttressed the east wall of the peribolos; they may have extended further north, where blocks tumbled along the steep unexplored slope now obscure whatever remains below.

Evidence of Steps over Time

The extant fourteen steps are steep (ranging from 0.20 to 0.28 m high, averaging 0.27 m), narrow (0.10–0.40 m at present, averaging 0.35 m), and irregular in their present state. Ascent and descent are possible but not easy, with a pitch of 51 degrees.[6] Orlandos envisioned a dual function for these steps as both retaining wall and access to the temple terrace. If the steps were intended solely to support the peribolos wall, one would expect them to extend along the entire east wall. As it is, they join the temenos between the temple and the altar, their south end aligned with the temple façade. It is worth noting that the sixth-century ramp to the temenos of Apollo at Corinth and the mid-fifth-century steps to the Middle Terrace at the Argive Heraion both intersected the sacred precinct in approximately the same relationship to temple and altar.[7] Since we assume that the steps permitted groups of worshippers to approach the temenos together in procession, this juxtaposition suggests that these sites had a preferred point of entry to the area where ritual would be carried out. The steps at Alipheira were far from the ideal physical proportions, but they are passable even now, and the local mountainous terrain indicates that their users in antiquity would have been quite accustomed to scaling steep slopes. Any theatral function can be dismissed, as the ground falls away steeply just beyond the lowest step.

Steps intended for viewing rites at the Amphiaraion at Oropos (Plate 32) on the northeast border of Attika have been identified as the τὸ θέατρον τὸ κατὰ τὸ[μ] βωμόν ("theater by the altar") cited in a fourth-century inscription.[8] The inscription records the reuse of the component blocks of the dismantled *theatron* in a water channel, part of a general refurbishing of the sanctuary. All that remains are three steps (0.25 m high, 0.30–31 m wide, ca. 20 m long) in a broadly curving arc close to the north side of the altar. The center of their arc aligns with the placement of the earliest of three successive altars, suggesting a late fifth-century date for their initial construction. We cannot be sure exactly what the original structure looked like, especially since the Greek theater did not assume a canonical form until the fourth century, and the term θέατρον could refer to a variety of venues from which people could observe.[9] The topographical specificity of the inscription may have been intended to distinguish the *theatron* by the altar from another theater at the site, perhaps a predecessor to the extant second-century theater.

In western Asia Minor, theatral steps 15 m wide cut in bedrock flanked a level open area identified (partly because of the steps) as the agora of the Karian site of Latmos (Plate 25). Amid great outcroppings of rock and irregular terrain, this rank of eight steps gave formal definition to the eastern edge of the area it faced.[10] Latmos must have been a city of moderate size in the fifth century, since it was a member of the Delian League, recorded as contributing one talent in the middle of that century.[11] These steps, ranging from 0.30 to 0.50 m in height and from 0.20 to 0.70 m in depth, probably to accommodate seated occupants, may have been used as early as the sixth century, with their use continuing into the fifth and fourth centuries. The site was abandoned by 300 B.C., when its inhabitants were moved to nearby Herakleia.[12]

More than at any other fifth-century site, steps were a striking feature of the renovations at the sanctuary of Hera 8 km outside the city of Argos. Situated on a hillside northeast of the city, the Argive Heraion (Plate 6) was active as an independent sanctuary from Geometric times until it was taken over by the polis of Argos in the fifth century.[13] A large pseudo-Cyclopean terrace wall presumably supported a seventh-century temple on its Upper Terrace and framed the primary focus

Steps in the Fifth Century

of ritual activity (perhaps including a large altar) on the Middle Terrace to its south. Its monumental scale attests to the resources allocated to this site from an early date.[14]

In the sixth century a ramp connected the terraces. Visible remains of its south retaining wall indicate that it sloped from the east end of the Upper Terrace downward and west along the face of the terrace wall until it turned south and descended to the Middle Terrace between two early porticos along the north side of the Middle Terrace.[15] Too little remains to determine whether the segment between the stoas was a ramp or a monumental staircase, as proposed by Lauter.[16] This symmetrically positioned broad pathway between two terraces, each a focus of religious activity, represents an early manifestation of the desire to create an architectural system for religious processions and rituals. At present, the ramp constitutes the best evidence for a festival procession as early as the sixth century, since Herodotus' account (1.31) of the Argive brothers Kleobis and Biton is no longer associated with the pair of sixth-century kouroi dedicated at Delphi.[17]

Massive renovations to the entire Heraion in the mid-fifth century (460–440 B.C.) transformed the entire site. The Middle Terrace was regularized, and retaining walls were built, as was a new South Stoa below the terrace. Some time after the Archaic temple of the Upper Terrace burned in 423 B.C., a new temple was constructed on the Middle Terrace.[18] The level of the terrace's surface was lowered and two steps were added below the crepis of the North Portico to compensate for the drop in ground level.[19] On the north side of the Middle Terrace, supplementary construction to the ramp and the two stoas flanking it gave the terrace a more regularly aligned border that integrated the opening of the ramp into the new plan. The ramp was probably given formal definition as monumental steps continuing above and beyond those added in front of the Northeast Portico. Lauter proposes a true staircase leading up to the east-west section of the ramp, but Billot is more circumspect. Lauter's monumental staircase would also furnish a fine grandstand for spectators to observe celebrations at the altar below them on the Middle Terrace—an attractive hypothesis, but without sufficient evidence in the form of preserved extended steps.[20]

These refinements of the Middle Terrace were part of a comprehensive rebuilding of the sanctuary that also entailed construction of the South Stoa and large stepped retaining walls on the south and east slopes of the Middle Terrace, as well as the new temple.[21] Amandry's close studies of the juxtaposition, materials, and technical similarities of these structures led him to conclude that all were part of a planned ensemble, starting with the South Stoa, followed by the stepped retaining walls, and then—eventually—by the temple.[22] Along the front of the South Stoa, a narrow terrace was supported by a rank of nine steps. They extended east beyond the South Stoa, forming an 80 m long stretch of poros steps until they abutted a large perpendicular retaining wall of local conglomerate running north-south, roughly parallel to the stoa's east wall. Between the east end of the South Stoa and the conglomerate retaining wall, poros steps continued north (uphill) all the way to the Middle Terrace, forming a large stepped hillside beside the South Stoa. The pitch changes partway up the steps, reflecting the underlying terrain.[23] The entire complex of stoa, terrace, and steps along the south edge of the Middle Terrace lies parallel to the refurbished north side of the terrace (the North Stoa with its two new steps, and the new steps in front of the Northeast Stoa), creating a rectangular frame for the Middle Terrace. After 423 B.C. the new temple was set in the center of the west end of the Middle Terrace and aligned with the rest of the complex. East of the conglomerate retaining wall, a spectacular array of taller poros steps formalized the slope of the entire hillside, extending another 80 m east, then continuing at an obtuse angle northeast for another 40 m.[24] This extensive remodeling resulted in a striking, dramatically defined sanctuary, whose superposed terraces gained a powerful sense of system from the topography of ordered ranks of monumental steps and connected terraces.

The primary purpose of this system of steps was to retain and formalize the hillside, an observation confirmed by the changing pitch and proportions of the steps in accordance with the existing slope. The 0.75 m height of the steps east and northeast of the conglomerate wall is too tall for stairs, but the height of the steps across the front of the South Stoa to the conglomerate wall and those continuing up to the Middle Terrace suggests that they could have served for human passage.[25] With risers ca. 0.30–0.36 m tall, the westernmost segment clearly provided access to the South Stoa, and they were probably intended as access to the Middle Terrace and its temple as well. Even though the risers seem inconveniently high for comfortable ascent or descent, the central placement of this segment of steps in the new configuration of the site suggests that ancient visitors were expected to take that route to the Middle Terrace. The location of their entry to the Middle Terrace—at the east façade of the temple—is worth noting. The same juxtaposition, with a steep approach arriving just at the façade of the temple, is seen at Corinth in the sixth century and at the early fifth-century sanctuary of Athena at Alipheira.[26] The steps are also nearly aligned with the approach to the ramp leading from the far (north) side of the Middle Terrace to the Upper Terrace, reinforcing the sense of symmetry and order of the Middle Terrace. Since there existed another, easier path to the Middle Terrace at its west end, these tall steps may have seen only occasional use for passage; they may have been as much symbolic as functional.[27] In addition, this segment of steps could have served as a grandstand, providing seats from which to observe processions or athletic contests at the base of the hill. The orientation of the South Stoa, facing downhill, also suggests that important activities took place to the south of the terraced complex, perhaps the athletic contests mentioned on six inscribed bronze objects of fifth-century date, and in later inscriptions.[28] The institution (or reorganization) of athletic contests, initially called the Hekatomboia, at the sanctuary is attested by three bronze hydriai of ca. 460 B.C. and another, slightly later hydria, a lebes, and a tripod, all six associated by inscription with the games of Hera Argeia.[29] Retrospective inscriptions of the fourth century at Delphi refer to athletic victors in fifth-century Hekatomboia, including Theagenes of Thasos, who is specified as having won at the Hekatomboia at Argos.[30] Moreover, an epigram inscribed on a Doric capital of ca. 500 B.C. found near the Heraion specifies its location as near the hippodrome, implying a prior history of contests in the plain below the hillside of the sanctuary.[31]

This refashioning of the Argive Heraion, with its extensive, continuing ranks of steps, gave order and definition not only to the sanctuary, but to the entire hillside, perhaps with the intent to turn it into a kind of man-made acropolis, a worthy successor to the citadels of Mycenae and Tiryns. More than any single structure, it is the regular arrangement and integration of forms of terraces, steps, and ramps together with buildings that convey a message of controlled space and therefore power. The magnitude of architectural change at the Argive Heraion appears to coincide with the assumption of control over the heretofore regional sanctuary by the polis of Argos in the 460s, a change characterized by J. M. Hall as a "disjuncture" rather than "continuity."[32] Literary and epigraphic

Steps in the Fifth Century

testimonia report Argos' destruction of Mycenae, Tiryns, and perhaps Nauplion at this time in a synoikism by conquest.[33] Substantial socio-political reorganization in the polis—perhaps the introduction of a democracy—can be inferred from references to tribes and phratries in inscriptions from after 460 B.C.[34] The major enhancement of both the festival of Hera and its physical setting in the sanctuary led Hall to propose that the Argives may have commissioned Pindar's Tenth Nemean Ode, dated 464 B.C., which explicitly links Hera and the city of Argos.[35]

The expanded wealth and authority of Argos was expressed in ceremonies and processes of both celebration and governance, which generated new architectural expression in city and sanctuary. The architectural embellishment of the Argive Heraion was paralleled by building activity in the center of the city of Argos, where the "Hypostyle Hall" and Odeion were constructed, furnishing facilities for meetings and assemblies that are considered further evidence that changes at Argos included democracy.[36] Information from an extraordinary cache of inscribed bronze plaques implies that some of the conquered territories of the newly incorporated cities were allocated as sacred land, with revenues directed to the Heraion and other shrines, mitigating the effects of defeat.[37] Kritzas has identified accounts of funds allocated for completing the doors and other details of the temple, perhaps even its chryselephantine statue.[38] These and other inscriptions document the recognition that shared traditions and rites associated with the sanctuary and its cult practices could maintain social connections during times of political rupture and upheaval. The rebuilt, reconfigured sanctuary would have accommodated new and expanded activities, such as processions, competitions, and performances, while still maintaining communal ties through shared ritual experience. The Heraion's conspicuous, integrated design gave tangible substance to the reconstituted polis of Argos even as it constituted an intermediary between conquered towns and Argos.

Broad steps were incorporated into major revisions of two sanctuaries at Corinth (Plates 14 and 15) in the fifth century: in the temenos of the Sacred Spring southeast of the temple of Apollo, and in the sanctuary of Demeter and Kore on the slopes of Acrocorinth. Beside the Sacred Spring (Plate 14d), lines of two or three poros steps defined a polygonal temenos and offered vantage points for observing animal sacrifice. In the early fifth century, three broad poros steps estimated to be 21.4 m or longer were installed opposite a small mudbrick altar that had several phases of renewal.[39] These steps were replaced by a similar construction within a generation or two, in the second half of the fifth century. Aligned slightly differently from their predecessors, they ran east-west for ca. 30 m, then (reduced from three to two steps) angled slightly northwest for 6.50 m, then north to a juncture with the two lowest steps of a staircase leading to a terrace atop the roof of the spring house of the Sacred Spring.[40] Adjacent to the Sacred Spring, these long steps gave formal definition to the underlying topography, which was still held in place by massive Geometric retaining walls to the west and north of these steps. Their primary purpose would appear to be theatral, offering places for viewing activities at and beside the mud altar to their north. While the excavator interpreted these as seats, the risers are too low (0.223, 0.244 m) and the treads proportionally too narrow (0.300 m) for adequate seating, and so observers would have stood.[41] There was small-scale animal sacrifice at the mud altar, indicated by bones of cow, pig, and sheep in small pieces, and auxiliary events presumably took place to its east as well, judging by the extension of the steps in that direction.[42] Subsequent use supports this interpretation, as wooden bleachers (with three phases of use) were erected in this area east of the mudbrick altar in the fourth and third centuries. In addition, these long steps may have demarcated the southern boundary of the temenos, as did a later curb set over part of their line.[43]

The sanctuary of Demeter and Kore (Plate 15) lies ca. 1 kilometer to the south of the temple of Apollo on the north slope of Acrocorinth. There is evidence of cult activity at the site from the seventh century and perhaps the eighth, and expanded use in the sixth.[44] However, it was in the fifth century that architectural structures gave durable form to the stages of ceremony at this sanctuary: processing, cultic enactment, and dining. Despite large gaps in our knowledge of cult practices at the site, the built environment of steps, terraces with viewing areas, and dining rooms suggests patterns of behavior on three terraces. Extensive deposits of miniature vases and terracottas support the interpretation of ritual activity throughout this site. Thousands of kalathiskoi, krateriskoi, and miniature hydriai, as well as figurines and model offering trays, were offered here to honor Demeter and Kore, concentrated on the Middle Terrace.[45] The most conspicuous addition was a monumental stairway from the rebuilt road at the lower limit of the sanctuary, on its north, which ascended the hillside to the Middle and Upper Terraces: 29 m long and 3 m wide (it ranges from 2.80–3.07 m). The stairway rose in flights of three or four steps punctuated by at least ten landings with entrances to buildings housing dining chambers, which flanked the stepped passage on either side.[46] Besides their width, the generous dimensions of the steps, with easily traversed low risers (0.14 m) and broad treads (0.30 m), encourage a slow and easy movement, suggesting that the stairway served for processions. While the stairs link the terraces and the dining facilities in an integrated, monumental design, the landings were placed according to the situation of the flanking buildings, and not according to an abstract plan or internal rhythm.[47] The organizing principle is human behavior rather than architectural aesthetics. This stairway may represent a constructed expression of a previous pathway (improved in order to reduce erosion) whereby participants moved to dining rooms aligned along the hillside or climbed up to the Lower, Middle, and Upper Terraces.

Throughout the history of the sanctuary, the Middle Terrace was evidently the primary focus of ritual, with an enigmatic oikos, an open platform for animal sacrifice, and stone-lined pits for votives in the fifth century. Quantities of votive pottery and figurines found here imply cult activity, but we lack written testimonia about the nature of the worship. From the fifth century on, and possibly as early as the sixth century, the Upper Terrace included stepped rock-cut areas for viewing whatever ceremonies did take place on the Middle Terrace. A "theatral area" of five steps provided standing room for about fifty spectators to view occurrences on the terrace below, according to the excavators: a limited capacity for an intentionally limited facility.[48] Carved out of the rough breccia that constitutes the local bedrock, now badly weathered and worn, three areas of steps can be discerned. The southernmost set was aligned with the processional stairway below, but was wider (4.8–5.0 m).[49] With risers averaging 0.20–0.29 m in height and treads averaging 0.40 m wide, these steps could accommodate either standees or seated observers. The dimensions also afford convenient passage up and down on this steep slope. The bedrock may have been faced with limestone in antiquity, but that need not have changed the proportions estimated for the steps.[50] The excavators estimated a capacity of about fifty people for this intentionally small facility. This small space was succeeded—or supplemented—by a more overtly theatral installation nearby, to the southeast, in the late fourth or early third century.[51]

Steps in the Fifth Century

The Upper Terrace was designed to provide a good view of processions making their way uphill as well as events below, especially rites conducted directly below it on the Middle Terrace. Unfortunately, we lack sufficient information to know what took place on the Middle Terrace that merited such attention. The excavators noted the narrow and restrictive entrances to the Middle Terrace and the small size of the theatral area and its successor, both suggestive of a mystery cult available to a limited number of eligible (perhaps initiated) participants.[52] Fragments of large terracotta statues, mostly of young men bearing offerings of small animals, were found on and near the Upper Terrace.[53] Such display in theatral areas would signal the importance of the restricted location and reinforce the privileged status of worshippers entitled to be there.

Turning to the repeated, extensive building projects of fifth-century Athens (Plates 8–12), we encounter examples of broad steps in different phases and structures on the Acropolis and also in the Agora. Traces of five or more steps beside the south wing of Mnesikles' Propylaia (Plate 9) reveal a late Archaic viewing area flanking the approach to the Acropolis.[54] This forecourt to an earlier gateway of the late sixth or early fifth century comprised poros steps and a marble bench, all part of a single installation that predated the Old Propylon, which itself preceded the Mnesiklean structure of 437–432 B.C.[55] The two lowest steps extended at least 10.24 m north-south, perhaps farther. While the built courses of poros limestone tapered at their north end into the rising surface of the rock, at their south end the steps turned west for 4.170 m, with a small return (1.345 m) at an oblique angle to the north-south steps.[56] The topmost step supported a bench of marble, 0.29 m high and 0.35 m deep, with a back made up of as many as eighteen marble slabs, all reused from a major mid-sixth-century temple on the Acropolis.[57] At its north end the marble bench abutted a square base with traces of three bronze legs and a central cylindrical marble shaft, commonly referred to as the "tripod base"; in fact, it probably supported a perirrhanterion, or else a triple-bodied Hekataion.[58] (The top step increased in width to accommodate this base, demonstrating that it was an integral part of the plan for the stepped area.) Since the steps have variable dimensions of risers and treads, some observers may have stood while others sat. This forecourt thus contributed formal articulation to the process of entry, framing the three-legged marker of transition (whether perirrhanterion or Hekataion) and offering a fine vantage point beside the ramp for watching the Panathenaic procession as it ascended to the sanctuary. The placement of seating just outside the sanctuary may also express restricted admission. At the last juncture, by the tripod marker, those ineligible to enter could at least sit on the bench.

Among the subsequent Periklean architectural projects of the mid-fifth century on the Acropolis, a new, larger ramp led up to the new Propylaia, and both the Parthenon and the Erechtheion made use of monumental steps. The broad ramp leading to the western end of the Acropolis (Plate 8a) was almost doubled to fill the entire width of the façade between the projecting wings of Mnesikles' Propylaia, attaining a width of more than 21 m over the same 80 m length as the earlier ramp it replaced. (The extant north retaining wall and cuttings in bedrock at its southern edge confirm its breadth and construction of isodomic blocks.) Although the surface is not preserved, it seems likely that steps would have helped mitigate the steep (30 degree) pitch, as seen in the ramps at Corinth and Aegina.[59]

Once through the Propylaia, worshippers would see the west end of the Parthenon set on a broad stepped platform (Plates 8a, 10). The number of rock-cut steps varies from two at the north end to nine at the south end. The steps carved into bedrock were augmented by constructed steps, achieving an impressive rank of up to nine (extant) steps ca. 2 m high. Stevens argued that seven additional steps built of limestone blocks, some reused from the earlier Peisistratid temple, would have continued above them, making a terrace wall of sixteen steps with a total height of 3.69 m.[60] Structurally and perceptually, this stepped retaining wall of either nine or sixteen steps established a base on which the unusually wide Parthenon was set. Its evident connection to the great temple is demonstrated by the fact that the steps display the same slight curvature that is seen in the crepidoma and entablature of the Parthenon.[61] The steps also affirmed the alignment of the Periklean Parthenon, which varied from the previous temple on the site, as shown by the line of the north retaining wall of the terrace, which meets the rock-cut steps at a slightly acute angle.[62] With risers of an average 0.227 m and treads estimated to average 0.291 m wide in the added steps, these steps offer reasonable access to and from the terrace, even though they are steeper than modern walkers are used to.[63] On the other hand, the closed west end of the Parthenon was never the destination. Cuttings for thirty-eight votive stelai and seven large bronze statues on the rock-cut steps, installed over several centuries, indicate that at this phase of ceremonies on the Acropolis, there was more attention to participation in the procession than observation of it.[64] The Parthenon's stepped platform was not primarily a route of access, nor a grandstand, but an imposing terrace for supporting and displaying the great temple and, over time, for displaying dedications to those approaching the Parthenon en route to the altar and rituals at its eastern end.[65]

Opposite the Parthenon, the area between the temple commonly called the Erechtheion and the north wall of the Acropolis, just east of the Erechtheion's North Porch, was originally a small theatral court, with steps for viewing solemn rites (Plates 8a, 11).[66] A flight of twelve marble steps between the ground level of the east façade of this irregular temple and the ground level adjacent to its North Porch 3.10 m below served for access and retaining, but its primary role in the fifth-century temple may have been to establish a secluded setting for the Plynteria, in which the ancient wooden image of Athena was brought from the temple and bathed.[67] These steps are more than a staircase, since they buttress the vertical face between the levels and so serve as a retaining wall. The dimensions of the twelve steps change mid-flight, introducing a risk of falling for those ascending and descending and suggesting that this staircase was less likely to have been a frequented passage and more likely to have served a theatral purpose.[68] The 0.078 m change in riser height mid-staircase reflects a close relationship to the temple and its construction. Each of the four lowest steps is 0.328 m in height and width, exactly the same as the crepidoma steps plus the molding course along the temple's north wall. The eight steps above them have risers 0.250 m tall (with treads 0.325 m wide), corresponding to half the height of adjacent wall blocks of the building, and the height of the steps of its East Portico.[69]

Adjacent ranks of steps and a rectangular area of marble paving at its foot confirm that a small court was part of the Erechtheion complex. The lower steps continued at right angles both north and south: on the north were eight steps along the inner face of the circuit wall of the Acropolis; and on the south, the three lowest steps extended as the Erechtheion's crepidoma along the north exterior side of the cella wall to where they met up with the three steps of the North Porch.[70] The theatral nature of these perpendicular stepped arrangements was emphasized by marble paving in the space framed by the steps and the temple, perhaps a successor to an earlier, pre-Periklean court on the site,

Steps in the Fifth Century

as indicated by the layer of poros blocks below.[71] Tightly fitted slabs of Pentelic marble were aligned at their northern edge with the euthynteria of the North Porch.[72] An interruption in the middle of the paved area suggests that a built feature may have given this theatral arrangement a permanently installed focus of attention.[73] An altar or base for ritual activities may have stood here, or a basin or cistern to collect water. Marble paving monumentalizes the horizontal plane and creates equivalence with adjacent structures so as to unify components into an architectural composition. The coordination of the theatral steps' measurements with the Erechtheion's own crepidoma and its wall blocks, plus the precisely aligned marble paving, make it clear that this open-air court was both contemporary with the temple and designed in close association with it. The stepped arrangement certainly looks like a setting for ritual, albeit one available to a limited number of observers, since the two banks of eight and twelve steps offer standing room for up to 150 onlookers.[74] In practice, the steps may not have been filled to capacity, since their size was apparently governed by the space between the temple and the north wall of the Acropolis.

This intimate North Court with limited access would be a suitable setting for the rites of the Plynteria and Kallynteria, in which the revered ancient wooden statue of Athena was brought out of the temple, undressed, cleaned, and adorned with fresh garments.[75] The day of the Plynteria was considered an ἡμέρα ἀποφράς, not to be mentioned, and therefore inauspicious, polluted. This temple was closed off, other temples were closed off, and no business was conducted.[76] Although no source reports where the disrobing, washing, and re-draping and re-ornamenting of the statue took place, the North Court's proximity and privacy make it a likely location for these rites. The stone paving, most often seen in fountain houses, suggests the use of water, as in bathing, and gives permanent indication of the practice in monumentalized form.[77] The steps also provide fine sightlines to the southeast corner of the North Porch, where the altar of the Thyechous may have stood, focus of yet another ancient ritual.[78]

Outside the walls of the roofed temple, yet still part of it, the North Court had steps that framed the rituals and furnished viewing facilities for officials of the cult. Few published plans of the Erechtheion include this formally constructed theatral area. Most present a cursory, often partial indication of the stairs between the east façade and the North Porch. This theatral court is not a building, but it is thoroughly coordinated with the temple, and potentially with its most important rites. Omitting it from plans and drawings of the Erechtheion compromises our ability to interpret how this enigmatic temple worked. A comparable issue accompanies the temenos of Pandrosos on the west side of the building, another constructed enclosure open to the sky. Must architecture have a roof? In the case of a structure as uncanonical as the Erechtheion, it is difficult to know how to draw the limits of the building, literally as well as figuratively.[79] With its irregular form and closely connected courts, the Erechtheion not only encompasses ancient sacred loci, but also anticipates subsequent architectural developments by incorporating varied built structures on multiple levels.

Visible from the North Court of the Erechtheion, on the west side of the Athenian Agora (Plate 12), four long bench-like structures stabilized the lower part of the hill of Kolonos Agoraios, even as they furnished seating. Set at the foot of the hill immediately north of the Old Bouleutereion, these "steps" were bracketed on the north by the addition of the Stoa of Zeus soon after their installation, dated to the mid-fifth century (Plates 12–13). They are aligned with the east façade of the

Hephaisteion, which dominates the hilltop above.[80] Their location afforded an excellent view over the Agora, including the route of the Panathenaic procession, and their dimensions (0.33–0.50 m high, 0.56–0.74 m wide) and spacing (1.55–1.60 m center to center) were well suited for seating. Estimates of their capacity in antiquity vary from 200 to over 400 seated occupants.[81] Boegehold proposed that they served as a law court, but others prefer a broader interpretation: that they furnished a gathering-place that could be used for a variety of institutional assemblies, a *synhedrion* ("meeting place," a term used in ancient sources).[82] Such flexibility is plausible, but some specific need, such as erosion control, may have stimulated the initial construction, since the excavator in the 1930s noted continuing difficulties with this slope, ameliorated by the benches.[83] Their horizontal alignment and specific placement centered symmetrically below the Hephaisteion, however, also express an intention to frame the façade of the temple uphill. These benches give the Hephaisteion a formally articulated stepped terrain on which to sit, perhaps echoing the stepped terrace for the Parthenon, or even the hillside steps of the Argive Heraion. A useful—and not unintended—consequence of these choices would be the four benches offering excellent facilities for spectating or for civic gatherings of whatever purpose. Later construction of the fourth-century temple of Apollo Patroos on the north and the Hellenistic Metroon on the south encroached on these benches so extensively as to eliminate all viewing capacity. A gap was nevertheless maintained between these later structures to preserve views of and access to the Hephaisteion, and an actual monumental staircase was later built uphill from the benches. The benches of the Athenian Agora thus served to retain the slope of Kolonos Agaoraios, even as they provided a visual base for the Hephaisteion above, and seating facilities in the Agora below.

In many ways the most transformative fifth-century uses of stepped structures were not the installations on the Acropolis but those at Selinus, and especially the Argive Heraion and Corinth. At both Selinus and the Argive Heraion, terraces were expanded on a grand scale. Existing topography, whether natural or constructed, was re-formed to create overtly man-made terrain, an intentional acropolis that impressed with both its size and its conspicuous message of order. These massive reconfigurations of the respective sacred precincts demonstrate the sanctuaries' interest in maintaining their identities at a time when poleis were gaining importance as centers of power in the Greek world.[84] At the Argive Heraion, the staircase to the temple terrace appears to be part of a larger scheme to build a comprehensive environment and create an impressive image for the sanctuary. At the much smaller sanctuary of Demeter and Kore at Corinth, adding the grand staircase not only stabilized the sloping site; it connected the three main areas of cultic observance: dining in the Lower Terrace, votive offering and sacrifice on the Middle Terrace, and spectating on the Upper Terrace. The new stairs brought organization and monumentality to the environment for ritual practice while contributing a visual image of system, order, and importance. On the whole, the formalization of landscape and the use of steps as connectors between zones of a temenos appear to be separate concepts in the fifth century. At the Argive Heraion (and Selinus), steps as terracing dominate the presentation of the site, subordinating the steps that are routes of access and possibly also grandstands. At Corinth, the great stair was primarily a route of access, although it did establish a tangible means of arranging the site that persisted for centuries.

CHAPTER 6

Steps in the Fourth Century

During the fourth century, specific functions became more directly expressed in distinct types of structure: for example, the theater evolves into a canonical form, and political buildings such as bouleuteria, prytaneia, and ekklesiasteria take on canonical form.[1] Hansen and Fischer-Hansen have demonstrated that "monumental architecture did not become a sign of power in public buildings ... until the late classical and early Hellenistic periods"; in the fourth century, they note, secular buildings are given monumental treatment heretofore reserved for sacred structures.[2] Meanwhile, in sanctuaries—at Perachora, Amyzon, and especially at Labraunda—we see more built pathways for processions. Stepped facilities for viewing at Lato, Olympia, Mount Lykaion, and Lykosoura all stabilize slopes while accommodating observers. We also see an expansion in the scope of stepped structures, bringing coherence to sites with many discrete components. At Lato, Mount Lykaion, and Olympia they serve to integrate varied structures and activities within the temenos. The role of the satrapal Hekatomnid family in Karia as patrons who appropriated Greek forms and concepts, and adapted them to suit their purposes, anticipates developments in later generations. My discussion of these sites is roughly chronological (many sites have uncertain chronology) and also reflects geography.

Early fourth-century renovations at the sanctuary of Hera Akraia at Perachora (Plate 33) included an elaborate new altar with baldachino in front of the temple by the harbor, and broad steps, perhaps a grand stair terrace, in the upper sector of the sanctuary.[3] Construction of the two-story L-shaped stoa by the harbor may also date as early as this phase of renewal.[4] The uphill sector of the site east of the harbor constituted an adjunct area, with dining chambers and deposits of previously dedicated votives.[5] From before Archaic times, north-south terrace walls perpendicular to the slope of this upper valley attest to the ongoing need for control of water drainage and soil slippage. Ca. 400 B.C. two ashlar walls, one labeled "the bastion," succeeded a polygonal terrace wall, possibly from the seventh century.[6] Seven steps, now in considerable disarray, remain of what was once a large staircase, perhaps as broad as 9 m wide if it reached the wall to its south.[7] This monumental stairway, probably punctuated by landings, is thought to have continued up and over the "bastion" 4 m to the east, and probably extended downhill to the west as well.[8] If the hypothetical restorations are correct, the seven tumbled steps at Perachora are a faint reminder of what could have been grand steps 9 m wide, well over 10 m long, that stabilized the site's upper terrain even as they furnished a stately route of access for festival processions leading up to banqueting chambers from the harborside temple and altar.

At the small site of Lato (Plate 26) in eastern Crete, two sets of broad steps have raised issues of interpretation with implications for other sites. In a saddle between two high points of the polis, an open space identified as an agora, with a small temple (perhaps Archaic in date) and a cistern in the middle, is bounded on the west by a small stoa and on the north by a rank of steps 8.4 m wide. The broad steps (nine on the east, ten on the west) vary in riser height from 0.20 to 0.36 m; most are over 0.30 m. The treads also vary: most are 0.34–0.37 m, with a few reaching widths of 0.56–0.60 m.[9] The rank of steps is divided into three sections by two rows of smaller steps for purposes of easier access to and from the stepped area and several rooms at their upper end. Fragments of an inscription found in one of the rooms stipulated that it was to be placed in the prytaneion, providing a relatively secure identification for the chambers atop the steps.[10] While logic suggests that another governing body met on the steps adjacent to the prytaneion, the capacity seems too small for a full ekklesiasterion and too large for a bouleuterion. Indeed, estimating the capacity of these steps presents problems in that most of them are too shallow for comfortable seating. As many as 180 people could be accommodated standing, but only 80 seated. Modern scholars have assumed that seated observers on these steps would feel cramped and crowded, but Hall's research on "proxemics" reveal that people's perception of what constitutes sufficient and appropriate space for and around the body is culturally determined.[11] We can only observe that these steps are noticeably smaller than seats in contemporary theaters. Ambiguity about the observers' posture at Lato complicates interpretation, as scholars have more often associated standing with religious ceremonies, presumably shorter in duration, and sitting with civic organizations (see above, pp. 23–24). For Lato, the excavators and most others have seen the "agora" steps as serving a group concerned with governance. On the other hand, Kolb prefers a religious function, with standing observers facing the small temple in the agora, and whatever rites were enacted in front of it; he also entertains the possibility that the steps served several functions, including political gatherings.[12] With a prytaneion at the top of the steps and a temple at the bottom, plus uncertainty about body posture and its implications, the primary purpose of these steps remains an open question.

Southeast of the "agora" at Lato, a second, larger rank of ten/eleven steps ca. 15 m wide was set below the terrace of a late fourth-century temple and altar. Hewn from bedrock at the west end, but mostly constructed of rectangular blocks, the steps are more regular than those beside the agora. Averaging 0.30 m high (ranging from 0.23 to 0.34 m) and 0.54–0.60 m wide, they are well suited for sitting. The dimensions were less appropriate for ascent and descent; since they abutted the terrace wall, there is no possibility that they gave access to the terrace in addition to their theatral function.[13] Allowing 0.40 m per spectator, the estimated capacity would be about 350, a more plausible figure for an ekklesiasterion.[14] A broad (15.3 by 8.3 m) terrace at the foot of these steps furnished room for either speakers or dramatic performers. An open-air rectangular "exedra" 12.0 m by 4.5 m, adjacent to and aligned with these theatral seats, could help interpret the primary function of the steps, but opinions vary. Was it a kind of loge for distinguished theatergoers (comparable to the *proedria*, elaborate theater seats)? Or could it have been a bouleuterion, conveniently close to the ekklesiasterion, if atypical in form?[15] We lack definitive evidence for dating either set of steps at Lato. The steps

Steps in the Fourth Century

by the "agora" have been assigned to the late fourth century, and those below the temple to slightly later, perhaps early in the third century.[16] Both served assembled groups of people, whatever their primary purpose was.

By contrast, the long stepped wall supporting the treasury terrace at the sanctuary of Zeus at Olympia (Plate 31) was clearly a retaining wall, controlling the lower slope of the hill of Kronos to the north while creating space for the array of small treasuries.[17] The repeated, extended lines of this *Stufenmauer* articulate the northern edge of the sanctuary and give coherence to the existing row of 12 (?) treasuries above. Originally, a nearly continuous stepped slope would have extended 185 m across the north side of the Altis in three connecting parts: the 48 m long segment of eleven steps beside the north flank of the temple of Hera, then 70 m of seven steps that continued east (including presumably 31 m of stepped slope later displaced by the nymphaeum of Herodes Atticus), until they make an oblique angle for another 67 m, at which point they taper into a vertical wall.[18] A water channel for drainage runs along the foot of the entire stepped wall, demonstrating the builders' concern for stabilizing the hillside and reinforcing the idea that the three segments of steps represented a single design.[19] The small Doric temple identified by Pausanias as the Metroon lies close beside this channel, which runs parallel with the temple platform until it makes the oblique angle opposite the temple's pronaos. A row of twelve bases for bronze statues of Zeus was set in front of the water channel from the northeast corner of the Metroon to the end of the terrace. These statues, called *Zanes*, were expiatory dedications financed by the fines levied on athletes who cheated. Behind the third through the seventh of these bases (counting from west to east), four additional steps extend below the water channel so as to compensate for the lower ground level. They may postdate the initial construction of the terrace steps.

Besides retaining the slope and defining the limit of the temenos, the steps at Olympia gave access to each and all of the treasuries. With a riser height ranging from 0.20 m to 0.29 m and a tread width of 0.23–0.27 m, the steps are steep but negotiable for ascent and descent; the tall risers and unusually narrow treads make descent especially awkward.[20] These steps probably also worked as grandstands, but only for standees, as the treads barely leave space for a foot, and certainly not for buttocks.[21] Spectators would have enjoyed an excellent vantage point from which to observe processions, rites, and rituals in the sanctuary, even if the Metroon blocked some parts of the view.[22] Their potential for viewing led scholars to interpret the steps of the treasury terrace as the θέατρον of Olympia mentioned by Xenophon (*Hell.* 7.4.28–31) in his account of combat between the Eleans and the Arkadians in the heart of the sanctuary in 365/4 B.C.[23] He described combat occurring between the bouleuterion and the sanctuary of Hestia, and the *theatron* nearby. Because no theater building has been located at Olympia, Xenophon's reference to a theater, and the specificity of its location, provoked a search for a suitably theatral structure. With the benefit of more topographical and stratigraphic information, recent opinion has favored locating the *theatron* in a different place: the sloping back side of the stadium facing the Altis, which could have been enhanced by wooden bleachers.[24]

Although the steps of the treasury terrace must have been in place by the last third of the fourth century, the time of their installation remains unresolved.[25] Their date has been related to that of the base for the bronze statue Zane VII. The bases for the Zanes are aligned along the steps from

Evidence of Steps over Time

the east end of the Metroon to the east end of the terrace by the entrance to the stadium. Pausanias (5.21.2–5) assigned the first six Zanes to the 98th Olympiad, or 388 B.C., and the seventh, dedicated by Kallipos of Athens, to the 112th Olympiad, or 332 B.C. Zane VII, embedded in the lowest of the treasury terrace steps (below the water channel), has been considered a *terminus ante quem* for the entire system of stepped walls. However, the segment of four steps below the water channel may be a supplementary addition to the original stepped terrace wall.[26] Herrmann asks whether the initial installation might have been built earlier, in the fifth century, preceding or contemporary with the Metroon.[27] There are traces of other stepped retaining walls of fifth-century date in the Altis: behind the Sikyonian Treasury (and perhaps others), south of the workshop of Pheidias, and supporting Stadium II, where Koenigs identified a stepped retaining wall for the second running track of the sanctuary, dated around 500 B.C., a wall of comparable form that may have been reconstructed for Stadium III in the fourth century.[28] It is now possible to consider an initial date in the fifth century for the long stepped terrace along the north edge of the Altis, but present evidence is not sufficient to reassign these steps to an earlier time. Their uses for access and viewing were opportunistic, secondary to their use as a retaining wall. It is the scope of Olympia's stepped wall that is striking, in that the steps delineate the entire northern side of this Panhellenic sanctuary. By providing a controlled, orderly setting that visually rationalized the temple of Hera, the treasuries, and nearby monuments, Olympia's stepped wall conveyed the importance of the several structures while reinforcing their collective identity.

High on a mountaintop in Arkadia, the sanctuary of Zeus on Mount Lykaion (Plate 30) housed another center for athletic competition. Fourth-century inscriptions with lists of victors document the widespread renown of the athletic contests held at the site, with victors from Argos, Athens, Sparta, Macedonia, Rhodes, and more. The sanctuary's fame is further demonstrated by references to victory at the Lykaia in fourth-century inscriptions from Delphi and Lindos.[29] The primary focus of cultic observance—perhaps including human sacrifice—was the ash altar and precinct of Zeus on the summit of Mount Lykaion, described by Pausanias and recently explored by D. G. Romano.[30] Early twentieth-century excavations on the slopes below the altar have revealed facilities for the Lykaian games, most assigned a fourth-century date. These include a hippodrome and stadium, a xenon, two fountain houses, an exedra, a long stoa, and a bank of four steps, plus bases for dedications.[31] In the area southeast of (uphill from) the hippodrome, a line of four steps extends ca. 38 m, roughly parallel to the front of the ca. 65 m long stoa running northeast-southwest.[32] Their dimensions (0.25 m high, 0.36–0.46 m wide) are tall but scalable for ascent and descent, and well suited for both retaining and viewing purposes, as the terrain slopes gently down in front of them (Romano calls them seats).[33] Romano notes that the line of the steps curves slightly to the west at their south (uphill) end, and that ca. 27 m northeast of their north end (toward the hippodrome) is a group of bases for statues and stelai aligned with the four steps.[34] These steps serve for retaining, access, and viewing, but their relationship to nearby structures awaits clarification. Pausanias (8.27.3–6) names the Lykaians among the residents of Arkadia who opposed the defensive synoikism against Sparta that led to the creation of the new city of Megalopolis in the second quarter of the fourth century. Although the Lykaians are listed as having been forcibly removed to the new polis, the sanctuary of Zeus Lykaios continued to operate as a major cult center. The cult was also represented by a

Steps in the Fourth Century

"doublet" precinct in the new polis.[35] Further exploration should provide more information about this remote sanctuary that remained an energized cult center at a time of political reorganization.

Residents of Lykosoura (Plate 28), by the sanctuary of Despoina, also rejected the Arkadian synoikism, but Pausanias (8.27.6) reports that they were given a reprieve when they took refuge in the sanctuary. Located 14 km south of Megalopolis, the sanctuary is set on a long, narrow plateau at the foot of a steeply sloping rocky hill. Excavated in the late nineteenth century, this important site has a temple flanked by a rank of broad steps against the hillside on the south, opposite a long stoa on the north, as well as three altars and several additional structures. The multiple phases of building at the sanctuary range from Archaic times (based on selected small finds) to Hadrianic revisions of the temple and its statue base. The small hexastyle prostyle Doric temple occupied the west end of the terrace, facing east toward altars to Demeter, to Despoina, and to the Great Mother. Along the northern edge of the temple terrace, the long stoa, whose date of construction is not certain, was shifted north (widening the terrace) in its second phase, perhaps to make room for the temple. A small rectangular enclosure was built into the hillside above the temple to the south, and a bank of ten long steps was built against the steep foot of the hill, set close along the temple's southern edge.[36]

These steps were an essential retaining wall (the excavators expressed concern about debris falling from the slope above onto the temple), but their dimensions offer ample space for sitting, and their architectural context suggests a theatral purpose. The height of the steps ranges from 0.27 m to 0.33 m, averaging about 0.32 m, and their depth, 0.710 m at the lowest step, progressively narrows to 0.463 m, and then expands to 0.788 m at the uppermost step, where the buttressing role gained importance over viewing.[37] The top step was about 21 m long, comparable to the length of the temple.[38] Each successive lower step was slightly longer at either end, resulting in a bottom step 28.92 m long.[39] The narrow (ca. 1.6 m) gap between the temple's side door and the lowest of the steps does not provide sufficient space for performances or for processions. While some scholars have proposed that the seating extended further east, to permit viewing ceremonies in front of the temple, spectators in the existing westernmost seats would not have had a clear line of sight to the temple's front, so that the steps could not have been built to observe that area.[40] The steps' apparent spatial coordination with the temple is further attested by a doorway in the south wall of the temple cella, facing the rank of steps. Although atypical in Greek temples, side doorways are known in Arkadian temples, at Bassai, Tegea, and Lousoi, but none had a grandstand opposite the door.[41] The architectural configuration suggests some sort of display or revelation by a religious official to a crowd of seated observers—but we should not rule out hymns, prayers, recitations, or pronouncements as well.[42]

There remain significant questions about the identification, dates, and building sequence of several key structures at this site. Pausanias (8.37.8) reports that the cult of Despoina was a sacred mystery, not to be divulged, and he mentions a structure called a "megaron" uphill and to the right of the temple.[43] Orlandini has argued that the stepped area should be considered the megaron, while Jost adheres to the excavators' attribution of that label to the rectangular enclosure on the hillside.[44] The *terminus ante quem* for the temple derives from its great sculptural group of Demeter and Despoina (Kore) flanked by the Titan Anytos and Artemis respectively, described in detail by Pausanias (8.37.1–6), who attributes it to the sculptor Damophon of Messene. Fragments of colossal statuary excavated at the site fit Pausanias' description. Themelis has narrowed the time of their creation to 200–190 B.C. Since traces of the group's installation are preserved (albeit disturbed by later renovations) within the cella, the temple must have been standing by the end of the third century.[45] Jost favors a fourth-century date for the temple based on comparisons of design and execution with fourth-century structures such as the temple of Zeus Sosipolis at Megalopolis, the limestone temple at Marmaria, Delphi, and the choregic monument of Nikias in Athens, while acknowledging the need for a more comprehensive study than has yet been undertaken.[46] Becker challenges the assumption that the steps and temple must be contemporary, proposing instead that the steps on the south and the stoa in its earlier phase on the north predate the temple, which he assigns to the second century.[47] He observes that the lowest step, just as finely finished as the others, underlies the steps of the temple's south door, and so must be earlier. His interpretation would also help explain the unusually narrow passage between temple and steps. If the temple predates 200 B.C., and if Becker is correct that the steps predate the extant temple, it is possible, if far from certain, that this sanctuary was given formal definition with monumental steps, a long stoa opposite them, and perhaps the three altars by the fourth century. Moreover, we cannot rule out the possibility of an earlier shrine beneath the existing temple. The presence or absence of a temple is critical to any explanation of this site. Becker's concept of rites in an open space between the steps and the stoa seems improbable for such a dark and mysterious cult, and the existing arrangement of steps and temple doorway is unusual enough to suggest that it reflected very specific rites.

Historically, Jost associates this monumental treatment of the sanctuary with the synoikism of Megalopolis in the third quarter of the fourth century.[48] Pausanias reports (8.27.6) that the inhabitants of Lykosoura refused to move at the time of synoikism and sought refuge in the sanctuary of Demeter and Despoina. T. H. Nielsen proposes that Lykosoura was allowed to maintain some sort of separate existence, presumably because of the inhabitants' association with the great sanctuary; we have noted the continuing vigor of the sanctuary of Zeus on Mount Lykaion as well.[49] As seen at Argos in the fifth century, the political disruption and actual displacement caused by a synoikism seem to have been mitigated by attention to sanctuaries. Although Pausanias (8.27.1) cites the precedent of Argos' synoikism for Megalopolis, his analogy warrants caution, as the concept of synoikism described a variety of processes of consolidation.[50] The forced fifth-century synoikism in the Argolid meant the end of civic life for the conquered poleis, yet the ostensibly voluntary synoikism of fourth-century Arkadia seems to have left established major sanctuary sites intact, even flourishing. In the Argolid, we have seen evidence that a regional cult center was taken over by Argos, then expanded and embellished to ameliorate political upheaval, whereas in Arkadia, dispersed existing sanctuaries were enhanced, and small mnemonic doublet shrines were set up in the newly created confederated polis. In both cases, a strategy of using religion to reinforce social ties during politically stressful times was expressed by monumental architectural additions, including stepped structures to promote and display shared participation in processions and rituals.[51]

The sanctuary of Zeus at Labraunda (Plate 24) in Karia, western Asia Minor, may represent another variation on this theme of sanctuary-based rituals and ceremonies as antidotes to polis-based disruption. Monumental architectural projects and epigraphic evidence from Labraunda and other sites under Hekatomnid rule in Karia, such as Amyzon and Halikarnassos, reveal political agendas

Steps in the Fourth Century

along with pious patronage. From a modest site with a sacred grove of plane trees and a temple on a hillside terrace (Hdt. 5.119), the sanctuary of Zeus at Labraunda was reconfigured by the addition of many conspicuous new structures dedicated by the Hekatomnid satraps Mausolos and his brother Idrieus.[52] Nearly all of the new construction at Labraunda occurred under these two rulers and so can be dated to the years 377/6–344/3 B.C.[53] The paved Sacred Way from Mylasa would have been essential for transporting large blocks of marble for construction in the temenos. Still visible along the modern road to the site, it was described by Strabo (14.2.23) as paved, nearly 60 stades (10.6–11.6 km) long, the route of sacred processions.[54] The 8 m wide Sacred Way reached a terminus on a terrace in the southeast corner of the temenos, south of the South Propylaia. Sparse traces beyond the sanctuary indicate that the paved road continued northeast toward Alinda.[55] Forty-two contemporary spring houses have been identified near the roadway throughout its length. An extensive necropolis of at least 80 tombs was situated along both sides of the roadway up to the sanctuary, attesting to its value for public display.[56]

The sanctuary of Zeus occupied a steep south-facing slope and extended over a succession of three terraces, each with a marble-faced *andron* (banquet hall) at the west end. The temple of Zeus stood on the uppermost terrace. At the southeast corner of the sanctuary, two marble propylaia, one oriented north-south, the other east-west, give access to a level area flanked on the south by the "Doric House," a small marble-faced fountain house, and on the north by the substructure of a large building of uncertain purpose. Turning from the Sacred Way, visitors walked through the South Propylaia and then encountered a flight of four broad steps over 10 m wide, leading up to a level enclosure. There, visitors joined those entering from the East Propylaia and turned 90 degrees left (west) to ascend the Great Stairway. The proportions of the four initial steps are taller than those of the Great Stairway but still quite easily negotiable: the risers range from 0.205 to 0.215 m, except for the topmost step, which is 0.290 m tall; the treads range from 0.49 to 0.53 m wide.

The grand 12 m wide monumental staircase of twenty-three steps ascends west to the first terrace (site of the early Roman Andron C). The Great Stairway was apparently set between two existing structures: Oikos L to the south and the massive substructure to the north.[57] With riser heights of 0.14–0.17 m and tread widths of 0.475–0.510 m, the steps are exceptionally easy for walking. Immediately at their top, visitors turned 90 degrees yet again, up nine or more steps 5–6 m wide to the middle terrace. (Nine steps are preserved, but there is room for two to four more.) The passage may have been broader in Hekatomnid times, since the sudden stenosis is caused by a retaining wall that has not been excavated.[58] Turning left (west), visitors faced Mausolos' imposing Andron B, whose marble façade dominated the terrace. The east end of the terrace consisted of a large open space faced by a Doric stoa with six rooms for dining.[59] In the northwest corner of this terrace, another broad staircase, originally 8 m or more wide, led (perhaps by way of an intermediate terrace no longer extant) to the uppermost terrace, site of the temple of Zeus, and, to its west, Andron A, also for dining, and the "oikoi," perhaps a treasury.[60] Subsequent alterations make it difficult to reconstruct the route from this stairway to the temple terrace.[61] Most of the buildings were constructed of local gneiss; however, the two propylaia are made of marble, and the Doric House, the androns, the oikoi, the columns of the dining stoa, and the peristyle of the temple all had marble façades.

Roman and later alterations include Andron C, a stoa on the north side of the upper terrace, rearrangements along the north side of the middle terrace, two bathing establishments, a late antique tetraconch in the southwest sector, and a Byzantine church beside the propylaia.[62] Additional Hekatomnid structures outside the sanctuary include a large built tomb further up the slope, a stadium, fortifications on the hilltop, and dozens of fountain houses and tombs along the Sacred Way from Mylasa.[63]

I believe that Mausolos initiated Labraunda's large-scale architectural expansion, as indicated by his documented expansion of the festival and his name on several structures. His name is inscribed on the architrave of Andron B, and on one of several anta blocks from an unidentified building, perhaps a stoa, reused in the Trajanic North Stoa that may have replaced it.[64] Idrieus' name is inscribed on the architrave of the temple, to which he added a marble peristyle, on the oikoi behind it, and on the south-facing façade of the South Propylaia. In addition, it is restored in inscriptions on Andron A and the small Doric House beside the South Propylaia.[65]

The relationship of the twin propylaia is unresolved. Both marble, Ionic, distyle in antis rectangles with three-door crosswalls, they are nearly—but not entirely—identical in form and unit of measure.[66] Investigations to date have not determined whether the construction and uselives of these gateways would have been simultaneous or sequential, and under what circumstances.[67] There are no traces of earlier buildings beneath either entry structure. Both propylaia, as well as the Doric House, were added under Idrieus, giving more formal definition—and control—to the process of approach.[68] Perhaps each was intended to receive visitors from a different direction: those who arrived on the paved way from Mylasa and coastal areas to the west, and those on the equivalent paved way from Alinda and inland points to the east. The stairs are unequivocally a route of access, a continuation of the impressive Sacred Way leading to the sanctuary. Within the temenos, the pathway was not paved between staircases, and its route made multiple 90 degree turns, yet the successive staircases are consistent enough in scale and treatment to define a distinct, continuous passage.

The net result of these Hekatomnid projects was an ostentatious sanctuary approached by a processional way leading visitors up to the temple of Zeus. The two propylaia were entirely of marble, and the Doric house, androns, oikoi, stoa, and the temple presented marble façades to those on the ceremonial route up through the temenos. All were articulated with the Greek architectural vocabulary, with occasional idiosyncrasies, such as the mixed Ionic columns and Doric entablature of the androns.[69]

Although inscribing a ruler's name on a building façade was an established practice in the Persian world, Umholtz has argued that the Labraunda inscriptions are also consistent with Greek practices.[70] Carstens emphasizes the royal, palatial nature of the site, with its processional way and extensive banqueting facilities.[71] However, labeling behavior as "Greek" or "Persian" emphasizes polarity rather than the hybridity that is more characteristic of Karia under the Hekatomnids.[72] Mausolos was an agile and resilient satrap, a Karian who manipulated diplomatic relations among Persian and Greek powers with skill and success. Vitruvius (2.8.10–11) and other ancient writers (e.g., Strabo 659 and Diodorus 15.18.1–3) report that Mausolos transferred the capital of Karia from Mylasa to Halikarnassos, which he reconstituted after a regional synoikism.[73] Mausolos' geopolitical shift to Halikarnassos may have been related to his expansion of the sanctuary at Labraunda to nearly Panhellenic scale.[74] Two Roman copies of fourth-century inscriptions indicate that Mausolos

Steps in the Fourth Century

extended the festival from one to five days, with specific prescriptions for the sequence of activities.[75] Beyond the literal and figurative veneer of Hellenism, Mausolos sponsored structures that suggest he promoted Greek modes of communal celebration as well, an appropriation equivalent to inventing tradition.[76] The 60–70 stade Sacred Way from Mylasa to Labraunda offered opportunities for grand processions and festive display. Within the sanctuary, the fine androns emphasized the privilege of the banqueting elite, and the stadium attests to athletic contests.[77] Processions, feasting, and contests in honor of Zeus brought residents of the region to a shared experience, bolstering the cultural prominence and economic well-being of the former capital Mylasa at a time when the political focus had shifted to Halikarnassos and the Aegean.[78]

Hellström characterizes Idrieus' embellishment of Labraunda as intended to consolidate the Karian base of Hekatomnid power, in contrast to his brother's use of architecture to draw international attention.[79] Unlike Mausolos, Idrieus explicitly identified himself in dedicatory inscriptions on buildings as *Mylaseus*, linking himself to the traditional capital down the road. The several marble structures bearing Idrieus' name on the architrave certainly constitute a display of his authority. However, it appears that his intended audience was more regional, as dedications at the sanctuary are predominantly from Mylasa and nearby.[80] Alexander's arrival in Karia and subsequent Macedonian rule put an end to Hekatomnid domination.[81] The sanctuary continued in use into Roman times, with periods of building in the Republic and under Claudius and Trajan.[82]

In northern Karia the sanctuary of Artemis at Amyzon (Plate 5) under Hekatomnid rule also had a fourth-century temple on a terrace approached by monumental stairs. An adjacent well-built ashlar wall created a terrace 168 m long to the south, perhaps the site of a sacred grove; traces of a small theater were identified nearby. About twenty steps 7.4 m wide and ca. 12 m long ascended the terrace wall (ca. 6 m high) to the level of the altar and temple, formerly interpreted as Doric prostyle, now considered Ionic distyle in antis. At the top of the staircase, distyle in antis propylaia extended the passage to the terrace. An architrave block inscribed with Idrieus' name, formerly attributed to the propylaia, has recently been assigned to the temple.[83] Although excavations yielded traces of sixth-century use, most extant structures appear to be fourth century in date, confirmed by Idrieus' name on the architrave block. We lack evidence as to whether Mausolos initiated construction of the temple, terrace, and stairs. At both Labraunda and Amyzon, it would be useful to know whether monumental stairs were normally associated with propylaia as components of a processional way when it reached its destined temenos. Coming late in the construction sequence of a multi-phase building project—after monumental approaches, including broad steps, were completed and operational—the propylaia at Labraunda dedicated by Idrieus and the ones at Amyzon may have been envisioned by Mausolos but not achieved until Idrieus resumed work. One can imagine Idrieus seeking to establish his own presence by essentially appropriating the roadway at the critical point of transition, through patronage of structures that marked and controlled access to the sanctuary.

At Mausolos' new capital, Halikarnassos (Plate 19), Pedersen reconstructed a hypothetical monumental staircase leading up to Building C, which he interpreted as propylaia to the terrace of Mausolos' monumental tomb. He envisioned thirty-two steps, 15.4 m wide, ascending 6.4 m to the exterior façade of the distyle in antis gateway.[84] An extant stairway 8.6 m wide led down to the doorway

Evidence of Steps over Time

to the actual tomb chamber. Partly rock-cut and partly constructed, these steps (0.24 m high and 0.44 m deep) would have accommodated the ruler's funerary cortège, but they were then filled in; animal bones and pottery fragments remain from sacrifices made after the closure of the great tomb.[85] There is also a pre-Mausolan rock-cut stairway 5 m wide that led down to earlier structures, whose function may or may not have been funerary.[86]

Among these examples of Hekatomnid architectural patronage, monumental steps consistently serve as routes of access to andron, temple, or tomb. The Great Stairway at Labraunda, the largest example, was not intended for architectural display in and of itself; rather, it is architecture *for* display. The stairs are a setting for processions and festival activities, for colorful garb, for music, and for movement up the terraces of the sacred hillside. The power that they express is in their potential capacity, implying grand celebrations with crowds of worshippers. The facilities Mausolos sponsored suggest that he adopted Greek traditional practices for Karia, recognizing the political benefits to be gained from the solidarity of shared ceremonies, even if they were imported. Among broad steps built in the fourth century, those at Labraunda stand out for their size and comprehensive scope. At Olympia, too, the monumental steps used as a retaining wall were conceived as one component of an architectural composition that brought both system and grandeur to a complex, varied site while serving practical needs. Earlier fifth-century projects at Selinus and the Argive Heraion had demonstrated a similarly ambitious vision, if more specifically focused on creating a setting for a temple.

As we observe a developing tendency to create architectural environments with spaces and structures that shape human experience, we need to consider to what degree such innovations are intentional, opportunistic, or even corrective. The theatral court of the Erechtheion may represent an opportunistic byproduct of a stepped retaining wall. The theatral steps of Lykosoura, surely intended as a retaining wall and for viewing, may predate the temple whose doorway facing them implies unusual cult activity. The breadth of the Great Stairway at Labraunda was apparently determined by its location between two existing buildings. In these and other instances, changes leading to more integrated architectural assemblages may be serendipitous, yet they had consequences that stimulated awareness of the potential of the built environment.

CHAPTER 7

Steps in the Third Century

Discussing sites with monumental steps under the arbitrary but neutral rubric of division by centuries allows us to give greater attention to cultural continuity and diminishes the generalized expectations tied to the term "Hellenistic," often characterized as "baroque," theatrical, or flamboyant in style. Most examples of broad steps built in the third century follow forms and uses established in earlier centuries, with a few notable exceptions. In this time of intense international political maneuvering, of shifting alliances and affiliations, the presence of monumental steps at sites such as Lindos and Morgantina represents recognition by cult officials and political leaders that shaping terrain on a large scale could present a public image of authority. The visual regularity, repetition, and size of grand steps, as well as their evident capacity for crowds, projected control and ambitious display. Less public but equally forceful in their message, the long ranks of steps in the sanctuary of Demeter at Pergamon proclaim the importance of the ceremonies within, and an awareness of the power of architectural form. Stepped structures at sites such as Rhodes and Kameiros, the hill of Kolonos Agoraios in Athens, Amphipolis, Argos, Thasos, Didyma, and Corinth demonstrate the ongoing use of broad steps for access and for framing within and around sacred precincts. The sites considered in this phase are many and varied; after beginning with several sites on the island of Rhodes, my account pursues themes from site to site instead of constructing a specific narrative sequence for this complex period.

In 408/7 B.C. a new polis of Rhodes (Plate 35) was formed through the synoikism of Lindos, Kameiros, and Ialysos. Nevertheless, the three cities did not disappear; extant architectural remains at these sites can be assigned to the fourth and especially the third centuries. Among the signal events of Rhodes's rich and varied Hellenistic history, a catastrophic earthquake of 227/6 B.C. is reported to have provoked international response. Polybius' (5.88–90) account of lavish donations to the Rhodians after the quake includes gifts in kind of building materials and skilled artisans, implying extensive rebuilding.[1] Although we lack physical evidence that can be attributed to that specific quake, the written sources suggest a magnitude of destruction and reconstruction that has led scholars to date several large-scale new structures on the island to this phase of recovery in the last quarter of the third century.

The acropolis of the new city of Rhodes was crowned by the temple of Apollo Pythios, set on a massive terrace 110 by 100 m adjacent to an odeion and a stadium on the east. A flight of twenty-seven monumental steps estimated to have been as much as 12 m wide (now restored in concrete) entered the terrace from the east, opposite but not aligned with the temple.[2] Remains of a long rectangular altar lie immediately north of the steps, aligned with the north and east walls of the terrace, but in no formal relationship to the temple. West of the altar (i.e., between the altar and the temple façade) is a large (38.5 by 34.0 m) quadrangular enclosure cut deep into the bedrock on the north. Hoepfner proposes an elaborate installation here for a colossal bronze statue of Helios in his quadriga, set in a pool.[3] Whether or not one accepts his hypothetical reconstruction, there was a large rectangular hollow between the temple and its altar. Bearing in mind the long use of such an important site, it is conceivable that a hole left from quarrying stone for the temple could have become a cistern (steps on the interior southeast corner lead to the bottom), which in turn could have been modified as a setting for a statue. Eventually, a church was built on the site.[4] The broad steps up to the terrace are symmetrically located in the middle of the terrace, and they lead in nearly direct alignment to the façade of the temple. However, the pathway is not direct, and the arrangement of structures in the temenos is far from symmetrical. Processions to the altar would have turned sharply to the right after ascending the stairs. The quadrangular enclosure would have restricted space around the altar, and any installation in it would have competed with the façade of the temple as the visual focus of those entering the terrace.[5] Acknowledging that the extant remains of the temple probably date to the first century B.C., Hoepfner nevertheless considers the temple's plan (6 by 11 without an opisthodomos) as indicative of a mid-fourth-century date for the original structure.[6] Others date the terrace and steps after 227/6 B.C., associating them with the reconstruction after the earthquake.[7] Given the altered state of the site after countless rebuildings, placing the construction of the several components of the sanctuary of Apollo Pythios chronologically with any degree of precision is unlikely.

The sanctuary of Athena at Lindos (Plate 27c–e) continued as an important site even after the Rhodian synoikism. Sometime in the late fourth or early third century, the temple was rebuilt, apparently in the form of its Doric amphiprostyle sixth-century predecessor. Epigraphic evidence from the Lindian Chronicle and a list of priests' names indicate that the old temple was destroyed by fire, along with most of the dedications, in 392/1 B.C.[8] An inscription on the architrave of the cella doorway, probably dated to 295 B.C., names Kleandrides and Timotheos sons of Aleximakhos as donors.[9] Reconstruction of the rest of the sanctuary presumably followed shortly after that of the temple, in the third century.

The sixth-century pathway (p. 38) was obliterated by a structure that was organized around a central flight of thirty-seven steps, 21.03 m wide (Plate 27d). This flight was crowned by a colonnaded façade with symmetrical projecting wings flanking intermediate doorways, which led to an interior portico with a perpendicular leg to the west in front of three dining chambers. Traditionally called the Propylaia, Lippolis' term "Upper Stoa" suits this multi-function structure better. The stairway was heavily restored in concrete in the late 1930s, limiting possibilities for reexamining remains.[10] Most of the blocks of the temple and other structures on the terrace have been removed, and little soil remains on the surface of the rock, so that it is difficult to assign dates to the various components of the sanctuary. The Upper Stoa is thought to date shortly after 300 B.C., following the reconstruction of the temple.[11]

The excavators envisioned Athenian influence in the projecting wings, drawing comparisons

Steps in the Third Century

with Mnesikles' Propylaia on the Acropolis; Dygve, in turn, cites the projecting wings of the Stoa of Zeus in the Athenian Agora and the late fifth-century stoa at Brauron as a comparison (prototype?) for the dining rooms.[12] While the Upper Stoa certainly adapted established forms, perhaps even from Athenian concepts, its significance lies in what was new, especially the scale of the staircase and the integrated complexity of the building. The conspicuous monumentality of these steps may have been intended to compensate for the unusually small scale of the temple at the apex of Lindos' precipitous acropolis by creating a strong horizontal base comparable to the stepped platforms of grand temples such as the ones at Didyma or Ephesos. The projecting wings of the portico atop the grand steps emphasized the central axis, and the broad steps themselves promoted symmetry, as most people will choose a path up the middle of a monumental stairway. Beyond the crosswall (restored with five symmetrical doorways), the architectural emphasis shifted away from linear axiality to a more traditional angled view of the temple. The visitor emerged into an L-shaped colonnaded portico, which faced the newly rebuilt temple at an angle across a small court. Three chambers, probably for dining, lay behind the colonnade on the north. This portmanteau Upper Stoa thus incorporated a variety of ceremonial activities into a single structure, using an established repertoire of forms to effect a transition from a grand and celebratory ambiance to a more intimate and intense ritual setting.[13]

The architectural changes at Lindos reoriented preexisting processional behavior even as they prepared visitors visually and physically to direct their attention to the upcoming ritual. The angle of approach—indeed, the entire approach—to the temple was changed. This Upper Stoa brought architectural coherence to a steep and difficult site with limited usable space. Processions would have ascended from the northern edge of the acropolis outcropping, where remnants of a contemporary flight of fifty-five steps 3 m wide are still visible beside the modern path.[14] Inside the temenos there was little room for an extended queue, but the breadth of the Upper Stoa's steps would have accommodated large numbers of worshippers. The *pompe* brought important vitality to the act of sacrifice, through the kinetic energy of people and animals in motion, through their anticipation, and through the collective energy of a crowd. Given the steep and uneven terrain, the exceptionally broad staircase captured and concentrated the drive of a procession that would have needed to be gathered for the final ascent. At the same time, the visual effect of the steps' long horizontal surfaces and the physical rhythm generated in ascending them introduced order and discipline to the process, and to the topography of the sanctuary.

Both the nature and the location of sacrifice at this sanctuary are controversial. No archaeological remains can be identified with confidence as an altar, but traces of an orthogonal feature in the inner court in front (northwest) of the temple may be remnants of one. The 18.20 by 12.80 m court would have been too small for the slaughter and butchering of more than one cow.[15] Archaic deposits of animal bones and ash found at the site indicate that animals were sacrificed somewhere at Lindos.[16] Moreover, the Lindian Chronicle records hecatombs sacrificed in honor of such luminaries as Alexander (330 B.C.), Ptolemy I (304 B.C.), and Pyrrhus (d. 272 B.C.).[17] Blinkenberg invoked a passage in Pindar (*Ol.* 39.71) stating that the sons of Helios sacrificed to Athena without fire (ἄπυρα ἱερά) at an unspecified site on Rhodes to assert that cattle were not sacrificed in front of this temple, an argument bolstered by his assumption that cattle could not scale the heights of this acropolis;

however, Pindar's comments were not explicitly about Lindos.[18] Defending the climbing abilities of Lindian cattle, Dygve restored a substantial altar in the court before the temple, while Kondis noted a potential location for a large altar in front of the northeast wing of the Lower Stoa.[19] The particularities of Lindian worship are not fully understood, and we lack a demonstrable focus of ritual activity, a terminus for the *pompe* whose route is clearly demarcated by the extant architecture.

The spectacular 87 m long stoa set symmetrically across the lower part of the third-century stairway may date from as early as the late third century, after the earthquake of 227/6 B.C.[20] Its long colonnade terminates in a short projecting wing at either end. The southeast end reaches the limit of buildable space on the acropolis, and the northwest end matches its dimensions. The stylobate of the central colonnade was set upon the two lowest steps of the monumental stairway.[21] Immediately inside the colonnade, the stylobate intersects the steps of the monumental stairway, so that worshippers would scarcely cross the threshold before facing a grand ascent. Recently scholars have emphasized the unity of concept with the Upper Stoa, proposing that the entire architectural assemblage of Upper and Lower Stoa was envisioned as an integrated composition from the beginning, even if several decades elapsed between the construction of the component structures.[22] However, I believe that both construction and design argue for a more evolutionary interpretation. The Lower Stoa was built of a reddish-gray poros limestone with shell inclusions, described as inferior in quality to the poros of the Upper Stoa and that of the temple.[23] The formal compression represented by the Lower Stoa's encroachment on the stairway is significant and profoundly changes the effect of the broad steps visually and experientially. The Upper Stoa was an innovative structure for the third century in its scale, its close coordination with other structures, and its domination of the landscape, but the form itself is a traditional Greek stoa with wings. Planning the entire assemblage of Upper and Lower Stoas linked by stairs seems improbable for the early Hellenistic period. The exaggerated scale of the Lower Stoa and its aggressive domination of terrain and view is most comparable to the 207 m long stoa across the acropolis at Kameiros, apparently constructed after the 227/6 B.C. earthquake. Without conclusive evidence, it is preferable to interpret the structures at Lindos as designed sequentially, as they were constructed.

The terrace created in front of the Lower Stoa was approached by a new stairway perpendicular to its façade, 10 m to its northeast. Becker estimated the breadth to be 11.5 m, with nineteen or twenty steps, each 0.160–0.166 m tall.[24] This prodrome to the monumental stairway screened by the Lower Stoa was replaced by narrower steps in the first-century enlargement of the terrace. While Becker interprets this staircase as a preliminary to the construction of the Lower Stoa, it could just as easily postdate construction, after the level of the terrace was firmly established. The stairway emphasized symmetry and axiality as it directed *pompai* through the Lower Stoa and on up the great stairway.

Of the three cities of the Rhodian synoikism, Kameiros (Plate 20) has received less scholarly attention after it was explored and restored by the Italians in the 1930s.[25] As at the city of Rhodes, Lindos, and Kos, broad steps at Kameiros were reconstructed in concrete, although ancient sections have been left in places. Extensive remains of houses line a major street, which slopes from a sanctuary and public structures at the lower end up to a third-century temple of Athena and a 207 m long stoa atop the ridge that delineates the upper boundary of the site. We lack information about processions to either sanctuary. At the foot of the road heading uphill, twelve broad steps diminish-

Steps in the Third Century

ing from ca. 9 m wide at the bottom to ca. 8 m wide at the top contribute authority to both temenos and street through their public scale. The steps are restored as 0.16 m high and 0.33–0.34 m wide, well suited for ease of ascent and descent.[26] At present, the best estimate of a date for this staircase is based on the assumption that it and associated architectural improvements to the lower sector of the town occurred after the earthquake of 227/6 B.C.—that is, in the late third or early second century.

Adjacent to the west edge of the monumental staircase is an open-air rectangular precinct on two levels oriented north-south. A doorway in the middle of the west wall (just before the foot of the staircase) gives access to the upper level, a long terrace with multiple statue bases and altars. It is separated from the lower terrace about 1 m below by three steps serving both as a retaining or terrace wall and as a means of access. The lower terrace likewise has altars and dedications to a variety of gods and heroes. Two kouroi were found here, and some monuments can be dated before the earthquake. Present evidence suggests that this space had been sacred for centuries, and that the Hellenistic renovation aligned existing monuments with the precinct and regularized the terrain by adding three long steps.[27]

Additional projects included construction of the lower sanctuary, the temple (of Apollo?), and the altar court, refurbishing the fountain house, and defining the precinct of the altars with long steps. Adjacent to the temple, an open temenos traditionally labeled "agora," lined with inscribed dedications and statue bases, includes a Π-shaped platform along its west wall with returns on north and south raised on three steps.[28] A large altar within this enclosure suggests that the raised platform provided viewing for ceremonies within the temenos, presumably focused around the altar. Heilmeyer proposes that this complex was dedicated to all the gods.[29] The dimensions of the steps (0.31–0.33 m high, 0.40–0.42 m wide) suggest that spectators may have sat; the platform area could have accommodated standees, but one cannot rule out the possibility that the steps were formerly extended upward with wooden benches or bleachers.

In Athens (Plate 13), third-century alterations on the hill of Kolonos Agoraios on the west side of the Agora present challenges of reconstruction and interpretation. Atop the northern end of the hill, minimal remains of an arsenal-like building have been dated to 272 B.C. on the basis of ceramic, epigraphic, and historical evidence.[30] Sometime after 225 B.C., a garden-like setting was created around the Hephaisteion, with bushes along the temple's south, west, and north sides.[31] Perhaps associated with these developments, a broad staircase as much as 9.52 m wide connected the hilltop with the Panathenaic Way outside the northwest corner of the Agora. Although these monumental steps were initially published as Roman, pottery from their bedding has since been dated to the first half of the third century, contemporary with the arsenal.[32] Covered over soon after they were excavated, these stairs are seldom shown on plans of the Agora.[33] The angles and spatial relationships between the top of the steps and the northwest corner of the arsenal do not suggest coordinated planning, but they may be contemporary. These stairs appear to have linked the Panathenaic Way with a poorly preserved roadway on the west side of the Hephaisteion precinct on Kolonos Agoraios.[34] Travelers and processions along the Panathenaic Way could angle uphill to the Hephaisteion before reaching the Agora, or those on the road behind the temple could gain direct access to the Panathenaic Way heading northwest to the Kerameikos.

Was there direct access from the Agora to the Hephaisteion? Many have assumed that some

Evidence of Steps over Time

sort of ramp of packed earth provided a route uphill above the fifth-century benches (p. 49–50). The early benches must have been buried by the time of the fourth century, when the temple of Apollo Patroos was built, and certainly by the second-century revision of the Metroon.[35] However, a gap stayed clear, offering a nearly symmetrically aligned view of the Hephaisteion's east façade, and interrupting the continuity among the various buildings along the west side of the Agora. A staircase ca. 10 m wide, of Roman date (first century A.D.) and incorporating reused material, has been restored leading up the hillside.[36] Might it have replaced a Hellenistic staircase given a monumental frame by second-century renovations to the Metroon? This slope of Kolonos Agoraios continues to present problems of erosion. Just as no trace of an altar remains east of the Hephaisteion, so we may never know what access, if any, was available from the Agora. Given the fragmentary evidence on the east slope, it is best to envision the actual steps on the north slope of Kolonos Agoraios as the documented path to the temple precinct during the Hellenistic period.

Continuing the theme of steps as routes of access, at the strategic site of Amphipolis (Plate 4) in northern Greece, a gymnasium complex in a prominent location in the southern part of the city was approached by a monumental staircase 8.70 m wide.[37] Coins and potsherds indicate that the steps could date to the earliest phase of construction, possibly as early as the fourth century, although a more conservative estimate places their introduction in the early third century; inscriptions from the palaistra attest to its use by the late third century.[38] The steps were a separate component, built against a continuous, distinctively finished wall face of isodomic masonry, with dressed margins and masons' marks. The steps must be contemporary with the palaistra, as they offered the sole access to it and the adjacent running tracks on the north side of the elevated terrace.[39] A gap at the top of the twelve steps in situ indicates that at least three (and possibly four or five) additional steps would have filled out the upper part of this impressive entrance, but it also leaves unclear the precise relationship between the steps and the palaistra building.[40] Elevation provided emphasis for the buildings, and the broad steps would have given grand expression to ceremonies and processions, as cited in a late first-century B.C. ephebic law inscribed on a stele found in front of the palaistra.[41] This inscription, and others from nearby, document the variety and importance of the athletic events held here, and the staircase offered a visual reminder of the scale of the festivities that took place.

The steps in the agora at the hellenized city of Morgantina (Plate 29) in east central Sicily are a spectacular example of steps that perform the three major functions of providing access, viewing, and terrain management—all on a grand scale. Morgantina's agora underwent a massive reorganization during the third-century rule of Hieron II of Syracuse (276–215 B.C.).[42] A great tripartite bank of steps 52 m wide incorporates a ca. 3 m difference in elevation between the lower south and the upper north sectors of an enormous agora. Their polygonal plan does not align with other structures in the agora and appears to have reflected the underlying topography. Built of local limestone, the individual steps range from 0.19 to 0.24 m high and 0.40 to 0.45 m wide, well suited for walking and standing, but too shallow for comfortable sitting. Details of construction suggest that the central section (A) was built first, then the western section (B), at a 130 degree angle, with a substantial stone drain built at the juncture of the two. While both sections have fifteen steps, the top two steps of each appear to be later additions, contemporary with the eastern section (C), whose thirteen steps align with all but the lower two steps of A and B.[43] Section C appears incomplete be-

Steps in the Third Century

cause of its irregular end, perhaps intended to extend to a retaining wall further east, and also some unfinished surfaces, including bosses on lower steps. Nevertheless, these truly monumental steps appear to represent a single concept, even if carried out over a generation or two in the mid-third century. Combining evidence from coins and stratigraphy, Bell proposes a date of 275–250 B.C. for sections A and B, and 250–211 B.C. for section C and the upper additions to A and B.[44] A complementary rank of eight steps tapering to ground level and serving as a retaining wall for a terrace in front of the south end of the east stoa is later in date (though still third-century), but part of the same overall plan for the agora.[45]

Among features in the lower agora, stone foundations of a rectangular structure (7.4 by 3.7 m) south of section C have been called a bema or speakers' platform by the excavation's directors.[46] A speaker standing in the middle of a platform on this base would be well placed to address listeners in sections A and B, who would be in direct line of sight, implying that the "bema" was a contemporary construction; however, it is not securely dated.[47] Interpreting this structure as a bema led to the hypothesis that Morgantina's steps served as an ekklesiasterion for public assemblies. Contending that participants in Greek assemblies sat because proceedings lasted so long, Kolb argues that these steps for standing must instead have been for observers of cultic rites associated with a sanctuary of the chthonian deities, but discrepancies of date and other factors make his explanation unlikely.[48] Morgantina's grand steps were central to the reconfiguration of the city's agora, first for topographical stabilization, second for access to and from key buildings, and third, perhaps opportunistically, for public assembly. The formality of the repeated horizontal lines would have given a visual base to the long stoas framing the north end of the agora, even as their central location meant that they were the place for traffic and movement up and down. We can imagine that Hieron II intended the monumental steps to reproduce the kind of architectural display represented by Selinus' retaining wall, the multi-stepped temple façades of Agrigento, or the Argive Heraion's man-made acropolis.[49] Brought to the heart of Morgantina, they became the site of public participation in governance.

Broad steps also furnish a formal transition between levels at the sanctuary of Pythian Apollo on the hillside known as the Aspis of Argos (Plate 7). The precinct is situated on a slope, with its scant remains located on two terraces rising from west to east and a third partial terrace. Ten steps 27 m wide carved out of bedrock, standing 1.48 m behind a large (14.32 by 3.31 m) rock-cut altar, create a transition between the open lower terrace and the upper terrace, on which there may once have been temples, as reported by Pausanias (2.24.1), and perhaps oracular structures as well.[50] The steps' low risers, 0.21–0.23 m tall, and treads 0.43–0.45 m wide would make for cramped seating, so that any use would involve walking or standing. A small well at the north end of the top step yielded Hellenistic pottery, indicating that it would have been in use during the active life of the steps and altar.[51] Vestiges of plaster and the absence of wear on the bedrock suggest that the steps were probably surfaced with plaster.[52] The steps and altar have been dated by a third-century inscription found at the site concerning improvements to the sanctuary of Apollo, but there is no trace of the temple it mentions.[53] The refurbishing described in the inscription involved moving the altar to the east and attention to the ὀφρύα, or brow (which may indicate the steps), and leveling the surface on the lower terrace. Most likely, the temple was also located on the lower terrace, perhaps facing the altar.

In addition to the altar and steps, the lower terrace has the foundations of an Archaic stoa along the north side, beside informal, irregular rock-cut steps giving access to a slope to the upper terrace. Another stoa, with a central row of columns, occupied the north side of the upper terrace, and there are meager remains of a quadrangular building with an interior peristyle, and also of a peripteral tholos on its own square terrace. The paucity of evidence makes identification and interpretation of these structures highly speculative. The quadrangular building has been called an Asklepieion by Roux, but Tomlinson prefers to consider it a dining facility; the tholos may have been dedicated to Athena Oxyderkes, based on Pausanias' account and a few figurines from the site. The two-aisled stoa has been assigned a fourth-century date, and the other two buildings have been called Hellenistic.[54]

The steps' close proximity to the altar would constrict a procession drastically, making a role as access to and from the upper terrace improbable. Roux argued that the steps were exclusively ornamental, "un simple artifice esthétique" between the terraces, reproducing the look of a stepped retaining wall while providing a visual frame for sacrifices at the altar.[55] Others interpret them as facilities for observing rituals at the altar, which seems more likely in the light of comparable examples at Selinus, Perachora, and Corinth.[56] The configuration of structures at this oracular sanctuary implies that the steps would be the terminus of a procession, gathering worshippers hard by the altar and defining a boundary for the upper terrace that may have been restricted to select visitors, or at least to visitors who did not arrive en masse. Pausanias (2.24.1) mentions a monthly oracular ritual in which a chaste woman prophesied after tasting blood from a sacrificial lamb. Such a practice could account for the accommodations for spectators at the altar.

In the northern Aegean, the sanctuary of Herakles on Thasos (Plate 39), located ca. 300 m southwest of the agora, was bounded on the west by a long (31.53 m) rank of six steps interrupted in the middle by a stepped base.[57] The site has yielded archaeological and architectural evidence of ceremonial banqueting in honor of Herakles from the seventh century on, but many questions remain about its later chronology. The broad steps of Thasos' Herakleion undoubtedly served as a retaining wall, and they also provided access up to the sanctuary, as well as a venue for displaying stelai and a large monument facing west. A large rock-cut altar stood in the approximate center of the temenos, apparently linked to the western steps by a paved area estimated to have been 14 m wide; however, since more of the temenos may have been paved, we cannot assume that this paving represents an ancient path. Along the south side of the precinct, five aligned rooms (oikoi), united by a colonnade along their façade, were apparently used for banqueting, as was an earlier structure beneath this complex.[58] The east side of the precinct was defined by a long north-south stoa-like building called the *lesche* by the excavators, constructed ca. 500 B.C. and later rebuilt.[59] On the north side, a peripteral rectangular building faced south toward the altar, but was not aligned with it.[60] While scholars differ as to whether an earlier structure beneath it (and its Classical successor) was a *hestiatorion* or a temple, the rectangular oikos that succeeded it on the same spot has been considered a temple in that phase of its existence because it was adorned with an added peristyle.[61]

The long steps along the east side of the temenos clearly served as a retaining wall, since their line continued in the form of vertical walls on both the north and the south ends. Their dimensions, 0.19–0.20 m high, 0.44–0.45 m deep, permit easy access up to and down from the platform of the temenos, elevated ca. 1.60 m, and they would have accommodated either seated or standing

Steps in the Third Century

spectators facing west, away from the altar. Small cuttings in the surface of the lowest steps, at the north and south ends of the long steps, may represent traces of a fence or balustrade.[62] In addition, cuttings in several steps indicate that stelai and other dedications were installed there so as to create a display like those at the east and west ends of the Parthenon on the Athenian Acropolis. Approximately (but not exactly) in the middle of the long rank of steps, a square base 6.63 m on each side was interpreted as a propylon by Launey, but as a large votive monument by Roux.[63] Remains of two steps on the west side of the base suggest that a total of six steps once led up to its top, reaching only the fourth of the six long steps—that is, below the level of the temenos.[64] A fragmentary shaft of a Doric column found nearby indicates a second-century date for whatever structure it embellished.[65] Judging by the limited evidence available, Roux's idea of a large, west-facing monument seems the most suitable interpretation. The formal frame provided by the steps, and their orientation, suggest that there were important spaces or structures to the west in areas that have not been excavated.

Explanations of the western steps of the Herakleion must be diachronic, and yet we lack crucial chronological information. Initial construction of the six steps of the terrace has been assigned dates ranging from the sixth to the second century.[66] Recent investigations have dated the north oikos (later recipient of the peristyle) to the early fifth century.[67] Dates for the five-chamber hestiatorion to its south range from the fifth to the third century. The monumental steps of Thasos' Herakleion were apparently designed to extend from the face of the not-yet-peripteral oikos in the north to the colonnaded façade of the five-room hestiatorion, bordering and giving direct access to the open space between these structures, where the altar was located.[68] Based on architectural details and an inscription that refers to building dining rooms, Roux proposed an early third-century date for the (re)building of this hestiatorion complex, together with construction of the steps on the west side.[69] Launey favors an Archaic and Martin a Classical date for this phase of monumentalizing enhancements, which may have included the new peristyle on the northern oikos.[70] Present information indicates that the steps were constructed, whatever the date, to delineate and enhance the western boundary in a general refurbishing of the Herakleion. Installation of stelai and monuments postdates that construction and may reflect activities in the unexplored area west of the sanctuary.

Stone retaining walls *cum* grandstands were erected alongside the great temple of Apollo at Didyma (Plate 16) to accommodate spectators at footraces. Three steps (of a possible seven) are preserved. The lowest, 0.360 m high, was probably intended as a level base; the next two are 0.470 m and 0.465 m. All three are set at levels that correspond to the levels and dimensions of the temple crepidoma opposite.[71] Parallel to the temple's south flank at a distance of 18.24–18.46 m, these bleachers continued the line of the adjacent retaining walls for ca. 13 m and offered clear viewing of competitions on the running track beside the temple.[72] The lowest steps of the temple platform would have provided parallel seating, as indicated by graffiti and inscriptions on their surface and face. Traces remain of intermediate smaller steps, which would have made it easier for spectators to ascend and descend the temple steps as they lined the south side of the temple platform to watch the footraces. The date of these grandstand steps is not certain, but style and circumstance suggest that they would have been built in the third century, when the temple was reconstructed.[73]

The self-contained sanctuary of Demeter on the slope below the acropolis of Pergamon (Plate 34) first achieved monumental form in the third century B.C. Closed off from the external world, it served as a Thesmophorion, to judge by inscriptions, finds, and architectural arrangement.[74] A sacred precinct may have existed on the site in the fourth century, represented by four small altars.[75] Inscriptions of Philetairos (281–263 B.C.) and his brother Eumenes in honor of their mother, Boa, on the temple and its new altar record a first phase of renovation in the second quarter of the third century; another dedication, by Queen Apollonis to Demeter and Kore, inscribed on a new propylon ca. 215 B.C., signals a second major refurbishing of the sanctuary.[76] The tetrastyle Ionic temple to Demeter, made of andesite except for its white marble frieze of boukrania and garlands, bore an inscription on its pronaos recording the dedication to Demeter on behalf of Boa.[77] A large new altar east of the temple and aligned with its façade was inscribed with the same message. The four existing small altars extend across the eastern sector of the sanctuary.

Under Philetairos the sanctuary was also endowed with a long stoa and a broad rank of steps 23.50 m long along its north side. While stabilizing the steep slope, these additions would have served worshippers at the Thesmophoria, including provision for hundreds of attendees seated on steps facing the open area east of the new altar. Piok Zanon's recent study credits Apollonis with a massive expansion of the sanctuary in the last decades of the third century. Besides the propylon with her dedicatory inscription, the west stoa, the upper and lower north stoas, and extensions of the steps of their existing nine rows to a length of 43.9 m long, all were added under the patronage of Apollonis as a counterpart to Attalos I's patronage of the temple of Zeus, in comparable architectural style.[78]

The dimensions of the steps themselves are well suited for seated spectators, with a horizontal depth of 0.408 m and a height of 0.373 m; they are not easily climbed, but are accessible from stairways at either end and a small intermediate passage 23.50 m from the west end and ca. 15 m from the east.[79] These steps could have accommodated 800–850 worshippers for viewing whatever took place in the open space between temple and propylon, at and near various altars.[80]

A similar arrangement—seats facing a terrace in front of a temple—at the sanctuary of Demeter in Corinth suggests comparable ritual activities, perhaps also associated with the Thesmophoria. Late in the fourth century, the sanctuary of Demeter and Kore at Corinth (Plate 15), with its monumental steps lined by rooms for dining, suffered a catastrophic destruction. In the rebuilding, the Middle Terrace remained the focus of cultic events, demonstrated in this phase by deposits containing quantities of votive figurines, miniature vases, animal bones and ash.[81] A well-built trapezoidal building was added along the northern edge of the Middle Terrace, facing an open courtyard, evidently a locus of important occurrences. Directly above it a small rectangular stepped theatral area was cut into the bedrock, affording a view of the court directly below to about eighty-five spectators.[82] While the rock-cut steps of this theatral area are quite irregular, ranging from 0.25 m to 0.35 m in height and from 0.40 to 0.60 m in width, there was sufficient room to sit. Noting the small scale of this area, Bookidis and Stroud suggest that, as with the theatral steps of the fifth century, admission must have been restricted to qualified participants.[83] Elsewhere in the sanctuary, most of the dining rooms were destroyed by the catastrophe and replaced with a smaller number of larger, more substantial dining halls. The uphill passage was broadened by adding an open ramp-like strip, perhaps for animals, along the west side of the intact stairway. A new propylon spanning this dual path controlled access from the Lower to the Middle Terrace.[84] Overall, the organization of the site

Steps in the Third Century

in the third century was essentially the same as earlier, but more clearly articulated, by emphasizing areas of activity: dining halls flank an uphill passage doubled in width; the added propylon marked the passage from the Lower to the Middle Terrace; and the expanded Middle Terrace gained emphasis from the small theater of the Upper Terrace focusing down on the Central Court. Processions uphill, performances—of sacrifice, ritual, drama—and participatory observation are implicit in the specific details and the revamped architectural configuration of these third-century modifications.

Nevertheless, rebuilding at Corinth repeated existing pathways, locations, and behaviors—in contrast to rebuilding at Lindos, where processions to the temple (in the same location) continued, but their route and the worshippers' experience underwent a dramatic change. Although Dygve attributed the grand staircase of the Upper Stoa to "oriental traditions" most immediately represented by the Great Stairway at Labraunda, we recall that a broad stepped route of approach was well established in Lindian tradition from Archaic times.[85] Moreover, the earlier steps at Lindos, and probably Labraunda as well were facilities for the human spectacle of processions, as well as architectural statements. The third-century renovations express both expanded festivities and also greater awareness of visual effects, perhaps to assert the importance of the sanctuary despite its small temple. The broad steps gave a metonymic presence in built stone to the festive *pompe*, with expansive size, yet sustained order in the repeated regular steps and the symmetry of the stoa itself. Their striking breadth allows for the accumulation of spectacular pageantry and processional energy, ordered and concentrated atop the acropolis en route to the sacrifice.

Reviewing other developments in the third century, we know more about patronage at Pergamon's sanctuary of Demeter and at Morgantina than at Lindos. While Philetairos and Eumenes advertised their beneficence by inscribing dedications on the temple and altar, Apollonis (and Attalos I) appear to have moved beyond donating individual structures to creating a comprehensive built environment for ritual. Their initiatives included not only framing the sanctuary with stoas and steps, but also adopting distinctive styles in architectural details such as capitals and components of the entablature so that their role as benefactors of many structures would have been visible and identifiable.[86] The broad steps of Morgantina's agora were part of larger revisions that brought order and system to public space. Serving to control the terrain of the grand rebuilt agora lined by long stoas and granaries, the scale of these steps added dramatic display to the space, as they also provided for both access and communal assembly. Besides the comprehensive designs of Lindos, Pergamon, and Morgantina, in the third century there are more examples of broad steps used as monumental pathways (Rhodes City, Kameiros, Amphipolis, Athens) or as grandstands with an intent to frame and focus on specific loci (Argos, Didyma, Corinth, perhaps Thasos). The proliferation of instances of incremental change bears witness to a growing recognition of the desirable effects of architectural definition. Even as these less ostentatious facilities give form to human activities, we note that they also bring increasing organization and spatial articulation to their respective cities and sanctuaries.

CHAPTER 8

Steps in the Second Century

Sanctuaries housed structures of many eras, so that it is an ongoing challenge to dissect how worshippers experienced a site at a particular phase in its history. Sites given monumental form in the third century, such as Lindos, Pergamon, and Morgantina, continued to flourish in the second century and beyond. On the other hand, sanctuaries such as the Asklepieion at Kos, or the sanctuary of Apollo at Knidos, may have had earlier origins but received such extensive additions in the second century that I have elected to discuss them at this stage. The shifting tides of political alliances, allegiances, and events in the second century undoubtedly affected the affairs of sanctuaries, cities, and towns, but caution is warranted in tying architectural developments too closely to specific events or rulers. In addition to the well-known sanctuaries of the west coast of Asia Minor, rich remains at sites in Pisidia, inland in southwestern Asia Minor, reveal the widespread adoption of Greek architectural forms for civic practices and prestige.

In the years between the Treaty of Apamaea in 189 B.C. (and the Seleucid withdrawal from western Asia Minor) and the ceding of Pergamon to Rome in 133 B.C., large building projects at many sites reveal widespread practices of patronage and euergetism, both internal and external. Beneficence came in many forms, with donors ranging from private citizens to kings, and gifts ranging from endowed feasts and festivities to temples and stoas. Patronage and euergetism involved complex processes of donation, decision making, and implementation; Apollonis' explicit inscribed dedication at Pergamon was exceptional, with few counterparts even at sites as well documented as Kos. Nevertheless, the second-century surge in construction coincides with epigraphic evidence of support for expanded display in both activities and architecture.[1]

The sanctuary of Asklepios on the island of Kos (Plate 23) has the best-known set of monumental steps in the Greek world. Set on a hillside, its three successive terraces linked by broad steps, the Asklepieion achieved its essential organization between the fourth and second centuries. Roman additions to the site did not change the configuration significantly. Quantities of contemporary inscriptions from Kos provide information about historical circumstances and religious activities that supplement testimonia from ancient written sources.[2] Although this sanctuary is often cited as the epitome of Hellenistic architectural compositions and discussed as if it were a single simultaneous creation, a diachronic view of stages in the formation of the Asklepieion correlated with contextual information from epigraphic evidence offers a more nuanced understanding of the site.

In 366/5 B.C. an island-wide synoikism resulted in the establishment of a city called Kos on the northeast coast of the island.[3] Located at or near an earlier polis, Meropis, the new city had a fine harbor with an agora nearby, sanctuaries, and other amenities of a fourth-century polis.[4] The sanctuary of Asklepios lies 3.5 km from this new city, on the slope of a north-facing hillside with natural springs. Its most renowned and revered feature was a sacred grove of cypress trees that may have existed as a holy place even before the synoikism. An epigram of the late fifth century or early fourth century, excavated on the Upper Terrace, refers to Paian, a healing god, "ἐν ἄλσει" (in the grove).[5] Fourth- and third-century inscriptions indicate that the sanctuary's cypress grove was sacred to Apollo Kyparissios (a site-specific *hapax epiklesis*, or sole occurrence of the name) as well as Asklepios.[6] It may be that Zeus as Alseios and Athena as Alseia were also worshipped in association with the cypress grove at the Asklepieion, and the grove served as a sacred focus for other Koan cults in the fourth century.[7] Epigraphic and literary references to processions to the cypress grove attest that it was a destination of continuing significance.

By the end of the fourth century, the cypress grove was well established as a sacred place associated with a variety of deities, several with healing powers. Paian and Apollo Kyparissios each had a healing function, the latter sometimes jointly with his son Asklepios. In addition, Machaon, son of Asklepios, was worshipped in the late fourth century at the sanctuary.[8] Although worship of Asklepios was not explicitly attested until the third century, when it became a state cult, at least one ancient source, a pseudo-Hippocratic letter, appears to confirm the presence of Asklepios at the sacred grove before the synoikism of 366/5 B.C.[9] He emerges as the dominant deity at the sanctuary in the third century, when it was developed into a major Panhellenic center. Logical as such a connection may seem, there is no evidence to link the preeminence of Asklepios with the act of synoikism.[10]

The architectural remains of the Asklepieion represent three main phases of pre-Roman construction. Unfortunately, important information has been lost as a result of the thirty-year delay in the publication of early twentieth-century excavations.[11] Architecture and some inscriptions were published, but not the associated small finds. Soon afterward key structures, such as the monumental steps, were extensively reconstructed in concrete, effectively eliminating prospects for much review of architectural details. Nevertheless, Schazmann's 1932 study, together with Becker's meticulous examination of the staircases, supplies useful information as to how the Asklepieion developed. Interdonato's recent analysis of the site and its cult, including a catalogue of architecture, sculpture, small finds, inscriptions and written testimonia, provides a comprehensive synthesis of the sanctuary and its ceremonies over time.[12]

The earliest structures of the sanctuary were situated on the Middle Terrace, where there was a source of water. A fourth-century marble slab, apparently an orthostate from an earlier altar inscribed to Halios, Hamera, Machaon, and Hekate, was found near the extant altar of the second century.[13] Asklepios' name does not appear. Major building on a large scale began early in the third century. While Schazmann, followed by others, insisted that the entire three-tier Asklepieion was conceptualized from the third century on, there is considerable latitude in defining whether that concept was a series of three terraces or a more extensive plan for construction; the former seems most likely.[14] The Middle Terrace and its altar remained the focus of cult activity. A small Ionic temple (Temple B) of Asklepios faced the altar from the west.[15] Along the temple's south side, Building D, sometimes identified as an *abaton* for incubating the sick, more likely housed dining chambers for officiants or elite worshippers; a spring house behind Building D would support either interpretation.[16] Another temple, perhaps dedicated to Apollo (beneath the later Roman Temple C), faced the altar opposite the temple of Asklepios.[17] Traces of additional structures—an exedra, a *lesche* (Building E), and others—have been noted southeast and east of this group. A terrace wall bordered this assemblage of buildings close by on the south, controlling slippage from above. Another terrace wall defined the northern (downhill) edge of the terrace.[18] In stabilizing the slope, three terraces from north to south up the hillside created a series of formal spaces, articulating preexisting usage and creating opportunities for expanded activities at the Asklepieion. On the uppermost terrace, three porticoes supported by tufa columns (later remodeled in marble) formed a Π-shaped building open to the north, framing the sacred cypress grove.[19] Stray fragments of poros architecture (two triglyphs, three geison blocks) suggest that there may have been another structure on this terrace, perhaps obliterated by the later Temple A.[20] Access to the Upper Terrace was presumably at either the east or the west end of the terrace, where the slope is reasonably gradual.[21]

North of the Middle Terrace, below the ca. 6 m high terrace wall, another Π-shaped stoa faced south (uphill), framing a large rectangular open space ca. 90 by 45 m.[22] The Doric colonnades, reconstructed in marble in the second century, had a series of rooms behind, perhaps associated with the healing process, or else used for communal feasting by festivalgoers. Over the centuries, rows of statue bases in front of the porticoes and the retaining wall came to line the four sides of this terrace.[23] Just west of center in the long northern segment of the colonnade, a propylon embedded in the stoa afforded a nearly symmetrical entrance to the large, open rectangular Lower Terrace. Leading up to the propylon are the foundations and side walls of a broad stairway over 13 m wide, but none of the actual steps are left in situ.[24] Across the terrace, opposite the propylon and slightly west, another set of broad steps 10.4 m wide ascended to the Middle Terrace, as indicated by side walls perpendicular to the terrace wall.[25] This bank of steps was built over and against the terrace wall between the Lower and Middle Terraces. It may have been associated with the initial phase of construction, based on traces of masonry not covered by modern restoration, although Interdonato prefers to assign it to the grand realignment of the second century.[26] Ascending worshippers would arrive at the heart of the sanctuary facing the altar-temple axis. Although Gruben questions whether the stoa complex and propylon of the Lower Terrace should be dated as early as the third-century phase of construction instead of the next major building program in the second century, the closest comparisons for architectural details appear among third-century buildings.[27]

By the mid-third century, worshippers would ascend the broad steps to the propylon and pass through the lower stoa to the open expanse of the Lower Terrace. From there they would see another broad stairway traversing a terrace wall to the altar and temple of Asklepios, with auxiliary buildings clustered nearby, accentuating the sense of a cult nexus. Close behind these structures was another terrace wall. Farther up the hillside, the sacred cypress grove would have furnished a visual backdrop for activities on the lower terraces; only the ends of the portico framing it may have been visible. This third-century architectural configuration suggests that people and processions moved purposefully to the altar and the Middle Terrace, which may have become the end point for processions to the grove; or there may have been additional passageways (no longer extant) up to the trees of the Upper Terrace around either end of the Middle Terrace.

Steps in the Second Century

The excavators based their dates on architectural styles and techniques together with epigraphic evidence. Inscriptions provide unusually specific information as to how the Asklepieion functioned. In 242 B.C. a Panhellenic pentateric festival, the Great Asklepieia, was established. Traveling *theoroi* solicited grants of *asylia* and contributions from cities and rulers. Processions, sacrifices (in detail), and competitions are recorded in inscriptions.[28] This newly grand sanctuary would have served daily needs, especially for healing; inscriptions tell of an annual festival (*panegyris*) with procession; and every five years the gala Great Asklepieia would attract visitors from far and wide to join festivities at the sanctuary. The success of Kos's Panhellenic venture is documented by the varied sources of *asylia* decrees found in Kos, and the varied origins of contestants whose names are preserved in victory lists from the Great Asklepieia. International contacts are attested from Sicily to Samothrace, from mainland Greece, Crete, and Asia Minor to Mesopotamia.[29] This expansion of the festival and subsequent additions to the sanctuary appear to result from Koan initiative and enterprise, combined with donations by major benefactors. Sumi notes that the festival's expansion followed Seleukos II's coming to power.[30] Hoepfner proposes that Ptolemy II Philadelphos, who was born on Kos in 309/8 B.C., contributed Temple B and underwrote the third-century expansion of the site, an attractive idea that lacks corroboration.[31] Ptolemy II Philadelphos seems to have conveyed his appreciation for his birthplace by not occupying or controlling the island as he did other nearby islands and cities, since Kos appears to have maintained its autonomy even after Ptolemaic rulers controlled Thera, Crete, Delos, and Halikarnassos.[32] Such a favorable political climate could have encouraged donations, but we lack information about any specific patron.

By the second quarter of the second century (ca. 170–150 B.C.), another major building phase transformed the Asklepieion. New construction on both the Lower and the Upper Terrace replaced the earlier porticoes with marble stoas with Doric columns and entablature on the same Π-shaped footprint.[33] A massive new terrace wall between the earlier Middle Terrace wall and the sacred grove gave sharp definition to the Upper Terrace. Most striking was the addition of a large new temple (A) set symmetrically toward the front of the Upper Terrace, and a truly monumental approach stairway, both broad and long, leading from the altar of the Middle Terrace through the terrace wall to just before the new temple.[34] The marble-faced steps, of which the six lowest are in situ, ascend in at least two flights. The lower flight, 11.25 m wide, of perhaps thirty-eight steps, passes over the old terrace wall to a horizontal landing in the intermediate space between old and new terrace walls. Bases for dedications flank the paved intermediate platform, and there are slots for holding posts, perhaps with banners, on either side wall of the upper flight. The second (upper) flight, 9.25 m wide (the same as the width of the temple's cella), of perhaps twenty-seven steps, penetrated the new terrace wall, then expanded to six steps 18.075 m wide, creating a visual base for the temple.[35] The entire height differential was more than 10 m.[36] The steps themselves were well suited for walking, with a height of 0.170 m and a depth of 0.335 m.[37] Their starting point, in close proximity to the altar and Temple B, suggests that the lower flight could have served double duty as a viewing stand for sacrifices and rituals at the altar, as well as access to the new temple above. Temple A was large, ostentatious, and dominant. Its 6 by 11 peripteral Doric form has been compared to the temple of Asklepios at Epidauros, only larger.[38] Hellström speculates that Temple A might be a banquet chamber in the guise of a temple, like the androns of Labraunda.[39] However, the addition of continuous marble paving in the center of the Middle Terrace and between the top step of the grand staircase and Temple A conveys an experiential message of cultic connection.[40] Within decades of this large-scale refurbishing, the altar was also rebuilt, around 130 B.C.[41]

These second-century additions projected the principles of axiality and symmetry onto the existing arrangement of the Asklepieion. In the third century, the ascent to the altar was phased, with a Labraunda-like rhythm of broad stairs and terraces. The implied passage from the propylon to broad steps to altar complex represented a necessary route of approach, arranged with an awareness of symmetry, as shown by the Π-shaped stoa of the Lower Terrace. But it is only the relentless alignment of second-century structures that suggests an intended formal axis from the propylon to Temple A. Some have speculated that the mortuary temple of Queen Hatshepsut at Deir el-Bahri in Egypt might have inspired the emphasis on linear axiality, based on comparable form and contemporary function, as well as Ptolemaic affiliations with the island.[42] However, even though a sanctuary to two healing deities associated with Asklepios—Amenhotep son of Hapu and (secondarily) Imhotep—was established within the upper terrace as early as the third century, the Egyptian site was not the grand integrated complex of Hatshepsut's time. Worship was situated solely in the reconstructed upper court, there were workshops in the middle terrace, and significant areas of the lower terrace were occupied by cemeteries, so that the effects of processional ramps ascending grand terraces would have been greatly diminished.[43] During the period of design and construction for Temple A at Kos, Hatshepsut's complex was operating as a local shrine; only in the second half of the second century, and in later Roman times, did it gain prominence for its healing and oracular functions.[44]

The new second-century structures would have affected the behavioral patterns of worshippers. Were the grand stairway and the Upper Terrace intended to articulate (and facilitate) processions that had always made their way to the sacred grove? Or were they entirely directed toward the temple? Who had authority to reconfigure such a major sanctuary and its essential practices so thoroughly? It is tempting to attribute such ostentatious changes to royal patrons seeking to make their presence known at a much-visited international shrine. Schwandner's notion of parallels of form between Temple A and a scarcely preserved temple in the gymnasium at Pergamon led him to conclude that Eumenes II gave Kos a replica of the Pergamene temple.[45] Although supporting evidence is scant for this hypothesis, there is epigraphic evidence for Koan worship of Eumenes II (197–159 B.C.) as Eumenes Soter.[46] In the town of Kos there was already a festival called the Attaleia after Attalos I, and there were processions for Eumenes II and Attalos II in the gymnasium there.[47] While a Pergamene patron is certainly plausible, Ptolemaic and other benefactors also appear in epigraphic and historical records.[48] Interdonato attributes the initial third-century expansion of the sanctuary to Ptolemy Philadelphos, and the second-century reconfiguration to the Attalid Eumenes II. Although there are sound historical reasons for assigning these large projects to the respective rulers, there may not have been a single patron, even for such grand improvements. Inscriptions from Kos record combined resources—from public subscriptions, state donations, contributions to the cult, and externally solicited funds—all used to carry out rituals and activities at the Asklepieion, so that patronage was undoubtedly a complex process with many actors.[49]

Such major renovations raise questions about agency. Who generated the initiative for such a

Steps in the Second Century

large building project? Would an external if friendly monarch be entitled to change worshippers' behavior by endowing the new temple and its setting? Did sanctuary supervisors solicit a patron or a group of benefactors to underwrite grand new facilities? The Middle Terrace must have become impossibly cramped as the Asklepieion's renown generated lavish processions and celebrations. Did primary agency lie with worshippers in procession? Even if the route of access changed, gala processions to sacrifice are amply attested as a key feature throughout the life of this sanctuary. It may be that participation in a kinetic performative ritual such as the procession counted for more than its particular route as it led to the culminating event of sacrifice at a fixed point (the altar) within the sanctuary. As they accommodated crowds of worshippers, the emphatic apex of temple and stairway themselves represented in built form the scale and practice of worship at the Asklepieion.

Stairs were for descending as well as ascending. It is possible that these monumental steps at Kos could also have served a theatral purpose for viewing sacrifice at the altar, whose ongoing importance is shown by its enlargement when the staircase and temple were built. Changes in the pathway were part of a larger modification of the sanctuary. The display and movement—and destination—were ultimately more important than a fixed or traditional route within the confines of the temenos. The meaning persisted in the act of processing even if the route changed. However, once the procession was given architectural articulation with monumental steps, the built path codified this behavior, bringing the *pompe* that much closer to ritual status. The order, rhythm, and organization intrinsic to the form of steps are essential traits of ritual, making the architecture and its activity mutually reinforcing.

Not far from Kos, at the west end of the city of Knidos (Plate 22), a rank of theatral steps looked down on the sanctuary of Apollo Karneios from above.[50] The sanctuary was entered through an Ionic propylon at the far west end of a major 10 m wide east-west city street.[51] On a lower terrace to the south was a Hellenistic Doric peripteral (6 by 11) temple.[52] A pair of buildings, at least one a nonperipteral temple, faced a large stepped altar ornamented with reliefs of nymphs. The altar had an inscribed dedication to Apollo Karneios, and also the names of two sculptors, providing both attribution and a second-century date.[53] The extant temple is Roman, but unexplored remains beneath it suggest that there may have been an earlier structure on the site.[54] Close parallels of architectural materials and execution indicate that construction of the round temple of Athena and its small altar on the terrace directly above the altar of Apollo must be contemporary with the altar, and so must date to the mid-second century.[55] Along the north side of the altar, an imposing retaining wall of ashlar masonry ca. 7 m high or more defines one side of that lower precinct. There was a spring at its foot, and above it a series of steps for seated observers ascends the steep slope on the north side. Beyond the seven rows of steps in situ, Bankel has restored a long, narrow terrace with a small shrine at its western end above the existing rows of steps.[56] Another retaining wall forms the border of the upper precinct, dedicated to Athena, with its round temple on the west, small rectangular altar, and a series of small treasury-like buildings continuing to the east.[57] Each of the existing steps is 0.35–0.37 m high and ca. 0.51 m deep. The longest row of steps is ca. 20 m long, but neither the east nor the west end of the steps has been located, so that they probably extended farther, especially to the west. With such limited information we can only speculate that the stepped facility could have accommodated 300 spectators or more. Observers were seated, as suggested by the dimensions of the steps, and confirmed by two intermediate aisles with smaller steps for ease of walking, like those at Lato or Pergamon's Demeter sanctuary, or the passages dividing the *kerkides* of a theater.

The close and integrated relationship with the temenos of Apollo below and that of Athena above implies that a stepped arrangement was part of the second-century configuration.[58] While recognizing that the steps contributed supplementary support to the two retaining walls on the steep terrain, we can also ask what observers watched in the precinct of Apollo.[59] The stepped seating affords spectacular views of the site of Knidos, which would have included processions making their way to the sanctuary for sacrifice, contests, and festivities associated with Apollo Karneios. Controversy continues as to whether this sanctuary was the site of contests in honor of Triopian Apollo mentioned by Herodotus (1.144), whether the Triopion should be located further east on the Datça peninsula, or whether the Triopion could have been moved to Knidos from another site on the peninsula.[60]

Far inland from the Aegean sites of Kos and Knidos, cities in Pisidia, the rugged highland region north of Antalya in southwestern Turkey, appear to have initiated and carried out a conscious strategy of adopting Greek practices.[61] There are many sites with substantial Hellenistic structures, followed by even more impressive Roman buildings. Few sites have identifiable traces of earlier structures. Sagalassos, Termessos, and Selge were major cities that adopted Greek practices, judging by physical remains and written testimonia; even small cities, such as Ariassos, Adada, Cremna, and Pednilessos have yielded evidence of what appears to be elective hellenization. Two unexcavated sites, Adada and Kapikaya (also called Kapilitas near Güynece) have monumental steps arranged so as to suggest that they held assemblies for governance, perhaps implying some form of democracy.[62] The array of architectural remains at each of these little-known sites indicates that they were less cut off from the ancient world than they are today.

Adada (Plate 1) lies 80 km north of Antalya and 40 km south of Lake Egridir. Hellenistic structures include fortification walls with towers, a large three-storey "market building," and a long rank of broad steps facing down toward an open "agora" while also furnishing access to the acropolis above.[63] Later additions include four Roman temples, the ruins of a Roman theater, and assorted inscriptions in situ. The steps at Adada performed all three functions of monumental stairs: they stabilized and supported the hillside, provided ample seating for several hundred people, and offered a means of ascent. They also brought a clear message of man-made order to the urban center. Ranging from thirty steps at the north end to nineteen or twenty steps at the south, this 24 m long bank comprised the entire east side of the agora and could have seated as many as a thousand people.[64] With riser heights of 0.330 m–0.345 m, and treads 0.590 m wide, the steps are well suited for seating, although they are not difficult to ascend, and they also afford access to upper areas. Details of the ashlar masonry of the fortification walls, and parallels between the market building and comparable buildings in Pisidia and western Asia Minor (e.g., Alinda, Aigai, Assos) indicate a date in the second century for these structures.[65] Since it appears that the fortifications adjacent to the steps received a fine finish to fit with the workmanship of the steps, Mitchell suggests that the steps and agora predated that section of wall.[66] Support for dating the steps before the mid-second century comes from an inscription found at Termessos, renewing a treaty between Termessos and Adada. The treaty refers explicitly to the democracy instituted in both cities, offering reason to

Steps in the Second Century

speculate that the steps at Adada were used for public assembly, perhaps associated with democratic governance. H. Brandt has proposed a date of 165–150 B.C. for the document on historical grounds, noting that it is a renewal of an alliance, implying comparable political conditions at an even earlier date.[67] To be sure, Adada could have had democratic governance prior to building a facility for assembly—if indeed that is how the steps were used.[68] At any one site, just what constituted democracy is not clear. Extrapolating from written sources and inscriptions elsewhere in Pisidia, "democracy" in the region was carried out by magistrates, councils of elders, and assemblies.[69]

The topographically spectacular but little-known site called Kapikaya (Plate 21), or Kapilitaş, southwest of Güynece, also has ranks of steps arranged in a way that implies public meetings, perhaps again to be associated with democratic practices.[70] A tall vertical rock face atop a high ridge marks this site, tentatively identified as the "city of the Typalliotai" cited in another inscription from Termessos.[71] The site's various well-built Hellenistic structures include fortifications, a market building, and several buildings whose scale and fine ashlar masonry suggest a public purpose.[72] Just south of the site's distinctive notch is a trapezoidal area flanked on three sides by freestanding banks of limestone steps: seven rows 17.2 m long on the north, four rows 13.3 m long on the opposite, south side, and four rows 8.8 m long on the east; the west side was open. With risers of 0.35 m–0.40 m and treads 0.50 m wide, the steps could accommodate up to 450 participants who stood or sat.[73] There is no indication of a roof. Unlike the single grand bank of steps facing a public space at Adada, this arrangement appears to be a separate structure for the purpose of meeting; like the steps at Adada, these steps, located among monumental buildings in what must be public space, convey a strong impression of civic participation. An additional example of monumental steps, along the east end of the agora at Sia, also in Pisidia, may represent another facility for Hellenistic democratic assembly. However, present evidence is insufficient to ascertain whether the steps are Hellenistic or Roman.[74]

With ample Hellenistic and Roman remains, few of them excavated, these Pisidian sites demonstrate what has been called strategic self-hellenization. Perhaps as early as the fourth century, and certainly by the second century, large and small cities in Pisidia appear to have adopted Greek political, economic, and cultural practices, to judge by monumental ashlar architecture in forms and configurations indicative of Greek behaviors, supported by epigraphic evidence.[75] Pisidia may have been remote, but it was not isolated, as it straddled a critical north-south route to the Pamphylian coast. Inscriptions and ancient authors record repeated examples of Pisidians in significant numbers serving as mercenaries in the forces of Seleucid and Ptolemaic rulers.[76] Greek language, institutions, and cultural practices can be identified in the region post-Alexander and undoubtedly spread from major centers to lesser towns and sanctuaries.[77] Fortifications, market halls, and assembly places that have been dated to the second century (in association with stabilized conditions under Pergamene rule after the Peace of Apamea in 189 B.C. and the Seleucid withdrawal from the region) in some cases may be datable to the third or even fourth century. Under both Seleucid and Pergamene rule, many Pisidian cities remained autonomous to some degree, as indicated, for example, by the persistence of local coinage.[78] The cities and towns of Pisidia were not truly independent but enjoyed significant autonomy as long as they provided funds and fealty to the king, and tolerated royal garrisons.[79] Their "spontaneous" hellenization leaves many questions about how and where such change originated. Constructing fortifications, market halls, and assembly places required major investment; the presence of such conspicuous public architecture implies energized economic and political activities. Pergamon was a pervasive but not all-controlling presence in Pisidia in the second century, and Pergamene patronage has long been seen as the reason for new construction throughout the region. However, scholars have recently emphasized the decentralized nature of Attalid rule.[80] Vanhaverbeke and Waelkens propose a model of peer polity interaction in which Pisidian cities and towns are seen to have sought prestige by adopting Greek and Pergamene cultural practices, including structures and styles of building derived from Greek buildings and forms.[81] While some buildings may represent patronage as a means of pacifying a particular town, competitive emulation among local elites may also account for many of the hellenizing structures of commerce, religion, and governance in Hellenistic Pisidia.

A temple and staircase at the major Pisidian city of Sagalassos (Plate 36) may also indicate connections with Pergamon. The "late Hellenistic" Doric temple of Zeus (probably associated with the indigenous deity Kakasbos) sits on a high promontory above a steep slope. A long flight of steps 12 m wide, now scattered on the hillside, provided formal access up the steep slope to the distyle in antis temple.[82] While the temple's low podium had only three steps, the building was set slightly east of center on a 20 m wide terrace approached by seven steps, below which was the long flight ascending the hill.[83] The effect has been compared to several third- and second-century temples at Pergamon, each set on a podium or terrace approached by a flight of steps at the front: the temple of Dionysos, the temple of Hera Basileia, the temple above the Upper Gymnasium, and the temple of Magna Mater at nearby Mamurt Kale.[84] Vandeput considers the podium to be indicative of a Roman Imperial date for the temple at Sagalassos, while Waelkens emphasizes Pergamene parallels and a late Hellenistic date, in the mid-first century B.C. or later.[85] Can we identify the Hellenistic podium temple in Asia Minor as a logical solution to sloping ground regularized with terraces and stairs? Or should the arrangement of podium and stairs always indicate contact with Rome, direct or indirect? Sagalassos and other sites in Pisidia are useful reminders of the complex processes and mechanisms implied by a term like "hellenization." The earlier, fourth-century Karian projects of Mausolos and Idrieus appear to represent a ruler-driven embrace of Greek styles and behaviors to foster political goals. By contrast, the Pisidian cities' second-century projects look more like local initiatives. After generations of exposure to and appropriation of Greek institutions, Pisidians seized economic and political opportunities to maximize the status of their cities, towns, and sanctuaries, undoubtedly encouraging external patronage when strategic.[86] Under Seleucid and especially Pergamene rulers, towns as remote as Kapikaya and Adada built large permanent buildings to serve administrative, economic, and political functions, and to present their own wealth and prestige to their neighbors and the world.

Conclusion

Taming terrain for humans is the fundamental purpose of every example of steps considered here. Control of topography is the primary effect. The intrinsic form—successive, regular horizontal surfaces accentuated by contrasting light and shadow—displays mastery of the challenge of sloping ground and the irregularity of nature. In addition, steps' open shape and monumental breadth project their inclusive function and their public role. In contrast to roofed buildings with doorways, broad steps convey an image of acceptance through their capacity to accommodate large numbers of people. To be sure, steps also control behavior: pathways prescribe routes, and grandstands define the number and placement of observers. In form and use, however, the message of broad steps in the Greek architectural tradition is communal.

Steps are participatory architecture. Close scrutiny of monumental steps in context across time and space provides useful evidence of behavior in antiquity, from individuals and groups to poleis and states. The biomechanics of the human body in relation to sloping ground and built form help to diagnose the several functions of broad steps, as retaining walls, pathways, and grandstands, permitting us to extrapolate group activities, especially in sanctuaries. The foot's repeated contact with a sequence of horizontal surfaces (treads) at regular, predictable intervals creates a sense of organization and system, affirmed by the visual formality of broad steps. This personal physical awareness fosters a phenomenological interpretation of architecture, in which space and form are understood and articulated as they are experienced. On the other hand, as we assess diachronic change in Greek public architecture, the increasing coordination and integration of structures into coherent complexes reflects a more abstract, Cartesian approach to design and construction that operates in a dynamic, often complementary relation to the initial phenomenological approach.

As we consider group design over time, coherence emerges from the clear definition of structures and spaces achieved in part by stepped pathways and framing grandstands. Symmetry is a fundamental trait of individual buildings in Greek architecture, but it is less evident in the arrangement of parts at most sanctuaries until the second century at Kos. Even then, the entry to the Lower Terrace at the Asklepieion at Kos does not line up exactly opposite the stairs to the Middle Terrace. Axiality, the dominance of a direct linear approach within a site, is not a major principle of design until the addition of Temple A and its steps at Kos. (Compare the symmetry we see in Italian sites built in one phase, as at Gabii, Praeneste, and Tivoli [see Appendix]. In central Italy, the alignment

Conclusion

of theater and temple at Gabii, Pietrabbondante, and Tivoli is not governed by a central passageway, in contrast to the pronounced axiality of Praeneste's sanctuary.)

What we do see in the Greek world is a developing realization of the symbolic power of built structures and complexes, beyond the scope of individual buildings such as temples or theaters, since each of the three uses for monumental steps implies a relationship to another space or structure: retaining walls exist to create stable horizontal areas; routes of access exist to achieve a destination or direct a procession; and grandstands exist for viewing events nearby. Even though broad steps may be seen as a discrete architectural component, their form is more relational and less self-contained than a closed building. Steps gain meaning from spatial relationships: topographical placement, adjacent structures, and objects or installations found or placed nearby.

Based on their form and the configuration of a site, steps may convey motion or stability. They may present a dominating visual effect, yet still be a means of access to a functionally more important structure, such as a temple. Some embody simultaneous upward and downward motion. Others shift roles between furnishing negative space and asserting a positive volumetric presence within an architectural site. Assertive and adaptable, monumental steps can be seen as catalysts whose presence profoundly alters how other structures and spaces—or groups of buildings—are experienced.[1]

In tracing changes in group design, discussion by century is arbitrary and sometimes awkward, but ultimately necessary. Avoiding the prejudicial labels of "Archaic," "Classical," and "Hellenistic" while elucidating phases of construction allows us to envision how sites operated at different times in their history, and to witness stages in the combination of structures into an architectural composition. At Corinth, Lindos, and Kos, parsing the sequence of building yields a more accurate picture of the respective sanctuaries than is possible with assignment to a single period, or a look at the totality of extant remains. Without presuming linear development, we can nevertheless identify patterns of use across the centuries at our various sites.

From the sixth century to the first, we have seen the connective role of broad steps recognized as they link and frame places and monuments in Greek sanctuaries. Early examples of steps and ramps at Lindos, Athens, Corinth, and Aegina demonstrate that the drive for monumentality extended beyond temples and altars to processional routes. These examples offer important evidence of grand *pompai* in the sixth century, while grandstands at Perachora and Eleusis signal the intensity of the experience of viewing ceremonies in a group. The fragmentary remains of Selinus' Temple M and environs anticipate later architectural design. As reconstructed, the alignment and coordination of temple, steps, and altar—all additionally oriented to a master urban plan—are without contemporary parallel.

In the next century, Selinus' spectacular early fifth-century retaining wall presumably originated to support grand renovations on the acropolis, but, intentional or not, its powerful display continues to impress modern visitors. On the other hand, the extensively stepped hillsides of the Argive Heraion look like a conscious exploitation of steps as display, an ashlar equivalent of the Cyclopean citadels of nearby Tiryns and Mycenae. The lack of crucial information about the means of access from the Middle to the Upper Terrace precludes our greater understanding of the role of steps in group design at the Heraion. In Athens, the theatral court along the north side of the Erechtheion was evidently not intended for display, but replaced an earlier paved court, perhaps as the site of

Conclusion

the Plynteria. Ancient authors and modern scholars consistently note how many special cultic loci the fifth-century temple sheltered, but in fact it encompassed even more; the precise architectural coordination between the theatral court and the adjacent temple building reveals the inclusion of unroofed structures and their rites in the planning, a remarkable integration of topography, architecture, and ritual in this fifth-century version of a building complex. The Erechtheion embodies multiple diverse objects and agendas, including the most sacred image in Athens, in a single architectural composition that anticipates later developments in sanctuary design. At Corinth, a central spine of broad steps connects and coordinates sectors of the sanctuary of Demeter and Kore, as well as individual structures, from the dining chambers of the Lower Terrace to the ritual areas of the Middle Terrace, and the theatral area of the Upper Terrace. This monumental stairway gave lasting expression to ceremonial processions while also defining an axis that brought a sense of system to the site and its appearance.

In the fourth century, monumental steps at Olympia and at Labraunda created coherence through architectural forms and associated behaviors. Olympia's stepped retaining wall that became an elongated grandstand created the long northern border of the temenos, linking the entrance on the northeast to the stadium on the northwest while incorporating the existing temple of Hera and treasury terrace. Continuity of line and consistency of form provide an intentional, ordered frame for activities within the Altis. The Great Staircase of Labraunda and the associated steps from terrace to terrace attest to Mausolos' appropriation of Greek processional practices, presumably to build solidarity in his political base. Whether or not he sought to emulate the zigzag Sacred Way of Delphi, as proposed by Hellström, he clearly intended to capture the social reinforcement of a crowd moving upward through a temenos of dedicated structures to a ritual focus.[2] In and of themselves, Labraunda's series of broad steps and marble-fronted androns and temples unify the site through repetition of form and material, together with the connection afforded by the pathway. The exceptionally wide steps in the lower part of the sanctuary may represent Mausolos' appreciation of the excitement and energy of parading worshippers, and perhaps also of the visual reminder represented by the steps' monumental scale when unoccupied.

Whereas the framing and linking steps at Olympia and Labraunda reveal an intent to affect the entire sanctuary, we begin to see steps as part of truly comprehensive planning in the third century, at Lindos, Morgantina, Pergamon, and Kos. The symmetrical wings flanking the broad steps of the Upper Stoa at Lindos may or may not refer to the Propylaia of the Athenian Acropolis. Like the Propylaia and the Erechtheion, Lindos' building gives articulation and emphasis to the ascent of challenging terrain while including multiple functions: entry and perhaps dining. The Upper Stoa not only controls the topography of Lindos' stark acropolis but dominates the worshipper's visual field, bracketing the monumental stairway so as to guide processions upward through its portico to the temple. The symmetry and scale of the Upper Stoa's façade creates a more completely encompassing setting for ritual and festivities than seen before. In an agora, not a temenos, Morgantina's steps likewise convert exigencies of terrain into a dramatic asset that would have highlighted the refurbishing of the civic center with their striking size and public function. While the steps at Morgantina serve as both pathway and grandstand (as well as *analemma*), the bema in the lower agora suggests that their social role, for gathering groups of people, predominated. The great triple bank

Conclusion

of steps spanning the central space proclaimed order and system in the new agora and enhanced community. At Pergamon's sanctuary of Demeter, the ruler's role is unequivocal, with the patronage of Philetairos (and Eumenes) and of Apollonis made explicit in inscriptions. The monumental theatral steps in both phases of construction are simply one element of a tightly organized, coherent scheme for the entire temenos. We see a comparable desire to create a complete setting for ritual and associated activities in the third-century development of the Lower Terrace at Kos, framed by three long colonnades and the terrace wall. The intention of symmetry is likely, even if the broad stairs of the propylaia do not quite line up with those rising to the Middle Terrace. Terracing was not new at this site or elsewhere (most notably Labraunda), since a sacred grove probably occupied a defined Upper Terrace as early as the fourth century. However, linking even the Lower and Middle Terraces with monumental steps leading to the altar and cultic center introduces axiality as a more overt trait in sanctuary design. It was later, in the second century, that the addition of Temple A and its enormous stepped approach brought ostentatious axiality to the Asklepieion at Kos, imposing a multi-stage linear ascent directed at an apex beyond and above the altar and its cluster of buildings on the Middle Terrace. This second-century version of the Asklepieion has come to epitomize Hellenistic architecture in standard handbooks, without acknowledgment of its preceding incremental development.

Evidence of large-scale building in second-century Pisidia appears to represent voluntary competitive emulation of Greek cities. Increasing archaeological exploration has revealed that Pisidia was less remote than modern scholars have assumed, and its inhabitants were more aware of Greek practices and governance, perhaps well before those appropriated behaviors were expressed in built facilities. In central Italy, emulation of Greek styles and forms in architecture extends from details such as capitals to components such as porticoes, and to sanctuary design, in which the alignment and symmetry of temple-theater complexes such as Gabii and Pietrabbondante apparently reflect local patrons' admiration for sanctuaries such as Lindos and Kos in the Greek East. At these Italian hillside sanctuaries, the frontal podium temple on an upper level was aligned with a theater below that embodied the concept of broad steps. However, alignment is not the same as axiality, which emphasizes a prescribed, symmetrically situated route to a distinct terminus. Neither Gabii nor Pietrabbondante had an identifiable processional way. In that sense, the dramatic successive stairways leading up from terrace to terrace at Praeneste are as striking a change in the existing tradition as the addition of Temple A at Kos.

In assessing these sites and structures, it is worth reviewing the experience of worshippers in a gala procession. Even local festivals would draw varied groups, often in flamboyant dress. The essential energy of a crowd in motion was intensified by music, rhythm, colorful garments, portable images and symbolic objects, heat, smells, and the suspense of escorting living creatures to their sacrificial death. Accompanying the beast(s), the crowd together anticipated and then witnessed the drama of killing a living animal, itself a compelling event, additionally invested with ritual meaning and history, subsequently affirmed by a feast for all at the end. Active participation in processing and viewing created a *communitas* of shared excitement and experience.[3] Stepped facilities at sanctuaries were intended to maximize the effects of the ceremony, and reinforce the solidarity engendered by these practices. Stepped structures in agoras likewise gained meaning by drawing people together

Conclusion

for shared endeavors, such as governance. The pathways and grandstands of cities and sanctuaries were not simply settings for ritual; their form and placement gave tangible expression to these group behaviors, and provided metonymic representation of the festivities.

Such solidarity was grounded in the traditions of a particular place, its specific terrain, its history, and the recurrent symbolic acts of ritual. The sanctuary's role as an alternative, often complementary authority to that of the polis is illustrated by the several versions of polis displacement discussed above. Whether we label the mid-fifth-century destruction of Mycenae and Tiryns by Argos "synoikism" or "conquest," the outcome—the allocating of conquered lands and their revenues to the Heraion—demonstrates the mediating effect of an authority perceived as separate from the political. Extensive rebuilding at the Heraion gave physical proof of these disbursements while enhancing the resources and appearance of the sanctuary itself.[4] The fourth-century defensive synoikism that created Megalopolis provoked enough resistance from Lykosoura that the sanctuary of Despoina was apparently embellished and a small doublet shrine established (along with others) in the new city; in this case, the importance of the sanctuary was acknowledged and its adjacent residents permitted to stay.[5] While Mausolos is known for his strategic synoikism of the peninsula's towns to form the city of Halikarnassos, his actions in the region of Mylasa and perhaps on the island of Kos demonstrate a shrewd awareness of sanctuaries' potential to mitigate political upheaval. He undertook a massive expansion of the sanctuary of Zeus at Labraunda, including the grand processional way from Mylasa to Labraunda and through the sanctuary, even as he transferred the Karian capital from Mylasa to his new city at Halikarnassos.[6] It is conceivable (but not provable) that Mausolos also brought about the synoikism of cities on Kos, and possibly the concomitant development of the nearby Asklepieion, so as to engender a sense of local identity and affinity separate from previous allegiances to individual poleis.[7]

The intense *habitus* of festivalgoers undoubtedly affected the architecture for such celebrations. Walking uphill was easier on a stepped path, and watching a sacrifice was more gratifying with a clear view from an elevated position. Monumental treatment of steps and other structures gave conscious validation to past practices, and created differential importance among components of a sanctuary.[8] Larger processions and ceremonies meant more wealth and renown for a sanctuary; grand facilities proclaimed the size of crowds by their size even when not in use, enhancing a site visually and conceptually. Display and prestige certainly accompanied these well-integrated sanctuary complexes, and many of the earlier monumental steps. Visitors to sites with such spectacular architecture presumably enjoyed a sense of added status from participating in festivities given importance by their constructed setting. Consistency of form, repetition, symmetry, and axiality all made for clearly articulated sites, often with dramatic displays of architectural control. Nevertheless, the primary agenda was always group experience, concentrated in prescribed pathways and captured by grandstands for assembled crowds.

In considering architectural changes, agency is always a question. By whose authority did change come about? Labraunda, Amyzon, and both phases of Pergamon's sanctuary of Demeter represent obvious examples of explicit royal patronage as dominant agency, donating structures with clearly prescribed purposes. Traditionally, the appearance of monumental architecture at outlying sites has often been assumed to represent the benefactions of such rulers—those of Pergamon in the Aegean regions, for example, or those of Rome at sites in Italy. However, as we recognize more complex cultural processes of emulation and appropriation of behaviors and built forms by local populations, we adjust our notion of agency and pay more attention to funding from multiple sources.[9] Construction of permanent facilities at a sanctuary codified activities; at sites such as Lindos, Labraunda, and Kos, changes in the processional route would significantly alter the scenario of the *pompe*, for example.[10] Changes such as the addition of the Upper Stoa at Lindos or Temple A and its stairway at Kos, as well as monumentalization in Italic sanctuaries, require a more nuanced interpretation of agency, starting with separating out the component parts of architectural patronage. Besides *habitus*, defining agency in these cases includes discerning whose initiative generates building, who funds new structures, who designs them, and who implements the planning. We have few answers, and these several roles may interact or overlap differently at different sites.

For royal and communal agency alike, funding drove changes both directly and indirectly. Most notably, the practice of euergetism by wealthy elites promoted increasingly numerous and lavish festivities and feasts from the fourth to the first century. Private benefaction in poleis and sanctuaries, in the form of donations to public and sacred institutions, was labeled "euergetism" as early as the fifth century; however, the preponderance of primary evidence for the practice dates to the fourth and especially the third and second centuries.[11] Donations by wealthy individuals took many forms, from funds for buildings (both construction and repairs) to support for festival activities such as processions and the purchase of animals for sacrifice, to the endowment of food, wine, or oil for entire populations.[12]

Processions, for instance, offered opportunities for wealthy patrons or kings to project their virtues in a traditional religious format that enabled collective reception by worshippers; there were also processions in honor of benefactors themselves.[13] Such contributions were freely given, often in a context of competitive self-representation for both the donor and the recipient institution. Kings, citizens, foreigners, even women by the third century—all could be *euergetai*, whose munificence (and rewards in the form of specific privileges) were recognized in honorary decrees, inscribed and erected as a public record.[14] As noted above, royal names such as those of Attalids and Ptolemies attract our attention, but crucial gaps in our understanding of agency remain, especially when it comes to the role of priests and administrators supervising the respective sanctuaries. Explanations for initiatives and change must necessarily differ for the various sites considered here, but most of the financial underpinnings of expanded functions and facilities from the fourth century on were likely assembled from a variety of sources: votive gifts, rent from leasing sacred land, sometimes public subscription (*epidosis*), as well as external and internal individual euergetism.[15] The epigraphic record of increasing euergetism from the fourth century on is reflected in architectural remains, including monumental steps. Competitive patronage meant larger processions, grander sacrifices, and more worshippers, requiring improved pathways, broad routes of access, and enhanced facilities for participatory viewing. The scenarios at each site will have differed. The sanctuary of Athena at Lindos, for instance, was an old sanctuary on a dramatic acropolis; the Asklepieion at Kos was a relatively recent foundation, with a special "market niche" for healing, that sought and achieved Panhellenic status in the third century.

Controlling terrain may be their core function, but the crucial asset embodied by these monu-

Conclusion

mental steps is social energy, the collective enthusiasm and solidarity of large festive groups performing and actively observing familiar yet immediate rites. A key source of religious power, this group vitality—and its continued reproduction from the past into the future—also represented political leverage, as reflected in our several examples of *metoikesis*, and as recognized by royal patrons and individual *euergetai*. Enhanced by sensory cues—visual, aural, olfactory—and the cultural legacy of ritual, the practices of processing and viewing at the heart of sanctuary function were given monumental treatment, commensurate with that of temples and altars, as broad stepped paths or theatral ranks of steps. Their grand scale, fine materials, and placement within sanctuaries established these broad steps as components expressing the importance of the rites and festivities they supported. Such "interanimation" of body and place, of behavior and built form, gave meaning to structures in the moment and beyond, even as they gave frame and shape to ceremony.[16]

APPENDIX

Hellenistic Italy

Characterizing second-century architecture in central Italy presents even more difficulty than hellenization in Pisidia. Hellenization, whether in Asia Minor or Italy, and Romanization in these and other regions represent distinct and variable processes of interaction between local societies and larger linguistic, social, economic, and political behaviors and institutions. At a time when Romanization (primarily political and economic) was taking place in Italy and in the Greek world, indigenous sanctuaries in Italy serving local cults were thoroughly reconstructed, with forms and configurations evocative of architecture in Hellenistic Greece and Asia Minor.[1] We face the challenge of determining whether this new monumentality was related to the Roman presence, directly or indirectly, or whether it was a direct result of Italic contacts in the Aegean. At any given site, the answer may include all three factors. Some of the most spectacular sanctuaries that were developed in the period after the Second Punic War and before the Social War began in 91/90 B.C., such as those at Gabii, Pietrabbondante, Praeneste, and Tivoli, achieved their architectural display with monumental steps or with stepped theaters that appear to link symmetrical structures. Each of these sites that expanded dramatically in the second century reflects a particular set of circumstances and a separate history, including relations with both Rome and the East. The mixture of local societies, hellenization, and Romanization expressed in these Italic sanctuaries includes key design features that have been attributed to Hellenistic Greek influence.

In central Italy, in sanctuaries and increasingly in urban centers, we see the appropriation of Greek ornament such as capitals, of building forms such as temples, porticoes, and theaters, and of principles of design such as axiality and symmetry on multi-level sites.[2] Questions remain as to whose initiative is to be credited with bringing Greek design to sanctuaries in central Italy and who executed specific designs. Since architectural planning is generally less tangible and portable than ceramics, metalwork, or sculpture, and since little contemporary written testimony survives on the subject, tracing mechanisms for transmitting building concepts is necessarily speculative. In central Italy, as well as in the city of Rome, hellenization was a cultural phenomenon, manifested in literature, material culture, and even festival practices.[3] The long-established, visible Greek cities and sanctuaries of Magna Graecia, including nearby Campania, undoubtedly provided models for structures such as theaters and the activities that took place in them.[4] From well before the second century, the Roman presence—economic, political, and military—in the Aegean region is well documented, as is Roman emulation of Greek literature and art, so that Greek forms, images, attitudes, and practices also reached Italy embedded in Romanization. Bernstein notes, for example, that *ludi scaenici* increasingly took the forms of Greek literary drama, and that overt Greek organization and practice were adopted for Roman processions and celebrations.[5] However, epigraphic evidence also reveals intensive economic connections between residents of central Italy and commercial centers in the eastern Mediterranean. Roman conquests and policies may have opened up opportunities, such as making Delos a free port, but we need not assume that the trade and exchange between agents in Italy and the Aegean was always Roman in nature.

Dramatic developments in the architecture of central Italian sanctuaries can be attributed to the patronage of wealthy local elites. Local aristocrats mentioned as benefactors at several second- and first-century sanctuaries in Italy are also named in inscriptions from Greek sites around the Aegean, especially the free port of Delos.[6] The commercial activities of these merchants in the Greek world included lucrative trade in wheat, wine, oil, and slaves, as well as booty from warfare and related profiteering.[7] In their ventures abroad, these Italians would have witnessed celebrations and festive display in monumental sanctuaries at cosmopolitan sites such as Rhodes, Kos, or Pergamon, impressive for the scale and formality of their constructed settings. They would have observed the practice of euergetism in its several forms, including instances of conspicuous patronage as a means of self-representation.[8] How and why such experiences were manifested in Italic sanctuaries is difficult to ascertain, and manifestations undoubtedly differed somewhat from one site to the next. Rome's political and economic presence in central Italy in the second century was substantial, and increasing.[9] The relationship of the respective sanctuaries to Rome varied significantly: Gabii, Praeneste, and Tivoli were literally and figuratively closer to Rome than Sulmona and Pietrabbondante (where details of the theater and of Temple B link it to Campania). The construction of grand sanctuaries and the appropriation of Greek forms, the visual vocabulary of prestige, represent local elites' statement of status, whether in resistance to Rome or competitive emulation of other sanctuaries or Rome itself.[10] Whatever the motivation, the architectural outcomes look similar, expressed as large complexes of colonnade-framed terraces, temples, and theaters, and presumably indicating a codification of behaviors as well.

What little we know of the processes of commissioning, design, and execution in the mid-second century comes from Rome. New construction of temples and basilicas in Rome would have demonstrated the effects of grand architecture near at hand. The presence in Rome of the architect Hermogenes' protégé, Hermodorus of Salamis in Cyprus, suggests that there was a market in Italy for his skills and expertise.[11] Referring to events a century later, Plutarch (*Pompey* 42.4) noted that Pompey so admired the theater at Mytilene that he had "sketches and plans" made in anticipation of emulating the Greek structure.[12] However, in the period before the Social War and more overt Roman domination afterward, we simply do not know precisely how designers of second- and first-century sanctuaries in central Italy conceived of combining components such as temples and theaters, stairs and stoas, into encompassing, controlled architectural compositions.

Early examples of monumentalized sanctuaries such as Sulmona and Gabii shed some light on the question. Extant structures at Sulmona reveal a process of monumentalization in which a sacred locus was given an increasingly larger and more distinctive form with a portico and broad steps,

Hellenistic Italy

presumably to accommodate expanded celebrations and greater numbers of visitors. The sanctuary of Hercules Curinus is located near ancient Sulmo (modern Sulmona) on a steep slope of Mount Morrone at the edge of a broad fertile plain, in the territory of the ancient Paeligni (Plate 43). Graves in an extensive cemetery nearby indicate occupation in the area in the fourth and third centuries. An early cult focus may have been a cave 300 m above the sanctuary, or a spring on the nearby slope, evidently a center of attention in subsequent centuries.[13] In the third or second century, a massive polygonal retaining wall over 40 m long and 4.25 m high created an upper terrace along the steep face of the rock just below the spring (now canalized). The retaining wall was aligned northwest-southeast along the rock face. Visitors to the sanctuary, entering on the north, would walk beside this imposing wall to its south end. They would then head east, uphill (perhaps up steps now built over), and turn 90 degrees left, to the north. A perpendicular rank of eight steps more than 10 m wide, each 0.20 m high and 0.37 m deep, led up to the spring and the terrace, where a first-century shrine is now located, presumably on or near the site of earlier cult activity.[14]

Modifications in the course of the second century contributed a monumental quality to the site. A long portico was created by adding a two-step stone base supporting a row of wooden columns in front of the existing polygonal retaining wall. Adjoining this new stoa on the south, but not aligned (angled slightly east), a broad flight of thirteen steps, from 18 m wide at the bottom to 14.5 m at the top, led from the level of the terrace in front of the stoa up ca. 2.6 m to the level of the lowest of the eight existing steps to the shrine. The grand new steps lay perpendicular to those approaching the shrine. The intermediate terrace thus formed was paved, accentuating the continuity between the two flights of steps so as to define a pathway, while also creating a sense of importance and sacred association by this monumentalizing treatment. The stoa and the lower stairs faced west onto a terrace, whose original dimensions have been obliterated by later expansion. Sometime in the first century, an enormous lower terrace framed by stoas along the north, east, and south edges was added here, supported by fourteen enormous vaults of concrete (*opus incertum* and *opus quasi-reticulatum*), giving this sanctuary the scale and grandeur seen at contemporary terraced sites in central Italy such as Terracina, Praeneste, and Tivoli.[15]

Although Sulmo's sanctuary of Hercules Curinus lacked the alignment and symmetry of those larger sanctuaries, its identifiable phases of development demonstrate the adoption of architectural enhancements that served practical needs. The portico made use of the existing polygonal retaining wall to provide shelter, while the broad steps helped retain the steep terrain and gave emphatic access to the focus of cult on the upper terrace. They also furnished a convenient grandstand from which to view festivities or convene an assembly. These added components can be seen as Greek-derived, less for details of their execution than for their purpose of giving grand and permanent form to the sanctuary and its ceremonies. The sanctuary's key components—shrine, steps, and portico—occur elsewhere in central Italy during the second century, aligned in a coherent architectural relationship that Hanson labels a "theater temple."[16] His label describes relationships of architectural structures based on principles of alignment and symmetry, but it does little to explain the behaviors and ceremonies served by these structures. Hanson and others have reasonably assumed that theater temples gave form to the rituals and celebrations associated with cult, including the *ludi*, or games, in their various manifestations, but at least one example, at Pietrabbondante, was used for political assembly.[17] Close scrutiny of a few early theater temples reveals variety in both function and design.

The sanctuary of Juno at Gabii (Plate 40), reliably dated to 160–150 B.C., is the earliest known example of the central Italic theater temple: an elevated podium temple flanked on three sides by porticoes, facing an altar above a semicircular theater-like structure.[18] The lower, theater-shaped sector of the sanctuary has not been completely explored; its shape and location, compared with other sites, suggest the existence of a theatral structure of about twelve rows of stepped seats on the slope below the temple. Regular cuttings in the rock of the upper terrace indicate that the temple was surrounded by a sacred grove.[19] The end walls of the porticoes are aligned with the façade of the temple, while the lines of the back walls of the porticoes continue (with a short jog in the wall on the east) as a temenos wall that brackets the theater. An intermediate wall bisects the temple-altar group and the theatral area, demarcating their respective precincts. In the center of this crosswall, a small opening lies on the axis of temple and theater, permitting controlled access in either direction and allowing limited visual linkage between the theater and the temple.[20] At ground level the crosswall would have severely restricted the visual experience of this complex as a unified entity. On the other hand, the view from the temple's porch would have presented more conspicuous coherence.

In this early example at Gabii, we can observe attention to symmetry and alignment. The frontality of Etrusco-Roman temples and their elevation on a podium lead logically to an emphasis on axiality, since access was feasible only by way of steps up to the front of the temple. However, the intermediate precinct wall at Gabii suggests that, rather than an extension of the temple's steps, the theater was considered a separate facility, placed in a formal alignment with the temple and altar above, but with separate meaning and activities, apparently focused downward, away from the altar.[21]

The theatral sector at Gabii may have been used for religious festivities, and it may have been used for political assembly.[22] As in the ongoing debate over the use of Greek theaters (above p. 24), it is possible to envision both activities, but it is harder to ascertain the primary motivation for constructing the facility. Inscriptions from the Samnite sanctuary at Pietrabbondante (Plate 41) indicate that political assemblies took place there in the theater below the temple of the late second century. With traces of earlier use in the third and possibly the fourth centuries, this sanctuary saw the construction of two temples in the second century, one atop a slope with a theater below. An earlier Ionic temple had been destroyed at the end of the third century, probably by Hannibal in 217 B.C. Oscan inscriptions on and in the nearby Doric Temple A of the early second century mention magistrates, revealing the political function of this sanctuary. In addition, they identify the ongoing patronage of the family of the Staii, known also from inscriptions on Delos.[23] About 50 m west of Temple A, a theater very similar to the one at Sarno and the small theater at Pompeii was constructed at the end of the second century. It had a high proscenium decorated with semicolumns and an Ionic cornice, faced by three rows of stone seats, defining the lower part of a sloping cavea.[24] The cavea was enclosed by a fine polygonal circuit wall; the remaining interior slope must have contained wooden benches or seats continuing the pattern of the stone built rows up to the circuit wall. Shortly afterward, ca. 100 B.C., the podium Temple B was built on a small framing

Hellenistic Italy

terrace immediately above the theater and aligned with it. Temple B was tetrastyle prostyle, with Corinthian capitals and a Doric entablature of terracotta-faced wood. The profiles of moldings from its podium have exact parallels in a temple at Capua.[25] Facing three altars (corresponding to its three cellas) set in front of the steps of its podium, the temple looked out over the theater.[26]

Like the sanctuary of Juno at Gabii, the building complex at Pietrabbondante features a large podium temple flanked by porticoes, facing an altar or altars, all set above a theatral area demarcated by an intervening wall with a single small doorway on the central axis of both theater and temple. At both sites the configuration of structures on a hillside is aligned and symmetrical. Despite the apparent unity of overall design, intermediate walls would have compromised visitors' visual perception of a connection between the upper and lower structures. Access to the theater seats was either through the *parodoi* at the bottom of the theater or through the narrow gap between temple and theater; only from the stylobate of the temple was there a comprehensive view of the aligned buildings. No such intervening structures affected the sanctuary of Fortuna Primigenia at Praeneste or the sanctuary of Hercules Victor at Tivoli, which appear to be unified architectural landscapes, combining porticoes, theaters, steps, and temples into symmetrical arrangements on multiple levels.

By the first century, the Roman combination of materials and methods generated an architecture of scope and control unprecedented in the Greek world. Extensive use of concrete and vaulting made it possible to construct great platforms and terraces so as to create entire architectural topographies. While there was minimal use of concrete at Sulmo, Gabii, and Pietrabbondante, sanctuary builders in the first century took advantage of their advanced structural capabilities to design entire settings for sanctuaries, such as those at Praeneste and Tivoli, and others at Terracina, Ferentino, Nemi, and elsewhere.[27] Stunning in their scale and comprehensive organization, accentuated by axial and symmetrical arrangement of monumental steps, porticoes, and theatral installations, the sanctuary of Fortuna Primigenia at Praeneste and that of Hercules Victor at Tivoli continue using Greek forms small and large, but their very completeness makes them more Roman than Greek.[28]

The sanctuary of Fortuna Primigenia at Praeneste (Plate 42) is the most spectacular of the central Italic sanctuaries. Now dated to 110–100 B.C., this grand hillside complex incorporated two existing cults and their separate locations into a unified axial complex of multiple terraces linked by a central monumental stairway.[29] Beneath its hellenizing veneer of Doric, Ionic, and Corinthian styles in trabeated colonnades, the sanctuary was based on successive terraces of concrete and vaulting, making possible its large scale. The distinctive polygonal masonry of a very long (over 100 m) and tall (7 m) wall at the base of this "upper sanctuary" establishes a physical and visual base for the terracing above.[30] From either end of this terrace, symmetrical diagonal ramps, walled on the downhill side, ascend to a dramatic point of convergence where a vista suddenly opens out over the countryside to the west.[31] The exedra of the east sector on this colonnaded fourth terrace (symmetrically replicated in form on the west) may have been the site for oracular consultation as described by Cicero (*Div.* 2.41, 2.86), unfortunately without reference to identifiable structures or terrain. From the center of Terrace IV, the steep central stairway 6.40 m wide rises in two ranks, interrupted only briefly at Terrace V, to the vast portico-framed court of Terrace VI.[32]

Opposite the top of the stairway, a semicircular theatral structure faced the court. It was crowned by a curving portico in front of a small tholos. The architectural forms—stairs ascending to

Appendix

Terrace VI and theater facing downward toward it—suggest that important events took place in its broad court, yet we lack information about group behavior at this important sanctuary. The monopteros atop the theater made a visual apex for the entire complex, yet the downward focus of the theatral steps below it suggests that its role was primarily symbolic. We remain ignorant of how the temple functioned and what kinds of ceremonies and celebrations occurred in the great court. The central broad stairway is reminiscent of monumental steps at sites such as Lindos and Kos, implying comparable processions, or at least an appreciation of the visual effects of such steps. However, the powerful axiality of Praeneste's central stair, emphasized by the converging ramps at its base, reflects an expanded version of the Italic tradition of stepped podium temples as much as it recalls Greek sanctuary architecture. The oracular cult of Fortuna was known to be wealthy from at least the second century. Cicero (*Div.* 2.87) quotes the second-century Greek philosopher Karneades as commenting that he had never seen Fortuna so fortunate as at Praeneste. As at Gabii, Pietrabbondante, and other central Italic sites, construction of Praeneste's sanctuary coincided with commercial activities of *mercatores* and *negotiatores* from Praeneste abroad, attested in inscriptions, especially from Delos.[33]

Epigraphic evidence from Delos also mentions the activities of *negotiatores* from Tivoli (ancient Tibur), site of another grand complex with a portico-framed temple above a theater.[34] Dated to 98–82 B.C., the oracular sanctuary of Hercules Victor at Tivoli (Plate 44) was set on a slope, yet controlled its own topography sufficiently to accommodate passage of the Via Tiburtina through its massive vaulted concrete (*opus incertum*) substructure. Much of the superstructure of this sanctuary is poorly preserved as a result of twentieth-century industrial works built on the remains.[35] Nevertheless, archaeological investigations have yielded sufficient evidence to restore an octastyle podium temple (*sine postico*) abutting a Π-shaped two-storey portico with arches flanked by Tuscan semi-columns framing a broad court.[36] The high podium of the temple was approached by a staircase 28 m wide in its second phase. Below the temple podium and aligned with it is a semicircular theatral cavea ca. 65 m in diameter; the topmost level of the cavea reached the level of the court.[37] No altar has been found. Although most reconstruction drawings of the sanctuary include a pair of symmetrically aligned monumental staircases on either side of the cavea, leading from the level of the orchestra to the portico-framed court, they are hypothetical restorations and do not appear in Giuliani's current reconstructions.[38]

The expansion of local shrines and sanctuaries to such a grand scale may be their most Hellenistic characteristic, along with specific forms of columns, porticoes, and theaters. Even if particular components are derived from the Greek architectural tradition, their recombination as theater temples is an Italian innovation. Theatral steps at Gabii, Pietrabbondante, and Tivoli face downward, away from the religious features—shrine, temple, and altars. Only Praeneste has an obvious formal pathway; in our other examples, the alignment of theater and temple seems more the result of a principle of design than of ceremonial behavior, such as a procession. The integration of architectural components and spaces at sanctuaries in central Italy suggests a Cartesian approach to place making, as the space of the respective hillsides was configured in symmetrical and systematic forms to create special places, centers for important human activities. The dramatic growth of local exurban sanctuaries into impressive architectural complexes reflects the initiative of wealthy

Hellenistic Italy

patrons from central Italy who observed the symbolic power of monumental stone architecture and the prestige of personal benefaction, both in nearby Magna Graecia and at sites around the Aegean, as they conducted business abroad. The proliferation of monumentalized sites may also represent competitive emulation in endowing both architectural structures and festival activities.

What are the models for these grand sanctuaries? No earlier structures at these sites compare with the size and scale of the second-century complexes. Pergamon, Lindos, and especially Kos are consistently cited as sources. At Pergamon, although construction of the Great Altar of Zeus in 165 B.C. would have featured broad steps framed by porticoes, the more general sense of sloping terrain articulated by architecture in multiple defined units (such as the terrace and altar, or the sanctuary of Demeter) may have impressed visitors from Italy, perhaps giving shape to their designs. Lindos produced an architecture of display as early as the third-century Upper Stoa, enhanced by the long screen of the Lower Stoa in the early second century. Filling up the small space of Lindos' acropolis, these buildings would have been experienced as a totally constructed environment. Both third- and second-century phases of the sanctuary at Lindos were dominated by symmetrically disposed architecture, at least until one reached the temple. The multi-level sanctuary of Asklepios at Kos is consistently cited as a prototype for the Italic sanctuaries, and yet it was not until the second half of the second century (contemporary with or later than Gabii) that Temple A was built, along with the monumental stairway that integrated the existing structures of the Asklepieion into a more coherent whole. Perhaps the sequence of terraces linked by stairs at Kos provided a general inspiration for the steep central stairway at Praeneste. Praeneste's steps, however, seem almost an independent passageway, with limited space for access to intermediate terraces in the ascent to the upper court. The axial spine of the stairway at Praeneste does not lead directly to a temple, as at Kos, but to the colonnaded court and theater.[39] While direct parallels of configuration are lacking, it seems most likely that visiting Italian aristocrats would have experienced sites such as Pergamon, Lindos, and Kos as total architectural environments and created their own versions at home of sanctuaries as monumental settings constructed and controlled by human intention.

Catalogue of Sites

SITES OF THE GREEK WORLD, SIXTH THROUGH SECOND CENTURIES

Adada
Dimensions
East side of agora steps: nineteen–thirty steps
    width: 24 m
    risers: 0.330–0.345 m
    treads: 0.59 m

Bibliography
Bean 1959, especially pp. 96–97; Belke and Mersich 1990; V. Bérard 1892; Bracke 1993; H. Brandt 2004, 2007; H. Brandt and Kolb 2005; Bresson and Descat 2001; Brewster 1993, pp. 112–13; Büyükkolanci 1998; Gruber 2007; Kosmetatou 1997; Lauter 1970; Mitchell 1991, especially pp. 123–25, 132, 134, 139–40; 1992; 1994; 1998; Sion-Jenkis 2001; Vanhaverbeke and Waelkens 2005; Waelkens 2002; 2004, especially pp. 457–58
    Plan: None available; site unpublished
    Photos: Plate 1a–b

Aegina: Sanctuary of Zeus Hellanios
Dimensions
Ramp to terrace: six or more steps
    width: 7.20 m
    risers: 0.16–0.26 m
    treads: 3.03–3.45 m

Bibliography
Becker 2003, pp. 92–95; Goette 1998; 1999; 2001a, pp. 345–48; 2001b; 2002; Welter 1938a, especially cols. 8–16; 1938b, pp. 91–92, 480–85
    Plan: Plate 2a
    Photo: Plate 2b

Alipheira: Sanctuary of Athena
Dimensions
Steps to terrace: ten or more steps
    width: 3.56 m
    risers: 0.20–0.28 m (most 0.23–0.25 m)
    treads: 0.10–0.40 m

Bibliography
Becker 2003, pp. 266–69; Jost 1985, pp. 77–82; R. Martin 1970; T. H. Nielsen 2002a, pp. 299, 550–51; Orlandos 1967–68, pp. 9, 29, 43–45; Papachatzis 1967, pp. 293–97
    Plan: Plate 3a
    Photo: Plate 3b

Amnisos
Dimensions
Steps atop Minoan structure: seven steps
    width: 3.66 m
    risers: 0.17–0.32 m
    treads: ca. 0.35–0.50 m

Bibliography
Becker 2003, pp. 219–20; Ginouvès 1972, p. 56; Hägg 1996; Kirsten 1940a; N. Marinatos 1996; S. Marinatos 1935, 1938; R. Martin 1951; Musti et al. 1991; Schäfer 1991; Schäfer et al. 1992; Sporn 2002, pp. 130, 133–35; E. Thomas 1984
    Plan: See Schäfer 1991, pl. 129
    Photo: See S. Marinatos 1938, p. 131 fig. 2

Catalogue of Sites

Amphipolis: Gymnasium
Dimensions
Steps to gymnasium: twelve or more steps
    width: 8.70 m
    risers: 0.19 m*
    treads: 0.37 m*
*Estimated by Becker (2003, p. 89 n. 462) from D. Lazarides' (1982, p. 44) plan

Bibliography
Becker 2003, pp. 89–91; Catling 1996–97; D. Lazarides 1980; 1982; 1984; 1997, pp. 52–59; K. Lazarides 1986, 1987
    Plan: Plate 4a
    Photo: Plate 4b

Amyzon
Dimensions
Steps to temple terrace: ca. twenty steps
    width: 7.40 m
    risers: not available
    treads: not available

Bibliography
Bean 1980, pp. 168–70; Carstens 2009a; Hellström 2009; Hornblower 1982, pp. 278, 313; Laumonier 1958; Marchese 1989, pp. 52, 63, 65, 69; Pedersen 1991b, pp. 66–67, 100–101; 2004; J. Robert and L. Robert 1983; L. Robert 1953
    Plan: Plate 5
    Photo: None available; site overgrown: see Robert and Robert 1983, p. 67 figs. 10–13

Argive Heraion
Dimensions
Steps east of South Stoa: number of steps unknown
    width: not preserved
    risers: 0.30–0.36 m
    treads: 0.25–38 m

Bibliography
Amandry 1952, 1980; Becker 2003, pp. 8–10, 42–47, 269–71; Billot 1997; Blegen 1937, pp. 19–20; Coulton 1982, pp. 35, 92, 135; des Courtils 1992; J. M. Hall 1995, 1997; Kritzas 1992, 2003–4, 2006; Lauter 1975; Morgan 2007; Pariente and Touchais 1990; Pfaff 1992, 2002; Piérart 1992; Piérart and Touchais 1996; Strøm 1988; Tilton 1902, especially pp. 130–31; Tomlinson 1972, pp. 203–4, 230–46, 275; Waldstein et al. 1902 and 1905; Williams 1993; Wright 1982
    Plan: Plate 6a
    Photo: Plate 6b

Argos: Aspis
Dimensions
Rock-cut steps behind altar: ten or more steps
    width: 27 m
    risers: 0.21–0.23 m
    treads: 0.42–0.45 m

Bibliography
Anti and Polacco 1969, pp. 173–75; Becker 2003, pp. 42–47; Bergquist 1967, pp. 18–19; Ginouvès 1972, pp. 65–66; Piérart and Touchais 1996, pp. 32–33, 52–53; Pouilloux 1958; Roux 1954; 1957; 1961, pp. 65–82; Rupp 1974, pp. 120–21; Tomlinson 1972, pp. 205–7, 247–49; Vollgraff 1956
    Plan: Plate 7a
    Photos: Plate 7b–c

Athens: Acropolis, Ramp to Acropolis
Dimensions
Ramp
    width: ca. 11 m in sixth century
    over 21 m in fifth century

Bibliography
Bradeen and McGregor 1974; Bundgaard 1957, pp. 19–30; Korres 1995; I. M. Shear 1999; Travlos 1971, pp. 482, 484, 487; Vanderpool 1974
    Plan: Plate 8a
    Photo: Plate 8b

Athens: Acropolis, Predecessor to the Propylaia
Dimensions
Steps at entrance to Propylaia: five or more steps
    width: 11 m or more
    risers: 0.23–0.31 m
    treads: 0.30 m (top)–2.00 m (lowest)

Catalogue of Sites

Bibliography
Brouskari 1997, pp. 57–61; W. B. Dinsmoor Jr. 1980, pp. 15, 17–31; Eiteljorg 1993; Tomlinson 1982
   Plan: Plate 9a
   Reconstruction drawing: Plate 9b

Athens: Acropolis, Steps West of the Parthenon
Dimensions
Steps on west of temple terrace: nine (sixteen?) steps
   width: over 30 m
   risers: 0.227 m (average)
   treads: 0.291 m (average)

Bibliography
Becker 2003, pp. 271–75; W. B. Dinsmoor 1947; Haselberger 2005; Hurwit 2005; Neils 2005; Osborne 1987; Reed 1987; Stevens 1940
   Plan: Plate 10a
   Section drawing: Plate 10b
   Photo: Plate 10c

Athens: Acropolis, Erechtheion, North Court
Dimensions
Theatral steps north of temple: eight–twelve steps
   width: 7–10 m (est.)
   risers: 0.328 and 0.250 m
   treads: 0.328 and 0.325 m

Bibliography
Becker 2003, pp. 229–32; Elderkin 1941; Holland 1924,1924b; Hollinshead 2012b, 2015; Korres 2002; Mansfield 1985; Papanikolaou (ed. Mallouchou-Tufano and Bouras) 2012; Paton et al. 1927; N. Robertson 1983, 1996, 2004; Stevens 1946; Weller 1921
   Plans: Plate 11a–b
   Photo: Plate 11c

Athens: Agora, Benches on West Side
Dimensions
"Benches" on west side: four benches
   width: 25 m or 37 m
   risers: 0.33–0.50 m
   treads: 0.56–0.74 m

Bibliography
Becker 2003, pp. 226–29; Boegehold 1967, 1995; Camp 1986, pp. 96, 100, 167; 2001; Ginouvès 1972, pp. 67–68; S. G. Miller 1995; Purchiaroni 1959–60; H. A. Thompson 1937, especially pp. 218–22; H. A.Thompson and Wycherley 1972, pp. 71, 80–81, 142, 149, 228
   Plan: Plates 12a, 13
   Photo: Plate 12b

Athens: Agora, Kolonos Agoraios
Dimensions
Steps on north slope: number of steps unknown
   width: ca. 8 m
   risers: not preserved
   treads: not preserved

Bibliography
Brogan 2003, especially p. 196 fig. 1; Pounder 1983; Rotroff 1982, p. 33; 1983; T. L. Shear 1938, especially pp. 339–41; 1940, especially pp. 266–68, 299–300; D. B. Thompson 1937–39, 1963
   Plan: Plate 13
   Photo: None available; site reburied after excavation

Corinth: Stepped ramp to early temple
Dimensions
Ramp southeast of temple: few steps preserved
   width: 7.45 m
   risers: 0.07–0.14 m*
   treads: 0.33–0.41 m*
*may represent substructure for stairs

Bibliography
Fowler and Stillwell 1932, pp. 204, 219–20; Robinson 1976a, 1976b; Romano and Schoenbrun 1993; Stillwell, Scranton, and Freeman 1941, p. 89; Williams 1993
   Plan: Plate 14a
   Photos: Plate 14b–c

Corinth: Steps by Sacred Spring
Dimensions
Steps beside Sacred Spring: three steps in early fifth century
   width: 21.4 m or longer

Catalogue of Sites

Two steps in later fifth century
    ca. 30 m and more
        risers: 0.223, 0.244 m
        treads: 0.30 m

Bibliography
Williams 1969, 1970, 1978; Williams and Fisher 1971, especially pp. 10–19
    Plan: Plate 14a
    Photo: Plate 14d

Corinth: Sanctuary of Demeter and Kore
Dimensions
Steps up through dining rooms: number unknown
    width: 2.80–3.07 m
    risers: 0.14 m
    treads: 0.30 m
Fifth-century theatral area: five steps
    width: 4.8–5.0 m
    risers: 0.20–0.29 m
    treads: 0.40 m (average)
Third-century theatral area: six steps
    width: 5.60–6.40 m
    risers: 0.25–0.35 m
    treads: 0.40–0.60 m

Bibliography
Becker 2003, pp. 235–39; Bookidis 1990, 1993, 2003, 2010; Bookidis and Fisher 1972; Bookidis, Hansen, and Goldberg 1999; Bookidis and Stroud 1987, 1997; Merker 2000; Pemberton 1989; Pfaff 1999; Stroud 1968
    Plans: Plate 15a–b
    Photo: Plate 15c

Didyma: Grandstand beside Temple
Dimensions
Grandstand south of temple: seven (?) steps
    width: ca. 13 m
    risers: 0.36–0.47 m
    treads: 0.682–0.868 m

Bibliography
Becker 2003, pp. 137–47; Cook 1975; Fontenrose 1988; Günther 1971; Haselberger 1996; Heilmeyer 1980; Hölbe 1984; Knackfuss 1941a, pp. 140–41; 1941b; 1941c; Montegu 1976; Naumann 1973; Parke 1985, 1986; Rehm, Wiegand, and Harder 1958; Tuchelt 1973, 1984, 1986; Voigtländer 1975, 1986
    Plan: Plate 16a
    Photos: Plate 16b–c

Dreros
Dimensions
Steps along "agora": seven or more steps
    width: ca. 23 m
    risers: 0.21 m (average)
    treads: 0.35 m

Bibliography
Becker 2003, pp. 218–20, 243 n. 1187, 283 n. 1404; Beyer 1976; Demargne 1933; Demargne and van Effenterre 1937, especially pp. 10–15, 333–48; Ducrey, Hadjmichali, and Picard 1970; Ducrey and Picard 1969a; Ginouvès 1972, pp. 56–58; M.-H. Hansen and T. Fischer-Hansen 1994, p. 62; Kolb 1976, especially pp. 296–97; 1981, p. 106; W. A. MacDonald 1943, pp. 66–67; S. Marinatos 1936; I. Nielsen 2000, pp. 110–11; Prent 2005, pp. 283–85; Sjögren 2003, p. 36; Sporn 2002, pp. 79–83; E. Thomas 1984; van Effenterre 1992; Willetts 1974, pp.198, 262
    Plan: Plate 17a
    Photo: Plate 17b

Eleusis: Sixth-Century Grandstand
Dimensions
Sixth-century stepped podium: three steps preserved
    width: 8.40 m preserved
    risers: 0.20 m
    treads: 0.41–0.58 m

Bibliography
K. Clinton 1993; Kourouniotes 1933–35, especially pp. 34–41; 1936; Kuhn 1985, pp. 281–82; Mylonas 1961, p. 71; Noack 1927, pp. 94–98, figs. 44, 46, pls. 34, 35; Palinkas 2008
    Plan: Plate 18a
    Photo: Plate 18b

Halikarnassos: Maussolleion Steps
Dimensions
Pre-Maussolleion southern steps: eighteen steps
    width: 4.7 m

Catalogue of Sites

    risers: not available
    treads: not available
Maussolleion western staircase: eleven steps
    width: 8.6 m
    risers: ca. 0.24 m (average)
    treads: ca. 0.44 m (average)

Bibliography

Becker 2003, pp. 13–15; Carstens 2009a, 2009b, 2011; Hoepfner and Schwander 1994, pp. 230–44; Jeppesen 1976, 1978, 1989, 2000, 2002; Jeppesen, Hojlund, and Aaris-Sorensen 1981; Jeppesen and Luttrell 1986; Pedersen 1988a, 1991a, 1991b; Vaag, Nørskov, Lund, Jeppesen, and Luttrell 2002; Waywell 1988; Zahle 1978; Zahle and Kjeldsen 2004
    Plan: Plate 19
    Photos: Pre-Maussolleion steps: Zahle and Kjeldsen 2004, fig. 2.6.1; western steps: Jeppesen 2000, figs. 3.2–3.3

Kameiros

Dimensions
Steps in street: twelve steps
    width: 8–9 m
    risers: 0.16 m restored
    treads: 0.33–0.34 m restored
Precinct east of street ("agora"): four steps
    width: ca. 22 m
    risers: 0.30–0.33 m
    treads: 0.40–0.42 m

Bibliography

Becker 2003, pp. 91–92; DiVita 1986–87, 1990, 1994; Heilmeyer 1999; Jacopi 1931, 1932; Kollias 1980, pp. 23–25; 1999, pp. 299–308; Konstantinopoulos 1971, pp. 40–63; 1986, pp. 168–78; Kypraiou and Zapheiropoulou 1999; Lauter 1982, 1986; Maiuri 1928, pp. 44–55; Petsa-Tzounakou 1996, pp. 78–82; von Hesberg 1994, pp. 152, 179
    Plan: Plate 20a
    Photo: Plate 20b

Kapikaya

Dimensions
Theatral structure: seven rows on north
    width: 17.2 m

Four rows on east
    width: 8.8 m
Four rows on south
    width: 13.3 m
    risers: 0.35–0.40 m
    treads: 0.50 m

Bibliography

Belke and Mersich 1990, pp. 287–88; Kosmetatou 1997; Mersich 1986, especially pp. 193–94 and fig. 2; Mitchell 1991, especially p. 138; 1992, especially p. 20; 1994a, especially p. 98; Waelkens 2004, especially pp. 457–58; Waelkens et al. 1997, especially pp. 21–29
    Plan: None available; site unpublished
    Photo: Plate 21

Knidos

Dimensions
Steps above retaining wall: seven steps
    width: over 20 m
    risers: 0.35–0.37 m (Roman)
    treads: ca. 0.51 m (Roman)

Bibliography

Bankel 1997, 1999, 2004, 2009; Bean 1980, pp. 147–52; Bean and Cook 1952; Becker 2003, p. 255; Berges 1994, 2006; Berges and Tuna 2000; Blümel 1992; Bruns-Özgan 1995; Demand 1989; M.-H. Gates 1994, 1995, 1996, 1997; I. Jenkins 2006, 2007; Love 1968a, 1968b, 1968c, 1969a, 1969b, 1971, 1972, 1973a, 1973b, 1978; Önen 1989, pp. 116–34; Stampolidis 1984; Tuna, Atici, Sakarya, and Koparal 2009; Yildirim and M.-H. Gates 1997
    Plan: Plate 22a
    Model: Plate 22b
    Photos: Plate 22c–d

Kos: Asklepieion

Dimensions
Steps to Lower Terrace: none preserved
    width: over 13 m
    risers: not applicable
    treads: not applicable
Steps to Middle Terrace: none preserved
    width: 10.4 m

risers: not applicable
treads: not applicable
Steps to Upper Terrace (three segments): thirty-eight (?) steps
   width: 11.25 m
Twenty-seven (?) steps
   width: 9.25 m
Six steps
   width: 18.075 m
   risers: 0.170 m
   treads: 0.335 m

Bibliography
Becker 2003, pp. 56–70; Blümel 1992; Bosnakis, Hallof, and Rigsby 2010; Buraselis 2004; Carlsson 2004, 2010; Coulton 1976, pp. 246–48; Crowther 2004; Fraser 1972; Gruben 1980; Hallof and Hallof 2004; Hellström 1990; Herzog 1899, 1903a, 1903b, 1906, 1928; Herzog and Klaffenbach 1952; Herzog and Schazmann 1932; Hoepfner 1984; Höghammar 1993, 2004; Hollinshead 2012b, especially pp. 41–46; Interdonato 2013, especially pp. 33–90, 265–348; Knell 1971; Kondis 1956; Laumonier 1958, pp. 691–94; Perrin-Saminadayar 2011; Rhodes and Osborne 2003, pp. 298–311; Rigsby 1996, 2004; Schwandner 1990; Senseney 2007, 2011; Sherwin White 1978; Shoe 1950, especially pp. 340, 347, 349; von Hesberg 1994, pp. 179, 182; Würster 1973; Zscheitzschmann 1936
   Plan: Plate 23a
   Reconstruction drawing: Plate 23b
   Photo: Plate 23c

Labraunda: Sanctuary of Zeus
Dimensions
Southeast Steps: four steps
   width: over 10 m
   risers: 0.205–0.300 m
   treads: 0.49–0.53 m
Great Stairway: twenty-three steps
   width: 12 m
   risers: 0.14–0.17 m
   treads: 0.475–0.510 m
Right-Angle Steps: nine–ten steps or more
   width: 5–6 m or more
   risers: 0.16–0.18 m
   treads: 0.33–0.39 m

Steps by Andron B: nine steps
   width: 8 m or more
   risers: 0.170–0.195 m
   treads: 0.50–0.51 m

Bibliography
www.labraunda.org; Baran 2009, 2010a, 2010b, 2011; Becker 2003, pp. 23–31; Carstens 2009a, 2011; Crampa 1969, 1972; Gunter 1985; Hellström 1985, 1988, 1990, 1991, 1996a, 1996b, 2009, 2011; Hellström and Alroth 1996; Hellström and Thieme 1982; Henry 2013a, 2013b; Hornblower 1982, 1990; Jeppesen 1955; Karlsson 2013; Karlsson and Carlsson 2011; Linders and Hellström 1989; Pedersen 1988, 1989; Roos 2011; Thieme 1989, 1993; Westholm 1963, 1978; Williamson 2013, 2014
   Plan: Plate 24a
   Photo: Plate 24b

Latmos
Dimensions
Steps lining "agora": eight steps
   width: 15 m
   risers: 0.30–0.50 m
   treads: 0.20–0.70 m

Bibliography
Peschlow-Bindokat 1977, especially p. 100; 1989; 1996; 2005, p. 21
   Photos: Plate 25a–b

Lato
Dimensions
Steps by "agora": nine–ten steps
   width: 8.4 m
   risers: 0.20–0.36 m
   treads: 0.34–0.37 m, some 0.56–0.60 m
Steps below temple: ten–eleven steps
   width: ca. 15 m
   risers: 0.23–0.34 m (average 0.30 m)
   treads: 0.54–0.60 m

Bibliography
Apostolakou 2003; Dilke 1948, p. 129; Ducrey, Hadjmichali, and Picard 1970; Ducrey and Picard 1969b, 1970, 1971, 1972;

Catalogue of Sites

Ginouvès 1972, pp. 56–57; Hadjimichali 1971; M.-H. Hansen and T. Fischer-Hansen 1994, pp. 63–65; Kolb 1976, 1981, p. 86; S. G. Miller 1978, pp.78–86; Picard 1992; Sporn 2002, pp. 62–65; E. Thomas 1984; Willetts 1965
  Plan: Plate 26a
  Photos: Plate 26b–c

Lindos
Dimensions
Sixth-century steps: twenty-three steps preserved
  width: at least 7 m
  risers: variable but low
  treads: 0.49–1.00 m (most 0.70 m)
Stairs to Upper Stoa: thirty-seven steps (thirty-five restored)
  width: 21.03 m
  risers: 0.174–0.175 m
  treads: 0.375 m

Bibliography
Becker 2003, pp. 78–97; Berthold 1984; Blinkenberg 1931; Blinkenberg and Kinch 1941; Coulton 1976, pp. 61, 172, 251–52; Dietz and Papachristodoulou 1988; Dygve and Poulsen 1960; Gabrielsen 1997; Higbie 2003; Hollinshead 2012a; Kondis 1963; Konstantinopoulos 1972; 1986, pp. 179–86; Kostomitsopoulos 1988; Lauter 1986, pp. 106–8, 290, 298; Lippolis 1988–89; Pakkanen 1998; V. Papadimitriou 1988; Reger 1999
  Plans: Plate 27a, 27c
  Photos: Plate 27b, 27d
  See also Lippolis 1988–89, p. 107 fig. 2 (photo of sixth-century steps)
  Model: Plate 27e

Lykosoura
Dimensions
Steps beside temple: ten steps
  width: 28.92 m (lowest)–ca. 21 m (top)
  risers: 0.27–0.33 (average 0.32 m)
  treads: 0.710–0.463 m at top, 0.780 m (topmost)

Bibliography
Becker 2003, pp. 233–35; Bruneau 1969; Coulton 1976, pp. 252–53; Daniel 1904; Demand 1990, p.115; Dickins 1905–6; Dickins and Kourouniotis 1906–7; Dillon 1997, pp. 72–73; Donnay 1967; Dörpfeld 1890; Glaser 1981–82; Jost 1973; 1985, pp. 172–79, 326–37; 1994; 2003; Kaltsas 2003 (translation Hardy); Kelly 1995; Kourouniotis 1906, 1907, 1912; Lehmann-Hartleben 1931; Leonardos 1896a, 1896b; Lévy 1967; Lévy and Marcadé 1972; Loucas and Loucas 1988; Loucas-Durie 1992; Matthaiou and Pikoulas 1986; Mitsopoulos-Leon 1992; T. H. Nielsen 2002a, pp. 566–67; Orlandini 1969–70; Orlandos 1911; Østby 1994; Papachatzis 1967, pp. 343–58; Reichel and Wilhelm 1901; Ridgway 2000, pp. 235–38; Scully 1979, pp. 202–3; Sokolowski 1969; Thallon 1906; Themelis 1993, 1994, 1996; Voyatzis 1990
  Plan: Plate 28a
  Photo: Plate 28b

Morgantina: Agora
Dimensions
Tripartite bank of steps in agora: thirteen–fifteen steps
  width: 52 m (all three segments)
  risers: 0.19–0.24 m
  treads: 0.40–0.45 m

Bibliography
H. L. Allen 1970; Becker 2003, pp. 70–73; M. Bell 1984–85, 1988; Fuchs 1964; Ginouvès 1972, p. 65; Holloway 2000, pp. 156–63; Kolb 1975; 1981, pp. 85–87; Sjövqvist 1964; Stillwell and Sjöqvist 1957, 1958; Tsakirgis 1995
  Plan: Plate 29a
  Photo: Plate 29b

Mount Lykaion: Sanctuary of Zeus
Dimensions
Stepped seats near stoa: three–four steps
  width: ca. 38 m
  risers: 0.25–0.36 m
  treads: 0.36–0.46 m

Bibliography
www.lykaionexcavation.org; Burkert 1983, pp. 84–93; Demand 1990, especially p. 115; Jordan, Valle, and Munsch 2007; Jost 1985, especially pp. 179–87, 548–49; 1994; 1996; 1999; 2002; 2007; Kourouniotis 1903, 1904a, 1904b, 1905, 1909; T. H. Nielsen 2002a; T. H. Nielsen and Roy 1999; D. G. Romano 1997, 2005; Voyatzis 1999

Plan: site not fully published; plan of steps: Plate 30c. For entire site, see Romano et al., http://lykaionexcavation.org/site/sanctuary (third image from top)
Photos: Plate 30a–b

Olympia: Sanctuary of Zeus
Dimensions
Steps along north edge of Altis: eleven, then seven steps
   width: ca. 185 m
   risers: 0.20–0.29 m
   treads: 0.23–0.27 m

Bibliography
Amandry 1952, p. 265; Arafat 1995; Becker 2003, pp. 275–79; Coulson and Kyrieleis 1992; Curtius, Adler, Dörpfeld, Graef, Partsch, and Weil 1966; W. B. Dinsmoor 1941b; Dörpfeld 1935; Dyer 1905, 1906, 1908; Gardiner 1925; Herrmann 1976, 1992, 1999; Hölscher 2002; Koenigs 1981; Krinzinger 1980; Kunze and Schleif 1938; Kunze and Weber 1948; Lehmann-Hartleben 1927; Mallwitz 1972, 1981a, 1981b, 1988, 1999a, 1999b; Mallwitz and Schiering 1964; Mallwitz and van de Löcht 1980; Moustaka 2002; Rups 1986; Schilbach 1984, 1992; Sinn 2002
   Plan: Plate 31a
   Model: Plate 31b
   Photo: Plate 31c

Oropos: Amphiaraion
Dimensions
Curved steps by altar: three steps
   width: ca. 20 m
   risers: 0.25 m
   treads: 0.30–0.31 m (bottom 0.46 m)

Bibliography
Anti and Polacco 1969, pp. 163–71; Arias 1934, p. 74; Coulton 1968, pp. 269–70; Dilke 1950, especially pp. 33–34; Fiechter 1930; Ch. Karouzos 1926; Leonardos 1925, 1926, 1927, 1928, 1929; Melas 1973, pp. 28–37; Petrakos 1967, 1968a, 1968b, 1974; Roesch 1984; Schachter 1981
   Plan: Plate 32a
   Photo: Plate 32b

Perachora: Sanctuary of Hera Akraia
Dimensions
Steps by altar: seven or more steps
   width: ca. 12 m
   risers: 0.23–0.24 m on east; 0.153, 0.205 m on west
   treads: 0.410–0.602 m on east; 0.280, 0.350 m on west
Steps in upper sanctuary: seven steps
   width: up to 9 m
   risers: 0.225–0.300 m
   treads: 0.45–0.48 m

Bibliography
Becker 2003, pp. 21–23, 221–24; Blackmon 1966; Coulton 1964; 1967; 1976, pp. 269–71; Kuhn 1985, especially pp. 257, 292–94; Menadier 1995, 2002; Morgan 1994; Payne et al. 1940; Plommer and Salviat 1966; Sinn 1990; Tomlinson 1977, 1992
   Plan: Plate 33a
   Photos: Plate 33b–d

Pergamon: Sanctuary of Demeter
Dimensions
Theatral steps: nine steps
   width: 43.9 m
   risers: 0.373 m
   treads: 0.408 m

Bibliography
Becker 2003, pp. 248–51; Bohtz 1981; de Grummond and Ridgway 2000; Deubner 1990; Dörpfeld 1910, especially pp. 355–84; 1912, especially pp. 235–56; Gruen 2000; Hepding 1910; Kästner 1998; Koester 1998; Kosmetatou 2003; Kron 1996; Pinkwart 1984; Piok Zanon 2006, 2007; Radt 1988, especially pp. 206–13; Raeck 1983; Rheidt 1992, 1996; Savalli-Lestrade 2001; Schalles 1985; Schwandner 1990; Stewart 2000; C. M. Thomas 1998
   Plan: Plate 34a
   Photo: Plate 34b

Rhodes City: Precinct of Apollo Pythios
Dimensions
Steps to temple terrace: twenty-seven steps
   width: ca. 12 m

Catalogue of Sites

risers: 0.19 m (est.)
treads: unknown

Bibliography

Becker 2003, pp. 87–89; Berthold 1980, 1984; Bresson 1988; Dietz and Papachristodoulou 1988; Fraser and Bean 1954; Gabrielsen 1997; Gabrielsen, Bilde, Engberg-Pedersen, Hannestad, and Zahle 1999; Gruen 1975, 1989; Higbie 2003; Hoepfner 1988, 1999, 2003; Hoepfner and Schwandner 1994, pp. 65–66; E. Kollias 1980, 1988, 1999; M. M. Kollias 2000; Kondis 1952, 1953; Konstantinopoulos 1968, 1972, 1973, 1974, 1986, 1988; Kypraiou and Zapheiropoulou 1999; Lauter 1972; Lippolis 1988–89; Momigliano 1936; V. Papadimitriou 1988; Pedersen 1988b; Rice 1995; Ridgway 2004; Segré 1949
  Plan: Plate 35
  Photo: See Konstantinopoulos 1986, p. 218 fig. 242

Sagalassos: Temple of Zeus

Dimensions

Steps uphill to temple: number not preserved
  width: 12 m
  risers: none in situ
  treads: none in situ

Bibliography

Mitchell 1991; 1992, especially p. 12; 1998; 2003, especially p. 33; Mitchell and Waelkens 1987, especially pp. 39, 42–43; Schwertheim 1992; Vandeput 1997; Waelkens 1989; 1992, especially pp. 49–50; 1993a; 1998, especially pp. 252–55; 2002; 2004; Waelkens and Loots 2000
  Plan: Plate 36a
  Reconstruction drawing: Plate 36b
  Photo: Plate 36c

Selinus: Temple M

Dimensions

Steps between altar and temple: number unknown
  width: 24 m
  risers: not preserved
  treads: not preserved

Bibliography

L. Pompeo 1999

Reconstruction drawing: Plate 37a
Photo: Plate 37b

Selinus: Acropolis

Dimensions

Stepped retaining wall: twenty-three or more steps
  width: 75 m
  risers: 0.42–0.52 m
  treads: 0.20–0.36 m

Bibliography

De Angelis 2003; DiVita 1984, 1985, 1996; Gabrici 1929; C. Marconi 2007, 2010; Mertens 1989; Østby 1995; Pace 1938; Pugliese Caratelli 1985–90; Tusa 1981–82
  Plan: Plate 38a
  Photos: Plate 38b–c

Thasos: Sanctuary of Herakles

Dimensions

Steps along west side: six steps
  width: 31.53 m
  risers: 0.19–0.20 m
  treads: 0.44–0.45 m

Bibliography

Alroth 1998; Becker 2003, pp. 47–52; Bergquist 1973, 1998; Daux 1967, especially pp. 70–74; des Courtils and Pariente 1985, 1986, 1987, 1988, 1991; Hägg 1998; Launey 1944, 1979; R. Martin 1978; Muller, Mulliez, and Blondé 1988; Perreault et al. 1988; Picard 1962; Pouilloux 1954; Queyrel et al. 1984; Roux 1979
  Plan: Plate 39
  Photo: See Roux 1979, p. 200 fig. 7

CENTRAL ITALIAN SITES OF THE SECOND CENTURY

Gabii: Sanctuary of Juno

Bibliography

Almagro-Gorbea 1982; Castagnoli 1977, 1980; Coarelli 1987, pp. 11–21; Gros 1973; Guaitoli 1981; Hanson 1959; Kähler 1962; Lauter 1968; Montero-Herreros 1983; Stek 2009, pp. 48–49
  Plan: Plate 40a
  Reconstruction drawing: Plate 40b

Pietrabbondante
Bibliography

Blanck 1970; Capini 1994; Cianfarani 1960; Coarelli 1984, pp. 489–92; 1987; Coarelli and La Regina 1984, pp. 230–57; Crawford 1981, especially pp. 159–60; La Regina 1965, 1966a, 1976, 1980; Salmon 1967; Stek 2009, pp. 39–52; Strazzulla and di Marco 1972; Tavano 2001; Wallace-Hadrill 2008, pp. 137–43

   Plan: Plate 41a
   Photograph: Plate 41b

Praeneste: Sanctuary of Fortuna Primigenia
Bibliography

Bodei Giglioni 1977, especially pp. 67–70; Coarelli 1978; 1987, pp. 35–84; 1993, pp. 137–48; Fasolo and Gullini 1953; Kähler 1958a, 1958b; Lauter 1979; Merz 2001; Wallace-Hadrill 2008, pp. 106–16

   Photo: Plate 42; see also Merz 2001, p. 11 fig. 1

Sulmo: Sanctuary of Hercules
Bibliography

Andreae 1959; Blanck 1970, especially pp. 344–45; Cianfarani 1960; Coarelli 1985, pp. 468–71; Coarelli and La Regina 1984, pp. 127–32; La Regina 1966b; La Torre 1989; Massineo and Pellegrino 1995; Mattiocco 1997; Stek 2009, pp. 75–76; Wallace-Hadrill 2008, pp. 115–16; van Wonterghem 1973; 1984, pp. 240–53; 1994

   Plan: Plate 43a
   Photo: Plate 43b

Tivoli: Sanctuary of Hercules Victor
Bibliography

Bodei Giglioni 1977, especially pp. 61–67; Coarelli 1987, pp. 85–112; 1993, pp. 77–85; Giuliani 1970, pp. 25–29, 164–201; 2009; P. Marconi 2008; Reggiani 1998; Wallace-Hadrill 2008, pp. 115–16, 128

   Plan: Plate 44a
   Model: Plate 44b
   Photo: See Giuliani 2009, pl. II, aerial view of the sanctuary

Plates

Many of the photographs include a pair of shoes placed on a step. Because taking measurements is not permitted at some sites, I have used the same pair of shoes 0.27 m long as a consistent scale and as a reminder of steps' use by people.

Shoes 0.27 m long, with metric scale. (Photo by M. Hollinshead)

Plate 1a. Adada, steps facing the "agora." (Photo by M. Hollinshead)

Plate 1b. Adada, profile of steps facing the "agora." (Photo by M. Hollinshead)

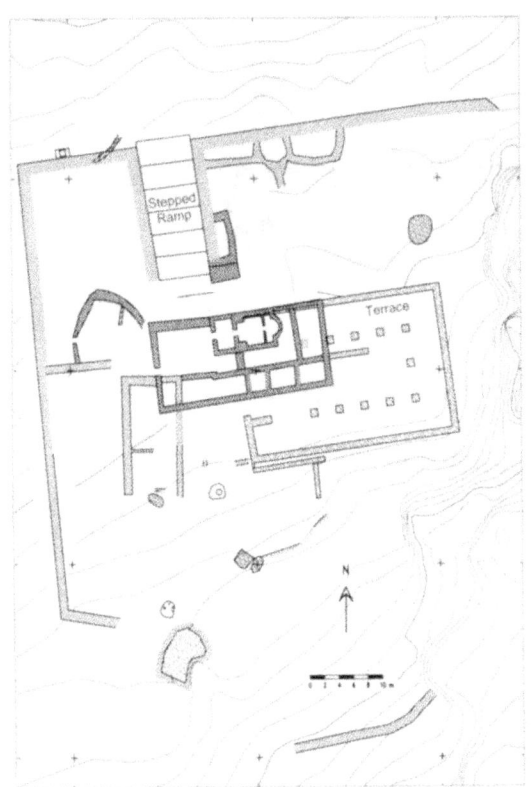

Plate 2a. Aegina, plan of the sanctuary of Zeus. (Courtesy of H. R. Goette, with H. Birk)

Plate 2b. Aegina, ramp to the sanctuary of Zeus. (Photo by M. Hollinshead)

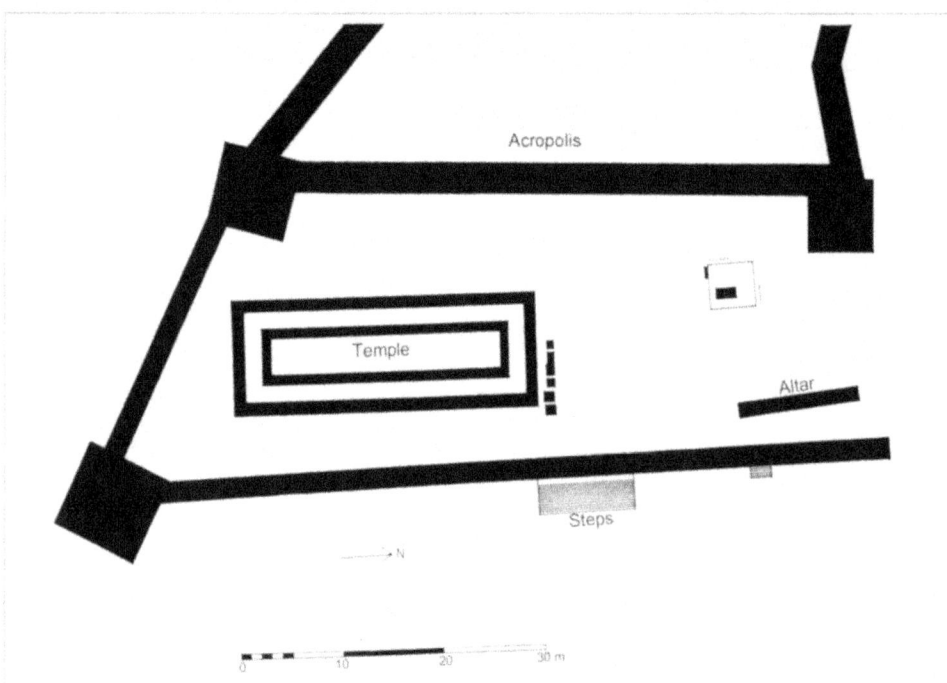

Plate 3a. Alipheira, plan of the sanctuary of Athena. (Drawn by C. Piok Zanon)

Plate 3b. Alipheira, steps to the sanctuary of Athena. (Photo by M. Hollinshead)

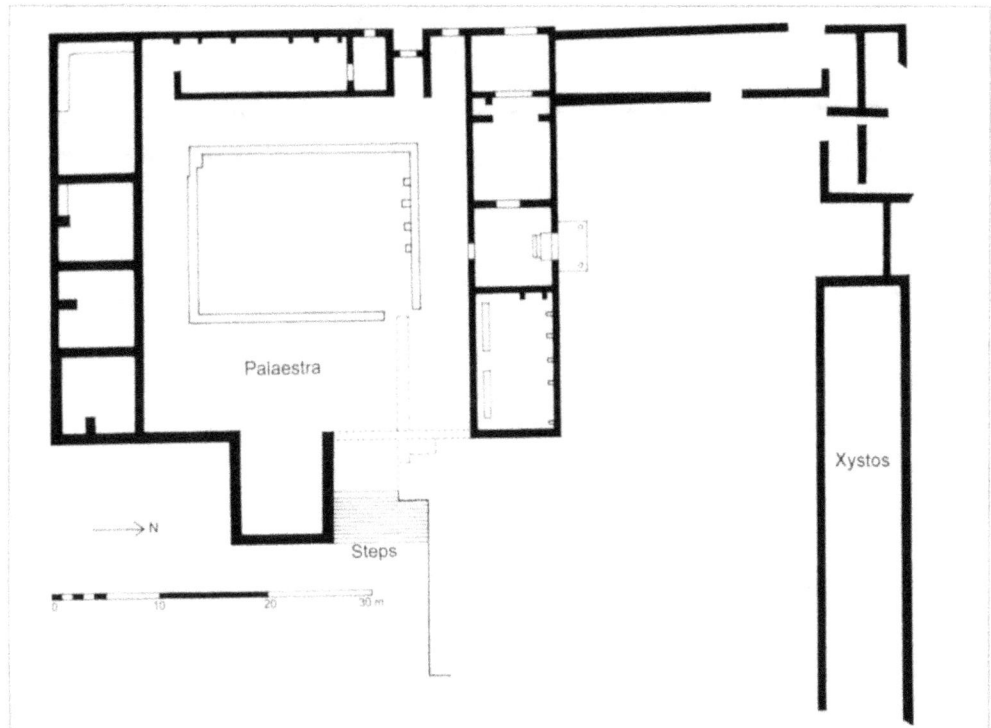

Plate 4a. Amphipolis, plan of the gymnasium complex. (Drawn by C. Piok Zanon)

Plate 4b. Amphipolis, steps to the gymnasium. (Courtesy of K. Lazarides)

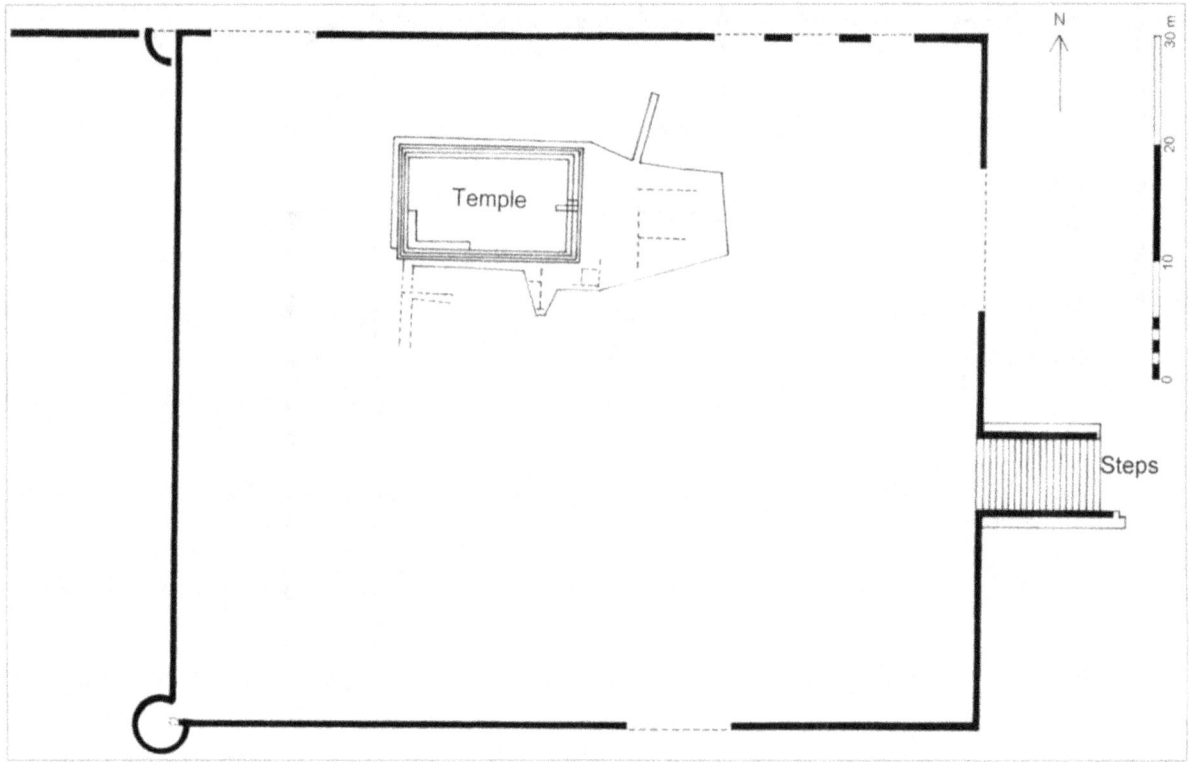

Plate 5. Amyzon, plan of the sanctuary. (Drawn by C. Piok Zanon)

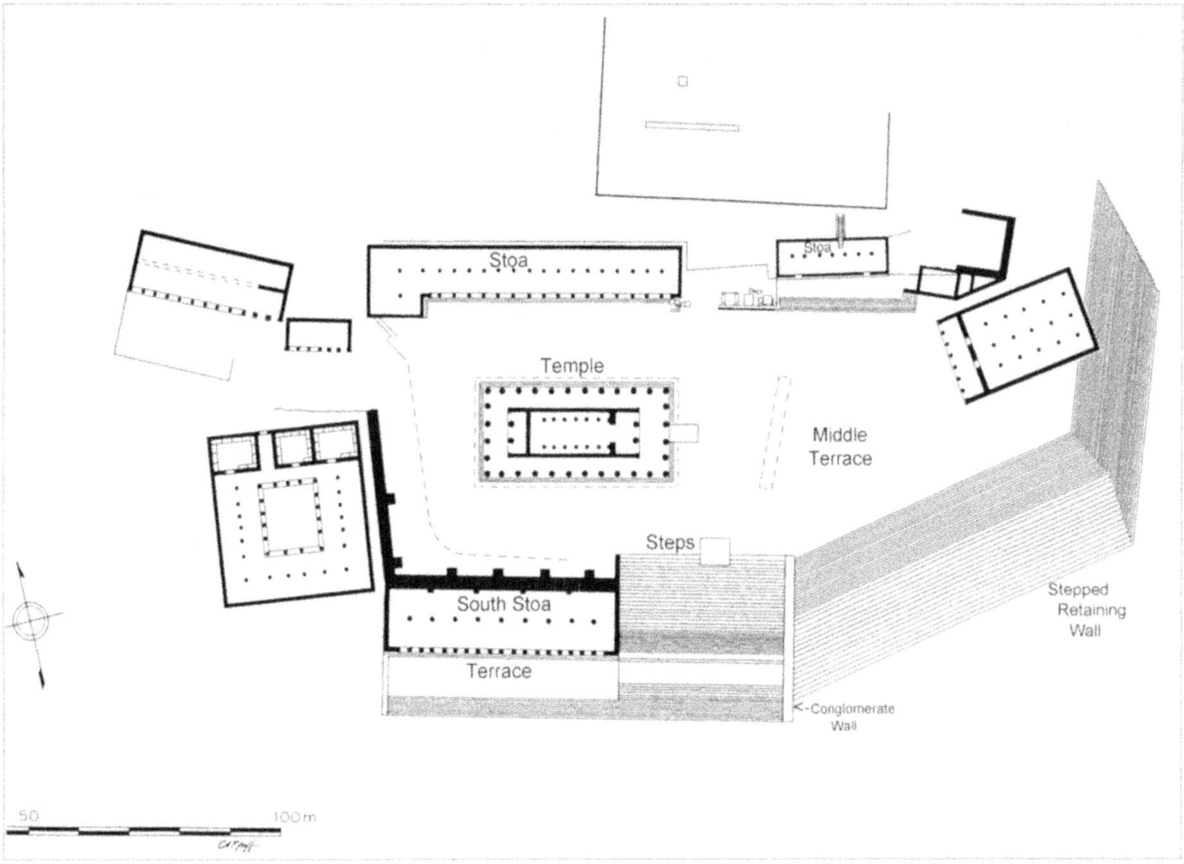

Plate 6a. Argive Heraion, plan of the Middle Terrace and retaining walls. From Pfaff 2002. (Courtesy of C. A. Pfaff and the American School of Classical Studies at Athens)

Plate 6b. Argive Heraion, steps south and east of the South Stoa, up to the Middle Terrace. From Amandry 1952, pl. 69b. (Courtesy of the American School of Classical Studies at Athens)

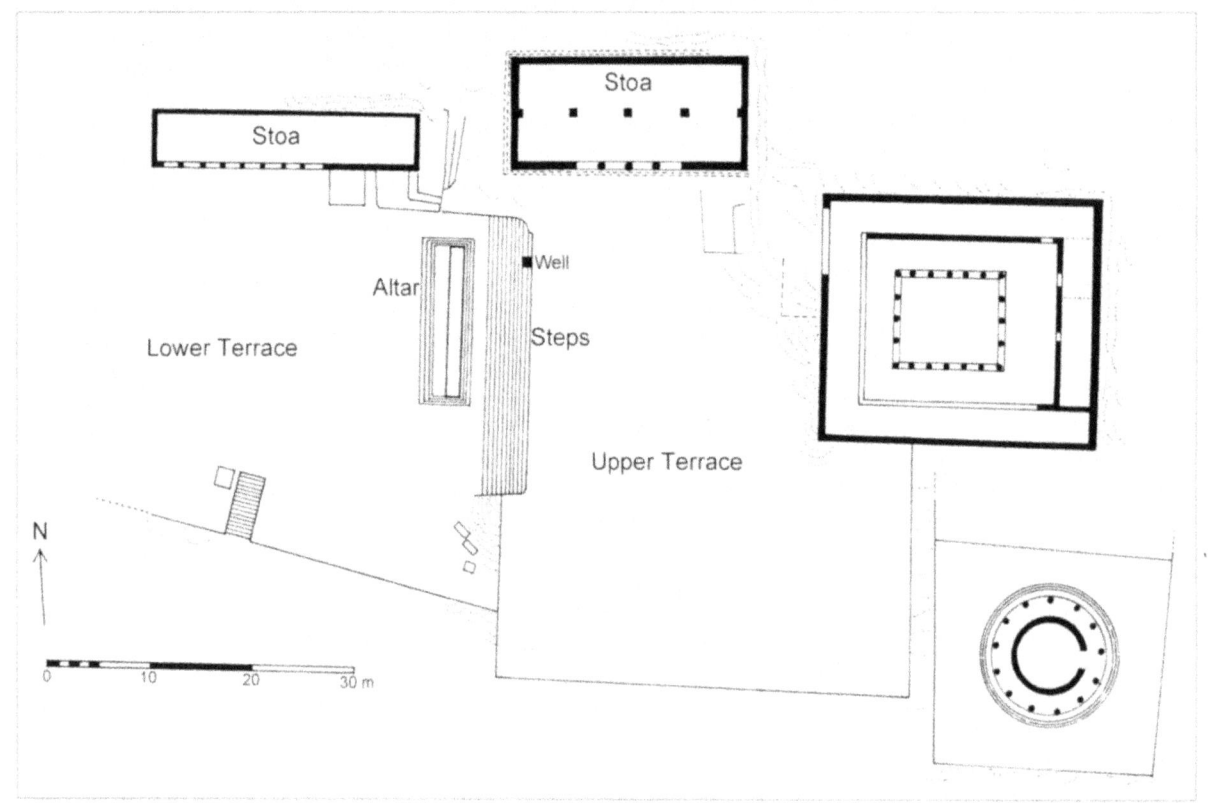

Plate 7a. Argos, Aspis, plan of the sanctuary. (Drawn by C. Piok Zanon)

Plate 7b. Argos, Aspis, general view of the altar and steps from the west. (Photo by M. Hollinshead)

Plate 7c. Argos, Aspis, steps and altar (on left) from the south. (Photo by M. Hollinshead)

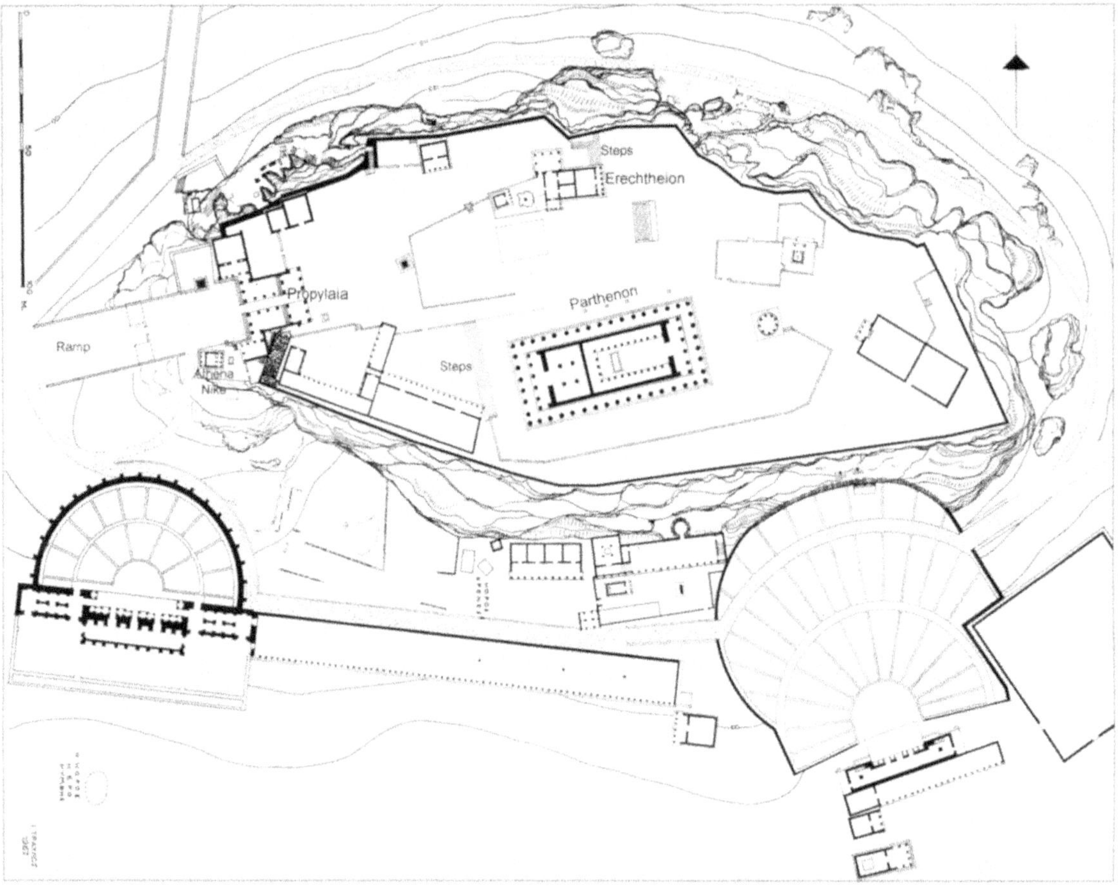

Plate 8a. Athens, Acropolis, plan with ramp. From Travlos 1971, p. 71 fig. 91. (Courtesy of the American School of Classical Studies at Athens)

Plate 8b. Athens, Acropolis, sixth-century ramp from the north. (Photo by M. Hollinshead)

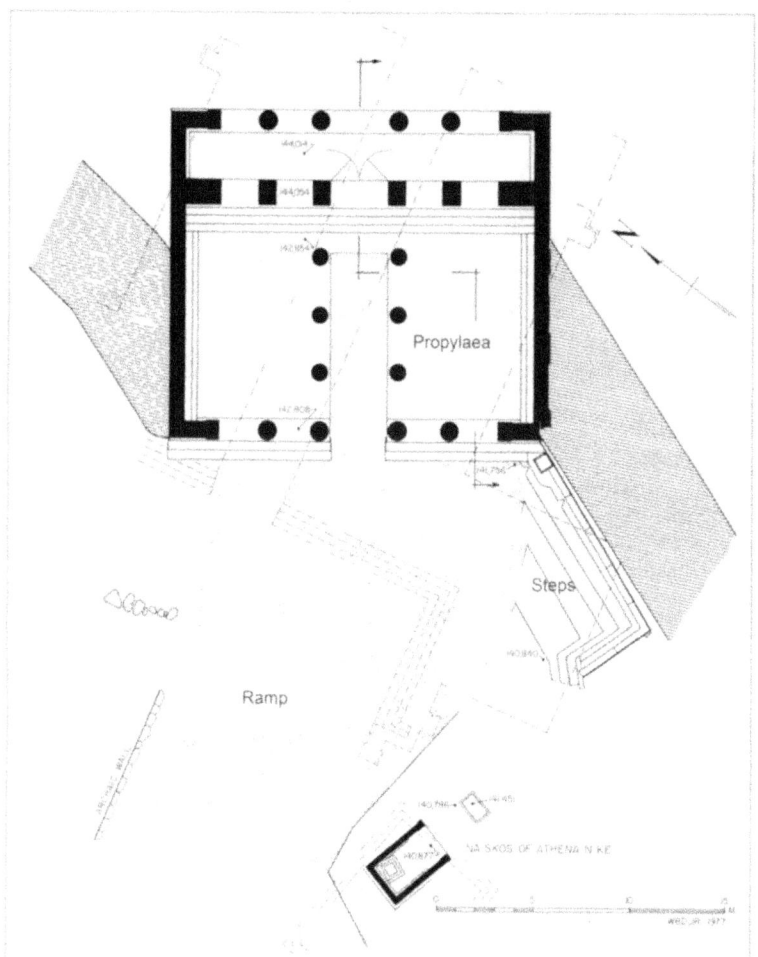

Plate 9a. Athens, Acropolis, plan of the predecessor to the Propylaia. From W. B. Dinsmoor Jr. 1980, pl. 16. (Courtesy of the American School of Classical Studies at Athens)

Plate 9b. Athens, Acropolis, reconstruction drawing of the predecessor to the Propylaia. From W. B. Dinsmoor Jr. 1980, pl. 3. (Courtesy of the American School of Classical Studies at Athens)

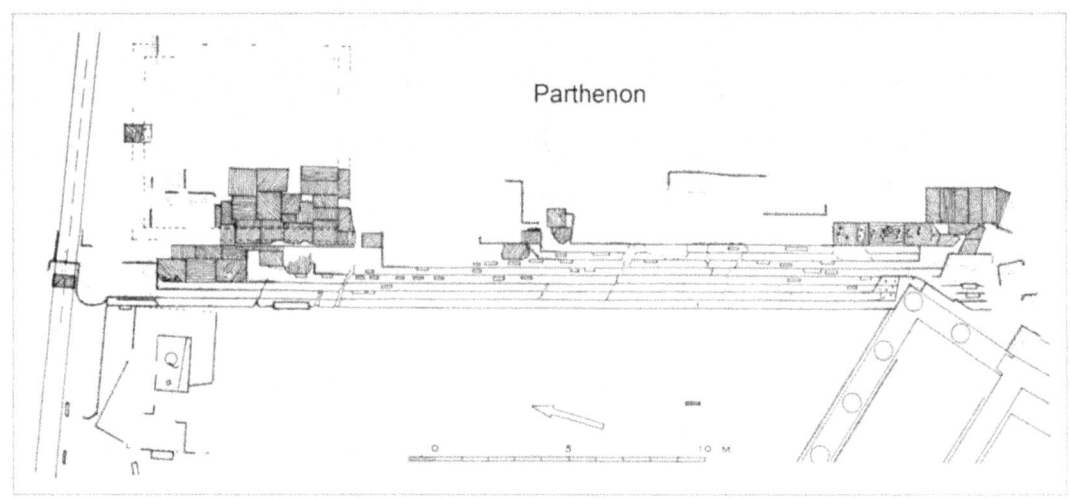

Plate 10a. Athens, Acropolis, plan of the steps west of the Parthenon. From Stevens 1940, p. 36 fig. 20. (Courtesy of the American School of Classical Studies at Athens)

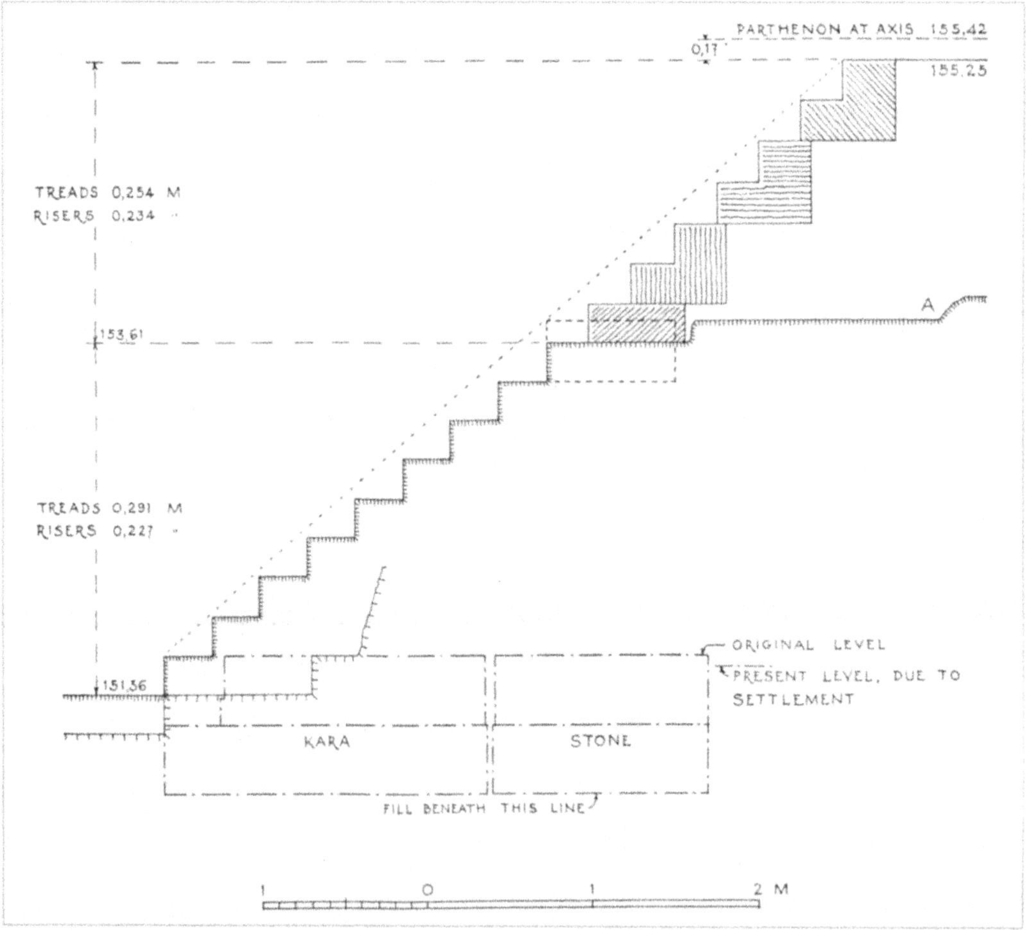

Plate 10b. Athens, Acropolis, section drawing of the steps west of the Parthenon. From Stevens 1940, p. 36 fig. 20. (Courtesy of the American School of Classical Studies at Athens)

Plate 10c. Athens, Acropolis, steps west of the Parthenon from the north. (Photo by M. Hollinshead)

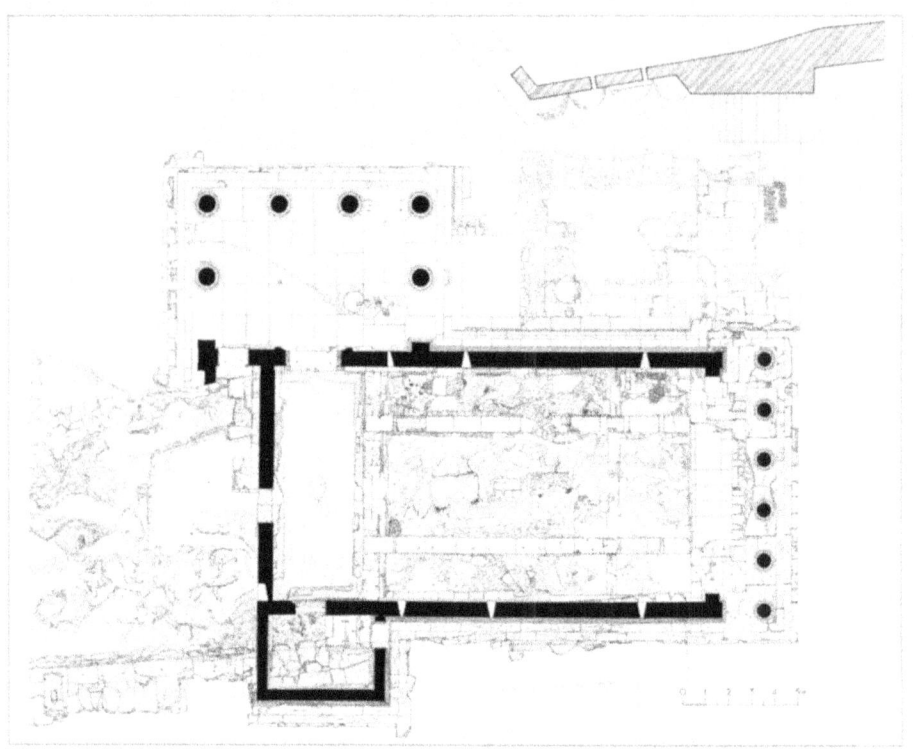

Plate 11a. Athens, Acropolis, Erechtheion, actual state plan. Plan: P. Psaltis. From Papanikolaou 2012, vol. 2, p. 502 fig. 129. (Courtesy of Athens: Acropolis Restoration Service, Hellenic Ministry of Culture and Tourism)

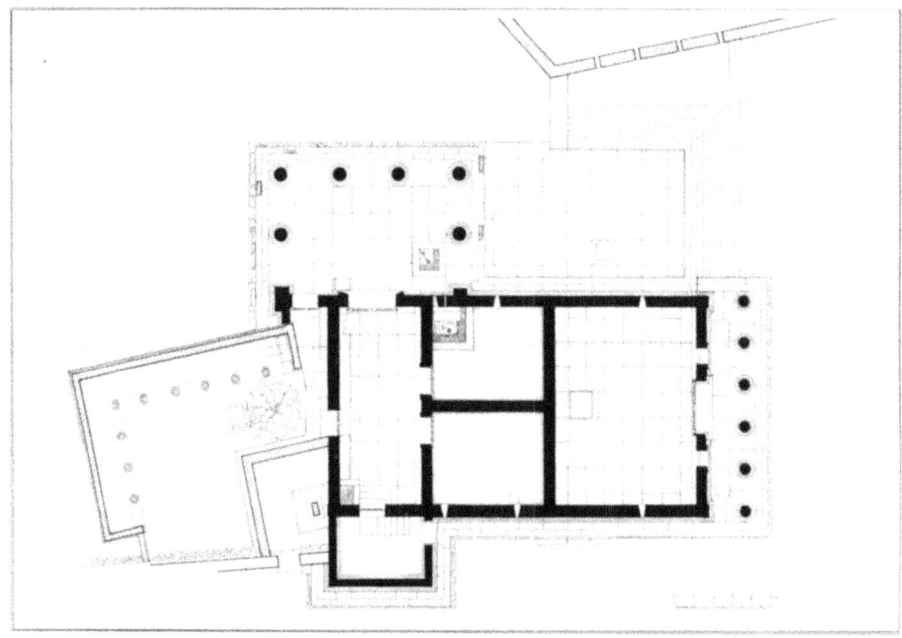

Plate 11b. Athens, Acropolis, Erechtheion, restored plan of the fifth century B.C. From Papanikolaou 2012, vol. 2, p. 503 fig. 130. (Courtesy of Athens: Acropolis Restoration Service, Hellenic Ministry of Culture and Tourism)

Plate 11c. Athens, Acropolis, Erechtheion, North Court from the east. (Courtesy of S. Henneberry)

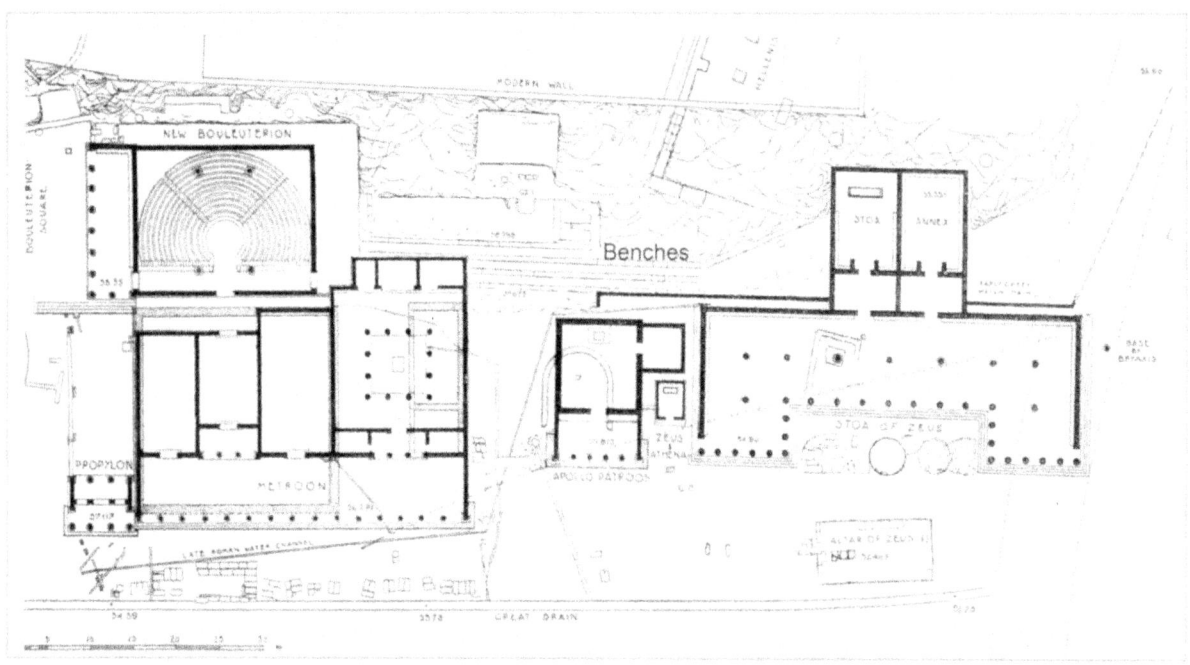

Plate 12a. Athens, Agora, plan of structures on the west side, with benches. From H. A. Thompson 1937, p. 219 fig. 126. (Courtesy of the American School of Classical Studies at Athens)

Plate 12b. Athens, Agora, benches on the west side below the Hephaisteion. From Boegehold 1995, pl. Ib. (Courtesy of the American School of Classical Studies at Athens)

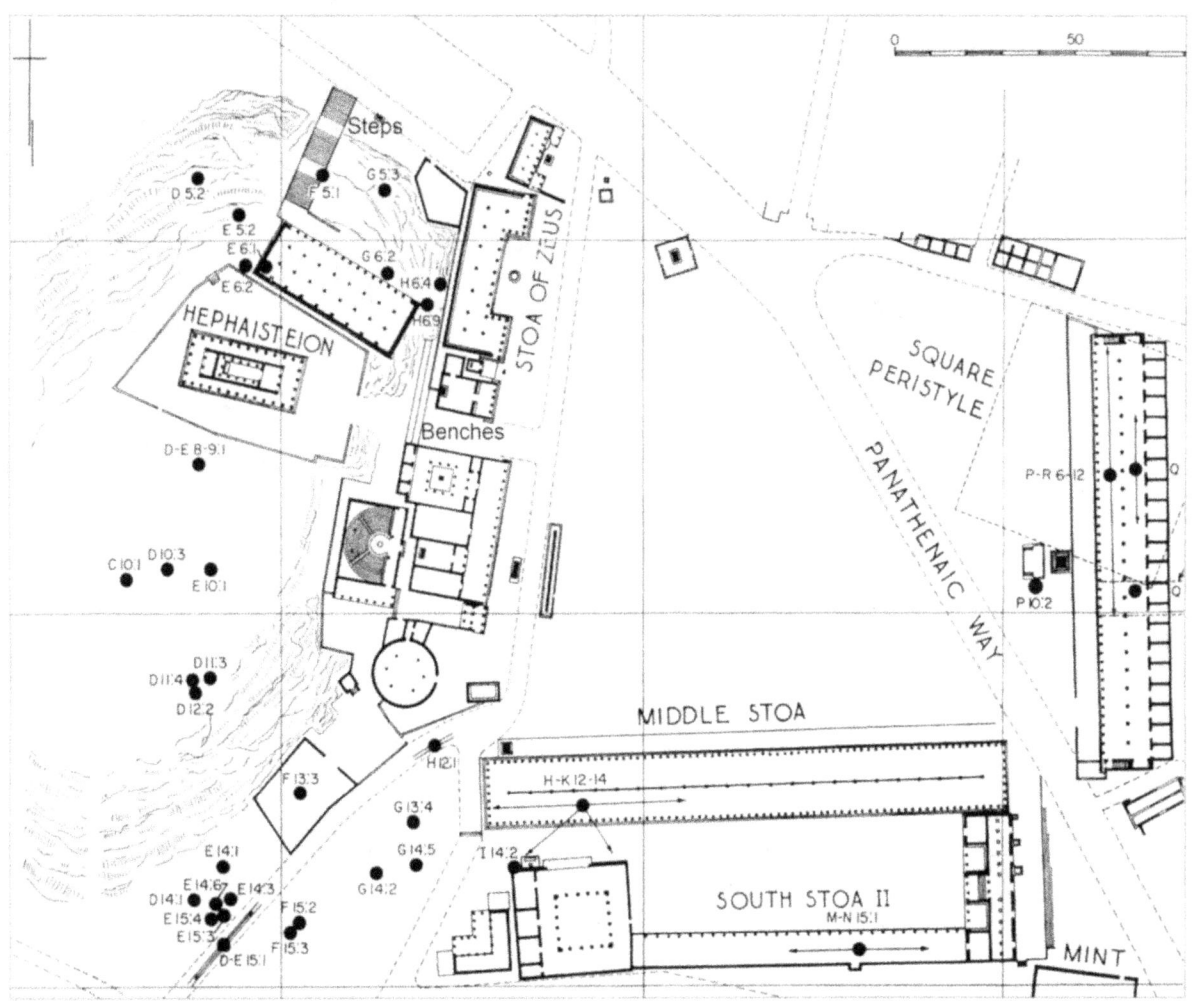

Plate 13. Athens, Agora, plan in the Hellenistic period, with steps to Kolonos Agoraios. From Rotroff 1982, pl. A. (Courtesy of the American School of Classical Studies at Athens)

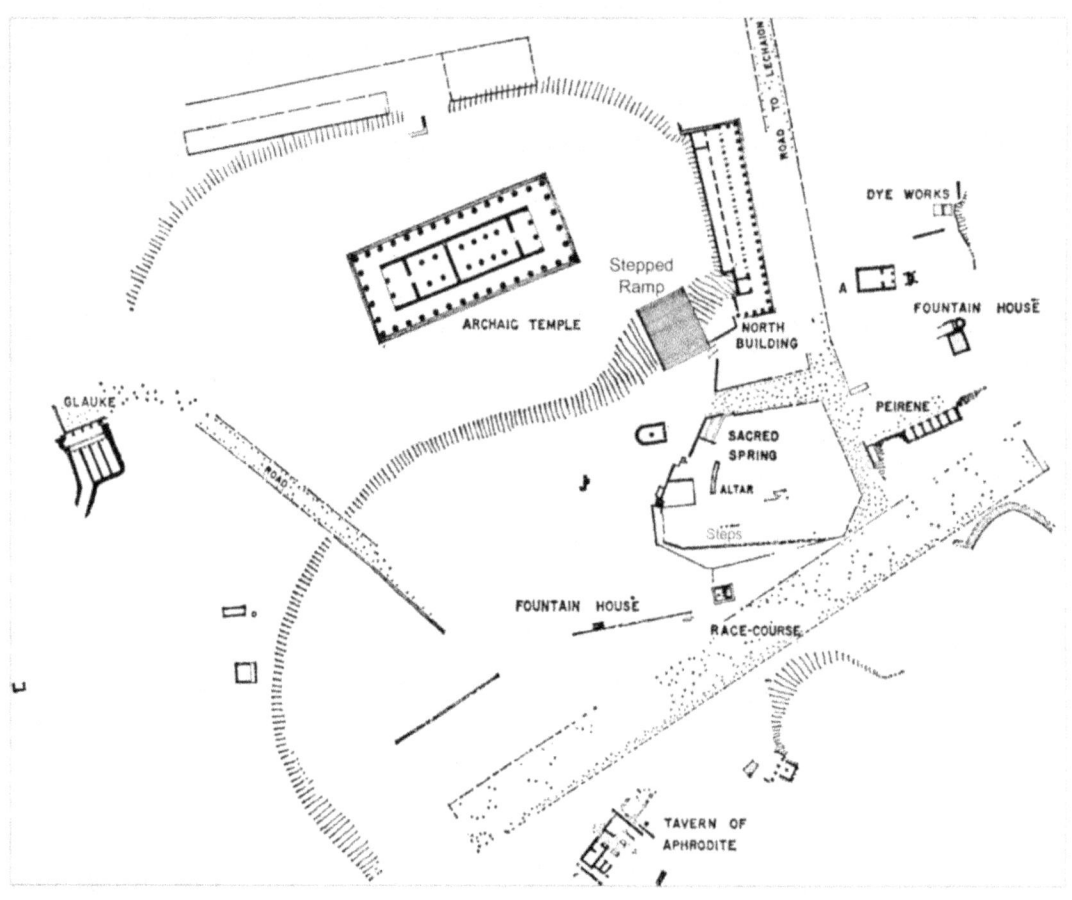

Plate 14a. Corinth, Temple Hill and the Sacred Spring, plan. From Williams and Fisher 1971, fig. 5. (Courtesy of the American School of Classical Studies at Athens)

Plate 14b. Corinth, general view of the ramp and temple from the southeast. (Photo by M. Hollinshead)

Plate 14c. Corinth, ramp to the temple from the southeast. (Photo by M. Hollinshead)

Plate 14d. Corinth, the Sacred Spring from the north. (Photo by M. Hollinshead)

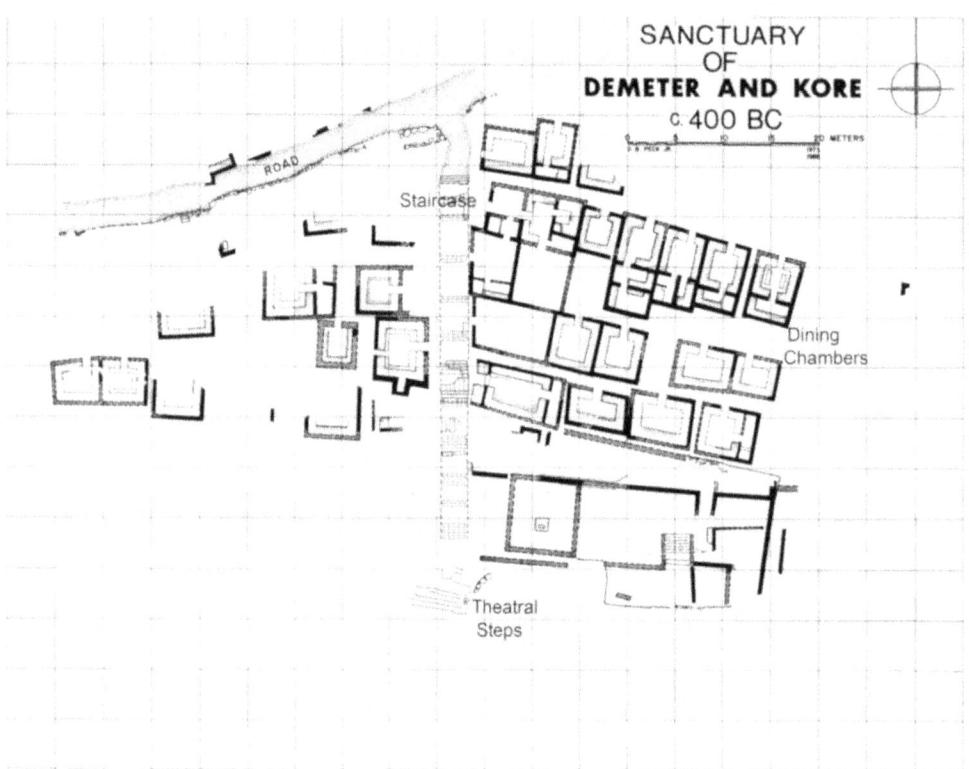

Plate 15a. Corinth, plan of the sanctuary of Demeter and Kore, 400 B.C. From Bookidis and Stroud 1997, plan 4. (Courtesy of the American School of Classical Studies at Athens)

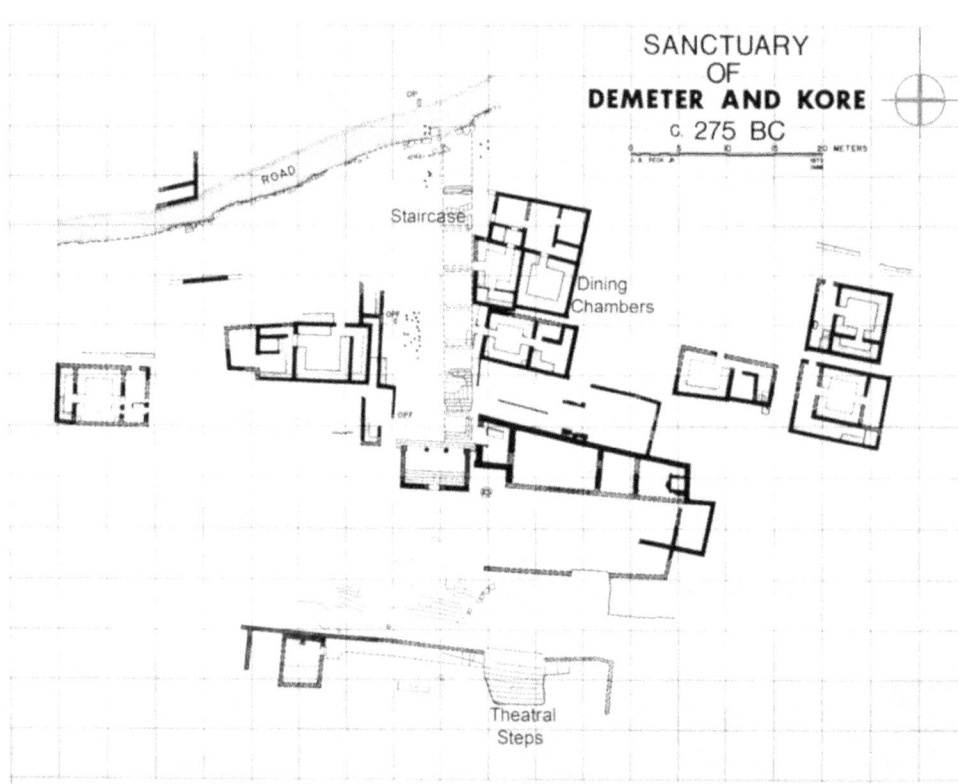

Plate 15b. Corinth, plan of the sanctuary of Demeter and Kore, 275 B.C. From Bookidis and Stroud 1997, plan 5. (Courtesy of the American School of Classical Studies at Athens)

Plate 15c. Corinth, sanctuary of Demeter and Kore from the northwest. From Bookidis and Stroud 1997, pl. 2. (Courtesy of the American School of Classical Studies at Athens)

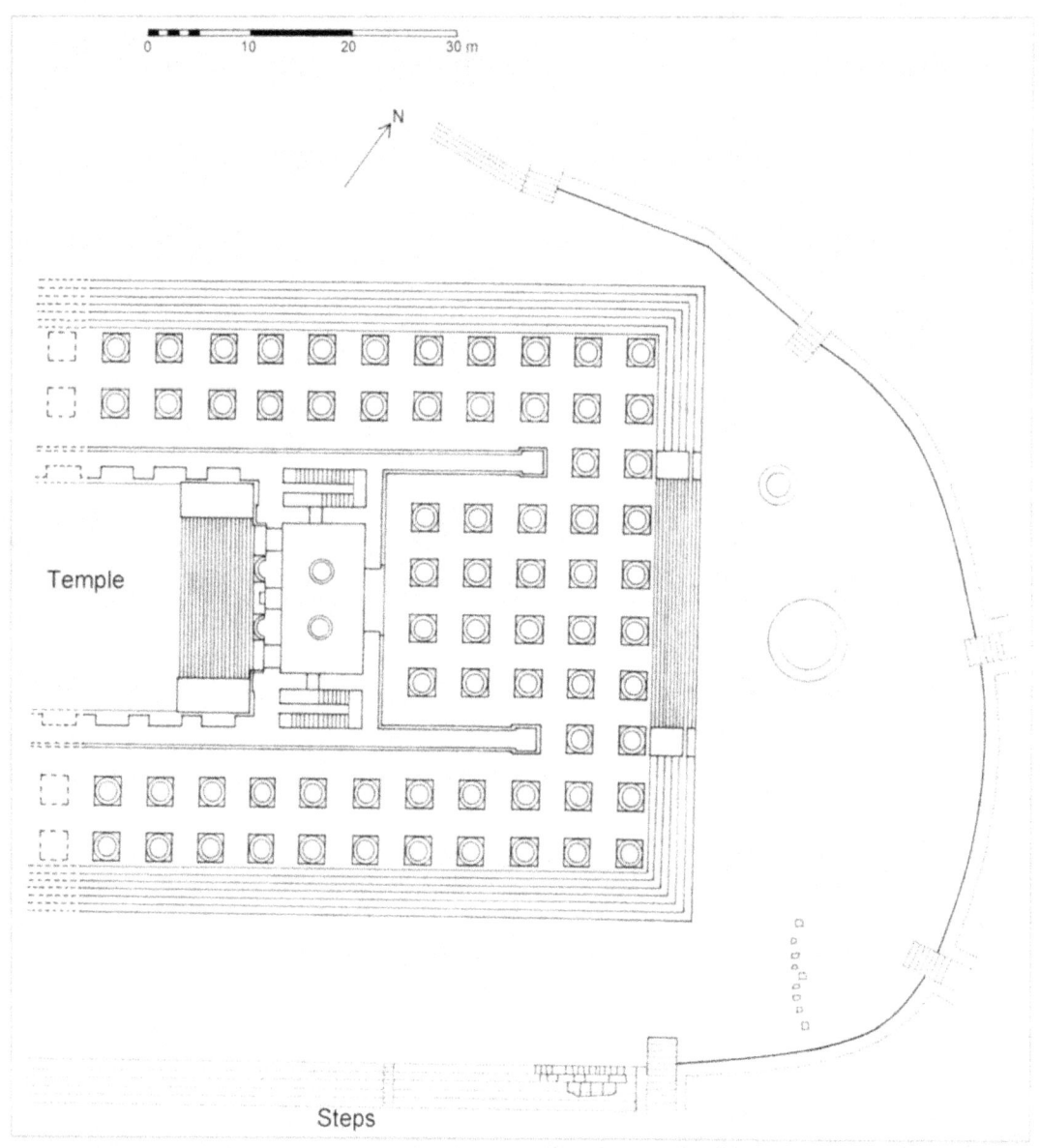

Plate 16a. Didyma, sanctuary of Apollo, plan with spectator steps. (Drawn by C. Piok Zanon)

Plate 16b. Didyma, upper edge of spectator steps (foreground) and temple from the southeast. (Photo by M. Hollinshead)

Plate 16c. Didyma, spectator steps from the west. (Photo by M. Hollinshead)

Plate 17a. Dreros, plan of the "agora." (Drawn by C. Piok Zanon)

Plate 17b. Dreros, steps facing the "agora" from the west. (Courtesy Ecole Française d'Athènes / H. Van Effenterre)

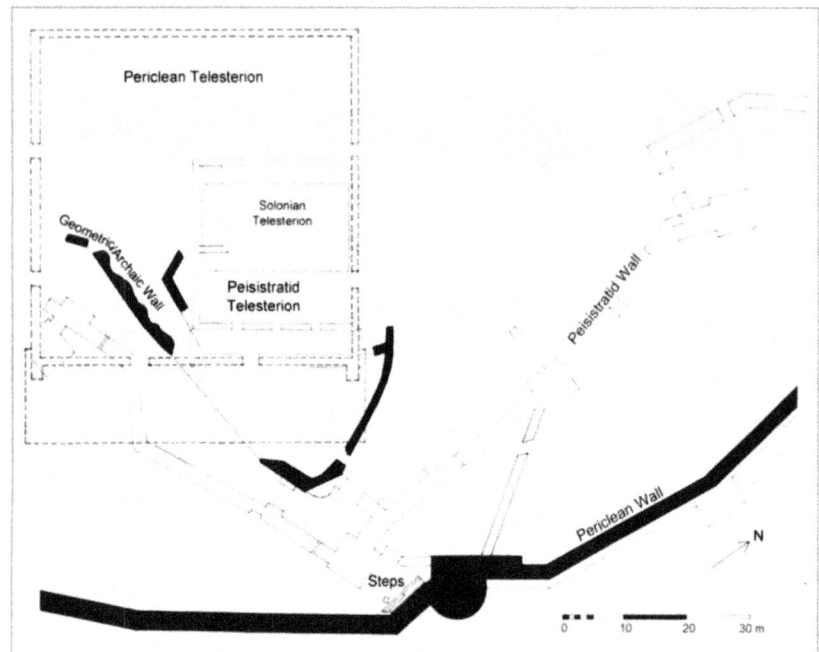

Plate 18a. Eleusis, plan of sixth-century structures. (Drawn by C. Piok Zanon)

Plate 18b. Eleusis, sixth-century grandstand (originally continued to the left). From Mylonas 1989, fig. 19. (By permission of the Princeton University Press)

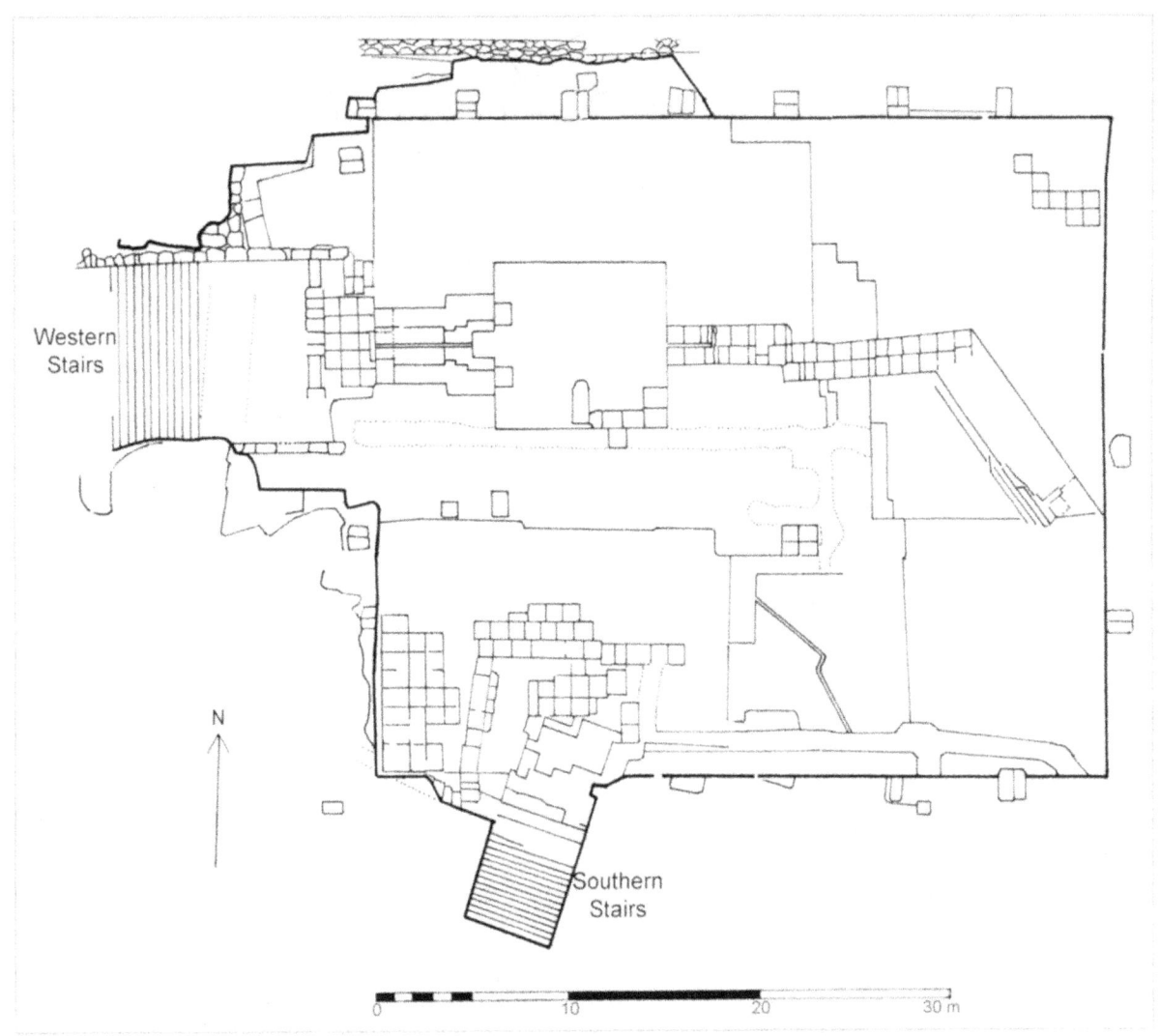

Plate 19. Halikarnassos, plan of the Maussolleion. (Drawn by C. Piok Zanon)

Plate 20a. Kameiros, plan of the lower sector of town. (Drawn by C. Piok Zanon)

Plate 20b. Kameiros, "agora," steps, and precinct from the south. (Photo by M. Hollinshead)

Plate 21. Kapikaya, grandstand steps from the north (note additional steps to the right). (Photo by M. Hollinshead)

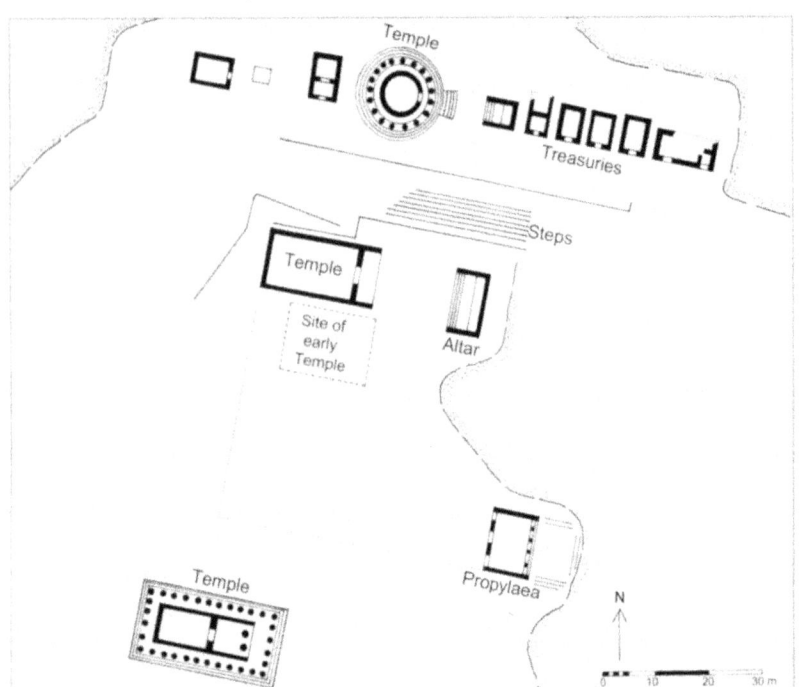

Plate 22a. Knidos, plan of the sanctuary of Apollo. (Drawn by C. Piok Zanon)

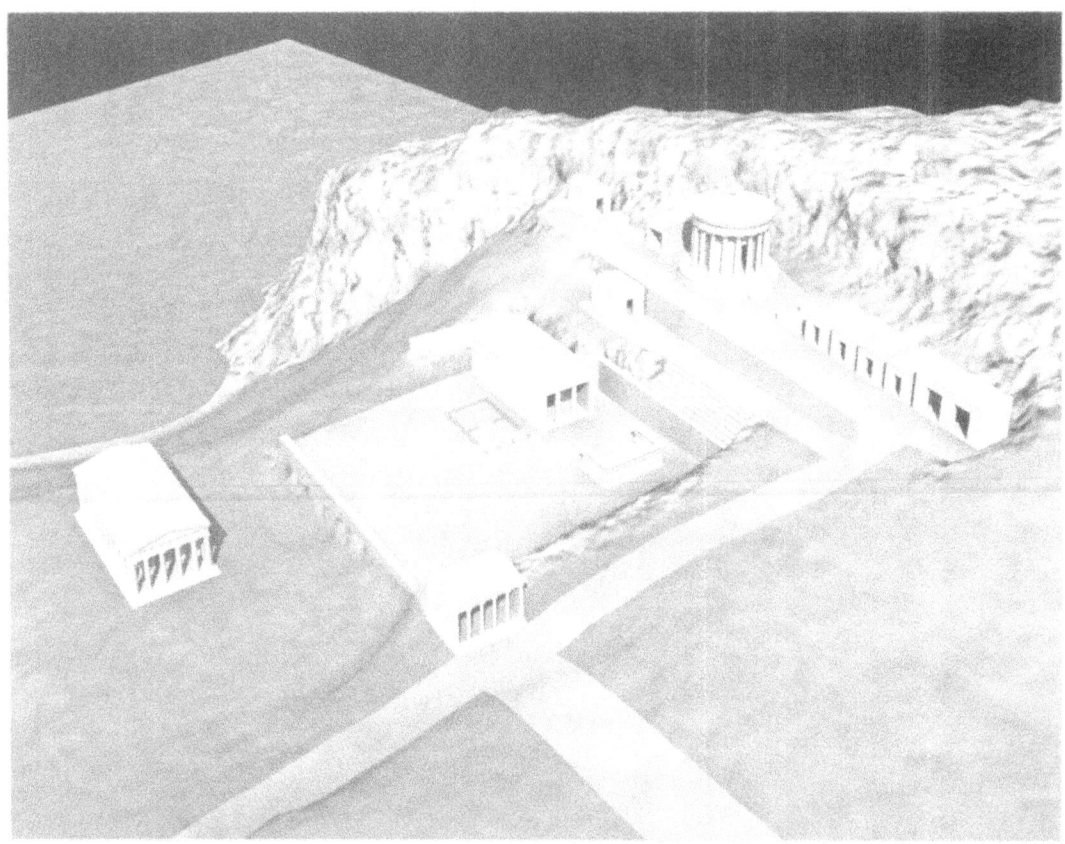

Plate 22b. Knidos, model of the sanctuary of Apollo. (Courtesy of H. Bankel)

Plate 22c. Knidos, spectator steps and altar (on left) from the southeast. (Photo by M. Hollinshead)

Plate 22d. Knidos, spectator steps from the east. (Photo by M. Hollinshead)

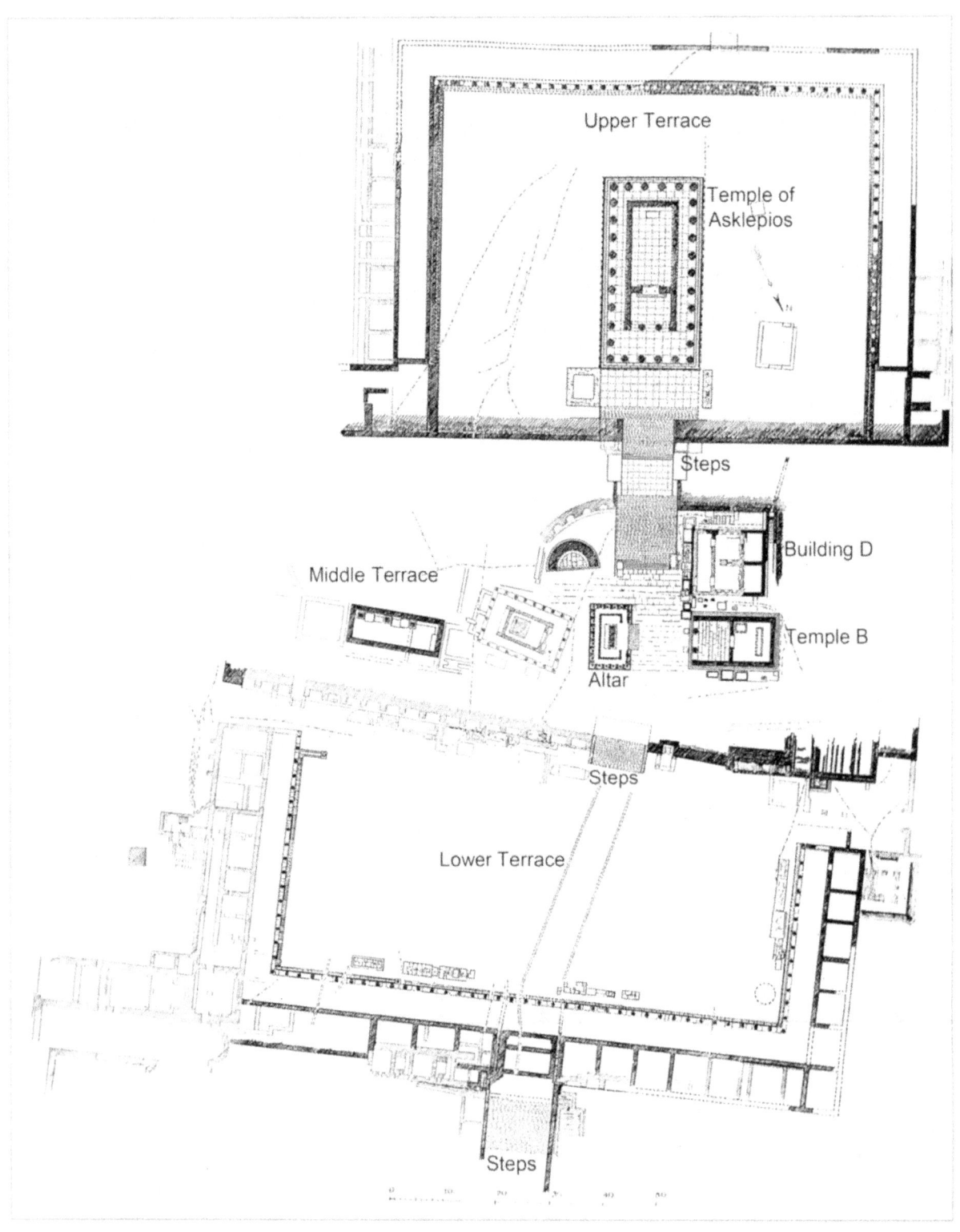

Plate 23a. Kos, plan of the sanctuary of Asklepios. From Herzog and Schazmann 1932, pl. 40. (Courtesy of the Deutsches Archäologisches Institut, Berlin)

Plate 23b. Kos, reconstruction drawing of the sanctuary of Asklepios. From Herzog and Schazmann 1932, pl. 38. (Courtesy of the Deutsches Archäologisches Institut, Berlin)

Plate 23c. Kos, steps to the Upper Terrace before restoration. From Herzog and Schazmann 1932, pl. 45. (Courtesy of the Deutsches Archäologisches Institut, Berlin)

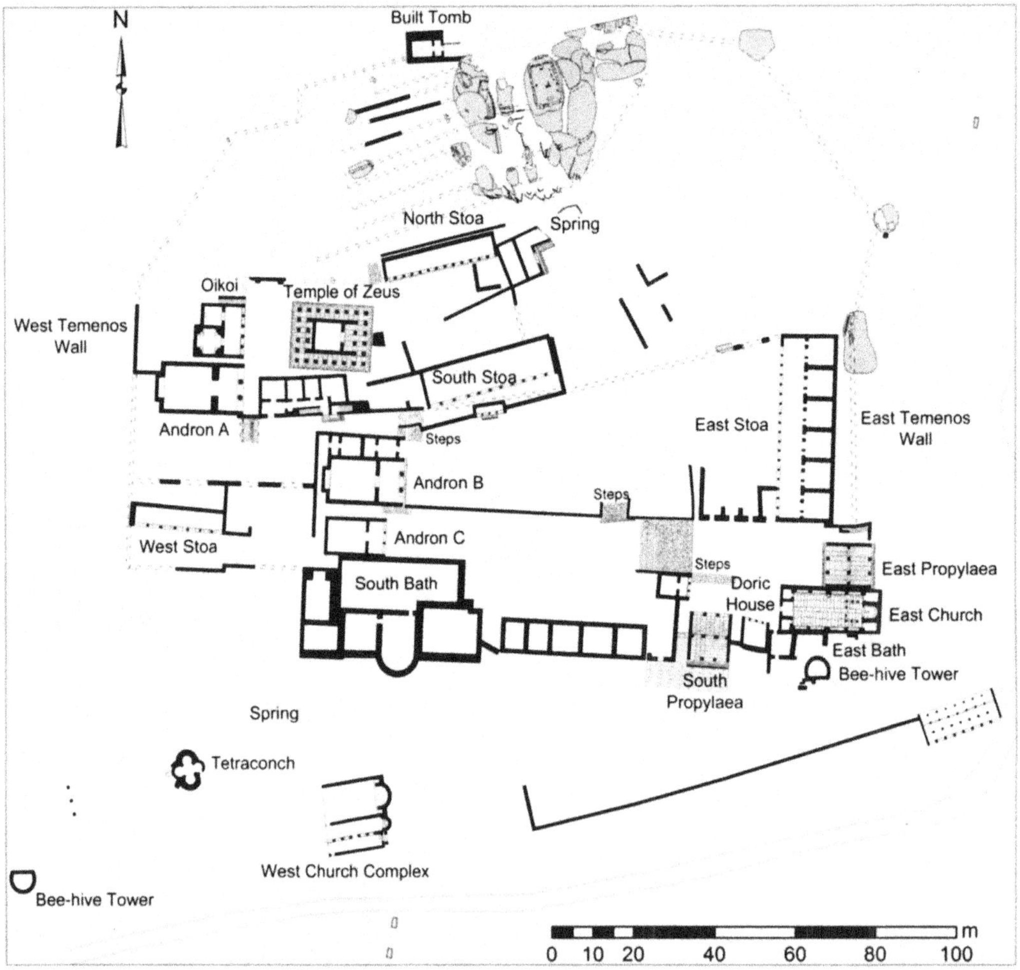

Plate 24a. Labraunda, plan of the sanctuary. (Drawn by J. Blid, courtesy of the Swedish Labraunda Expedition)

Plate 24b. Labraunda, Great Stairway from the southeast. (Photo by M. Hollinshead)

Plate 25a. Latmos, distant view of the "agora," with steps in the middle. (Courtesy of A. Peschlow)

Plate 25b. Latmos, steps along the "agora." (Courtesy of A. Peschlow)

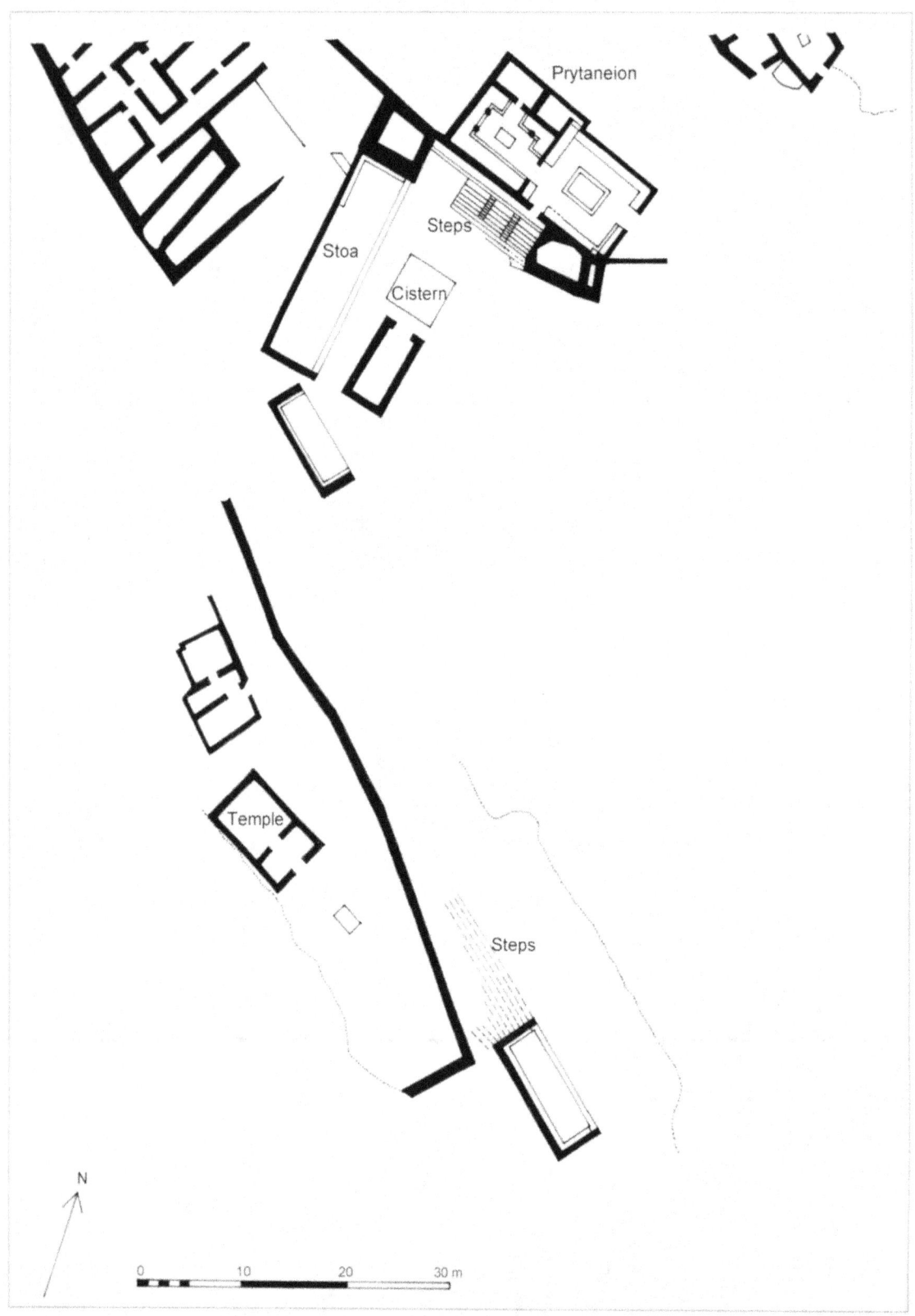

Plate 26a. Lato, plan of the "agora" and temple area. (Drawn by C. Piok Zanon)

Plate 26b. Lato, steps to the prytaneion. (Photo by M. Hollinshead)

Plate 26c. Lato, theatral steps below the temple. (Photo by M. Hollinshead)

Plate 27a. Lindos, plan of the sixth-century steps. From Dygve and Poulsen 1960, p. 75 fig. III.29. (Courtesy of the National Museum of Denmark)

Plate 27b. Lindos, sixth-century steps as excavated. From Dygve and Poulsen 1960, p. 75 fig. III.32. (Courtesy of the National Museum of Denmark)

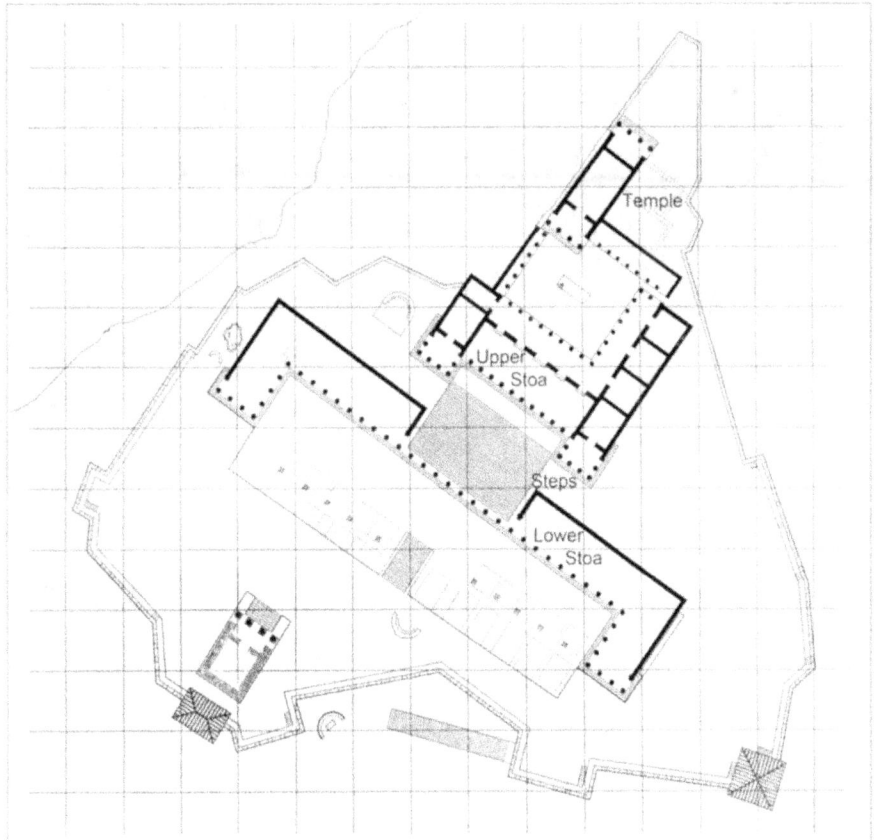

Plate 27c. Lindos, plan of the sanctuary of Athena in the third century and later. From Dygve and Poulsen 1960, p. 532 fig. XIV.6. (Courtesy of the National Museum of Denmark)

Plate 27d. Lindos, third-century steps before restoration. From Dygve and Poulsen 1960, p. 259 fig. VI.1. (Courtesy of the National Museum of Denmark)

Plate 27e. Lindos, model of the sanctuary of Athena. (Courtesy of the National Museum of Denmark)

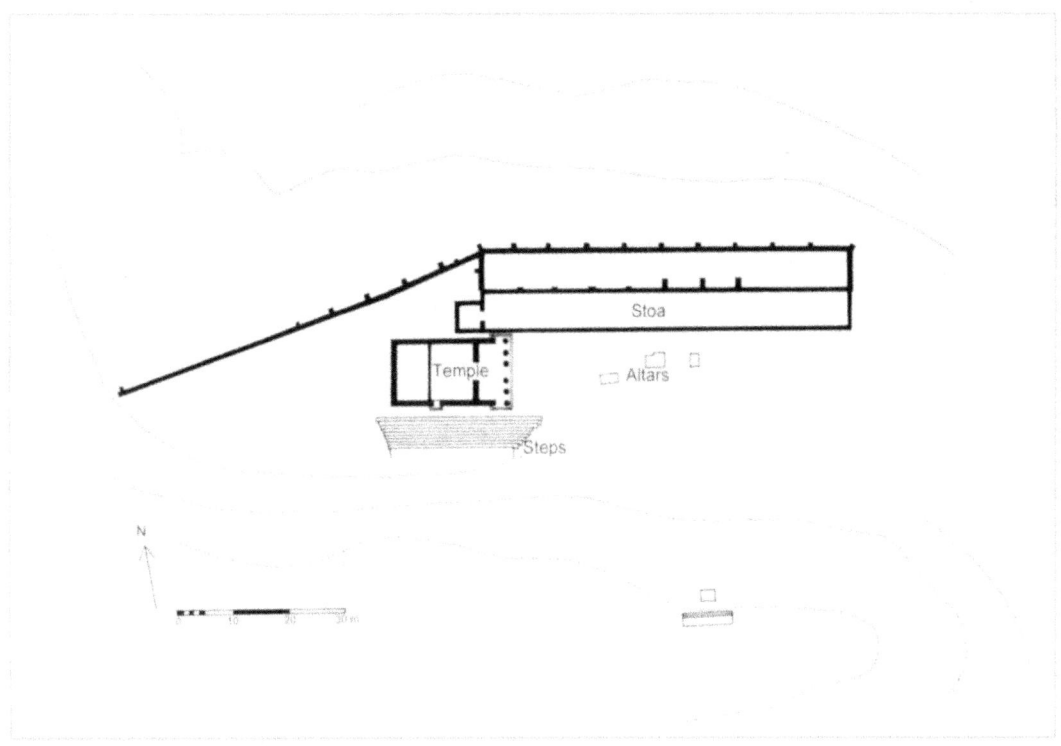

Plate 28a. Lykosoura, plan of the sanctuary. (Drawn by C. Piok Zanon)

Plate 28b. Lykosoura, steps and south side of the temple from the east. (Photo by M. Hollinshead)

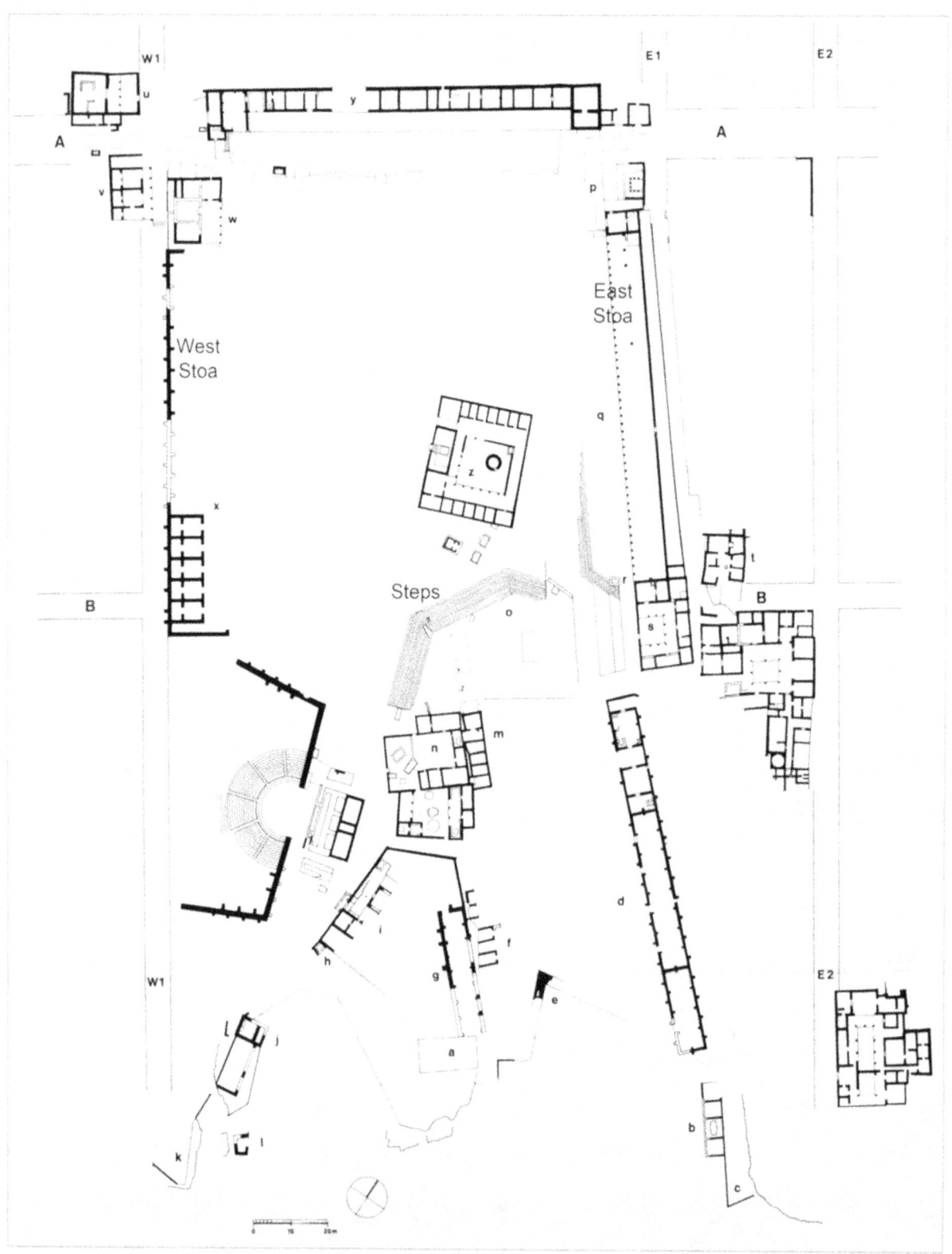

Plate 29a. Morgantina, plan of the agora. From M. Bell 1988, p. 315 fig. 1. (Courtesy of American Excavations at Morgantina)

Plate 29b. Morgantina, agora steps from the east. (Photo by M. Hollinshead)

Plate 30a. Mount Lykaion, steps from the west before excavation. (Photo by M. Hollinshead)

Plate 30b. Mount Lykaion, excavated steps from the northeast. (Courtesy of Mount Lykaion Excavation and Survey Project)

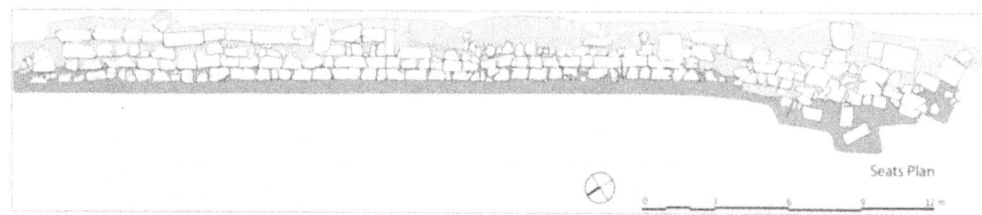

Plate 30c. Mount Lykaion, plan of the steps. (Courtesy of Mount Lykaion Excavation and Survey Project)

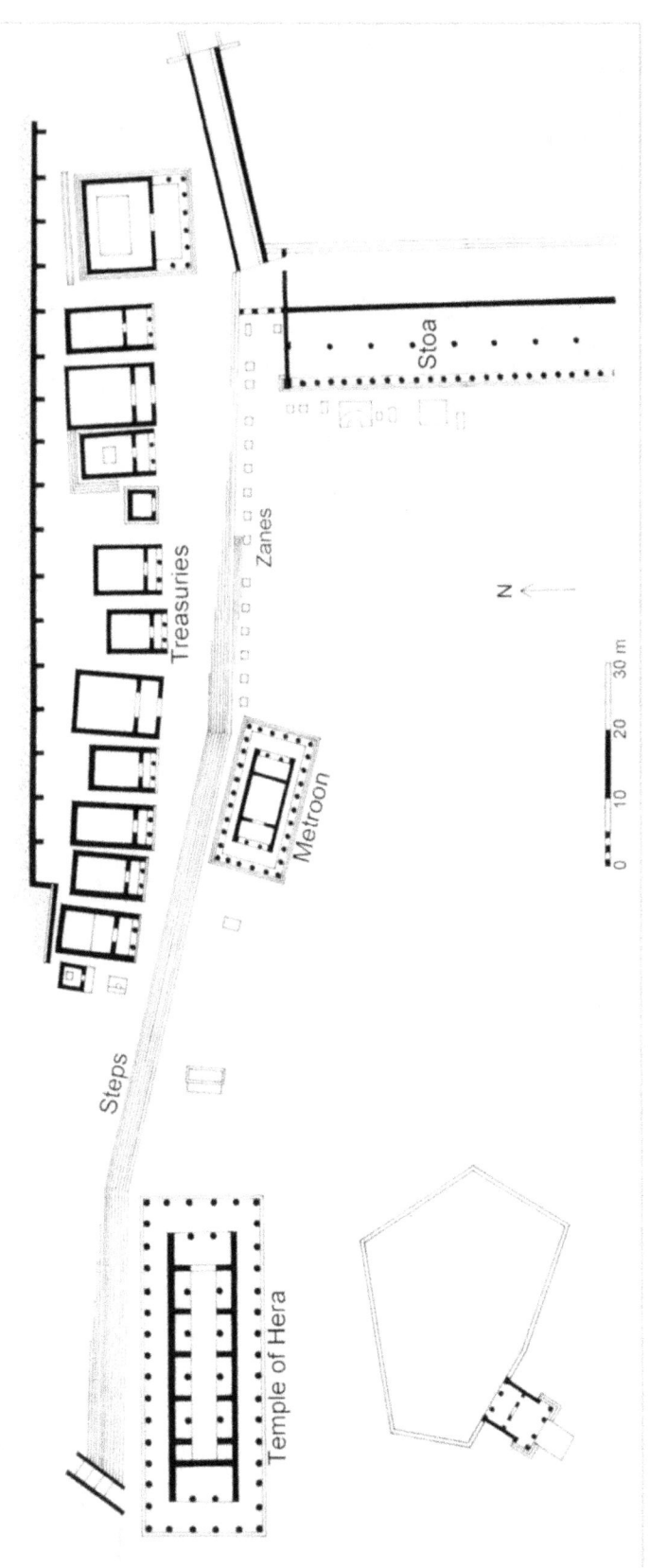

Plate 31a. Olympia, plan of the northern sector of the sanctuary of Zeus. (Drawn by C. Piok Zanon)

Plate 31b. Olympia, model of the north side of the sanctuary of Zeus. (Courtesy of H. R. Goette)

Plate 31c. Olympia, steps along the north side of the sanctuary of Zeus, from the east. (Photo by M. Hollinshead)

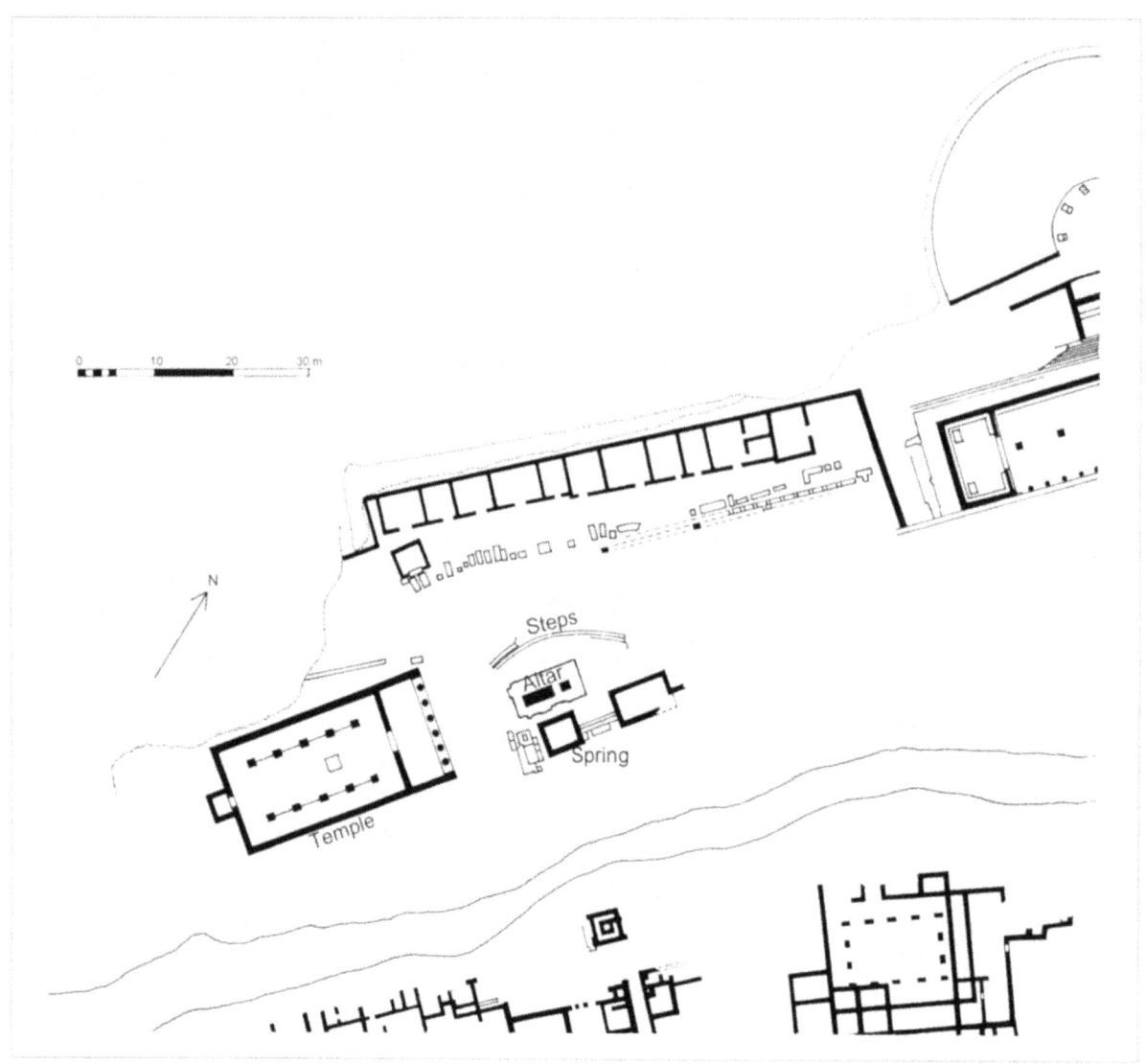

Plate 32a. Oropos, Amphiaraion, plan of the temple and altar area. (Drawn by C. Piok Zanon)

Plate 32b. Oropos, Amphiaraion, steps facing the altar (on the left). (Photo by M. Hollinshead)

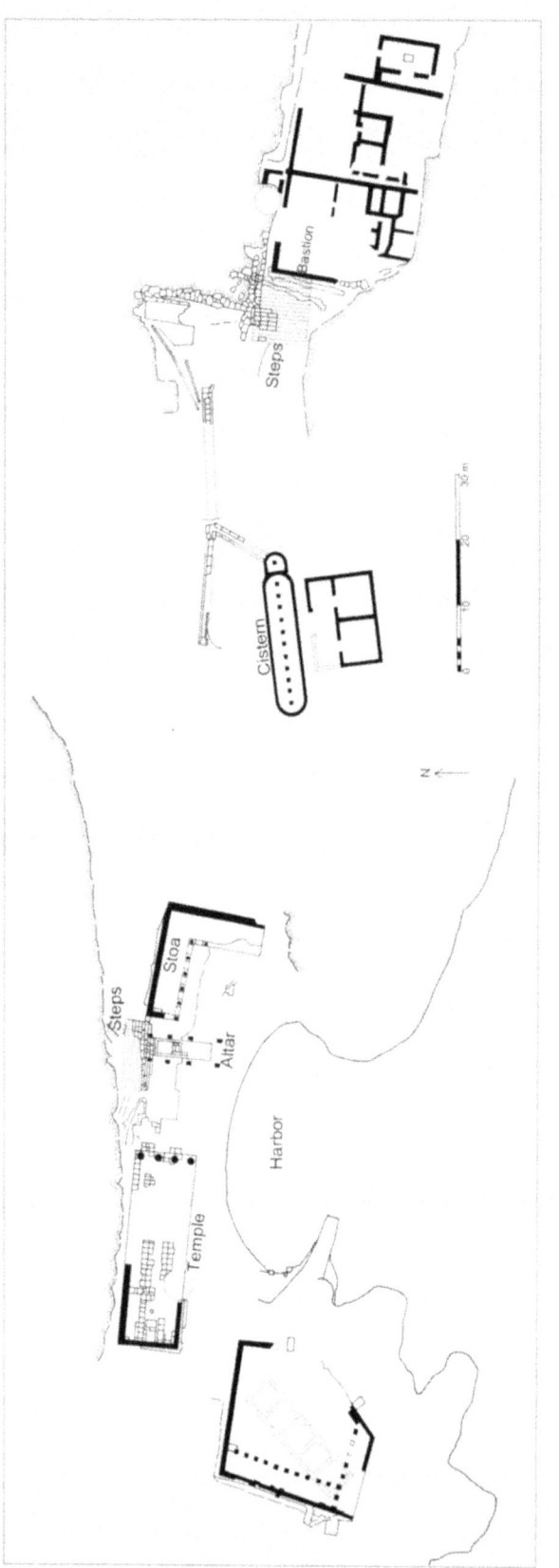

Plate 33a. Perachora, plan of the sanctuary of Hera, lower and upper sectors. (Drawn by C. Piok Zanon)

Plate 33b. Perachora, aerial photo of the sanctuary, lower and upper sectors, from the west. From Sinn 1990, pl. 11. (Courtesy of U. Sinn)

Plate 33c. Perachora, steps by the altar from the southwest. (Photo by M. Hollinshead)

Plate 33d. Perachora, tumbled steps in the upper sanctuary from the south. (Photo by M. Hollinshead)

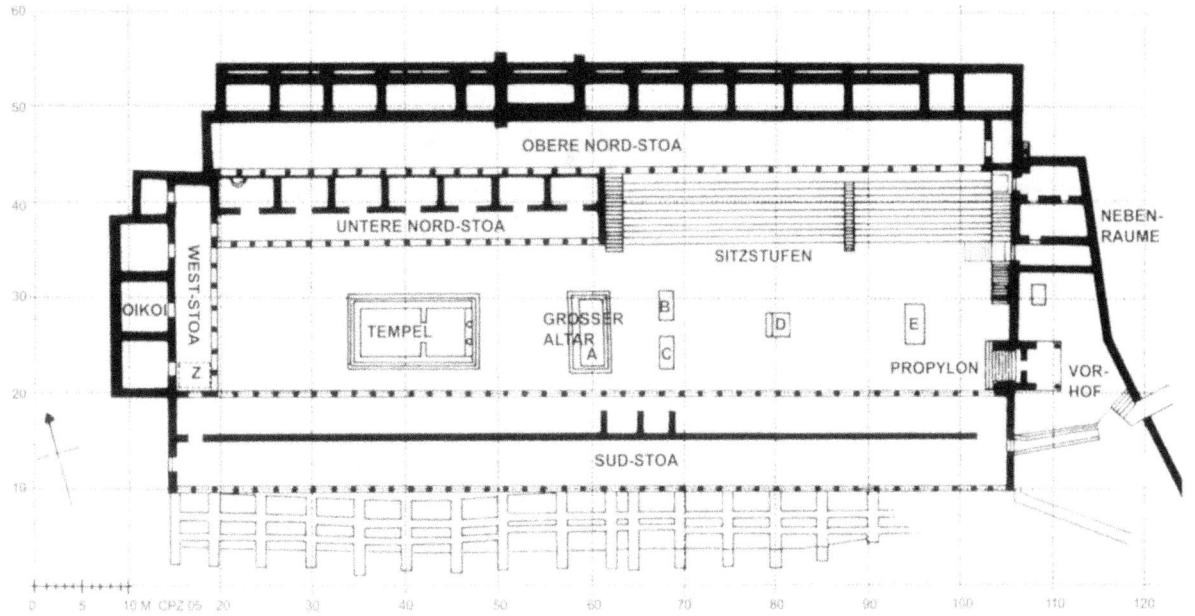

Plate 34a. Pergamon, plan of the sanctuary of Demeter. From Piok Zanon 2007, p. 326 fig. 1. (Courtesy of C. Piok Zanon)

Plate 34b. Pergamon, sanctuary of Demeter from the east. (Courtesy of C. Piok Zanon)

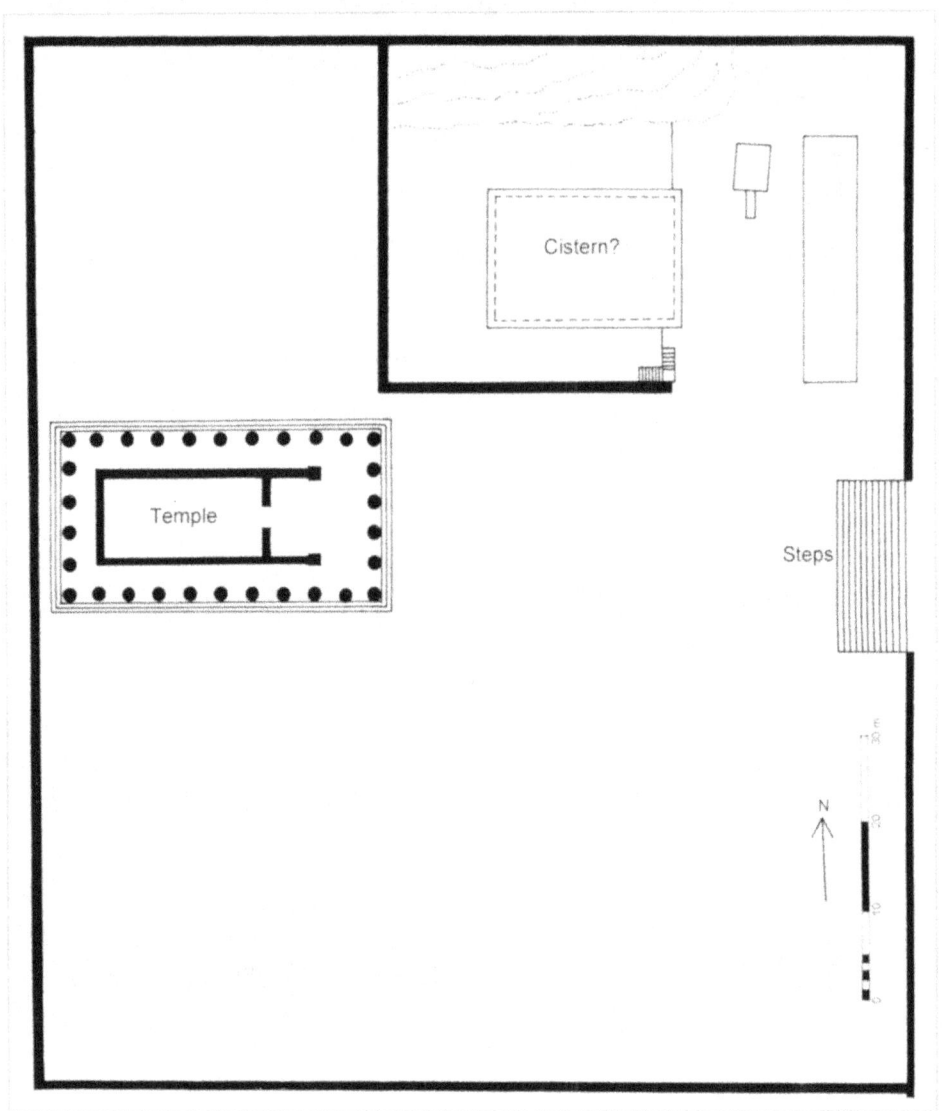

Plate 35. Rhodes City, plan of the sanctuary of Apollo. (Drawn by C. Piok Zanon)

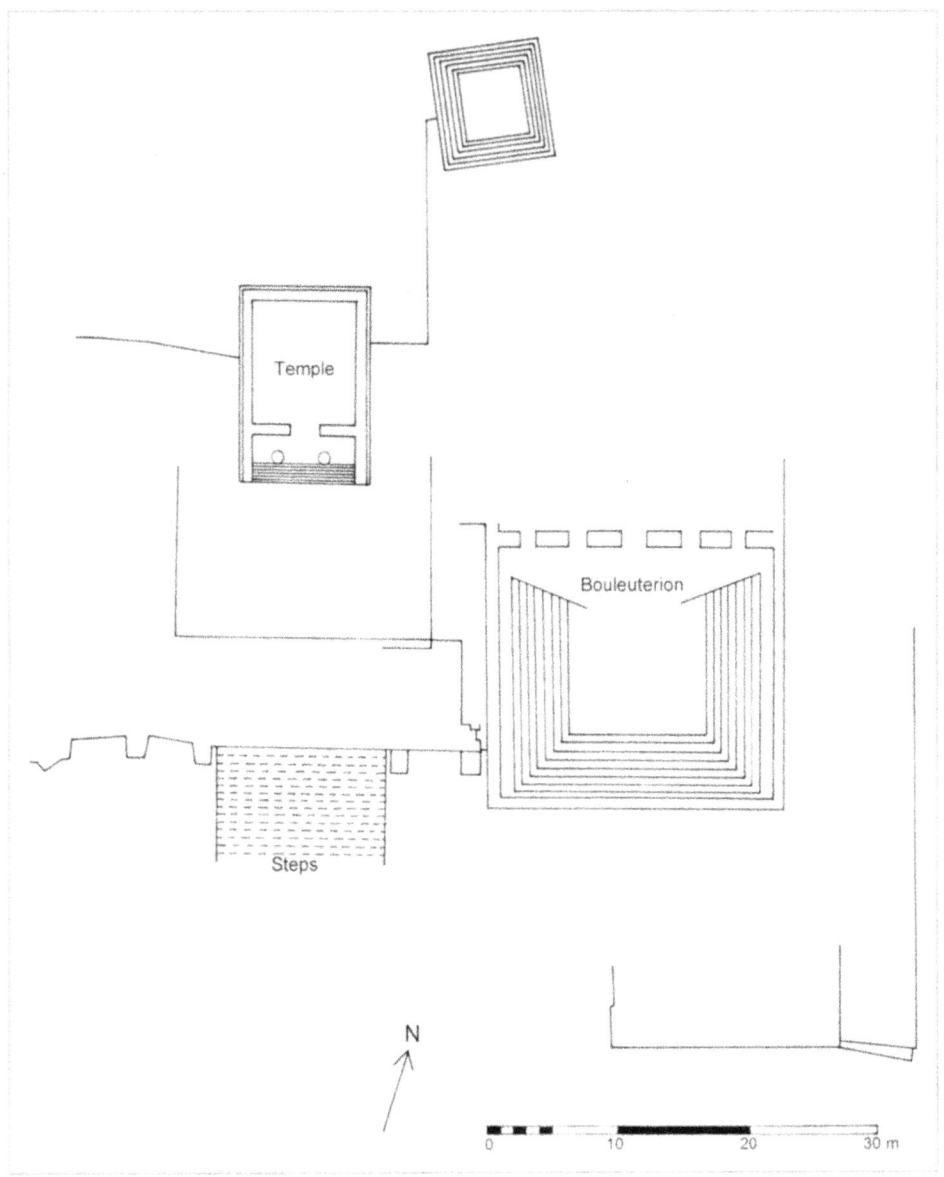

Plate 36a. Sagalassos, plan of the temple area. (Drawn by C. Piok Zanon)

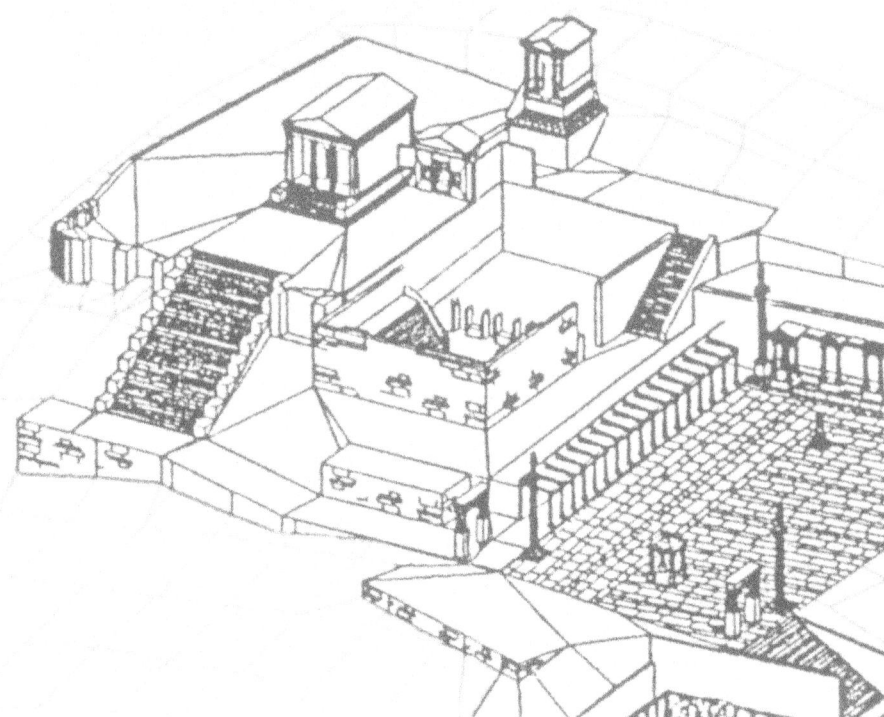

Plate 36b. Sagalassos, reconstruction drawing. (Courtesy of M. Waelkens, Sagalassos Archaeological Project)

Plate 36c. Sagalassos, profile of the steps from the east. (Photo by M. Hollinshead)

Plate 37a. Selinus, reconstruction drawing of Temple M. From Pompeo 1999, pl. VI. (Courtesy of L. Pompeo)

Plate 37b. Selinus, steps and base of Temple M from the southeast. From Pompeo 1999, fig. 53. (Courtesy of L. Pompeo)

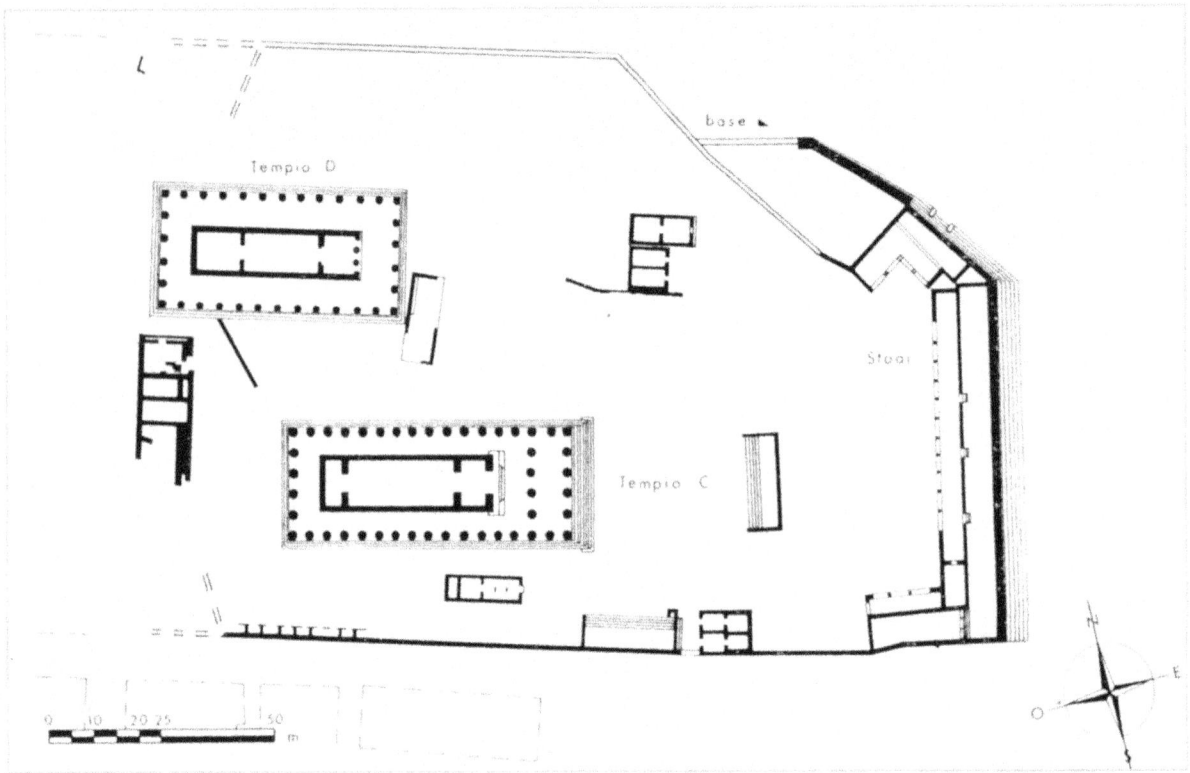

Plate 38a. Selinus, plan of the acropolis. From Di Vita 1984, p. 34 [28] fig. 18. (Courtesy of the Scuola Archeologica Italiana di Atene)

Fig. 38b. Selinus, aerial view of the acropolis from the northeast. From Di Vita 1984, pl. III.b. (Courtesy of the Scuola Archeologica Italiana di Atene)

Plate 38c. Selinus, acropolis, stepped retaining wall from the southeast. (Photo by M. Hollinshead)

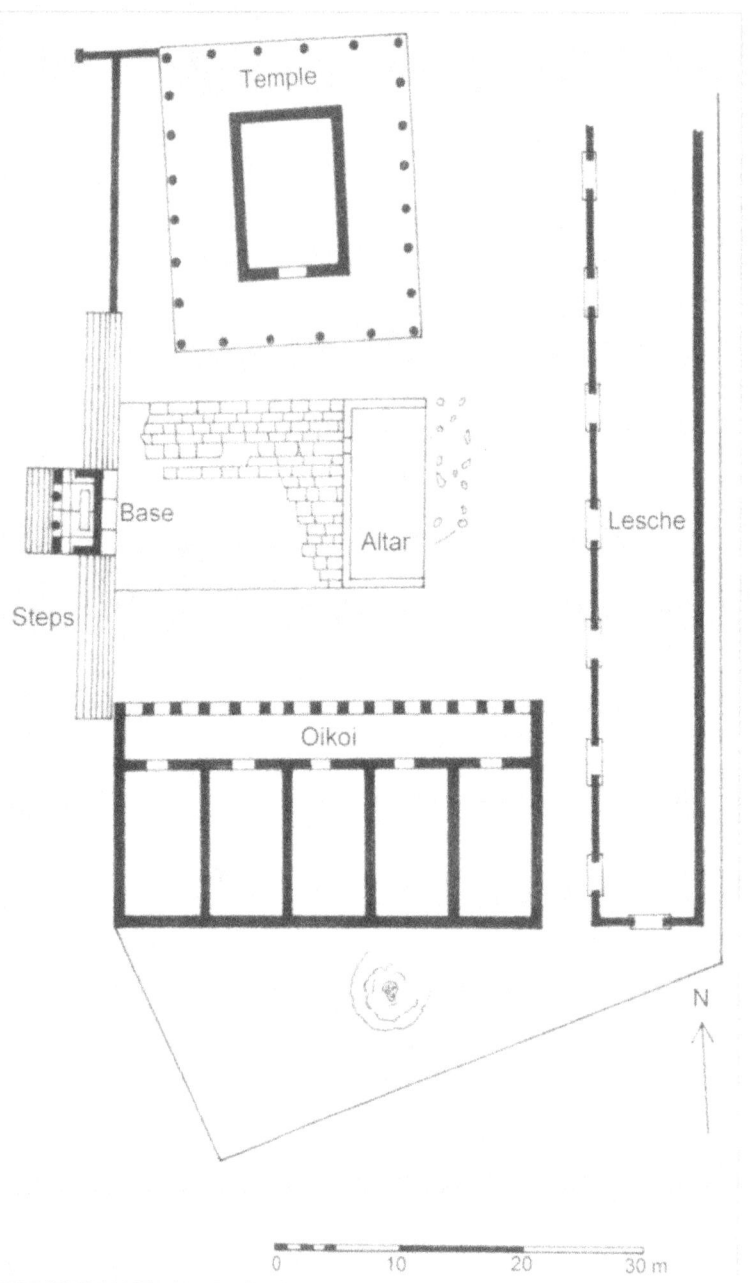

Plate 39. Thasos, plan of the Herakleion. (Drawn by C. Piok Zanon)

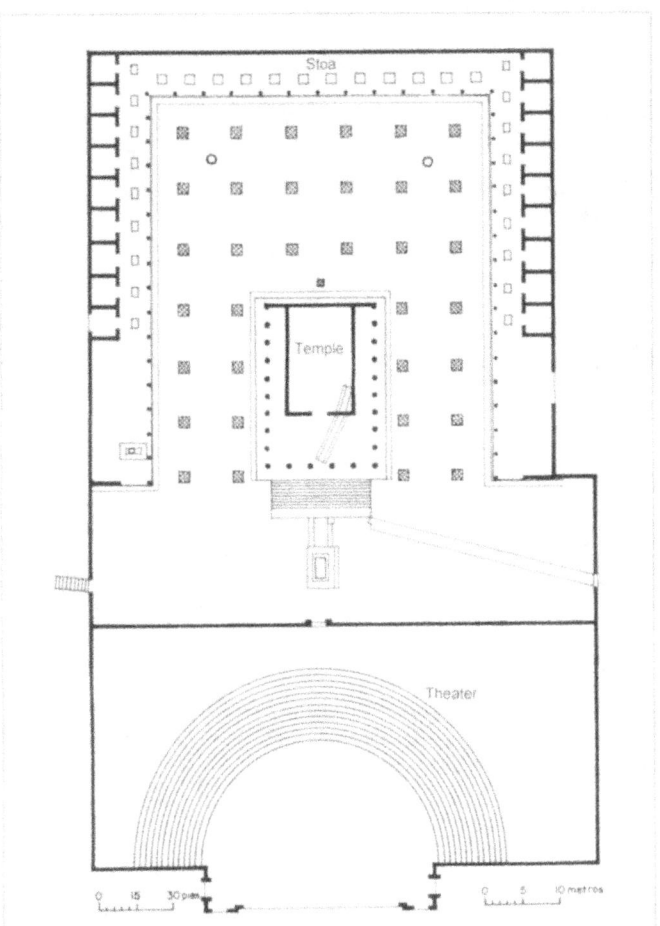

Plate 40a. Gabii, plan of the sanctuary of Juno. From Almagro-Gorbea 1982, p. 584 fig. 1. (Courtesy of M. Almagro-Gorbea)

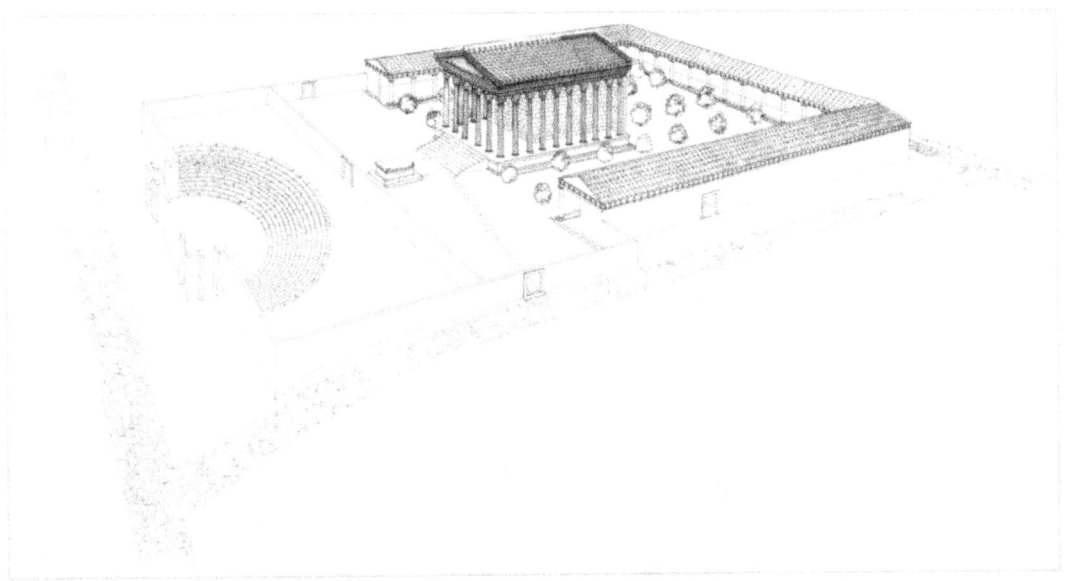

Plate 40b. Gabii, reconstruction drawing of the sanctuary of Juno. From Almagro-Gorbea 1982, p. 585 fig. 2. (Courtesy of M. Almagro-Gorbea)

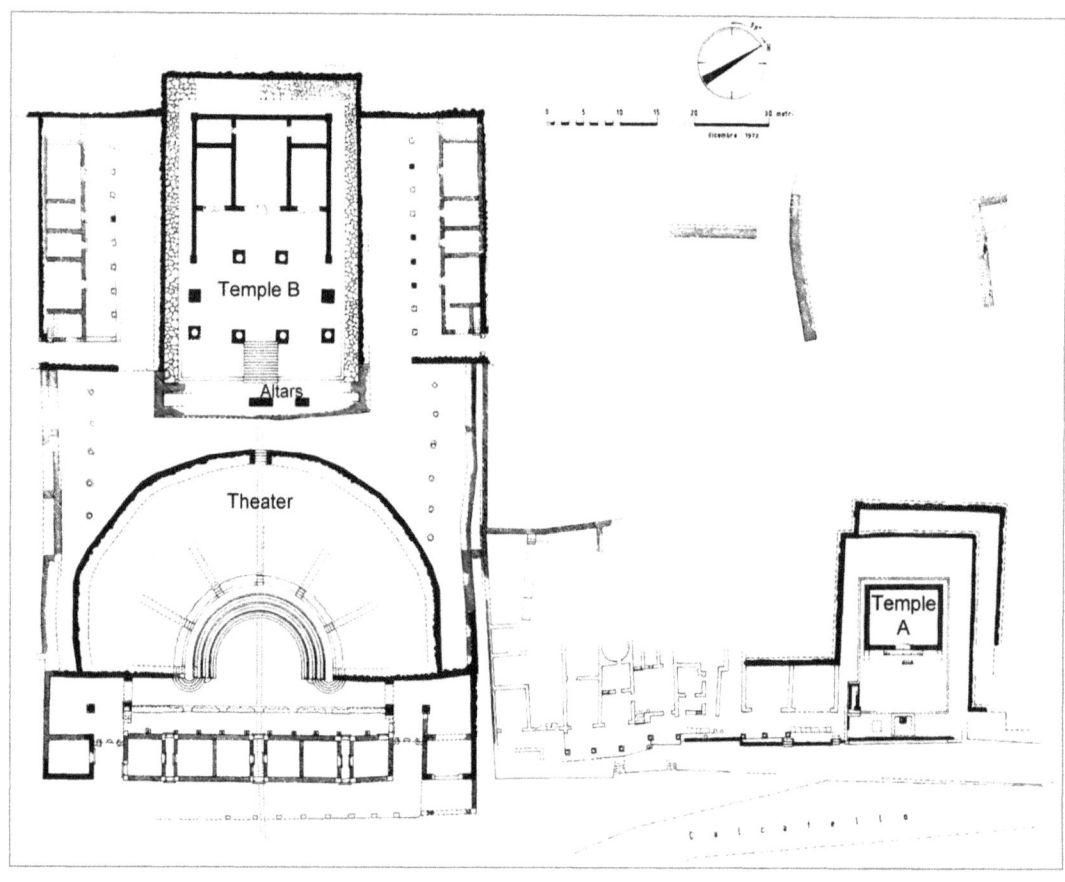

Plate 41a. Pietrabbondante, plan of the sanctuary. From Strazzulla and di Marco 1972, p. 11 fig. 1. (Courtesy of A. La Regina)

Plate 41b. Pietrabbondante, the sanctuary from behind the temple (from the northwest). (Photo by M. Hollinshead)

Plate 42. Praeneste, aerial view of the sanctuary of Fortuna from the west. (Courtesy of Pro Loco Palestrina, Comune di Palestrina)

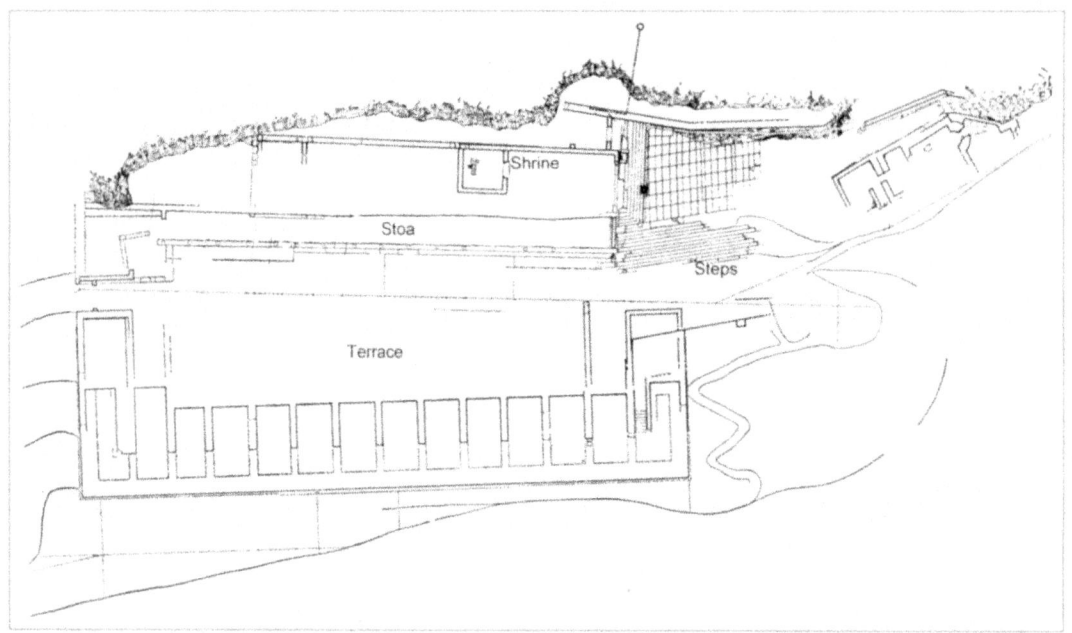

Plate 43a. Sulmo, plan of the sanctuary of Hercules. From van Wonterghem 1984, p. 242 fig. 327. (Courtesy of A. La Regina)

Plate 43b. Sulmo, sanctuary of Hercules: terrace (on left) and steps to the shrine from the south. (Photo by M. Hollinshead)

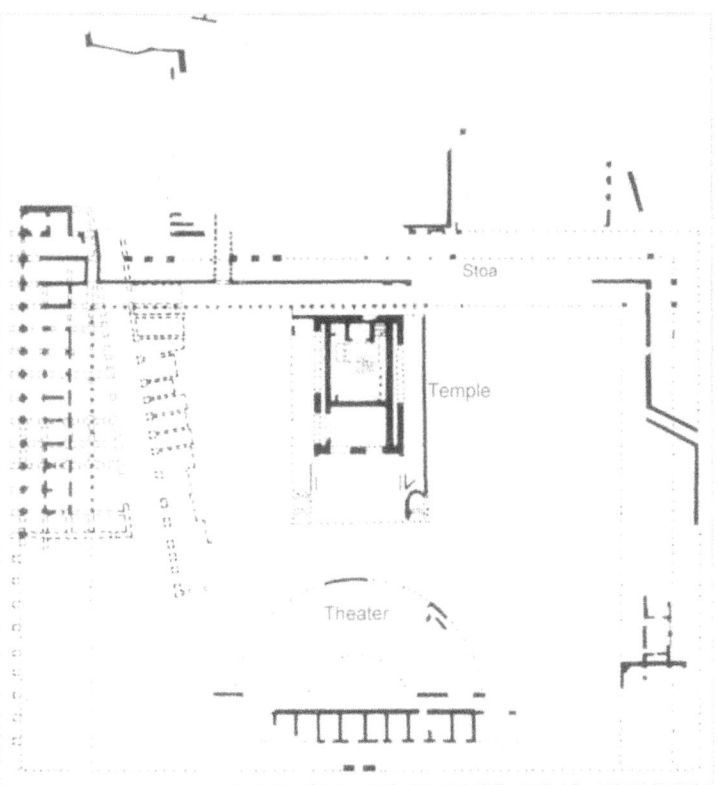

Plate 44a. Tivoli, plan of the sanctuary of Hercules. From Giuliani 1970, p. 193 fig. 218. (Courtesy of C. F. Giuliani)

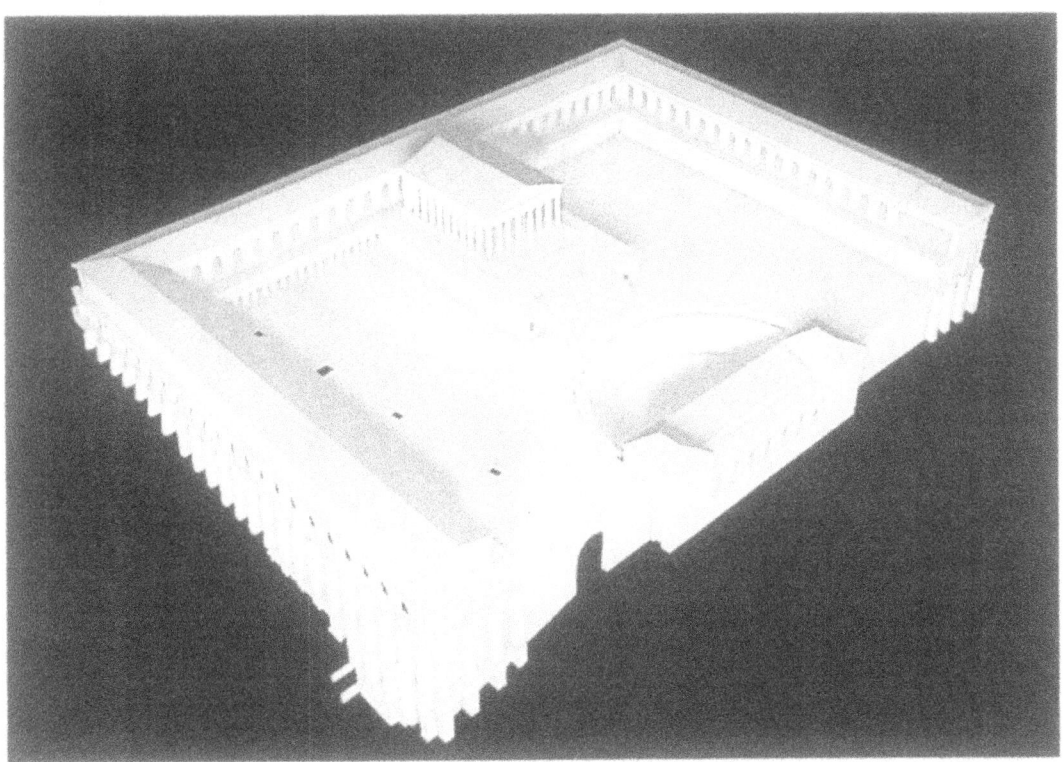

Plate 44b. Tivoli, model of the sanctuary of Hercules. From Giuliani 2009, p. 7 fig. 7. (Courtesy of C. F. Giuliani)

Notes

ABBREVIATIONS

Abbreviations of journals and standard works follow the usage of the *American Journal of Archaeology* (http://www.ajaonline.org/submissions/abbreviations) and the *Oxford Classical Dictionary*, ed. S. Hornblower and A. Spawforth (Oxford: Oxford University Press, 1996).

INTRODUCTION

1. For monumentality see Letesson and Vansteenhuyse 2006, pp. 92–93; Hansen and Fischer-Hansen 1994; Parker Pearson and Richards 1994, p. 3. In my opinion, Lefebvre's assertion (1991, p. 143) that monumentality indicates political dominance does not apply to the structures discussed here.

2. Mylonopoulos 2008, p. 52.

3. Zedeño 2000; A. Nielsen 1995, pp. 55–56, 59; Parker Pearson and Richards 1994, pp. 30, 65–66; Lawrence 1990; Lawrence and Low 1990, p. 485; McGuire and Schiffer 1983, pp. 282–84.

4. See Ashmore and Knapp 1999, pp. 18–19, for comments on the uselives of architecture in ruins.

5. Rowland 1994 on orders; Bauer 1973 on capitals; Shoe 1936 on moldings.

6. Temples: Gruben 1980. Theaters: Bieber 1961. Altars: Ohnesorg 2005; Etienne and Le Dinahet 1991; Yavis 1949. Tombs: Fedak 1990. Typology in general: W. Adams 1988; Adams and Adams 1991.

7. Zedeño 2000, p. 107.

8. Martin 1973, p. 69. Maré (2013, p. 157) asserts that monumental stairs represent conspicuous display of the wealth and power of patrons. For Roman uses of steps, W. L. MacDonald 1986, pp. 66–73.

9. Hollinshead 1992 represents early thoughts on this subject. See also Hollinshead 2012a.

10. Becker 2003.

11. I. Nielsen 2002. See also Frederiksen 2003.

12. Frederiksen 2002; Hansen and Fischer-Hansen 1994; Kolb 1981; Ginouvès 1972; Dilke 1948; W. A. MacDonald 1943.

13. Bergquist 1967, 1992; Doxiadis 1972; Martiensen 1956; P. W. Lehmann 1954; Scranton 1949. See also Stillwell 1957; Plommer 1956; von Gerkan 1938. Other studies of sanctuary space include Tanoulas 1991; Smithson 1958; Matz 1953–54.

14. E.g., Naiden 2013; Patera 2012; Brandt and Iddeng 2012; Goldhill and Osborne 1999; Hägg 1998; Dougherty and Kurke 1993; Marinatos and Hägg 1993; Linders and Nordquist 1987; Van Straten 1981. Acropolis: e.g., Neils 1996b.

15. Hölscher 2002. For spatial aspects of ritual, see Balthis 2006 on monumental altars.

16. Scott 2010, 2013.

17. Dickenson and van Nijf 2013; Williamson 2013.

18. Mylonopoulos 2006, 2008; see also Stavrianopoulou 2006a.

19. McMahon 2013.

20. Wescoat and Ousterhout 2012.

21. Graf 1996; Chaniotis 1995; Sourvinou-Inwood 1994; Connor 1987. See also Rutherford 2013; Mylonopoulos 2006; 2008; P. Wilson 2007; Elsner and Rutherford 2005; Kavoulaki 1999.

22. Moser and Feldman 2014b.

23. Cole 2004; Alcock and Osborne 1994; Jost 1985. See also Ashmore and Knapp 1999 for a more cross-cultural sample of studies. For spatial aspects of ritual see Balthis 2006 on monumental altars.

24. DePolignac 1994;1995. While his work has been revised and refined (and rejected by some), the attention it brought to political and spatial aspects of sanctuaries has stimulated productive discussion, as in Alcock and Osborne 1994. Polinskaya

2006 argues vehemently against the binomial polarity of city and country. See also comments in Stek 2009, pp. 58–59.

25. P. Wilson 2007, p. 3.

26. Mylonas 1961, p. 161. For an excellent photograph of the site and its many steps, see Kourouniotis 1938, p. 9, fig. 4.

27. A Hellenistic or Roman date is likely, but no greater precision is possible at present; see Kane and White 2007, pp. 41–43; Applebaum 1957, p. 161. Scott (2013, pp. 14–44) summarizes historical developments in the agora at Cyrene but does not mention these steps.

28. See below p. 79. Waelkens 2004, pp. 457–58; Mitchell 1991, pp. 135, 139; 1998, p. 251; 1999, pp. 173–74; Waelkens et al. 1997, p. 23; Bean 1960, pp. 74–75; V. Bérard 1892, pp. 434–36.

29. Becker 2003, pp. 109–80 (temples), 181–216 (altars).

30. I. Nielsen 2002.

31. Knackfuss 1941; Becker (2003, pp. 137–47) presents a detailed discussion of this temple and its steps.

32. Voigtländer (1975, p. 33) proposed that a linear progression through the temple was initially planned but subsequently altered, noted by Parke (1986, p. 125) but countered by Heilmeyer (1980, p. 738) and others. See Becker 2003, pp. 137–47.

33. Rehm, Wiegand, and Harder 1958, pp. 41–49 no. 39 line 13, 165 no. 217 line 8, 255–56 no. 424 lines 51–52, 257 no. 427 line 8, 295 no. 493 line 11. See Hollinshead 1985, 1999 on *adyton*.

34. Ohnesorg 2005; Becker 2003, pp. 181–216; Linfert 1995; Etienne 1992; Etienne and Le Dinahet 1991, pp. 267–306 on typology; Rupp 1974; Şahin 1972; Yavis 1949.

35. Pergamon: Becker 2003, pp. 200–207; Stewart 2000; Kästner 1998; Hoepfner 1991, 1996, 1997b; M. Kunze 1991; Schrammen 1906. Cape Monodendri: Şahin 1972, pp. 43–44; von Gerkan 1915. Samos: Kienast 1991; Walter 1976; Şahin 1972, pp. 44–45; Ziegenaus 1959; Buschor 1957; Schleif 1933. Priene: Carter 1983, pp. 16–17, 181–209; von Gerkan 1924; Wiegand and Schrader 1904, pp. 120–26. Tenos: Becker 2003, pp. 211–13; Etienne 1996b; Etienne and Braun 1986; Şahin 1972, pp. 65–66. Magnesia: Balthis 2006; Becker 2003, pp. 181–216; Bingöl 1998, pp. 36–40; Hoepfner 1989; Özgan 1982; Linfert 1976, pp. 28–30, 164–78; von Gerkan 1929; Humann, Kohte, and Watzinger 1904, pp. 91–99.

36. Balthis 2006.

37. Noack 1927, pp. 6, 95, 98. He notes that the existing rock-cut steps represent only the bedding for blocks that formed the steps used by worshippers. Clinton 1993, 1994; Kuhn 1985, pp. 281–82; T. L. Shear 1982; Mylonas 1961, pp. 88, 112, 115, 121. For the biomechanics of sitting on steps, see below p. 23.

38. Frederiksen 2002; Rossetto and Sartorio 1994.

39. Hansen and Fischer-Hansen (1994) observe that public buildings (as opposed to overtly religious buildings such as temples) did not receive monumental treatment until the fourth century. See also Frederiksen 2002, p. 86.

40. For the continuing debate as to whether theaters also served as places of civic and political assembly, see Frederiksen 2002, pp. 80–87, and also pp. 66, 75, 90–92; Hansen and Fischer-Hansen 1994, pp. 48–53, 88 n. 9; Kolb 1981, pp. 88, 90, 98.

41. Translation Wycherley 1957, p. 220 no. 726, also p. 97 no. 276. For a list of relevant Greek texts, see Martin 1957, p. 73.

42. *LSJ* s.v. ἴκρια. M. H. Hansen 1983b describes comparable wooden structures erected as temporary apparatus for public assemblies (*Landsgemeinde*) in Switzerland. See also Paga 2010, p. 373 n. 85; Csapo 2007, pp. 93, 103–8.

43. I. Nielsen 2002, pp. 117–18; Camp 1986, pp. 45–46; Kolb 1981, pp. 20–61; Wycherley 1978, pp. 204–6; Thompson and Wycherley 1972, pp. 126–29; Martin 1957, especially pp. 72–74; Dilke 1948, pp. 146–49.

44. Wycherley 1957, pp. 161–63, 220–21.

45. Bieber 1961, p. 64; Martin 1957, pp. 72–81; Rogers 1924.

46. I. Nielsen 2002, pp. 117–18; Neils 1992a, pp. 18–20. Camp 1986, pp. 45–46; Thompson and Wycherley 1972, pp. 126–29. Kerameikos: Ohly 1965.

47. Pollux 7.125. Cf. Athenaeus 4.167; Wycherley 1957, p. 105 no. 302 (Athenaeus) and p. 163 no. 528 (Pollux). Also Martin 1957, p. 76.

48. I. Nielsen 2000, p. 143; Hansen and Fischer-Hansen 1994, pp. 65–66; Mertens and de Siena 1982, pp. 22–24, 55 n. 53; Kolb 1981, pp. 110–11.

49. Williams and Fisher 1971, pp. 16–20; I. Nielsen 2002, p. 103.

50. For other post-holes at, e.g., Olympia and Naxos see Moustaka 2002.

51. Athens NM 15499: *ABV* 39.16. *Paralipomena* 18; *Addenda²* 10; BAPD 305075; Mylonopoulos 2006, pp. 93–94; Kuhn 1985, pp. 282–83; Bakır 1981, pp. 5–6, 65 no. A.3; Arias 1962, pp. 285–86 no. 39. The painter's name and his subject are identified by inscriptions on the vase.

52. E.g., Bieber 1961, p. 54; Dilke (1948, p. 131) suggests stone. See also I. Nielsen 2000, pp. 117–18.

53. Florence 3773 (and Berlin 1711), attributed to the Castellani Painter, dated 560 B.C.: *ABV* 95.8, 683; *Paralipomena* 34, 36; *Addenda²* 25; BAPD 310008; *LIMC* 7.1, p. 279, 7.2, p. 217

Notes

no. 11 (s.v. "Peliou Athla"); Kluiver 1996, p. 9 no. 180; Pfuhl 1923, pp. 248–49 fig. 206, with an image of the entire scene; Thiersch 1899, pp. 58–65 no. 54.

54. R. Martin (1951, p. 255) calls it stone. J. P. Small suggests that it could depict a funeral mound, such as that of Patroklos (personal communication).

55. Vatican Astarita 565, ca. 560 B.C. Kaltsas and Shapiro 2008, pp. 196–97 no. 79 (M. Sannibale) with bibliography; Hansen and Fischer-Hansen 1994, pp. 47–48; Amyx 1988, p. 264; Bérard 1977; Beazley 1957.

56. Paris, Cabinet des Médailles 243: *CVA* France 10 Bibliothèque Nationale, Cabinet des Médailles 2 (Paris 1931) III.H.e p. 68 and pls. 88.4, 89.1–2 (E. Pottier); BAPD 1047; Stansbury-O'Donnell 2006, pp. 17–19; Bentz and Eschbach 2001, p. 191 no. 275; Shapiro 1989, p. 33; 1992, p. 56.

57. Neils (1994, p. 154; 2007, p. 48) reads κάδος (jug) instead of κάλος (fine, good). Shapiro 1989, p. 33.

58. Kyle 1992, pp. 89–91; Shapiro 1989, p. 33; 1992, p. 56; Reed (1987) prefers to associate the hoplite's action with the *euandria*, after Davison 1958. Schultz (2007) does not include this vase in his list of images of the *apobatai*.

59. For picks, see S. G. Miller 2004, p. 66. Picks in images of jumping and the pentathlon are consistently represented with a head that is a long slender arc, as opposed to the shorter axelike head of this implement.

60. Neils 1994, p. 154. For the skyphos from the Noble collection in Tampa (86.93) see Neils 1992b, no. 47, p. 176 with bibliography, illustrated p. 96.

CHAPTER 1. BIOMECHANICS

1. Stevens 1940, pp. 6, 27, 52–53, 55. See also Hurwit 2005, p. 17 and n. 21.

2. S. Fox, personal communication (male body). Bourbou and Tsilipakou (2009, p. 122) report mean living stature in the sixth–seventh centuries A.D. as 1.70 m for males and 1.52 m for females.

3. Vitr. 3.4.4; Rowland and Howe 1999, pp. 16, 51, 190, 200.

4. On the Roman foot, see Rowland and Howe 1999, p. 167 n.

5. Palladio's figures were publicized and explained by the seventeenth-century Englishman Sir Henry Wotton and also by John Evelyn. Scamozzi's 1615 treatise *Idea della architettura universale* was translated into Dutch, French, and German in the course of the seventeenth century. For more on this history see Habermann 2002, pp. 14–15; Templer 1992b, pp. 26–27.

6. Habermann 2002, pp. 15, 42–43, and see also p. 216 for sources of information about current standards in France, Germany, Switzerland, the United Kingdom, and the United States. See also Templer 1992b, pp. 26–28. For Blondel, see Gerbino 2002.

7. Templer 1992b, pp. 25–39, especially pp. 29, 38–39; Fitch, Templer, and Corcoran 1974, pp. 85–90. For an earlier analysis see Olmsted 1910.

8. Packard 1981, p. 7.

9. U.S. Department of Labor, Occupational Safety and Health Administration (OSHA) Regulations, Standard number 1910.24e. http://www.osha.gov/pls/oshaweb/owadisp.show_document?p_table=STANDARDS&p_id=9716 (accessed July 5, 2013).

10. Templer 1992b, pp. 35–36, 84–86; Fitch, Templer, and Corcoran 1974, pp. 87–88.

11. Olmsted 1910, p. 87: "the optimum size varies not only for different individuals, but for the same individual at different times." See also Fitch, Templer, and Corcoran 1974, p. 84: "gait and posture (are) distorted by the customs and costumes of the culture."

12. Mauss 1934. See also Bremmer 1992, p. 15, p. 29 nn. 1, 2; K. Thomas 1992, p. 3.

13. Templer 1992b, pp. 33–34.

14. Templer 1992b, p. 34.

15. Templer 1992b, pp. 9, 34, 43–57, especially p. 45 with table. Packard (1981, p. 7) recommends a pitch of 5–15 degrees for ramps.

16. Templer 1992b, p. 44; Fitch, Templer, and Corcoran 1974, p. 90.

17. Travlos 1971, p. 482.

18. Fitch, Templer, and Corcoran 1974, p. 84.

19. The German terms "Stutzmauer," "Schautreppen," and "Sitzstufen" are admirably economical. While "Schautreppen" lacks the sense of movement I associate with steps as a route of access, it expresses a greater sense of public display.

20. Selinus: Becker 2003, pp. 262–63, 266; Di Vita 1996, pp. 286–88. See below p. 41. Brauron: Papadimitriou 1948, pp. 84–86; 1949, pp. 76–79; 1950, p. 177; 1963, pp. 113–14. Athens: LaFollette 1986, pp. 80–82; Stevens 1940, pp. 24–40. See below pp. 47–48.

21. As demonstrated by repeated stumbles on an irregular step at a New York subway station: Matt Flegenheimer, "A Step to Lose Face Over," *New York Times*, June 29, 2012.

22. Petrakos 1968a, pp. 98–99; 1974, p. 49; see Frederiksen

2002, pp. 69–76 on the meaning and use of θέατρον. See below p. 53 for a discussion of the *theatron* at Olympia.

23. Packard 1981, pp. 5, 532, 576–79; Dilke 1948, pp. 153–61.

24. Pergamon: Becker 2003, p. 249; Bohtz 1981, p. 36. See below pp. 69–70.

25. Lato: Dilke 1948, p. 129, for measurements of each step; Becker 2003, p. 241; Ducrey and Picard 1972; Ginouvès 1972, p. 56; and see below p. 52. In estimating numbers of seated bodies in any given space, Ducrey and Picard (1971, p. 528) allow 0.40 m per person, while Bookidis and Stroud (1997, p. 257) allow 0.50 m. Having compared actual practice in Switzerland with seats and markings in Greek theaters, M.-H. Hansen (1983b) favors 0.40 m per person in antiquity. See E. T. Hall 1966 and 1968 on the cultural aspects of personal space.

26. On standing versus seated viewers, see Rups 1986, pp. 74–75 n. 302; Mallwitz and van de Löchte 1980; Kunze and Schleif 1938. See below p. 52 (sitting and standing) and p. 53 (Olympia).

27. On Lato see Ducrey and Picard 1972, p. 591 and n. 42. See also Dilke 1948, pp. 127–29.

28. Homer *Od.* 2.239; Thuc. 1.67; 1.87.3, 6.13.1, 8.76; Xen. *An.* 7.1.33; Cic. *Flac.* 16; Hansen and Fischer-Hansen 1994, pp. 63, 74; Kolb 1978; 1981, pp. 88, 90, 98; Vischer 1873.

29. Scullion 2005; Parker 2004; Goldhill 1999, pp. 10, 20; Bremmer 1992, 1998; Jameson 1998, pp. 171, 175–76; Dougherty and Kurke 1993, pp. 1–6; Connor 1988.

30. Frederiksen 2002, pp. 80–87; Hansen and Fischer-Hansen 1994, pp. 48–53; Kolb 1981, pp. 88, 90, 98. On rituals in theaters, see Chaniotis 1997, 2007.

CHAPTER 2. THEORETICAL OBSERVATIONS

1. This discussion can be characterized as "empirical theory." This kind of middle-range theory, according to Smith (2011, pp. 167–73), includes a higher proportion of empirical information than does social theory and grounds its theoretical statements in actual cases. See also Dovey 2010, p. 8.

2. The Greek mathematician Euclid produced ca. 300 B.C. the earliest known comprehensive account of geometry. The seventeenth-century French philosopher and mathematician René Descartes conceived of space as all-encompassing and established the system of locating a point in a plane using numerical coordinates, a contribution that gave expression to Euclid's geometric theorems in the form of algebra.

3. The vast literature on space and place includes: Dovey 1999, pp. 39–52; 2010, pp. 3–6, 11; Meskell and Preucel 2004b; Low and Lawrence-Zúñiga 2003; Casey 1993, 1996; Relph 1985; Merleau Ponty 1962, p. 148: "the experience of our own body teaches us to realize space as rooted in existence."

4. Pred 1984, 1990.

5. McGuire and Schiffer 1983, p. 280.

6. Hillier and Rooksby 2002; Dovey 1999, pp. 17–19, 48–49; Bourdieu 1990; Giddens 1984. For practice theory applied to archaeology, see McMahon 2013, pp. 163–64; Smith 2011, p. 184; Fisher 2009, pp. 439–40; Maran 2006; Kavoulaki 1999; Barrett 1988, 1994a, 1994b; Garwood 1991, pp. 13–14; Donley-Reid 1990, pp. 114–17; Sanders 1990. For its application to ritual, see C. Bell 1992; 1997, pp. 76–80.

7. Giddens 1984, p. 25 and passim; Bourdieu 1990.

8. Referring to the built environment, Maran (2006, p. 10) observes, "Space structures action, but is in itself realized through action and patterns of perception." See also Rapoport 1990, 1976.

9. Basso 1996, p. 55. See also Casey 1993, pp. 22–24.

10. Casey 1993, p. 23 (emphasis in original).

11. Parker Pearson and Richards (1994, p. 5) warn against "architectural determinism," the assertion of behavior based on form, without regard for specific context. See also Wright 2006, p. 64.

12. Casey 1993, p. 34. See also Bremmer 1992 and Mauss 1934 regarding cultural influence on posture and movement.

13. A. Nielsen (1995, p. 52), based on Skibo and Schiffer 1995, defines performance characteristics as "the behavioral capabilities that artifacts possess by virtue of their design" (see Nielsen 1995, pp. 52–59). His list of characteristics (which I have modified) is heavily oriented to his theme of differentiating power. Zedeño (2000, p. 108) cites formal properties, performance characteristics, and life histories (she adds formation processes) as useful concepts from behavioral archaeology for studying landmarks and landscapes.

14. Bourdieu 1993, 1986, 1984. See also Dovey 2010, pp. 34–35; Dovey 1999, pp. 35–38; R. Jenkins 1992, p. 85.

15. McGuire and Schiffer 1983. Thanks to Foucault's celebrated commentary on the panopticon (1977, pp. 26, 145–53, 202, 217), Bentham's eighteenth-century design for prisons, hospitals, and factories has come to epitomize architecture as an instrument of social manipulation by means of controlling the space occupied by individuals or groups. In fairness, Foucault himself (p. 217) contrasts the panopticon with the

Notes

Greek theater. See also Hodder and Hutson 2003, pp. 84–85; J. Thomas 2000, pp. 152–53; Goldhill 1999, pp. 16–19; Parker Pearson and Richards 1994, p. 3; Lawrence and Low 1990, summary on pp. 484–85; Giddens 1984, pp. 145–59; A. Nielsen (1995, p. 56) applies the idea of performance characteristics to concentrating rituals in specialized buildings or places.

16. Crumley (1999, p. 272) notes that "the ability to control distance across time, space, and states of existence is an enduring definition of political power."

17. Dovey 1999, pp. 9–16; 2010, p. 14; Hodder and Hutson 2003, pp. 84–85; Foucault 1990; Shanks and Tilley 1987, p. 109; Miller and Tilley 1984.

18. Stavrianopoulou 2006b. Some (e.g., Gero 2000) have protested that the value placed by contemporary researchers on these traits reflects dominant Western male values of independence, action, and authority, and therefore is inappropriately ethnocentric.

19. Barrett (1994b, p. 4) asserts that "the individual is not an analytically useful unit of archaeological study." He defines agency (p. 5) as "the means of knowledgeable actions" but maintains that it is not reducible to the actions of a single individual. See also Barrett 2001; Dobres and Robb 2000, p. 11; Gero 2000, pp. 36–37; Shanks and Hodder 1995b, p. 17; Kent 1990, p. 3; Johnson 1989, p. 190. For agency in general, see Hitchcock 2004; Dobres and Robb 2000. Some have maintained that objects or monuments, especially those with high aesthetic and symbolic content, can affect social activities enough to merit the label "agent," but many are reluctant to ascribe interactive roles to inanimate objects. See Gell 1998; also Osborne and Tanner 2007b; Stavrianopoulou 2006b; Corbet, Layton, and Tanner 2004, pp. 359, 368–69.

20. Since agency theory attempts to describe the relationship between an agent and the society of which it is a part, Barrett and Johnson have argued that such theory needs to emerge from a particular context. See Barrett 2000; Johnson 2000, p. 213: "Forms of agency . . . must be seen as historically particular, specific, and changing." Brumfiel (2004) does not agree, warning (p. 254) of "the projection of our own values onto past societies," an error presumably mitigated by cross-cultural theorizing.

21. C. Bell 1997, pp. 150–53; Zuesse 1975. For useful summaries of approaches to ritual and a companion annotated bibliography, see Kreinath, Snoek, and Stausberg 2006, 2007. For archaeology and ritual across cultures, see Kyriakides 2007.

22. C. Bell 1992, p. 92.

23. Participants in the project on Ritual Dynamics at the University of Heidelberg have played leading roles in this conversation: Chaniotis 2006, 2011; Mylonopoulos 2008; Kreinath, Snoek, and Stausberg 2006, 2007; Stavrianopoulou 2006a, 2006b, 2006c; Kreinath 2004; Kreinath, Hartung, and Deschner 2004. See also C. Bell 1992, pp. 221–22; 1997, pp. 210–52.

24. Kreinath 2004, p. 275.

25. Buraselis 2012; Chaniotis 2011, p. 10; Kreinath 2004. For transfer of ritual, see Langer et al. 2006.

26. Bookidis 2003, pp. 255–56; Alroth 1998.

27. For architectural expression of changes in ritual, see J. R. Brandt 2012; Mylonopoulos 2008.

CHAPTER 3. SOCIAL EFFECTS AND POLITICAL CONSEQUENCES

1. *ThesCRA* 1 (2004) s.v. "Processions," pp. 1–20 (M. True et al.); Goldhill 1999; Kavoulaki 1999; Jameson 1998. All discuss Athens. See also Mylonopoulos 2006, pp. 103–9; Köhler 1996.

2. Chaniotis 1995, 2006; Chankowski 2005; Parker 2005, pp. 162, 178–80; Kavoulaki 1999; Dillon 1997; Graf 1996; Köhler 1996; Wikander 1992; Connor 1987; Burkert 1985, pp. 99–101; Bömer 1952; Nilsson 1916.

3. Panathenaia: Neils 1992a; 1992b; 1996a; 2001; 2007, pp. 44–45; 2012; Palagia and Choremi-Spetsieri 2007; Valavanis 2004, pp. 354–57 (model on p. 354); I. Jenkins 1994. See also Sourvinou-Inwood 1994 on the City Dionysia in Athens.

4. Neils 2007, p. 45; 2012; Connelly 2007, pp. 187–89; Mylonopoulos 2006, pp. 73–74; Price 1999, pp. 30–31; Marangou et al. 1995, pp. 86–93, with additional references; van Straten 1995, pp. 14–15 no. V55. Scenes on ancient vases represent an ideal selection of representative images, not literal reporting of events: Stansbury-O'Donnell 2006, pp. 37, 90. Cf. van Straten 1995, pp. 14–31, for other images of processions; and van Straten 1981, pp. 83–88, for images of objects carried. A Boeotian black-figure lekane of the mid-sixth century in the British Museum (GR1879.10–4.1, vase B80) also depicts a full and lively procession; see Kaltsas and Shapiro 2008, pp. 232–33, with bibliography.

5. Procession of Ptolemy Philadelphos: Ath. *Deipnosophistai* 197C–203B; date based on Foertmeyer 1988. See also D. J. Thompson 2000, with bibliography p. 367 n. 4; Köhler 1996, pp. 35–45; Stewart 1993, pp. 252–60; Wikander 1992; Rice 1983.

6. *LSAM*, pp. 88–92 no. 32; *I. Magn.* 98.32–46; translation: Price 1999, pp. 174–75 no. 3; Köhler 1996, pp. 46–53; Ebert 1982. The instruments referred to are the *syrinx*, *aulos*, and *kithara*: Sumi 2004, p. 86; Kern 1900, no. 98. Lines and labels have been identified in the pavement at Magnesia, naming contingents and their order in procession: Balthis 2006, pp. 35–36; Bingöl 1998, pp. 41–43; 2005, p. 166. See Chankowski 2005 and Sumi 2004 for the political context of this and comparable contemporary inscriptions.

7. Slater 2007.

8. Tilley 1994, pp. 16–17. See also Snead, Erickson, and Darling 2009.

9. De Certeau 1984. He characterizes walking as "a process of appropriation of the topographic system," and "a spatial acting out of the place" (pp. 97–98). Cf. Tilley 1994, pp. 27–31, on paths. See also above, p. 26.

10. Sourvinou-Inwood 1994, especially pp. 287–88.

11. On flexibility of ritual, see Iddeng 2012; Chaniotis 2011; Stavrianopoulou 2006b; Kreinath, Hartung, and Deschner 2004; Jameson 1999; C. Bell 1992, 1997; Garwood 1991.

12. *ThesCRA* 2 (2004) s.v. "Greek Music," pp. 345–90 (E. Simon et al.); Brand 2000. *Aulos*: R. P. Martin 2003; P. Wilson 1999. Music in processions: Bundrick 2005; Landels 1999; Bélis 1995; Nordquist 1992, 1994; West 1992; Haldane 1966. Images of procession and sacrifice on Athenian vases of the sixth and fifth centuries include musicians playing the *aulos*, and sometimes additional instruments such as the *kithara*: Bundrick 2005; van Straten 1995; Nordquist 1992; Shapiro 1992; Peirce 1984. *Kithara*: Bélis 1995. See also Kowalzig 2005.

13. Nordquist 1994, p. 91. Eretria: *IG* XII.9, lines 236, 237; Sokolowski 1969, no. 92. Kos: Sokolowski 1969, no. 163.

14. Furley 1995, 2007; Kowalzig 2005; West 1992, pp. 15–16; Bremer 1981. See also Rutherford 2013, pp. 237–49; Burkert 2012.

15. Cross and Watson 2006; Scarre 2006; Scarre and Lawson 2006. See also Kavoulaki 1999, p. 295. Lind (2009, p. 204) stressed the social context and sense of belonging produced by music.

16. Kavoulaki 1999, p. 302.

17. McMahon 2013; Chaniotis 1995, 2006; Stansbury-O'Donnell 2006; Stavrianopoulou 2006b; Goldhill 1999, pp. 15–23; Jameson 1999, p. 323; Kavoulaki 1999, pp. 311–12; Bell 1997, pp. 159–69; Schafer 1985, p. 94.

18. Bell 1997, p. 161, referring to the work of Don Handelman.

Note that "framing" is used metaphorically, as opposed to my usage, which includes the literal architectural meaning as well as the metaphorical one. For the metaphorical use of "frame," see Handelman 2004, 2006; and also Goldhill 1999, p. 13, based on Goffman 1974. See also Stavrianopoulou 2006a, p. 7.

19. Chaniotis 1995; De Polignac 1995.

20. Rutherford 2013, pp. 250–58, 277–80; Mylonopoulos 2006; Chankowski 2005; Kowalzig 2005.

21. Hansen and Nielsen 2004, pp. 114–19; Mackil 2004; Reger 2001, especially pp. 161–62; Demand 1990; Moggi 1976. See also Hornblower 1982, pp. 78–105.

22. J. M. Hall 1995; Kritzas 1992. See below pp. 44–45.

23. Jost 1985, 1994. See below pp. 54–56.

24. *Pace* Hellström 2011. See Hellström 1991; Westholm 1963; and see below, pp. 56–59. There were undoubtedly economic factors in play as well.

CHAPTER 4. EARLY STEPS

1. Schäfer et al. 1992, p. 353. Becker (2003, pp. 218–21) also denies the connection. Ginouvès (1972, pp. 53–56) expresses reservations about continuity, as does Dilke (1948, pp. 127–28). See also I. Nielsen 2000, pp. 69–74, 110; Kolb 1981, pp. 103–6. E. Thomas (1984) argues for continuity of practice on Crete.

2. Dated to 110–70 B.C. based on epigraphic evidence: Schäfer et al. 1992, pp. 165–66, 183–84, 352–54; Schäfer 1991. See also Prent 2005, pp. 332–36, 527–29, and pl. 66; Becker 2003, pp. 218–20; Sjögren 2003, p. 114; Sporn 2002, pp. 130, 133–35; N. Marinatos 1996; E. Thomas 1984; S. Marinatos 1935, 1938.

3. Schäfer et al. 1992, pp. 352–54; Schäfer 1991. On the larger question of continuity and building on earlier ruins in Crete, see Prent 2005.

4. For a current plan, see Rose and Darbyshire 2011, p. 8 fig. 0.7. Sams 1994; DeVries 1990, pp. 381–82.

5. Sams and Voigt 2011, p. 161 and p. 8 fig. 0.7.

6. Rose and Darbyshire 2011; Voigt 2005; DeVries 2003; Voigt and Henrickson 2000, p. 48; Sams 1994. They were subsequently cut off by a Middle Phrygian enclosure wall. Berndt-Ersöz 2006, p. xxi; DeVries 1990, p. 382; 2005.

7. Berndt-Ersöz 2006, 2009; Haspels (1971, pp. 38–39, 91, 93–97) refers to them as "so-called altars." Berndt (1997) lists types of Phrygian monuments and sites with steps. He rejects the proposal by Ayiter 1978 that the broad rock-cut "stairs" at Inli were Phrygian steps with special significance, arguing

Notes

convincingly that they are traces of Byzantine quarrying. For steps as elements of Phrygian design, see, e.g., Midas City: Berndt 2002; Akurgal 1990, pp. 274–76; Haspels 1971.

8. Hornblower 1982, pl. 1; Radt 1970, 1978. I was unable to identify this structure at the site in 2000. For a computer-generated model of the site, see Cavalier and Mora 2011, especially p. 379.

9. Radt 1970, 1978. Kuhn (1985, p. 284 n. 754) subsequently suggested that the broad, shallow building across the open space was a sheltered portico, since it had steps along the back wall suitable for seated onlookers.

10. Hdt. 1.171; Strabo 7.7.2; 13.1.58–59; 14.2.27; Carstens 2009a, pp. 101–2; Rumscheid 2009b; Flensted-Jensen and Carstens (2004) discuss both literary and archaeological evidence, with bibliography. Peschlow-Bindokat 1996, pp. 3–5, 22–23; Hornblower 1982, pp. 9–14; Bean 1980, pp. 2–3; Bean and Cook 1955.

11. Ratté 1993, 2011; Roosevelt 2009; Curtis 2005a, especially pp. 44–46; Boardman 2000, pp. 53–60; M. C. Miller 1997, pp. 91–95; Nylander 1970.

12. Stronach (1978, p. 43) also notes the Lydian nature of the structure's design and construction; cf. pp. 24–43. Nylander (1970, pp. 91–102) earlier considered the overall concept of Cyrus' tomb Achaemaenian; see especially pp. 93, 101. See also Carstens 2009a, pp. 42–43; Fedak 1990, pp. 32–33, 186–87. A similar but smaller Persian tomb at Buzpar, set on three steps, perhaps in emulation of Cyrus' tomb, may date to the fifth or fourth century: Boardman 2000, p. 57; Stronach 1978, pp. 300–302.

13. Ratté 2011, pp. 40, 49, 65, 94–99, 207–13. He earlier (1992) speculated that the Pyramid Tomb may have been built for an eminent Persian in the West, in emulation of the tomb at Pasargadae. Citing additional examples of house-shaped tombs on stepped bases: Carstens 2009a, pp. 52–53; Roosevelt 2009, p. 140; Boardman 2000, pp. 53–56; Stronach 1978, p. 41; Nylander 1970, p. 93. Kleiss (1996) reasserts the Persian and Mesopotamian antecedents for the stepped base. Hanfmann (1972, p. 261 fig. 192) proposed that it commemorated a Persian nobleman killed in the conquest of Sardis in 547 B.C., as recounted by Xenophon (*Cyr.* 7.4.5, 16).

14. Cahill 1988, pp. 483 and 487 fig. 6. See also Boardman 2000, pp. 55–56; Carstens 2009a, pp. 52–53. Stepped roofs reappear in subsequent monuments; M. C. Miller (1997, pp. 237–38, 337–38) reconstructs a hypothetical stepped roof for the Odeion of Perikles in Athens. Pyramidal stepped roofs also occur in the (late-fourth–early-third-century) Lion Tomb at Knidos and its near-twin, the Lion Tomb at Amphipolis, as well as in Pliny's description of the roof of the Maussolleion at Halikarnassos (*NH* 36.4.31). Miller (ibid.) denies the Persian nature of such a roof design. See also Fedak 1990, pp. 72–73, 76–78, 200–203. For other examples of stepped pyramidal roofs, see Hellman 2002, pp. 292–93, who does not discuss possible Phrygian or Lydian or Ionian prototypes, but looks to Egypt for predecessors.

15. Cahill 1988; see also Bean 1966, pp. 96–97; Perrot and Chipiez 1892, pp. 65–67; Weber 1885, pp. 132–36 no. 2. Akurgal (1990, p. 118) proposed a fourth-century date based on a comparable rock-cut tomb nearby with datable pottery.

16. Henry 2013; Rumscheid 2009b.

17. Borchhardt 1970, 1976. See also Carstens 2009a, pp. 59–60; Fedak 1990, pp. 52, 193.

18. The date (late Archaic) is based on an unfinished Archaic relief found built into the steps: Demargne and van Effenterre 1937. Becker (2003, pp. 218–20, 243 n. 1187, 283 n. 1404) expresses skepticism at this early date and believes that the steps of Dreros, like those at Lato, may be Hellenistic. Renewed excavation at Dreros should clarify the date and the arrangement of the site. See also Prent 2005, p. 285; Sjögren 2003, p. 36.

19. Demargne and van Effenterre (1937, p. 15) note that the steps of the "agora" are different from those leading to the temple. Van Effenterre (1992) assigns them a date in the sixth century.

20. Willetts (1974, pp. 68–69) cites an inscription to Zeus Agoraios from the site as an indication of the area's function. See also Hansen and Fischer-Hansen 1994, p. 62; Kolb 1976, pp. 296–97; Ginouvès 1972, p. 56 n. 3; W. A. MacDonald 1943, pp. 66–67.

21. See above, pp. 23–24. Frederiksen 2002, pp. 80–87; I. Nielsen 2000, pp. 110–11; Hansen and Fischer-Hansen 1994, pp. 50–51. The steps are 0.40 m wide according to Nielsen's measurements, 0.35 m by mine.

22. Date: Plommer and Salviat 1966, pp. 207–15, by juxtaposition and material. See also Becker 2003, pp. 221–24; Menadier 1995, pp. 75–78, 120; Payne et al. 1940.

23. The width, 0.41–0.50 m, is just adequate for sitting, but is cramped in combination with the low risers. Contrast these dimensions with those of the bench within the nearby hall to

the southwest: 0.35 m high and 0.50 m wide. Menadier 1995. See also Kuhn 1985, pp. 292–93.

24. For the harbor see Blackmon 1966.

25. The figure 8.40 m is the length of the preserved north end; the south end was cut off by the construction of the Classical wall around the sanctuary: Kourouniotis 1938. See also Palinkas 2008; Mylonas 1961, pp. 70–72. I am grateful to Jennifer Palinkas for bringing these steps to my attention.

26. Dygve and Poulsen 1960, pp. 59–62, 75, 79, 191. See also V. Papadimitriou 1988, p. 169; Kondis 1963, pp. 394–95.

27. Date: Vanderpool 1974. See also I. M. Shear 1999, p. 105; Tanoulas 1987, p. 468; Travlos 1971, pp. 482, 484 fig. 608, 487 fig. 614; Bundgaard 1957, pp. 19–30. The reported width of the ramp varies from 10 m (Travlos) to 12 m (Vanderpool, Shear); Bundgaard is the most specific, noting that the ramp measured over 11 m at the Mycenaean pyrgos. Camp (2001, p. 31) describes the dimensions as 11 m wide and 90 m long.

28. Bundgaard 1957, p. 30.

29. The estimated width is based on measuring from the farthest extent of the ramp's eastern edge to the west edge along the retaining wall that overlies the ramp; the retaining wall may be built of blocks pirated from the ramp: Stillwell, Scranton, and Freeman 1941, p. 89. See also Robinson 1976a, 1976b. The slope of this ramp is steep enough that it seems equally possible that it was originally a substructure for a staircase for most of the ascent. The extant ramp is comparable in appearance to the remaining substructure for the broad steps from the middle to the upper terrace at Kos in the second century, as shown in Herzog and Schazman 1932, pls. 45, 46. See below p. 75 and Plate 23c. B. Millis has observed traces of what could be an earlier ramp southeast of the lower part of the sixth-century ramp. These remains are noted in Fowler and Stillwell 1932, pp. 219–20; also Becker 2003, pp. 5–6.

30. Goette 1999, pp. 19–20 (date); 2001a, pp. 345–48 fig. 105 and pl. 91; 2001b, pp. 642–43; 2002, pp. 18–19; Welter 1938a, cols. 1–33, especially 8–16; 1938b, pp. 91–92. Becker (2003, pp. 92–95) questions the sixth-century date and prefers the early second century.

31. Goette 2001a, pp. 345–48.

32. Lolos 2003, pp. 161–62, 173.

33. Pompeo 1999, p. 73 (dimensions); for photos, see pls. 16.2, 17.1, 2. See also Marconi 2007, pp. 70, 74, 83–84; De Angelis 2003, p. 134; Becker (2003, pp. 52–56) does not include Pompeo's publication.

34. Pompeo 1999, p. 36 (railing).

35. Pompeo 1999, pp. 83–85. See also Marconi 2007, pp. 65 (plan), 83.

36. Pompeo 1999.

CHAPTER 5. STEPS IN THE FIFTH CENTURY

1. The extant wall is 9.8 m high; Becker (2003, p. 262) suggests that it may have extended 2 m higher. Pace (1938, p. 379) imagines a wall as much as twice the extant height. For an excellent image, see Pugliese Caratelli 1985, fig. 498. Marconi (2007, p. 72) dates its construction to the second half of the sixth century.

2. Becker 2003, pp. 262–63, 266; DiVita 1984; 1996, p. 286. The south wall of the terrace is essentially vertical.

3. Becker 2003, pp. 115–19, 265; Østby 1995, pp. 90, 98. Recent excavations have revealed that the base for a large rectangular structure along the south retaining wall was neither an altar (Gabrici 1933) nor a grandstand (Becker 2003, pp. 149, 224–25; Mertens 1989), but most likely supported a hall for votive gifts (Marconi 2010). For a fine aerial photograph, see De Angelis 2012, p. 190 fig. 42.

4. DiVita 1985, pp. 394–95, is the clearest account. See also Becker 2003, p. 265; Tusa 1981–82, pp. 837–38 pls. 209, 210.1.

5. Orlandos 1967–68. See also Becker 2003, pp. 266–69; Martin 1970. The long, narrow temple with its unpartitioned cella looks earlier in form but seems to reflect a lingering Archaic style in this mountain region.

6. For a staircase height of 2.84 m across a horizontal distance of 5.56: Orlandos 1967–68, p. 44 fig. 25. Becker (2003, pp. 266–69) doubts the steps' use as a stairway because of the exceptionally tall topmost step, double the usual height; however, this step is also double in width, and so an intermediate fifteenth step could have fit into the gap and filled out the sequence of steps to the terrace.

7. To be sure, there are difficulties with the sequence of building at the Argive Heraion. This hypothesis presupposes that the location of the second temple at the Heraion was established well before the building was constructed. See below, p. 43.

8. *IG* VII 4255 line 29. Petrakos (1968a, pp. 98–99, 179–182 [text of inscription]) dates the inscription 338–322 B.C. See also Frederiksen 2002, pp. 69–76; Roesch 1984, pp. 180–81; Petrakos 1974; Travlos 1988, pp. 301–3 fig. 380.

Notes

9. *LSJ* s.v. θέατρον; Frederiksen 2002, especially pp. 74–76 and note p. 121.

10. Peschlow-Bindokat 1996, pp. 27–32; 2005, p. 21. She refers to them as "Sitzstufen."

11. Peschlow-Bindokat 1989; 1996, pp. 4–5; 2005, pp. 4–6. For comparison, Priene, Myus, and Mylasa each contributed the same amount: Meritt, Wade-Gery, and McGregor 1939–53, vol. 1, pp. 328, 510; vol. 3, p. 24 line 101.

12. Peschlow-Bindokat 1989; 1996; 2005, pp. 4–6.

13. J. M. Hall 1995.

14. There is disagreement over the date of the Cyclopean wall: Billot 1997; Wright 1982; Amandry 1952; Blegen 1937.

15. Tilton 1902. See also Billot 1997, p. 33; Amandry 1952, pp. 225, 239. Blegen 1937, p. 20. The date of the northeast building is controversial: Billot 1997, pp. 32–33 n. 206.

16. Lauter 1975.

17. Summarized by Morgan 2007, pp. 250–51. See also J. M. Hall 1995, pp. 594–95.

18. Pfaff 1992. The date is based on Thuc 4.133.2. Amandry (1952) argued that this temple had been planned well before the fire as part of a comprehensive plan begun decades earlier. Pfaff (pp. 6–7, 191) is more cautious about when the idea was conceived.

19. A separate rank of perhaps two or three steps down would have continued east across the opening of the Archaic ramp, extending along the front of the Northeast Stoa, creating a small trapezoidal terrace that absorbed the front alignment of the portico with the newly emphasized line of the terrace's border: Billot 1997, pp. 42–44; Lauter 1975, pp. 178–80, 182–83; Amandry 1952, pp. 238–39.

20. Lauter 1975, especially fig. 5. Cf. comments by Billot 1997, p. 43 and n. 300.

21. Billot 1997, pp. 39–41; Des Courtils 1992; Lauter 1975; Amandry 1952, 1980.

22. Amandry 1980. Billot (1997, pp. 41, 43) does not take a position on when the temple was planned.

23. For a section of the steps with elevations see Amandry 1980, p. 239 fig. 17.

24. Amandry 1952, pp. 261–63.

25. The steps at the far eastern end are lower, but they butt up against a vertical masonry wall, precluding any use for access: Amandry 1952, pp. 264–65.

26. To be sure, this observation applies to the Heraion only if one accepts Amandry's hypothesis that the temple was planned well before it was built: Amandry 1952, pp. 269–72. Cf. Pfaff 1992, pp. 6–8. What seems like a rather rough comparison in terms of formal architectonic relationships must have been quite comparable experientially. Participants in a procession would expect to arrive in a certain area of the sacred precinct as they approached the temple building and the altar in front of it. For an aerial view of the Argive Heraion, see Pfaff 1992, p. 5. For an aerial photograph of Corinth, see Williams 1993, p. 35. For Alipheira, see Orlandos 1967–68, plan on p. 29.

27. Amandry (1952, p. 263) doubted that the monumental steps are Greek. Lauter (1975, pp. 183–85) supports the interpretation of these steps as a route of access. The conglomerate wall constitutes a clear demarcation from the steps to the east, which are certainly too tall for human use, implying that the steps west of the wall were indeed intended as a route of access.

28. Kuhn 1985, p. 294; Amandry 1980, p. 244; Tomlinson 1972, pp. 240–41.

29. Morgan 2007, pp. 255–57; Kritzias 1992; Amandry 1980, p. 242. The competitions were later moved to Argos and called the Heraia, subsequently known as the Aspis: J. M. Hall 1995, pp. 611–12.

30. Morgan 2007, pp. 250, 255–57; Amandry 1980, pp. 220–23; 1992, pp. 220–21. Several victors at the Hekatomboia are listed in third-century inscriptions, but without a specific location.

31. Argos E 210; *CIG* 136: Morgan 2007, pp. 249–50; Kritzas 2006, p. 414; McGowan 1995, pp. 628, 632; Jeffery 1990, no. 15, p. 168; Daly 1939.

32. J. M. Hall 1995, p. 613.

33. J. M. Hall 1995; Kritzas 1992; Demand 1990, pp. 59–60; Moggi 1976.

34. Phratries: Kritzas 1992, 2006; J. M. Hall 1995.

35. Morgan 2007, pp. 249–63; J. M. Hall 1995, pp. 596, 612; Kritzas 1992, p. 235 n. 8.

36. Morgan 2007, pp. 251–54; Des Courtils 1992.

37. Kritzas 1992, 2006. See also Morgan 2007, pp. 254–55.

38. Kritzas 2006.

39. Williams 1978, pp. 92–93, 95, 99, 110–11; Williams and Fisher 1971, pp. 10–13, 17–19. See also Morgan 2007, pp. 245–47; Bookidis 2003, p. 250.

40. Williams 1978, pp. 92–93, 95, 112–14; Williams and Fisher 1971, pp. 11–19.

41. Williams and Fisher 1971, p. 13.

42. Williams 1970, p. 24; 1978, pp. 114–18; Williams and Fisher 1971, p. 19.

43. Williams 1978, pp. 122–25; Williams and Fisher 1971, pp. 16, 19–21.

44. Bookidis and Stroud 1997, pp. 423–28. See also Mylonopoulos 2006, pp. 80–83; Pfaff 1999.

45. Merker 2000; Bookidis and Stroud 1997, pp. 16–17, 53–83, 153–70, 425, 428–29; Pemberton 1989. Cf. Patera 2012, 133–39.

46. Bookidis and Stroud 1997, pp. 94–98, 167, 429. The excavators speculate that there could have been as many as seventeen landings, but only eight to ten are preserved and attributable to the fifth century. For dining chambers and foodstuffs, see Bookidis 1990; 1993; 2003, p. 255; Bookidis, Hansen, and Goldberg 1999.

47. Bookidis and Stroud 1997, p. 429.

48. Bookidis and Stroud (1997, p. 257) estimate a width of 0.50 m per person. See above p. 23 and n. 25 regarding differing estimates for seating and proximity.

49. Steps 7–11 in sector Q–R 19–20: Bookidis and Stroud 1997, pp. 253–60, 429–30.

50. Bookidis and Stroud 1997, p. 257.

51. Bookidis and Stroud 1997, pp. 260–66, 433.

52. Bookidis and Stroud 1997, pp. 2, 247, 433.

53. Bookidis 1990, pp. 90–91; 1993; 2010; Bookidis and Stroud 1997, pp. 259–60, 428–30.

54. Dinsmoor (1980) refers to this arrangement as a "theatral area." I. M. Shear (1999) and Eiteljorg (1993) call it a "forecourt." Brouskari (1997) calls it an "exedra."

55. I. M. Shear 1999, pp. 108, 109; Eiteljorg 1993, pp. 15–24; Dinsmoor 1980, p. 15. For the date of the steps, Dinsmoor (1980, p. 15) proposes 489 B.C., but Tomlinson (1982, 1990) and I. M. Shear (1999) have both expressed reservations, implying that they prefer an earlier date. Eiteljorg (1993, pp. 59–67) favors a post-Persian date. Completed at one time: Eiteljorg 1993, p. 22; Dinsmoor 1980, p. 30.

56. Eiteljorg 1993, p. 19; Dinsmoor 1980, p. 18.

57. Their material, size, and decoration indicate that they came from the same source as the two slabs on which the Hekatompedon inscription was inscribed: I. M. Shear 1999, pp. 106, 108–10; Dinsmoor 1980, pp. 21–27.

58. I. M. Shear 1999, p. 108 and n. 122; Eiteljorg 1993, p. 20; Dinsmoor 1980, pp. 31–34.

59. Dinsmoor and Dinsmoor 2004, pp. 66, 70. The ramp rises 25 m over its 80 m length, yielding a pitch of just over 30 degrees: Tanoulas 1987; Travlos 1971, p. 482; Bundgaard 1957, pp. 19–30. I. M. Shear (1999, pp. 108–9 n. 129) emphasizes the challenge of transporting large heavy blocks of stone for construction projects on the Acropolis. See also Korres 1995, pl. 18, with explanation of the process of moving stone blocks.

60. Stevens 1940, pp. 24–40; dimensions: p. 27. See also Hurwit 2005, pp. 17–19; LaFollette 1986, pp. 80–82; Stevens 1936. Reused blocks: Dinsmoor 1947, pp. 135–36, based on Dörpfeld's observations.

61. Stevens 1940, pp. 6, 25. See also Haselberger 2005.

62. Stevens 1936, pp. 480–81.

63. Stevens 1940, p. 25. Cf. Travlos 1971, p. 213.

64. A substantial, nearly square base, perhaps supporting a dedication to Athena Ergane (as noted by Pausanias 1.24.3) may have occupied the north end of the steps, balancing a group of statues on the south: Stevens 1940, pp. 55–57.

65. See also Hurwit 2005, pp. 15–18. On a much smaller scale, the stepped wall of a terrace temple base for the temple of Artemis at Brauron was also used to display votive stelai: J. Papadimitriou 1948, 1949, 1950, 1963.

The exact route of the Panathenaic procession between the Propylaia and the east end of the Acropolis is not known. Stevens (1936, pp. 479–83) hypothesized that participants in the Panathenaic procession would have turned south through a small propylon, at which point cattle and other quadrupeds would continue directly below the north side of the temple platform. After arriving in a small forecourt, the people would have ascended these steps and divided to complete the procession along the terrace beside both flanks of the Parthenon. However, Hurwit (2005, pp. 15–16) correctly asserts that there was a greater focus during the procession on the rituals at the east end of the Acropolis.

66. Erechtheion: Papanikolaou 2012; Paton et al. 1927. Identification: Jeppesen 1987. See also N. Robertson 1996, pp. 29–44; Ridgway 1992, pp. 126–27; Mansfield 1985, pp. 245–52.

67. Hollinshead 2012b; 2015. Unfortunately, identification of this venue for rites involving the wooden image does not help locate the interior chamber that the venerated object occupied.

68. Templer 1992b, pp. 108–16. See above p. 21.

69. Paton et al. 1927, pp. 15–18, 216. Cf. Stevens 1946, pp. 97–102.

70. Paton et al. 1927, pp. 16, 18, 216, 427. Cf. Stevens 1946, pp. 97–102.

71. The marble paving occupies an area slightly larger than

Notes

and slightly to the west of the roughly rectangular area of the poros paving, as seen in Plate 11a–b; Holland 1924a, 414–23; 1924b, 431–32. Cf. Paton et al. 1927, p. 15 n. 5 and pp. 427–29.

72. Paton et al. 1927, pp. 15–16, 18. Cf. Travlos 1971, p. 213; Stevens 1946, pp. 97–102. Only a small amount of this paving has survived, along the temple's north wall and at the northern end of the North Porch's east side.

73. Stevens 1946, p. 97; L. Holland 1924a, pp. 422–23. The north-facing vertical edge of a slab along the gap in the paving is smooth, with no anathyrosis (unlike other paving slabs), suggesting that it delineated an open space.

74. My estimate of 150 is based on an average row length of 8 m and an allowance of 0.50 m per person standing, as well as subtraction of some places at the angle where the steps converge, and hard up against the temple wall, with no expectation that the purpose was to maximize capacity. The length of the rank of the eight steps inside the Acropolis perimeter wall is not known. See Stevens 1946, pp. 101–2. The dimensions and proportions of the steps suggest that onlookers stood, as the treads are quite narrow for sitting.

75. Sourvinou-Inwood 2011; Parker 1996, pp. 307–8; 2005, p. 478; N. Robertson 1983, pp. 277–82; 1996, pp. 31–34, 48–52; 2004; Dillon 2002, pp. 133–34; B. Nagy 1991, 1994; Christopoulos 1992; Ridgway 1992, p. 124; Brulé 1987, pp. 105–10; Mansfield 1985, pp. 366–423; Simon 1983, pp. 46–48; Parke 1977, pp. 152–55, 186; Mikalson 1975b, pp. 160–61, 163–64; L. Deubner 1932, pp. 17–22. There is ongoing debate among scholars about details of these rites. See Hollinshead 2015.

76. Mikalson 1975a.

77. The Klepsydra spring house on the north slope of the Acropolis (475–460 B.C.E.) had a paved court of poros slabs: Hurwit 1999, pp. 142–43; Travlos 1971, pp. 323–27; Glaser 1983, pp. 8–9 no. 2; Parsons 1943. The early fourth-century B.C. fountain house beside the Dipylon Gate was paved with Hymettos marble: Travlos 1971, pp. 302–4; Knigge 1991, pp. 74–75; Glaser 1983, pp. 64–65 no. 47; Gruben 1969, p. 39. At Delphi, two fountain houses by the Castalian spring, one Archaic and one Classical, had paved surfaces: Glaser 1983, pp. 97–98 no. 68, pp. 98–100 no. 69; Amandry 1977, 1978.

78. Hurwit 2004, p. 170; N. Robertson 1996, pp. 32–33, based on *IG* I³ 474 lines 77–79, 202–8, and *IG* I³ 476 lines 218–20; Mansfield 1985, pp. 217–18; Paton, Stevens, et al. 1927, pp. 105–9, 290–91, 296–97, 318, 478.

79. Travlos (1971, p. 214) called the Pandroseion "organically linked to the Erechtheion and an inseparable part of it." His plan (p. 218 fig. 281) includes the Pandroseion, but not the North Court, whose relationship to the roofed part of the Erechtheion is equivalent.

80. Becker 2003, pp. 226–29; Thompson and Wycherley 1972, pp. 71, 149; H. A. Thompson 1937, p. 219.

81. Boegehold 1967, p. 118; in Boegehold 1995, pp. 14, 95, he would like to add a fifth bench in front to reach a potential capacity of 500, suitable for his interpretation of these benches as a venue for a law court; however, there is no trace of an additional bench. These differing estimates also depend on whether the benches' length is understood to be 25 m or 37 m. See also Camp 1986, p. 100; H. A. Thompson 1937, p. 218.

82. Hansen and Fischer-Hansen (1994, p. 65) support Boegehold. Cf. Camp 1986, p. 100. Thompson and Wycherley (1972, p. 71) object to the lack of privacy for Boegehold's law court.

83. H. A. Thompson 1937, p. 218.

84. Hansen and Nielsen 2004. Kindt (2009; 2012, pp. 12–35) describes aspects of Greek religion and its practices that are not tied to the patronage of the polis, as articulated by Sourvinou-Inwood (1988, 1990) and others.

CHAPTER 6. STEPS IN THE FOURTH CENTURY

1. Frederiksen 2002; Hansen and Fischer-Hansen 1994.

2. Hansen and Fischer-Hansen 1994, p. 85.

3. Payne 1940. See also Becker 2003, pp. 21–23, 221–24; Menadier 1995; Tomlinson 1977, 1992; Sinn 1990.

4. Becker (2003, p. 21), Menadier (1995, pp. 123–24), and Sinn (1990, p. 104) argue that Coulton's date later in the fourth century is too low and that the stoa need not be linked to Demetrius Poliorcetes. See Coulton 1967, p. 369.

5. This section of the site is no longer considered a second sanctuary, to Hera Limeneia, as it was by Payne. See Tomlinson 1977.

6. Becker 2003, pp. 19–21; Menadier 1995, pp. 84, 123–24; Tomlinson 1992, pp. 339–40; Sinn 1990, pp. 101, 103–4; Payne 1940, pp. 116–21.

7. Becker 2003, p. 21.

8. Becker 2003, pp. 19–21; Tomlinson 1977, p. 198: "they obviously once extended further to the east and higher"; Tomlinson 1992, p. 339; Sinn 1990, pp. 103–4; Payne 1940, pp. 119–20.

9. Ducrey and Picard 1972, pp. 583–85. See also Hansen and Fischer-Hansen 1994, pp. 63–65; Kolb 1976; Ginouvès 1972, pp. 56–57; Dilke 1948, p. 129.

10. S. G. Miller 1978, pp. 78–86, 192 (A321),196 (A346). A third-century treaty between Lato and Gortyn, its eleven fragments were found in the agora, on the steps, and in Room 37, which was apparently lined with couches: Kirsten 1940b; Demargne 1901.

11. Ginouvès 1972, p. 56; E. T. Hall 1966, 1968.

12. The excavators favored a bouleuterion: Ducrey and Picard 1972, pp. 591–92. Hansen and Fischer-Hansen (1994, pp. 63–65) propose that the steps were for jurors, and served as a dikasterion, comparable to the benches below the Hephaisteion. Kolb's proposal (1976; 1981, p. 86) of religious rites in this sector is not unreasonable in the light of the temple at the base of the steps, and the examples cited here of stepped structures viewing temple-altar areas. I. Nielsen (2002, pp. 111–12) interprets both stepped areas at Lato as "cultic theaters."

13. Ducrey and Picard 1971, pp. 527–28; 1972, p. 592. Cf. Kolb 1976, pp. 296–97. For theaters with rectilinear orchestras, see Paga 2010, pp. 366–71, with additional references; Gebhard 1974.

14. Ducrey and Picard 1970, p. 573.

15. Ducrey and Picard 1971, pp. 528–29. Cf. Kolb 1976, pp. 298–300.

16. Ducrey and Picard 1972, pp. 588–91.

17. Mallwitz and van de Löcht 1980; Kunze and Schleif 1938. Becker (2003, pp. 275–79) firmly asserts its role as a retaining wall, and is skeptical about other uses.

18. Figures from Amandry 1952, p. 265 n. 83. For a plan representing this concept, see Sinn 2002, p. 55 fig. 7; Hölscher 2002, p. 335 fig. 2.

19. Most scholars consider the steps of the northern edge of the Altis as two segments, without addressing the date or relationship of the westernmost segment by the temple of Hera. In the absence of more complete information, I take the close similarities in dimensions of the steps north of the temple of Hera to those of the treasury terrace as a reasonable indication of contemporaneity. See Herrmann 1999; Amandry 1952, p. 265; Becker (2003, p. 276) estimates that the western segment would have accommodated thirteen steps. He notes a small difference in dimensions and material between this segment and the eastern one, implying separate construction, which could mean different dates as well.

20. Becker (2003, p. 275 nn. 1359, 1360) includes step-by-step measurements reported by several scholars, all within this range, confirmed by my own measurements.

21. Rups 1986, pp. 74–75 and n. 302.

22. Hölscher 2002; Mallwitz 1988.

23. Dyer 1908. See also Rups 1986, pp. 73–79.

24. Frederiksen 2002, pp. 74–75; Koenigs 1981; Krinzinger 1980. Cf. Hölscher 2002, pp. 332–36, 338; Herrmann 1999, p. 367; Mallwitz 1972, pp. 202–4; 1981a, pp. 105–6; 1988, pp. 94, 103; 1999b, pp. 256–57 and n. 288.

25. Original date: Kunze and Schleif 1938; questioned by Dinsmoor (1941b), who favored a date in the second century. Those arguments were refuted by Kunze and Weber 1948.

26. Becker 2003, pp. 276–78; Mallwitz and van de Löcht 1980; Kunze and Schleif 1938.

27. Herrmann 1999, p. 367 n. 2. The Metroon dates to the first decade of the fourth century: Mallwitz 1972, p. 162.

28. Herrmann 1999, pp. 368–69, 378–80. He also notes traces of stepped retaining walls behind the treasuries of Selinus (IX) and Gela (XII). The wall south of Pheidias' workshop: Herrmann 1981, pp. 353–69; 1999, p. 380 n. 39; Mallwitz and Schiering 1964, pp. 48–53. See also Schilbach 1992, pp. 33–34.

29. Jost 1985, p. 184.

30. Paus. 8.38.9; Romano 2005. For the most current information, see www.lykaionexcavation.org.

31. Romano 2005; Kourouniotis 1903, 1904a, 1904b, 1905, 1909.

32. Coulton (1976, p. 252) lists its exterior dimensions as 70 by 11 m. Romano (2005) argues that the stoa faced northwest; Coulton supposes that it faced south. See also Jost 1985, pp. 182–83; Kourouniotis 1904b, 1909.

33. Romano 2005. Measurements by author.

34. Romano 2005, p. 386.

35. Jost 1985, pp. 148–49; 1992, pp. 229–31; 1994, pp. 226–28; Demand 1990, pp. 114–15. See Paus. 8.30.2 for the shrine in Megalopolis. For the early renown of the sanctuary, see T. H. Nielsen 2002a, pp. 61, 67, 84, 86, 87, 148–52, 153; Jost 1985, pp. 548–49; 1994, pp. 225–30.

36. Mylonopoulos 2006, pp. 95–96; Becker 2003, pp. 233–35; Jost 1985, p. 176; Papachatzis 1967, pp. 343–58, plan pp. 344, 345; Leonardos 1896a, 1896b.

37. Measurements from Becker 2003, p. 233 n. 1138; Amandry 1952, pp. 266–67 n. 33. Cf. Jost 2003 p. 149; Leonardos (1896a) reports a reduction in depth from 0.85–0.43 m. View: Orlandini 1969–70, p. 355 fig. 8. Loucas-Durie (1992, p. 87) suggests that observers on the upper steps stood, while those on the lower steps sat.

Notes

38. Becker 2003, p. 233 n. 1137; Becker is skeptical about Leonardos' measurement and its equivalence to the temple.

39. Jost 1985, p. 174; Leonardos 1896a, especially pp. 99, 115, and pl. 1.

40. I. Nielsen 2002, pp. 106–8; Ginouvès 1972, p. 68; Orlandini 1969–70, pp. 354–57. Contra these scholars: Jost 2003, p. 149.

41. The Archaic temple at Bassai is also thought to have had an opening in the flank, as did the fifth-century temple: Kelly 1995. Tegea: Østby 1994. Lousoi: Jost 1985, pp. 46–51; Reichel and Wilhelm 1901. Mitsopoulos-Leon 1992 summarizes recent work at the site.

42. Jost 2003, p. 149, on *deiknumena*; Loucas-Durie (1992, pp. 87–96, especially pp. 88–89) suggests that spectators viewed a revelation of some sort.

43. Jost 2003, p. 149.

44. Jost 1985, pp. 176–77; 2003; Orlandini 1969–70.

45. Date: Themelis 1993; 1994; 1996, especially pp. 170–72. The sculptures are now divided between the National Archaeological Museum in Athens and the museum at the archaeological site. See Kaltsas 2003, pp. 279–81 nos. 584–91. See also Ridgway 2000, pp. 235–38; Stewart 1990, pp. 94–96. Inside the temple: Lévy and Marcadé 1972; Lévy 1967.

46. Jost 1985, pp. 175, 178. She compares the attachments for the statuary group to those in the mid-fourth-century Philippeion at Olympia and finds details of the akroteria reminiscent of the tholos at Epidauros. Daniel (1904, p. 55) also suggests a possible fourth-century date for the temple. Akroterion: Themelis 1996, p. 164. Jost's arguments have merit, but a fourth-century date also suits her historical interpretation of the role of this sanctuary.

47. Becker 2003, p. 235.

48. The date, ca. 370 B.C. (372/1–368/7 B.C.), is controversial: Jost 1992. Synoikism: T. H. Nielsen 2002a, pp. 413–510, 520–25, 572–76.

49. T. H. Nielsen (2002a, p. 566) proposes that Lykosoura survived as "a dependent polis in charge of an important sanctuary inside the polis of Megalopolis."

50. Hansen and Nielsen (2004, pp. 115–19) offer a nuanced view of what constituted synoikism and criticize Demand's (1990) narrower interpretation. See also Reger 2001, pp. 161–62; Moggi 1976.

51. Jost 1985, pp. 176, 548–49; 1992, pp. 224–38; 1994, pp. 225–28. Processions: Jost 1992, pp. 233–37; 1994, pp. 228–29.

52. The website www.labraunda.org has the most current information. Karlsson (2010, pp. 54–61) summarizes the origins and cult of the sanctuary. See also Williamson 2013, pp. 6–19; 2014, pp. 90–96; Baran 2009, pp. 301–4; Thieme 1993; Hellström 1991, p. 297; Westholm 1963. Hellström recently (2011, p. 155) proposed, on the basis of his historical interpretation, that "all of the Hekatomnid buildings at Labraunda were part of a single major dynastic project" that included a massive expansion of feasting. For a summary of work to date with excellent photographs, see Edgü, Kuzucu, and Ural 2010.

53. See Hornblower 1982, pp. 38–40, for dates. Upon his death in 353/2 B.C., Mausolos' immediate successor was his wife, Artemisia, who had shared his rule for a period of time. She ruled alone until her own death in 351/350 B.C., when Idrieus became satrap.

54. Baran 2010a, 2010b, 2011. Aelian's estimate (*On Animals* 12.30) of 70 stadia (12.4–13.5 km) seems to be more accurate than Strabo's: Hellström 1996b, p. 134. Shortly before his comments about the Sacred Way, Strabo notes the quarries for white marble near Mylasa and observes that the stone is suitable for temples and public structures: Westholm 1963, pp. 9–10. Improvements to the modern road have obscured some of the details of the ancient route described by Westholm. Cf. Bean 1980, p. 47 and pl. 11; www.labraunda.org/Sacred_Way. For another image, see www.labraunda/Report_2007. Carstens (2009a, 2011) emphasizes the potential for a royal procession afforded by the paved way.

55. Baran 2010a, 2010b, 2011; Westholm 1963, p. 10.

56. Baran 2010a, 2010b, 2011; www.labraunda.org/Sacred_Way. Tombs: Henry 2009, 2010b; www.labraunda.org/Tombs.

57. Jeppesen 1955, p. 43 n. 12. Oikos L, a small rectangular structure west of the four broad steps, is described as antedating them and the Great Stairway abutting it to the north.

58. Hellström (1991, p. 302) observes that "what is visible does not look properly Hecatomnid."

59. Karlsson 2010, pp. 26–27; Hellström 1988; 1990; 1991, p. 302; 1996a.

60. Karlsson 2010, pp. 30–37; http://www.labraunda.org/Labraunda.org/Oikoi_Building_eng.html. See also Hellström 1991, pp. 303–4; 1996a, p. 168; 2011, p. 154; Westholm 1963. It is not clear whether the oikoi served as additional dining facilities, archives, a prytaneion, a priests' house, a treasury, or some other function.

61. Hellström 1991, pp. 303–4.

62. Blid 2006–7, 2010, 2011; Hellström 1991, p. 297; Westholm 1963.

63. For the most current information see www.labraunda.org. Large tomb: Henry 2006, 2010a, 2010b, 2011; Carstens 2009a, pp. 82–83; 2009b, pp. 383–84; Fedak 1990, p. 76; Westholm 1963, pp. 101–5. Stadium: Roos 2011; Westholm 1963, pp. 19–20. Fortifications: Karlsson 2011. Fountain houses and Sacred Way: Baran 2010a, 2010b, 2011; Westholm 1963, pp. 9–10. Tombs: Henry 2009, 2010a, 2010b, 2011.

64. I have doubts about Hellström's (2011) revised interpretation: the entire sanctuary as a grand plan that began under Hekatomnos. See also Hellström 1991, p. 299; 1996b, p. 134. He assumes that the fourth-century predecessor to the Roman stoa would have occupied the same space. Cf. Umholtz 2002, pp. 273–76; Crampa 1972, pp. 8–10 nos. 13, 14.

65. Hellström 1991, 1996a, 1996b; Crampa 1972, pp. 13–18 nos. 16–19.

66. Thieme 1989, pp. 86–90; Jeppesen 1955.

67. Hellström 1996b; Jeppesen 1955. More of the South Propylaia is preserved. Based on its juxtaposition with the back wall of the Doric (fountain) House, it appears to antedate that structure, also attributed to Idrieus epigraphically: Jeppesen 1955, p. 43 n.12.

68. Control takes many forms. Crampa (1972, p. 197) cites a later (second-century) inscription forbidding camping in the shrine and gathering animals in buildings. Current excavators also mention efforts to keep cattle from the archaeological zone: www.labraunda.org/Report_2008.

69. Hellström 1988, 1990.

70. Umholtz 2002. See also Karlsson 2013; Hornblower 1990; Gunter 1985. M. C. Miller 1997 offers valuable comments on connections between Greece and Persia.

71. Carstens 2009a, 2011; Hellström (2011) places greater stress on the royal nature of the site.

72. Carstens 2013 emphasizes the "creole" nature of Hekatomnid Karia. See also Henry 2013b.

73. Demand 1990, pp. 120–26; Hellström 1988, p. 74; Pedersen 1988b, p. 98; Hornblower 1982, pp. 78–105, 188, 297–98. Epigraphic evidence suggests that the Macedonian satrap Asander moved it back in the early Hellenistic period: Hornblower 1982, pp. 78 n. 5, p.103 and n. 192.

74. Williamson 2013, pp. 6–19; 2014, pp. 90–96. Hellström (1988, p. 74; 1990, p. 243; 1991, pp. 304, 308) finds strong spatial correlation with Delphi, perhaps intentional; cf. Hornblower 1982, p. 312. For a cross-cultural comparison, of sites purposely configured in emulation of the major Inka sanctuary at Cuzco, see Coben 2006.

75. Crampa 1972, pp. 81–89 nos. 53–54a. Two Roman inscriptions of imperial date appear be to be copies of fourth-century prototypes.

76. Hobsbawm and Ranger 1983.

77. Roos 2011; Hellström 2009; Mylonopoulos 2006; www.labraunda.org/Stadion; Westholm 1963, pp. 19–20; Crampa (1972, p. 196) notes the reference to *agones* in a post-Hekatomnid inscription: no. 11 lines 7, 10.

78. For a summary of Mausolos' activities in the Aegean, including possibly controlling trade routes, see Hellström 1996b, p. 134. The subject is more fully covered by Hornblower 1982, pp. 107–37. Cf. Crampa 1972, pp. 194–95, on Mylasa's authority over the sanctuary.

79. Hellström 1996b.

80. Crampa 1972, pp. 191–97.

81. Westholm 1963, p. 112.

82. Blid 2010; Hellström 1991, p. 297; Crampa 1972; Westholm 1963, pp. 112–14.

83. Robert and Robert 1983, pp. 63–68, 76, 83; Robert 1953; Hellström (2009, pp. 272–90) reexamined the site and R. Martin's unpublished notes from his work with the Roberts in 1950. Hellström's revised interpretations are necessarily speculative, as there have been no excavations since the Roberts'. See also Carstens 2009a, pp. 107–8; Pedersen 1991, pp. 66–67; Marchese 1989, p. 52; Hornblower 1982, pp. 278, 313; Bean 1980, pp. 168–70.

84. Pedersen 1991b, pp. 66–67.

85. Carstens 2009a, pp. 69–74; Jeppesen 1976, pp. 52–53; 1978; 2000, pp. 37–39.

86. Carstens 2009a, pp. 65–69; 2009b, pp. 389–91; Zahle and Kjeldsen 2004; Jeppesen 1989, p. 15; 2000, pp. 141–43; Zahle 1978.

CHAPTER 7. STEPS IN THE THIRD CENTURY

1. Polyb. 5.88–90; Diod. Sic. 26.8.1; Strabo 14.2.5; Plin. *HN* 34.41; Berthold 1980; 1984, pp. 92–93. While some structures may reflect a fourth-century plan or even predecessor, absent tangible physical traces or explicit epigraphic testimonia, it is prudent to consider the Rhodian sites as third-century and later in date. Synoikism: Reger 2001; Gabrielsen 2000; Hornblower 1982, pp. 104–5.

Notes

2. Becker 2003, pp. 87–89; Hoepfner 1999, 2003; von Hesberg 1994, p. 181 no. 6.1.14; Kondis 1953, pp. 283–84.

3. Hoepfner 1999. His date is also based on a lion-headed water spout and a Doric capital, both presumably from the first temple; see Konstantinopoulos 1973, pp. 131–33. Hoepfner (2003, pp. 33–42) conjectures that this would be the setting for the statue of Helios made by Lysippus, as reported by Pliny (*HN* 34.60). He dismisses (p. 34) Segré's 1949 hypothesis of an oracle within the temple. See also Ridgway 2004; Becker 2003, pp. 87–89; Konstantinopoulos 1973, pp. 129–34.

4. Hoepfner 2003.

5. *Pace* Hoepfner (2003, p. 34), who emphasizes the priority of this Rhodian example of aligning the monumental approach to what he calls propylon and temple façade.

6. The first-century date is based on Josephus' account of a fire in the time of Herod: Hoepfner 1999, pp. 54, 56.

7. E.g., Becker 2003, pp. 87–89.

8. Blinkenberg and Kinch 1941, pp. 60–147 no. 1 (priests of Athena Lindia) and pp. 148–99 no. 2 (temple chronicle). Other epigraphic testimonia about adorning a (the?) statue of Athena are less securely dated; indeed, the presumed date of the temple has been used to place them chronologically: Higbie 2003, pp. 11–12, 146–47, 256–58; Lippolis 1998–99, pp. 127–32; Gruben 1980, pp. 413–14.

9. Blinkenberg and Kinch 1941, cols. 287–88 no. 71. It is not clear whether these men donated the doors or the temple itself. Blinkenberg thought that the gift was limited to the doors, supporting a fourth-century date for the temple. See also Dygve and Poulsen 1960, pp. 180–81. With the benefit of more epigraphic information, Lippolis' 1998–99 supposition (pp. 127–32) that the inscription refers to donors of all or part of the temple building makes more sense.

10. For the Italian policy in 1938–1940 of restoration with reinforced concrete, considered a prestigious modern material at the time, see V. Papadimitriou 1988, pp. 169–71. Similarly enthusiastic restorations were carried out at this time at the sanctuary of Apollo Pythios in the city of Rhodes and at the Asklepieion on Kos: Kondis 1963, p. 392; Dygve and Poulsen 1960, pp. 25–26.

11. Hollinshead 2012a; Higbie 2003; Lippolis 1988–89, p. 134; Coulton 1976, pp. 172, 251–52; Kondis 1963; Dygve and Poulsen 1960, pp. 276–80.

12. Blinkenberg 1931, col. 16; Athenian influence denied by Kondis 1963, p. 397. See also Becker 2003, p. 78 n. 398; Lippolis 1988–89, p. 136; Gruben 1980, pp. 415–17; Dygve and Poulsen 1960, pp. 181–82.

13. A narrow Ionic stoa was added along the south wall in the late second century, further enclosing the temple court: Dygve and Poulsen 1960, pp. 184–89.

14. The dimensions and execution of these steps are similar to those of the Upper Stoa, and pottery fragments beneath them were called Hellenistic. The steps appear to have turned left at the top, but modern steps have obliterated their uppermost sections and continuation: Dygve and Poulsen 1960, pp. 57–58, 73, 76–77. Cf. Becker 2003, pp. 85–86, with dimensions.

15. Dygve and Poulsen 1960, p.179. Cf. Kondis 1963, pp. 398–99.

16. Kostomitsopoulos 1988; Lippolis 1988–89, pp. 137–38; Dygve and Poulsen 1960, pp. 177–78; Blinkenberg 1931, col. 183.

17. Blinkenberg and Kinch 1941, cols. 149–99, especially cols. 177–82.

18. Blinkenberg 1931, col. 11, cited in Dygve and Poulsen 1960, pp. 112, 176–80. See also Becker 2003, p. 86; Higbie 2003, p. 236; Kostomitsopoulos 1988.

19. Kondis 1963, pp. 398–99. Cf. Dygve and Poulsen 1960, p. 297.

20. Lippolis 1988–89.

21. Dygve and Poulsen 1960, pp. 159, 220.

22. Becker 2003, pp. 79, 82–83; Lippolis 1988–89, pp. 134, 150; Pakkanen (1988, pp. 150–54) adopts Lauter's position (1986, pp. 106–8).

23. Dygve and Poulsen 1960, p. 218. He reports (p. 40) that the stone was said to come from the island of Phanos, across the bay from Lindos.

24. Dygve and Poulsen 1960, p. 43 (pl. IIA), pp. 225, 286–87 (pl. VI P). See also Lippolis 1988–89; Gruben 1980, pp. 420–21. Becker (2003, pp. 83–85) estimates their depth at 0.35–0.40 m by comparison with the steps of the Upper Stoa.

25. Becker 2003, pp. 91–92; DiVita 1986–87, 1990, 1994; von Hesberg 1994, pp. 152, 179; Konstantinopoulos 1986, pp. 170–71; Lauter 1982; 1986, p. 79.

26. Becker 2003, p. 9; von Hesberg 1994, p. 179 no. 6.1.6, pls. 38d, 39a. The remains of the original steps measure 0.12–0.16 m high and 0.32–0.34 m wide.

27. Tataki 1997, p. 52; Konstantinopoulos 1986, pp. 173, 176–77.

28. The dates of inscriptions on the bases are consistent with a post-earthquake date, in the late third/early second century:

Becker 2003, p. 92; Petsa-Tzounakou 1996, pp. 78–82; von Hesberg 1994, p. 152 no. 3.1.5; Konstantinopoulos 1986, pp. 174–76; Lauter 1982, p. 708.

29. Heilmeyer 1999.

30. Pounder 1983, p. 252. Cuttings for foundations and well beddings, a few foundation blocks, and two cisterns are all that remains of this structure: Camp 1986, p. 167; Thompson and Wycherley 1972, pp. 80–81, 149, 228.

31. Pounder 1983, especially p. 242. The date is based on Rotroff's ceramic studies of mold-made relief bowls (1982, p. 33). See also Thompson and Wycherley 1972, p. 149; D. B. Thompson 1937, 1963.

32. I am grateful to the late Judith Binder for bringing these steps to my attention. Pounder 1983, pp. 240–41 n. 20; T. L. Shear 1938, p. 339; agora excavation daybooks section LL 1937–39, where a slight divergence of alignment from the Augustan road on the north is also noted. Despite pottery dates recorded by the excavator, D. B. Thompson, as fourth–second century, she assigned the stairs a Roman date based on comparisons with the (very partial) staircase on the east side of Kolonos Agoraios between the Agora and the Hephaisteion. This interpretation may have been based on an underlying assumption that monumental stairs must be Roman, not Greek.

33. Pounder (1983, pp. 240–41 n. 20) explains that John Travlos, who drew so many of the official plans of the Agora, was skeptical that there were steps here. They do appear in Rotroff's plan A (1983) and Brogan 2003, p. 196 fig. 1 and p. 204 fig. 11.

34. Pounder 1983, p. 240; Thompson and Wycherley 1972, pp. 80, 149.

35. Camp 1986, pp. 159–62; 2001, p. 156; Thompson and Wycherley 1972, pp. 36–38, 136–39, 149.

36. H. Thompson 1937, pp. 221–22.

37. D. Lazarides 1982; 1984; 1997, pp. 52–59. See also Becker 2003, pp. 89–91; Catling 1986–87, p. 43.

38. K. Lazarides (1986, pp. 58–59) favors a third-century date; and see D. Lazarides 1980, pp. 13–14; 1982, p. 47; 1997, p. 54. See also Becker 2003, p. 91.

39. D. Lazarides 1982, pl. 45; 1997, p. 52. See also Becker 2003, p. 91. After a major fire, the grand staircase went out of use (a drain was laid across it in the east); then, in the mid-first century A.D., a new propylaia was constructed on the north side of the palaistra to give access to the rebuilt athletic complex: D. Lazarides 1997, pp. 54, 57; K. Lazarides 1986, pp. 59, 60.

40. Becker (2003, p. 89 n. 462) estimates steps 0.19 m high and 0.37 m wide, based on D. Lazarides' plan and section (1982, plan B and p. 44). The stairs are now covered in sand for protection.

41. D. Lazarides 1984, pp. 23–25; 1997, pp. 57–58. The ephebic law of the ephebarch Adaios son of Euemeros, dated to the last quarter of the first century B.C., incorporates earlier rules. Other inscriptions add information about laws concerning the games, and there are votive inscriptions to Hermes and Herakles as well.

42. Becker 2003, pp. 70–73; Holloway 2000, pp. 156–63; Tsakirgis 1995; M. Bell 1988.

43. The angle between sections B and C is ca. 137 degrees, slightly wider than that between sections A and B: M. Bell 1988; Stillwell and Sjöqvist 1957. It appears that the ground level was raised as much as 0.35 m when the steps were built: M. Bell 1988, p. 328. Cf. Becker 2003, pp. 70–74.

44. M. Bell 1988, pp. 338–39. See also H. Allen 1970; Stillwell and Sjöqvist 1957.

45. Stillwell and Sjöqvist 1957, p. 152. Cf. Becker 2003, pp. 73–74.

46. M. Bell 1984–85, 1988; Stillwell and Sjöqvist 1958.

47. M. Bell 1988, and M. Bell, personal communication, February 15, 1988; Stillwell and Sjöqvist 1958, p. 161.

48. Kolb 1975; 1981, p. 85–87. He makes the same argument for the steps below the prytaneion at Lato as cultic in nature; see above p. 52 and n. 12. For M. Bell's rebuttal, see 1984–85, p. 510 n. 22.

49. Agrigento: Becker 2003, pp. 163–80.

50. Pausanias (2.24.1) calls the site that of Apollo Deiradiotes, after its location on the *deiras*, or ridge. Vollgraff (1956, pp. 43–49) also points out that there is room at the top for another step or two. Cf. Becker 2003, pp. 42–47; Ginouvès 1972, p. 66; Tomlinson 1972, pp. 23–24, 247–49; Roux 1961, pp. 65–82.

51. The well is 0.90 m in diameter and 17.80 m deep. It appeared to be for collecting rainwater: Vollgraff 1956, pp. 47–48. Cf. Roux 1961, p. 78.

52. A veneer of applied stone slabs would have left marks in the bedrock where clamps fixed them in place, as seen on the altar: Roux 1957, p. 481; Vollgraff 1956, p. 43.

53. The early third-century date is based on letter forms and prosopography: Pouilloux 1958; Vollgraff 1956, pp. 109–17.

54. Tomlinson 1972, pp. 247–49; Roux 1957, especially p. 481; 1961, pp. 66–71; Vollgraff 1956. For the attribution to Athena

Notes

Oxyderkes, see Roux 1957, p. 484; see Vollgraff 1956, pp. 51–84, on the finds.

55. Roux 1957, p. 480; 1961, pp. 77–78.

56. Rupp 1974, pp. 120–21; Anti and Polacco 1969, pp. 173–75; Pouilloux 1958.

57. Bergquist 1973, 1998; Roux 1979; Launey 1944. Cf. Becker 2003, pp. 47–52.

58. Roux (1979, p. 199) notes that the pattern of paving may simply represent what is preserved from a more fully paved temenos. Beneath the oikoi lay a small earlier (mid-sixth-century) structure of polygonal masonry with an interior hearth. A well lay in a triangular court just south of the oikoi: Bergquist 1973, 1998.

59. Bergquist 1973, 1998; Launey 1944.

60. Recent excavations have revealed a seventh-century structure beneath the peripteral building: Des Courtils and Pariente 1985, 1988, 1991; Brunet et al. 1987. Cf. Bergquist 1998.

61. Bergquist 1998, pp. 69–71; Des Courtils and Pariente 1988, 1991. Cf. Becker 2003, pp. 47–52.

62. Bergquist 1973, 1998; Roux 1979; Launey 1944. Cf. Becker 2003, pp. 47–52.

63. Roux 1979, pp. 195–99, supported by Bergquist 1998, p. 71. Launey 1944.

64. Roux 1979, pp. 196–97. Cuttings across the lowest step of the base may indicate a barrier.

65. Roux (1979) says second century.

66. Des Courtils and Pariente (1986, p. 806) identified sixth-century pottery and debris beneath the stepped wall, providing only a *terminus post quem* for its construction. Bergquist (1998) favors a fifth-century date, but entertains other possibilities. Roux (1979) proposes a date in the third century.

67. Des Courtils and Pariente 1988.

68. Roux 1979, pp. 204–5.

69. The date of the colonnaded oikoi should provide a *terminus post quem* for the broad steps: Roux 1979, pp. 206–11, adopted by Becker 2003, pp. 47–52.

70. Des Courtils and Pariente (1985, 1986, 1987) support a post-sixth-century date. Bergquist (1998) acknowledges uncertainty but tilts toward the fifth-century date favored by Martin (1978). Launey 1944, pp. 19–21.

71. Knackfuss 1941a, pp. 140–41. The bottom step is 0.868 m deep, the middle step 0.732 m, and the top step 0.682 m deep: Becker 2003, pp. 252–54; Akurgal 1990, p. 231; Naumann 1973, pp. 47–49.

72. Starting blocks have been preserved east of the passage between the stepped bleachers and the temple platform. The race probably followed an out-and-back format: Naumann 1973, pp. 47–49; Knackfuss 1941a, p. 141.

73. Knackfuss 1941a, pl. 79 Z618, pl. 80 Z619, pl. 84 Z638. Cf. Becker 2003, pp. 253–54.

74. Piok Zanon 2007; Bohtz 1981. See also Mylonopoulos 2006, pp. 96–97; Becker 2003, pp. 248–52; C. M. Thomas 1998; Kron 1996, pp. 173–75; Radt 1988, pp. 206–14; Dörpfeld 1910, 1912.

75. Bohtz (1981, pp. 56–57) identified traces of an early temenos wall and propylaia, but Piok Zanon (2007, p. 325 and n. 6, p. 340) is skeptical. See also Becker 2003, p. 251; C. M. Thomas 1998, pp. 284, 286–87; Radt 1988, pp. 206–7.

76. For the date of Apollonis' dedication, see Piok Zanon 2007, pp. 342–48; Schalles 1985, pp. 146–49.

77. Dörpfeld 1910, pp. 355–84 nos. 22 and 23; 1912, pp. 235–56 no. 5. See also Piok Zanon 2007, p. 325; Kron 1996, pp. 174–75; Hepding 1910, p. 439.

78. Piok Zanon 2007, pp. 349–59; Rheidt 1996; Schalles 1985; Rumscheid 1994, pp. 118–24.

79. Bohtz 1981, p. 36; Dörpfeld 1912, p. 240. Piok Zanon (2007, pp. 336–41, 358) argues that the earlier steps built under Philetairos extended 23.50 m, from the altar to the temenos perimeter wall, and that the additional 15 m section was added with the expansion and rebuilding under Apollonis.

80. The estimated number is from Becker 2003, p. 250.

81. Bookidis and Stroud 1997, pp. 231–52, 432–33.

82. Located in area S-T 21: Bookidis and Stroud 1997, pp. 253–72.

83. Bookidis and Stroud 1997, pp. 246–47, 260–66, 433.

84. The cleared area beside the stairway was marked by boundary stones and a retaining wall, indicating that the absence of rebuilding there was intentional: Bookidis and Stroud 1997, pp. 231–52, 432–33. A small room just before the propylon housed two stelai and a pit, presumably for votive offerings: ibid., pp. 216–17.

85. Dygve and Poulsen 1960, p. 182. He presumably had difficulty considering the form of monumental steps as Greek, since he also explicitly linked such steps at Athens to the Roman presence.

86. Piok Zanon 2007, pp. 251–59; Rheidt 1996; Rumscheid 1994, pp. 118–24.

CHAPTER 8. STEPS IN THE SECOND CENTURY

1. Thoneman 2013b, p. 43; Dignas 2002; Ma 1999; Kron 1996; van Bremen 1996, pp. 182–94; Bringmann 1993; Gruen 1993; Veyne 1990; Gauthier 1985.

2. Interdonato 2013 has assembled evidence of many types for the site and its ceremonies. After a long delay in publication, the extensive array of inscriptions from Kos is now receiving scholarly study and publication: Bosnakis, Hallof, and Rigsby 2010; Crowther 2004, p. 21; Hallof and Hallof 2004; Höghammar 2004, p. 7. See also Perrin-Saminadayar 2011 for a summary of the publication history of these inscriptions.

3. Strabo 14.2.19 (657); Diod. Sic. 15.76.2; Reger 2001, especially pp. 171–74; Sherwin-White 1978, pp. 43–74; Herzog and Schazmann 1932, p. 72.

4. Sherwin-White 1978, pp. 24–25, 68–70. There is not sufficient evidence to know whether Mausolos had any role in the synoikism of Kos.

5. Interdonato 2013, pp. 108, 210–11 (no. 2), 381; Sherwin-White 1978, pp. 55, 338–40; Herzog 1903b, p. 198; 1928, p. 33.

6. Interdonato 2013, pp. 108–111, 212–14 (no. 4), 381; Jordan and Perlin 1984, pp. 155–57; *LSCG* 150 A and B; Sherwin-White 1978, pp. 55, 340–41; Laumonier 1958, pp. 691–94.

7. Interdonato 2013, p. 108; Sherwin-White 1978, pp. 294–95, 341; Laumonier 1958, pp. 692–93; for groves sacred to Apollo, see Birge, 1994; Jordan and Perlin 1984, pp. 155–57; *LSCG*, pp. 251–53 nos. 150A and B.

8. Interdonato 2013 pp. 114–15, 217 (no. 6); Sherwin-White 1978, pp. 334 n. 395, 338.

9. Sherwin-White 1978, pp. 338–39, 356; Herzog and Schazmann 1932; Herzog 1928, p. 9 (*LSCG* 165). The pseudo-Hippocratic letter to the residents of Abdera refers to a lavish procession to the cypress grove (πομπὴ πολυτελὴς ἐς κυπάρισσον) as part of the annual festival of Asklepios. Sherwin-White (1978) maintains that the specificity of other rituals described in the passage means that it is more likely to contain accurate information. For the text, see Sherwin-White 1978, p. 339 n. 423; see also pp. 15, 74–75, 334–35, 340, 346–47. See also Interdonato 2013, p. 120.

10. Sherwin-White 1978, pp. 74–75.

11. Interdonato 2013, pp. 21–29; Herzog and Schazmann 1932, pp. xxii–xxxi.

12. Interdonato 2013; Hollinshead 2012a, pp. 41–46; Becker 2003, pp. 56–70; Herzog and Schazmann 1932. For the history of investigations at the site, including restoration, see Interdonato 2013, pp. 20–29.

13. Interdonato 2013, pp. 114–15, 217 (no. 6); Sherwin-White 1978, pp. 334–35, 344; Herzog and Schazmann 1932, pp. 25–26, 73.

14. Interdonato 2013, p. 39; Becker 2003, pp. 56–70; Lauter 1986, p. 106; Sherwin-White 1978, pp. 341–42; Zscheitzschmann 1936; Herzog and Schazmann 1932, pp. 1–2.

15. Interdonato 2013, pp. 45–48, 75, 91–94, 280–83, 382; Sherwin-White 1978, pp. 342–43; Herzog and Schazmann 1932, pp. 34–39. This structure is assumed to be the temple of Asklepios described in Herodas' fourth mime.

16. Interdonato 2013, pp. 49–50, 82,124, 283–88, 382, 386; Hellström 1990; Sherwin-White 1978, p. 343; Herzog and Schazmann 1932, pp. 49–51. For comparable structures, see Bergquist 1998.

17. Interdonato 2013, p. 74; Sherwin-White 1978, p. 343; Laumonier 1958, p. 693; Herzog and Schazmann 1932, pp. 42, 47–48.

18. Interdonato 2013, pp. 37–45, 265–73; Sherwin-White 1978, p. 343; Herzog and Schazmann 1932, pp. 47–48.

19. Interdonato 2013, pp. 41–43, 265–73, 299–303; Sherwin-White 1978, p. 342; Herzog and Schazmann (1932, pp. 14–16) reconstructed this phase with wooden posts, but Interdonato has identified fragmentary tufa blocks as coming from this initial stage of construction.

20. Interdonato 2013, pp. 44, 76, 269; Herzog and Schazmann 1932, p. 15.

21. Interdonato (2013, pp. 41, 77, 299, 382) proposes that access to the various terraces has a distinct east-west orientation, which was radically altered with the addition of the stairways in the second century. She suggests that the route from the Middle to the Upper Terrace was located at their east end. Cf. Becker 2003, p. 68.

22. Interdonato 2013, pp. 37–49, 277–79, 294–303, 381–82; Sherwin-White 1978, p. 342; Herzog and Schazmann 1932, pp. 61–67.

23. Interdonato 2013, pp. 84–87, 96–99; Höghammar 1993; Sherwin-White 1978, pp. 358–59; Herzog and Schazmann 1932, p. 61.

24. The steepness of the 26 degree slope, once thought to be a ramp, led excavators to restore steps as more feasible for ascent and descent. The stairs ascend 5 m across a 19 m distance. Interdonato 2013, p. 309 proposes two flights, of five

Notes

and thirteen steps respectively, separated by a paved landing. Becker (2003, pp. 56, 58 n. 286) proposes twenty-nine to thirty steps with landings.

25. Interdonato 2013, pp. 298–99. Steps B. Only side walls and foundations remain of these steps, estimated to have been 10.4 m wide, rising ca. 6 m high. For an early photograph see Herzog and Schazmann 1932, pl. 54. Becker (2003, pp. 59–61) proposes thirty-six steps, extending farther south into the middle terrace than in published restorations based on Schazmann's publication.

26. Between scant remains and aggressive reconstruction, too little remains for a definitive interpretation; nevertheless, details of masonry suggest that a stairway existed here in the third century. Interdonato 2013, pp. 298–99, 310; Becker 2003, pp. 59–60; Herzog and Schazmann 1932, pp. 61–62.

27. Interdonato 2013, pp. 41–44, 299–303, 308–10; Gruben 1980, pp. 405–6; Shoe 1950; Herzog and Schazmann (1932, pp. 64–67, 74) cite the harbor stoa in Miletos and the older palaistra in Pergamon as parallels. See also von Hesberg 1994, p. 179 n. 1486; Coulton (1976, p. 246) added a question mark to the date.

28. Interdonato 2013, pp. 120–33; Buraselis 2004; Rigsby 1996; Sherwin-White 1978, pp. 111–14, 357–59; *LSCG*; Herzog 1928. For *theoroi*, see Rutherford 2013, pp. 77–82. Musical, athletic, and equestrian contests are mentioned, but they may not have taken place within the Asklepieion precinct.

29. Interdonato 2013, pp. 123, 173–89; Buraselis 2004; Rigsby 1996, 2004; Sherwin-White 1978, pp. 111–14, 357–58; Herzog and Klaffenbach 1952.

30. Sumi 2004, p. 81. He also notes that Magnesia had failed in a comparable undertaking, the introduction of a pentateric Panhellenic festival of Artemis.

31. Hoepfner 1984. See also Interdonato 2013, pp. 45, 47, 184, 382; Höghammar 1993, pp. 21, 86–87.

32. Carlsson 2004, p. 114; Höghammar 1993, p. 20; Sherwin-White 1978, pp. 90–111.

33. Interdonato 2013, pp. 51–57, 265–73, 299–303; Herzog and Schazmann 1932, pp. 14–21.

34. Interdonato 2013, pp. 55, 75–76, 273–80; Becker 2003, pp. 65–70; Sherwin-White 1978, p. 344; Herzog and Schazmann 1932, pp. 3–5, 22–24.

35. Herzog and Schazmann 1932, pp. 22–24 and pls. 10, 11, 45, 46, 47, 48, 54. See also Interdonato 2013, pp. 279–80, who notes runs of thirty-seven steps and twenty-six steps. Becker (2003, pp. 61–66) would add additional landings. He questions whether there is sufficient evidence for this broadening before the temple. The issue probably cannot be resolved in the light of remains now accessible.

36. Interdonato 2013, p. 279 describes the height as ca. 12 m, while Becker (2003, p. 65) says 10.865 m.

37. Becker 2003, p. 63; Herzog and Schazmann 1932, p. 22. Interdonato (2013, pp. 279 n. 335) observes that there was variation in the dimensions of the steps, perhaps reflecting ancient rebuilding. Like other structures at the Asklepieion, these steps have been extensively reconstructed in concrete, with only small samples of their ancient form now visible.

38. Senseney 2007; 2011, pp. 45–49. Epidauros: von Hesberg 1994, pp. 54, 179; Gruben 1980, pp. 408–9; Würster 1973; Knell 1971, p. 210.

39. Hellström 1988.

40. Interdonato 2013, p. 279. Becker 2003, p. 66; Herzog and Schazmann 1932, pp. 22–24.

41. Interdonato 2013, pp. 83, 288–90, 383; Becker 2003, pp. 207–9; Herzog and Schazmann 1932, pp. 73, 75.

42. Merz 2001, p. 25. See also Interdonato 2013, p. 382; Coulton 1977, pp. 122–23.

43. The corpus of Greek inscriptions from the second-century phase of the site led Lajtar (2006, p. 84) to describe it as "a small cult place of local importance which drew adherents from among inhabitants of the closest neighbourhood, mainly belonging to the lower strata of society." Evidence of embalmers' workshops in the portico of the middle terrace indicates a diminution of the multi-level character so often associated with the site. Lajtar 2006, pp. 10–11, 94; see also Strudwick 2003, pp. 172–73, 182–83; Szafranski 2001.

44. Lajtar 2006; Strudwick 2003, pp. 172–74, 182–84; also Laskowska-Kusztal 1984.

45. Schwandner 1990, pp. 92–93. Cf. Radt 1988, pp. 27–28.

46. Probably after 183 B.C.: Höghammar 1993, p. 24; Sherwin-White 1978, p. 369.

47. Sherwin-White 1978, pp. 132–33, 369; Herzog 1928, p. 9.

48. Interdonato 2013, pp. 45, 47, 57, 76, 132–33, 184, 188–89, 382–83 on rulers as patrons, pp. 159–67 on evidence for the administration of the sanctuary; Sherwin-White 1978, pp. 135–38.

49. Dignas 2002, pp. 20–25; Migeotte 1992, 1995; Debord 1982; Sherwin-White 1978, pp. 344, 358.

50. Ehrhardt 2009; Berges et al. 2006, pp. 24–34; Bankel

2004; Becker 2003, p. 255; Love 1968a; 1968b; 1969a; 1969b; 1972b, pp. 404–5; 1973a, p. 423.

51. Love 1972a, pp. 69–71; 1972b, pp. 397–98;1973b, pp. 100–105; 1978; Bankel (1999; 2004, p. 112; 2009) dated this structure to the early third century. Cf. Ehrhardt 2009.

52. Ehrhardt 2009; Bankel 2004, pp. 103–4.

53. Berges 2006, pp. 24–29; Bankel 1997, pp. 53, 69; Bruns-Özgan 1995; Stampolides 1984; Love 1973a, p. 423.

54. Bankel 1997, p. 69. Cf. I. Jenkins 2006.

55. Ehrhardt 2009; Bankel 1997, pp. 53, 69.

56. Bankel 2004, p. 104. This reconstruction also addresses Becker's (2003, p. 255) question about whether spectators in upper rows could see the altar.

57. Bankel 1997, pp. 59, 67. See Bankel 2009 and Ehrhardt 2009 for views of a model reconstructing this area of the site.

58. Bankel 1997, p. 68.

59. Bankel 1997, p. 69; see also Bankel 2004 for a model of the Apollo sanctuary in the second century. Cf. Ehrhardt 2009.

60. The controversy is summarized by Tuna et al. 2009; Berges. 2006, pp. 19–34; Bankel 2004; Berges and Tuna 2000; Berges 1994; Bean 1980, pp. 111–27; Demand 1989; Bean and Cook 1952, pp. 208–12.

61. Waelkens and Vandeput 2007. For a summary of written testimonia about the Pisidians, see Vanhaverbeke et al. 2010, p. 122.

62. Waelkens and Vandeput 2007, pp. 100–101; Carlsson 2004.

63. H. Brandt 2004; Waelkens 2004, pp. 457, 461; Büyükkolanci 1998; Bracke 1993, p. 23; Mitchell 1991, pp. 132, 134, 139–40; 1992, p. 16; Belke and Mersich 1990, p. 170.

64. A fortification tower interrupts the steps along their upper edge, accounting for the inconsistent number of steps at either end.

65. Lauter 1970; Waelkens (2004, pp. 461–66) speculates whether earlier dates are possible for these buildings.

66. Mitchell 1991, p. 132.

67. H. Brandt 2004; *TAM* III.2. See also Waelkens and Vandeput 2007, p. 101; Kosmetatou 1997, p. 28; Mitchell 1991, pp. 123–25; Bean 1959, pp. 96–97. For the nature of "democracy" and "autonomy" in such inscriptions, see Ma 1999, pp. 160–62, 235–42; 2000, pp. 109–10, on conventions of epigraphic language. Cf. Carlsson 2004, pp. 112–13, 2010; Gruen 1993, pp. 340–43.

68. Mitchell 1991, pp. 135, 139; 1998, p. 251; 1999, pp. 173–74; Waelkens et al. 1997, p. 23; Bean 1960, pp. 74–75; V. Bérard 1892.

69. Carlsson 2004, 2010; Ma 1999, pp. 160–62, 235–42; Bracke 1993, pp. 22–23; Mitchell 1991, pp. 124–25.

70. Waelkens 2004, pp. 457–58; Waelkens et al. 1997, pp. 21–29; Belke and Mersich 1990, pp. 287–88; Mersich 1986, pp. 193–94. See also Waelkens and Vandeput 2007, p. 101.

71. Mitchell 1994a, p. 98.

72. Waelkens et al. 1997, pp. 22–23.

73. Waelkens 2004, pp. 457–58; Waelkens et al. 1997, pp. 23–25.

74. Waelkens and Vandeput 2007, p. 101; Waelkens 2004, pp. 457–58; Mitchell 1991, pp. 135, 139; 1998, p. 251; 1999, pp. 173–74; Waelkens et al. 1997, p. 23; Bean 1960, pp. 74–75; V. Bérard 1892.

75. Inscriptions in the Greek language reinforce the sense of hellenized political practices: Waelkens and Vandeput 2007, pp. 449–50; Vanhaverbeke and Waelkens 2005; Waelkens 2002, pp. 314–15, 317–21; 2004; Kosmetatou 1997; Bracke 1993, p. 28; Mitchell 1991, p. 143; 1998, pp. 243, 248.

76. Waelkens and Vandeput 2007, p. 99; Vanhaverbeke and Waelkens 2005, pp. 55–57; Waelkens 2002, p. 314; Kosmetatou 1997, pp. 8, 13–15, 19, 20, 22; Bracke 1993, pp. 17–20; H. Brandt 1992, pp. 33, 87–93. In the fourth century, Alexander may have founded the city of Kretopolis in Pisidia for mercenaries from Crete who had served in his army: Mitchell 1999, p. 175; Kosmetatou 1997, pp. 10–11; Sekunda 1997, pp. 217–22; D. French 1994, pp. 129–36. On mercenaries, see Sion-Jenkis 2001 with bibliography p. 19 n. 2. For military settlements, see Ma 2013, pp. 64–74.

77. Vanhaverbeke and Waelkens 2005, pp. 52–54; Waelkens 2002, pp. 314–15; 2004, pp. 46–66.

78. Thoneman 2013b. Kosmetatou (1997, pp. 24–36) notes the absence of honorary inscriptions for Pergamene officials and the persistence of some local coinage as indicative of local autonomy. See also Thoneman 2013a; Vanhaverbeke and Waelkens 2005, pp. 59–64.

79. Vanhaverbeke and Waelkens 2005, pp. 60–61.

80. Thoneman 2013b; Waelkens and Vandeput 2007, pp. 99–101; Ma 2000, pp. 160–82; on Pergamon specifically, see Virgilio 2008; Gruen 2000; Schalles 1985.

81. Vanhaverbeke and Waelkens 2005; Waelkens 2002, pp. 317–20. See also Thoneman 2013b, p. 43; H. Brandt 2004; Mitchell 1991, p. 143; 1998, p. 248; Kosmetatou 1997, especially pp. 24–36; Bracke 1993, pp. 17–18. For a broader discussion of Hellenistic peer polity interaction, see Ma 2003.

Notes

82. The width of the stairway can be determined from side walls that are still in situ. Waelkens (1993b, p. 9) reports that the steps were later replaced by three terraces. See also ibid., pp. 9–12, 19;Waelkens 1998, pp. 252–55; 2002, pp. 316–17; Vandeput 1997, pp. 21–22; Mitchell 1991, pp. 130, 131; Mitchell and Waelkens 1987, pp. 39, 42–43.

83. Mitchell and Waelkens 1987, p. 42. Vandeput will publish a study of the temple.

84. Waelkens and Vandeput 2007, p. 463;Waelkens 1989, pp. 84–85; 2002, pp. 316–17; Waelkens and Loots 2000, pp. 217, 227–28, 231, 246; Vandeput 1997, pp. 21–22; Mitchell and Waelkens 1987, pp. 42–43. Pergamon: Mengoli 2007; Becker 2003, pp. 154–62; Radt 1988, pp. 214–16, 218–22, 272–74; 1998, pp. 27–28; Schwandner 1990. Mamurt Kale, where an inscription of Philetairos on the temple's architrave provides a secure *terminus ante quem* and link to Pergamon: Ohlemutz 1940 (1968), pp. 174–81; Conze and Schazmann 1911. See also Williamson 2014, pp. 96–105; Agelidis 2009, pp. 49–51; Whitney 1994; Radt 1988, pp. 272–74.

85. Waelkens 1989, pp. 84–85; 1998, pp. 252–55; 2002, pp. 316–17; Waelkens and Loots 2000, pp. 217, 228–31. Waelkens has acknowledged the potential for Roman influence on architectural form during the Republic, but generally he has favored a Pergamene source for this kind of podium temple. See also Waelkens and Vandeput 2007, p. 101.

86. Waelkens 2002, p. 314.

CONCLUSION

1. Arnheim (1977, pp. 71–72) comments that "interspaces can be, and often are, visual objects in their own right."

2. Hellström 1988, p. 74; 1990, p. 243; 1991, pp. 304, 308.

3. Turner 1977, pp. 96–97, 126–65. Pilgrimage: Mylonopoulos 2006, 2008; Chaniotis 1995, especially pp. 154–63; 2006; Chankowski 2005; Elsner and Rutherford 2005; Kowalzig 2005.

4. Above, p. 45. Kritzas 1992, 2006.

5. Above, p. 56. Jost 1985, 1992, 1994.

6. Above, pp. 58–59. Williamson 2013, pp. 6–19; 2014, pp. 90–96; Hornblower 1982, pp. 13, 90–105. See also Dignas 2002, p. 3; Demand 1990, pp. 120–27.

7. Demand 1990, pp. 127–32 and n. 90; Hornblower 1982, pp. 103–4; Sherwin-White 1978, pp. 65–68.

8. Garwood 1991, p. 25.

9. Dignas 2002; Debord 1982.

10. Kreinath 2004.

11. Gauthier 1985, pp. 20, 25–26; Carstens 2009a. Herodotus (3.140, 8.85) and Thucydides (1.129.3) apply the term *euergetes* to those recognized by Persian kings for their generosity, but see also Meiggs and Lewis 1988, nos. 12, 15–17, for fifth-century inscriptions documenting more general use for an individual given recognition for his beneficence, often in the formulaic honorific phrase πρόξενος καὶ εὐεργέτης.

12. On the bonding effects of processions, with special attention to Hellenistic poleis: Chankowski 2005; Chaniotis 1995, 1997; Köhler 1996. Euergetism: Dignas 2002; Bringmann et al. 1995–2000; Kron 1996; van Bremen 1996, pp. 19–20 nn. 24–25; Bringmann 1993; Migeotte 1992; Veyne 1990 (1976); Gauthier 1985; Debord 1982.

13. Wikander 1992, p. 145 n. 18; Gauthier 1985, p. 57.

14. Cf. Thoneman 2013b, p. 43. Women as *euergetai*: Kron 1996. Van Bremen (1996, pp. 8, 12, 25, 37) dates the earliest examples of non-royal female *euergetai* to the late third century.

15. Migeotte 1992, 1995 on *epidosis*; Debord 1982. See also van Bremen 1996, p. 37. Dignas 2002 explains the three-way relationship among poleis, sanctuaries, and kings in Hellenistic Asia Minor.

16. Basso 1996, p. 55; Casey 1996, pp. 22, 24, 36.

APPENDIX: HELLENISTIC ITALY

1. The scholarship on Romanization is extensive and still growing. For a brief summary, see Stek 2009, pp. 1–34; van Dommeln and Terrenato 2007b. Recent attention has shifted away from viewing events and practices outside of the city of Rome in relation to Roman models, and toward an approach that considers indigenous behavior first, before describing the effects of interaction with Rome. See articles in Colivicchi 2011; Wallace-Hadrill 2008, especially pp. 17–28; Dench 2003; Curti, Dench, and Patterson 1996, especially pp. 181–88.

2. Colivicchi 2011; Gros 1996, pp. 127–40.

3. Bernstein 1998, especially pp. 227–311; 2007; Curti, Dench, and Patterson 1996; Coarelli 1987, pp. 29–30.

4. Mitens 1993; Lauter 1976. Cf. Sear 2006, pp. 49–50.

5. Bernstein 1998, 2007.

6. Italians from central Italy in the Aegean: Hatzfeld 1912, 1919; see A. J. N. Wilson 1966, pp. 85–126, 152–64, for perspective on Hatzfeld. On Italian merchants on Delos, see Stek 2009, pp. 44–45, 48; Lomas 1996, pp. 52–53, 66–68; 2004, pp. 218–19; MacKay 2004, pp. 92, 100; Coarelli 1987, pp. 30,

66, 79–80, 101; Keaveney 1987, pp. 3–19; Bodei Giglioni 1977, pp. 72–76; La Regina 1976, pp. 229–30; van Wonterghem 1976, p. 146. Scholars continue to identify families and individuals known from written testimonia in central Italy (Pietrabbondante, Praeneste, Tivoli, and elsewhere) who are also recorded in inscriptions from Delos in its floruit (167–88 B.C.), as well as other sites in the Aegean region: Wallace-Hadrill 2008, pp. 113–16, 126, 143; Cébeillac-Gervasoni and Lamoine 2003; Müller and Hasenohr 2002; Le Dinahet 2001; Solin 1982.

7. Wallace-Hadrill 2008, p. 113; Cébeillac-Gervasoni 2002; Deniaux 2002.

8. Dench 1995, pp. 150–51, 218–21; Kuttner 1995. The papers in Colivicchi 2011 document the physical remains of comparable developments elsewhere in south Italy and Sicily.

9. Emphasized recently by Stek 2009 as a correction to assertively postcolonial views of Italic autonomy.

10. Stek 2009, especially pp. 52, 220–21. Many of Campagna's (2011) observations about circumstances in northwest Sicily pertain to elites in central Italy as well.

11. *Vitr.* 3.2.5; La Rocca 2011; Coarelli 1987, p. 13; Almagro-Gorbea 1982, pp. 87–124, 614; Gros 1973, 1976, 1978. See n. 18 below.

12. The terms are εἶδος and τύπον: ἡσθεὶς δὲ τῷ θεάτρῳ περιεγράψατο τὸ εἶδος αὐτοῦ καὶ τὸν τύπον, ὡς ὅμοιον ἀπεργασόμενος τὸ ἐν Ῥώμῃ, μεῖζον δὲ καὶ σεμνότερον. "And being pleased with the theatre, he had sketches and plans of it made for him, that he might build one like it in Rome, only larger and more splendid" (translation Perrin 1968).

13. Van Wonterghem 1973; 1976, pp. 145–47; 1984; 1994. Cf. Coarelli 1985, pp. 468–71.

14. Van Wonterghem 1976, p. 151; 1984, pp. 246–47, 250–51; La Regina 1966b. The shrine is a 5 by 6 m building on a stone socle with mudbrick walls. It has a mosaic floor and remains of first-style wall painting.

15. Coarelli 1987.

16. Hanson 1959. He described the form less in terms of its origin and more in terms of its outcome in later Roman architecture, especially the Theater of Pompey. See also I. Nielsen 2002, pp. 180–96; Almagro-Gorbea 1982, pp. 62–63, 615.

17. Stek 2009; Bernstein 1998, 2007; Sear 2006, p. 23; Hanson 1959.

18. Date: Almagro-Gorbea 1982, pp. 610–11. Almagro-Gorbea proposes that the architect Hermodorus of Salamis on Cyprus was the agent who contributed such a unity of vision to Italic sanctuaries. See also Coarelli 1987, pp. 11–21, especially p. 13.

19. Coarelli 1987, pp. 16–18; Almagro-Gorbea 1982, pp. 48–55; Lauter 1968. I. Nielsen (2002, pp. 181–83) extrapolates from published dimensions of the cavea-shaped area to estimate space for 1,200 spectators.

20. Coarelli 1987, p. 15; Almagro-Gorbea 1982, pp. 58, 583, 586.

21. We have no evidence that builders in central Italy knew of Temple M at Selinus, set above a stepped slope leading to an altar: Pompeo 1999.

22. Almagro-Gorbea 1982, pp. 591–92, 616.

23. Stek 2009, pp. 40–46; Wallace-Hadrill 2008, pp. 137–43; Coarelli and La Regina 1984, pp. 240–41; La Regina 1976, pp. 223–30, 244–48; Strazzulla and di Marco 1972, pp. 35, 49–56; Hatzfeld 1912, 1919.

24. I. Nielsen (2002, p. 183) estimated a capacity of 1,000. See also Sear 2006, p. 138; Crawford 1981 p. 159; La Regina 1976, p. 233; Lauter 1976.

25. Torelli 1995 [1986], p. 11; Coarelli and La Regina 1984, p. 252; Strazzulla and di Marco 1972.

26. Dench 1995, pp. 136–39. The largest (central) altar is preserved, and one of the (presumably two) symmetrically placed smaller altars. Torelli (1999, pp. 129–30) noted the combination of Campanian and Latin features in this Etruscan-style temple as indicative of the complexity of Romanization in architecture; see also La Regina 1976, pp. 229–33.

27. Lancaster 2007, pp. 3–6; Coarelli 1987. Parallels with construction at these sites suggests that Sulmo's terrace was extended during the first century, as it was supported by massive vaults in *opus incertum* and *opus quadratum*: van Wonterghem 1976, p. 151; 1984. The second-century sanctuary of Asklepios at Fregellae, another large complex with minimal use of concrete (but no known monumental steps), also has documented connections with the Aegean: Coarelli 1987, p. 30.

28. Gros 1996, pp. 138–40.

29. The scholarship on this site, especially its date, is extensive: Wallace-Hadrill 2008, pp. 106–16; Merz 2001; Coarelli 1987, pp. 35–84; Bodei Giglioni 1977, pp. 67–70; Kähler 1958a; 1958b; Fasolo and Gullini 1953.

30. Fasolo and Gullini 1953, pp. 53–56, 201–8.

31. Lauter 1979, p. 412; Kähler 1958a; Fasolo and Gullini 1953, pp. 20, 67–70. Merz (2001, pp. 20–21) questioned whether the ramps were in fact a later addition to the sanctuary.

Notes

32. Kähler 1958b, pp. 375–76.

33. Hatzfeld 1912. See also Wallace-Hadrill 2008, p. 113; Coarelli 1987, pp. 66, 79; Bodei Giglioni 1977, pp. 73–76; A. J. N. Wilson 1966, p. 110. See above n. 6 for additional references.

34. Inscriptions: Giuliani 1970, 2009; Coarelli 1987, p. 101; 1993, pp. 78–79; Hatzfeld 1912, p. 113. Sanctuary: Giuliani 1970, pp. 190–97; 2009; Reggiani 1998; Gros 1996, pp. 139–40; Coarelli 1987, pp. 85–112; 1993, pp. 77–85; Bodei Giglioni 1977, pp. 61–67, 72–76.

35. Giuliani 2009; Reggiani 1998, pp. 30–37.

36. Giuliani 1970, p. 194; 2009; Coarelli 1987, p. 91. The fact that the temple is not precisely in the center of the framed court suggests that its location may reflect a sacred spot established at an earlier time.

37. Restoration of the theater: P. Marconi 2008; Reggiani 1998, pp. 38, 42–61.

38. For current reconstructions of this complicated, poorly preserved site, see Giuliani 2009; also Giuliani 1970, pp. 196–97; Coarelli 1993, p. 80.

39. This arrangement has been compared to that of the sanctuary of the Syrian Gods at Delos (built 128–108 B.C.), but Will describes it as reflecting widespread Hellenistic eclecticism in combining formal elements such as porticoes, courts, and theaters, to which I would add stairs: Will 1985, especially pp. 113, 121–22.

Bibliography

Adams, W. Y. 1988. "Archaeological Classification: Theory versus Practice." *Antiquity* 61, pp. 40–56.

Adams, W. Y., and E. W. Adams. 1991. *Archaeological Typology and Practical Reality: A Dialectical Approach to Artifact Classification and Sorting.* Cambridge.

Agelidis, S. 2009. "Cult and Landscape at Pergamon," in Gates, Morin, and Zimmerman 2009, pp. 47–54.

Akurgal, E. 1961. *Die Kunst Anatoliens.* Berlin.

———, ed. 1978. *The 10th International Congress of Classical Archaeology, Ankara-Izmir 23–30/IX/1973.* Ankara.

———. 1990. *Ancient Ruins and Civilizations of Turkey.* 7th ed. Istanbul.

Alcock, S., and R. Osborne, eds. 1994. *Placing the Gods: Sanctuaries and Sacred Space in Ancient Greece.* Oxford.

Allen, H. L. 1970. "Excavations at Morgantina (Serra Orlando) 1967–1969: Preliminary Report X." *AJA* 74, pp. 359–83.

Almagro-Gorbea, M., ed. 1982. *El Santuario de Juno en Gabii.* Rome.

Alroth, B. 1998. "Changes in Votive Practice? From Classical to Hellenistic: Some Examples," in Hägg 1998, pp. 217–28.

Amandry, P. 1952. "Observations sur les monuments de L'Héraion d'Argos." *Hesperia* 21, pp. 222–74.

———. 1977. "Notes de topographie et d'architecture delphiques." *BCH Suppl.* 4, pp. 179–228.

———. 1978. "Notes de topographie et d'architecture delphiques." *BCH* 102, pp. 221–41.

———. 1980. "Sur les concours argiens," in *Études Argiennes. BCH Suppl.* 6, pp. 211–53.

Amyx, D. A. 1988. *Corinthian Vase Painting of the Archaic Period.* Berkeley, Los Angeles, and London.

Andreae, B. 1959. "Funde und Grabungen in Mittelitalien 1949–1959: Sulmona." *AA*, pp. 255–58.

Anti, C., and L. Polacco. 1969. *Nuove ricerche sui teatri greci arcaici.* Padua.

Apostolakou, V. 2003. Λατώ. Athens.

Applebaum, S. 1957. "A Lamp and Other Remains of the Jewish Community of Cyrene." *IEJ* 7, pp. 154–62.

Arafat, K. W. 1995. "Pausanias and the Temple of Hera at Olympia." *BSA* 90, pp. 461–73.

Arias, P. E. 1934. *Il teatro greco fuori di Atene.* Florence.

———. 1962. *A History of 1000 Years of Greek Vase Painting.* Translated and revised by B. Shefton. New York.

Arnheim, R. 1977. *The Dynamics of Architectural Form.* Berkeley and Los Angeles.

Ashmore, W., and A. B. Knapp, eds. 1999. *Archaeologies of Landscape: Contemporary Perspectives.* Oxford.

Ayiter, K, 1978. "Treppen und Stufen bei phrygischen Felsdenkmälern," in Şahin, Schwerthein, and Wagner 1978, pp. 99–106.

Bagnall, R. S., and P. Davoli. 2011. "Archaeological Work on Hellenistic and Roman Egypt, 2000–2009." *AJA* 115, pp. 103–57.

Bakır, G. 1981. *Sophilos: Ein Beitrag zu seinem Stil.* Mainz.

Balthis, A. C. 2006. "Built Altars and Religious Ritual in Hellenistic East Greece," in *Visualizing Rituals: Critical Analysis of Art and Ritual Practice*, ed. J. K. Werts. Cambridge, pp. 34–43.

Bankel, H. 1997. "Knidos, der hellenistische Rundtempel und sein Altar Vorbericht." *AA*, pp. 52–71.

———. 1999. "*Scamilli inpares* at an Early Hellenistic Ionic Propylon at Knidos—New Evidence for the Construction of a Curvature," in Haselberger 1999, pp. 127–38.

———. 2004. "Knidos: Das Triopion—Zur Topographie des Stammesheiligtums der dorischen Hexapolis," in Schwandner and Rheidt 2004, pp. 100–113.

———. 2009. "Versatzmarken am Propylon des Heiligtums für Apollon Karneios in Knidos." *Byzas* 9, pp. 1–19.

Baran, A. 2009. "Karian Architecture Before the Hekatomnids," in Rumscheid 2009a, pp. 291–313.

———. 2010a. "The Sacred Way to Labraunda and Ancient Spring Houses," in Edgü, Kuzucu, and Ural 2010, pp. 121–35.

———. 2010b. "The Sacred Way to Labraunda and Ancient Spring Houses," in van Bremen and Carbon 2010, pp. 121–37.

———. 2011. "The Sacred Way and the Spring Houses of Labraunda," in Karlsson and Carlsson 2011, pp. 51–98.

Barrett, J. C. 1988. "Fields of Discourse: Reconstructing a Social Archaeology."*Critique of Anthropology* 7, pp. 5–16.

———. 1994a. "Defining Domestic Space in the Bronze Age of Southern Britain," in Parker Pearson and Richards 1994, pp. 87–97.

———. 1994b. *Fragments from Antiquity: An Archaeology of Social Life in Britain 2900–1200 B.C.* Oxford.

———. 2000. "A Thesis on Agency," in Dobres and Robb 2000, pp. 61–68.

———. 2001. "The Duality of Structure and the Problem of Agency: The Archaeological Record," in *Archaeological Theory Today*, ed. I. Hodder. Oxford, pp. 141–64.

———. 2002. Review of M. B. Schiffer, *Social Theory in Archaeology*. *AJA* 106, pp. 317–18.

Basso, K. H. 1996. "Wisdom Sits in Places: Notes on a Western Apache Landscape," in Feld and Basso 1996, pp. 53–90.

Bauer, H. 1973. *Korinthische Kapitelle des 4. und 3. Jahrhunderts v. Chr.* Berlin.

Bean, G. E. 1959. "Notes and Inscriptions from Pisidia: Part I." *AnatSt* 9, pp. 67–117.

———. 1960. "Notes and Inscriptions from Pisidia: Part II." *AnatSt* 10, pp. 43–82.

———. 1966. *Aegean Turkey*. London.

———. 1980. *Turkey beyond the Maeander*. 2nd ed. New York and London.

Bean, G. E., and J. M. Cook. 1952. "The Cnidia." *BSA* 47, pp. 171–212.

———. 1955. "The Halicarnassus Peninsula." *BSA* 50, pp. 85–171.

———. 1957. "The Carian Coast." *BSA* 52, pp. 58–146.

Beard, M., and M. Crawford 1985. *Rome in the Late Republic*. Ithaca.

Beazley, J. D. 1957. "ΕΛΕΝΗΣ ΑΠΑΙΤΗΣΙΣ." *ProcBritAc* 43, pp. 233–44.

Becker, T. 2003. *Griechische Stufenanlagen: Untersuchungen zur Architektur, Entwicklungsgeschichte, Funktion und Repräsentation*. Munster.

Bélis, A. 1995. "Cithares, citharistes, et citharodes en Grèce." *CRAI*, pp. 1025–65.

Belke, K., and Mersich, N. 1990. *Phrygien und Pisidien: Tabula Imperii Byzantini 7. DenkschrWien* 211. Vienna.

Bell, C. 1992. *Ritual Theory, Ritual Practice*. New York and Oxford.

———. 1997. *Ritual: Perspectives and Dimensions*. New York and Oxford.

Bell, M. 1984–85. "Recenti scavi nell'agora di Morgantina." *Kokalos* 30–31, pp. 501–20.

———. 1988. "Excavations at Morgantina, 1980–1985: Preliminary Report XII." *AJA* 92, pp. 313–42.

Bell, S., and G. Davies, eds. 2004. *Games and Festivals in Classical Antiquity. BAR International Series* 1220. London.

Bentz, M., and N. Eschbach, eds. 2001. *Panathenaïka: Symposion zu den Panathenäischen Preisamphoren, Rauischholzhausen 25.11.–29.11 1998*. Darmstadt.

Bérard, C. 1977. "Architecture et politique: Reception d'une ambassade en Grèce archaïque," in *Études de Lettres* series 3, vol. 10, pp. 1–25.

Bérard, V. 1892. "Inscriptions d'Asie Mineure." *BCH* 16, pp. 434–36.

Berges, D. 1994. "Alt-Knidos und Neu-Knidos." *IstMitt* 44, pp. 5–16.

Berges, D., et al. 2006. *Knidos: Beiträge zur Geschichte der archaischen Stadt*. Mainz am Rhein.

Berges, D., and N. Tuna. 2000. "Das Apollonheiligtum von Emecik: Bericht über die Ausgrabungen 1998 und 1999." *IstMitt* 50, pp. 171–214.

Bergmann, B., and C. Kondoleon, eds. 1999. *The Art of Ancient Spectacle*. Washington, DC.

Bergquist, B. 1967. *The Archaic Greek Temenos: A Study of Structure and Function*. Lund.

———. 1973. *Herakles on Thasos: The Archaeological, Literary and Epigraphic Evidence for His Sanctuary, Status and Cult Reconsidered*. Uppsala.

———. 1992. "The Archaic Temenos in Western Greece," in Schachter 1992, pp. 109–52.

———. 1998. "Feasting of Worshippers or Temple and Sac-

Bibliography

rifice? The Case of Herakleion on Thasos," in Hägg 1998, pp. 57–72.

Berndt, D. 1997. "Keine kultische Treppe." *IstMitt* 47, pp. 449–51.

———. 2002. *Midasstadt in Phrygien: Eine sagenwobene Stätte im anatolischen Hochland*. Mainz.

Berndt-Ersöz, S. 2006. *Phrygian Rock-Cut Shrines: Structure, Function, and Cult-Practice*. Leiden.

———. 2009. "Sacred Space in Iron Age Phrygia," in Gates, Morin, and Zimmerman 2009, pp. 11–20.

Bernstein, F. 1998. *Ludi publici: Untersuchungen zur Entstehung und Entwicklung der öffentlichen Spiele im republikanischen Rom*. Stuttgart.

———. 2007. "Complex Rituals: Games and Processions in Republican Rome," in *A Companion to Roman Religion*, ed. J. Rüpke. Oxford, pp. 222–34.

Berthold, R. M. 1980. "Fourth Century Rhodes." *Historia* 29, pp. 32–49.

———. 1984. *Rhodes in the Hellenistic Age*. Ithaca and London.

Beyer, I. 1976. *Die Tempel von Dreros und Prinias A und die Chronologie der kretischen Kunst des 8. und 7. Jhs. v. Chr.* Freiburg.

Bieber, M. 1961. *The History of the Greek and Roman Theater*. 2nd revised ed. Princeton.

Billot, M.-F. 1997. "Recherches archéologiques récentes à l'Héraion d'Argos," in *HÉRA: Images, espaces, cultes*, ed. J. de la Genière. Naples, pp. 11–81.

Bingöl, O. 1998. *Magnesia am Mäander*. Ankara.

———. 2005. "Neue Forschungen in Magnesia am Mäander," in Schwertheim and Winter 2005, pp. 165–69.

Bintliff, J., ed. 2004. *A Companion to Archaeology*. Oxford.

Birge, D. 1994. "Sacred Groves and the Nature of Apollo," in *Apollo: Origins and Influences*, ed. J. Solomon. Tucson and London, pp. 9–19.

Bispham, E., and C. Smith, eds. 2000. *Religion in Archaic and Republican Rome and Italy: Evidence and Experience*. Chicago and London.

Blackmon, D. J. 1966. "The Harbour at Perachora." *BSA* 61, pp. 192–94.

Blanck, H. 1970. "Funde und Grabungen in Mittelitalien 1959–1969: Pietrabbondante (Campobasso), Sulmona." *AA*, pp. 335–45.

Blegen, C. W. 1937. *Prosymna*. Cambridge.

Blid, J. 2006–7. "New Research on Carian Labraunda in Late Antiquity." *OpAth* 31–32, pp. 231–55.

———. 2010. "Roman and Byzantine Labraunda," in Edgü, Kuzucu, and Ural 2010, pp. 81–92.

———. 2011. "Recent Research on the Churches of Labraunda," in Karlsson and Carlsson 2011, pp. 99–107.

Blinkenberg, C. 1931. *Lindos: Fouilles de l'Acropole 1902–1914*, vol. 1.1: *Les petits objets*. Berlin and Copenhagen.

Blinkenberg, C., and K. F. Kinch. 1941. *Lindos: Fouilles de l'Acropole 1902–1914*, vol. 2.1: *Inscriptions*. Berlin and Copenhagen.

Blümel, W. 1992. *Die Inschriften von Knidos. Inschriften griechischer Städte aus Kleinasien* 41. Bonn.

Boardman, J. 2000. *Persia and the West: An Archaeological Investigation of the Genesis of Achaemenid Art*. New York.

Bodei Giglioni, G. 1977. "Pecunia Fanatica: L'incidenza economica dei templi laziali." *RivStorIt* 89, pp. 33–76.

Boegehold, A. L. 1967. "Philokleon's Court." *Hesperia* 36, pp. 111–20.

———. 1995. *The Athenian Agora*, vol. 28: *The Lawcourts at Athens*. Princeton.

Bohtz, C. H. 1981. *Altertümer von Pergamon*, vol. 13: *Das Demeter-Heiligtum*. Berlin.

Bömer, F. 1952. *RE* s.v. "*Pompa*," cols. 1878–1994.

Bookidis, N. 1990. "Ritual Dining in the Sanctuary of Demeter and Kore at Corinth: Some Questions," in Murray 1990, pp. 86–94.

———. 1993. "Ritual Dining in the Sanctuary of Demeter and Kore at Corinth," in Marinatos and Hägg 1993, pp. 45–61.

———. 2003. "The Sanctuaries of Corinth," in Williams and Bookidis 2003, pp. 247–60.

———. 2010. *Corinth 18.5: The Sanctuary of Demeter and Kore; The Terracotta Sculpture*. Princeton.

Bookidis, N., and J. E. Fisher. 1972. "Sanctuary of Demeter and Kore on Acrocorinth." *Hesperia* 41, pp. 283–331.

Bookidis, N., J. Hansen, and P. Goldberg. 1999. "Dining in the Sanctuary of Demeter and Kore at Corinth." *Hesperia* 68, pp. 1–54.

Bookidis, N., and R. Stroud. 1987. *Demeter and Persephone in Ancient Corinth*. Princeton.

———. 1997. *Corinth 18.3: The Sanctuary of Demeter and Kore; Topography and Architecture*. Princeton.

Borchhardt, J. 1970. "Das Heroon von Limyra: Grabmal des lykischen Königs Perikles." *AA*, pp. 353–90.

———. 1976. *Die Bauskulptur des Heroons von Limyra*. *IstForsch* 32. Berlin.

Bosnakis, D., K. Hallof, and K. Rigsby, eds. 2010. *Inscriptiones Coi insulae: Decreta, epistulae, edicta, tituli sacri. IG* XII 4.1. Berlin and New York.

Bourbou, Ch., and A. Tsilipakou. 2009. "Investigating the Human Past of Greece during the 6th–7th centuries A.D.," in Schepartz, Fox, and Bourbou 2009, pp. 121–36.

Bourdieu, P. 1984. *Distinction: A Social Critique of the Judgment of Taste*. London.

———. 1986. "The Forms of Capital," in *Handbook of Theory and Research for the Sociology of Education*, ed. J. G. Richardson. New York, Westport, and London, pp. 241–58.

———. 1990. *The Logic of Practice*. Translated by R. Nice. Cambridge.

———. 1993. *The Field of Cultural Production: Essays on Art and Literature*. New York.

Bracke, H. 1993. "Pisidia in Hellenistic Times (334–25 B.C.)," in Waelkens 1993a, pp. 15–32.

Bradeen, D. W., and M. F. McGregor, eds. 1974. *ΦΟΡΟΣ: Tribute to Benjamin Dean Meritt*. Locust Valley NY.

Brand, H. 2000. *Griechische Musikanten im Kult: Von der Frühzeit bis zum Beginn der Spätklassik*. Dettelbach.

Brandt, H. 1992. *Gesellschaft und Wirtschaft Pamphyliens und Pisidiens im Altertum*. Bonn.

———. 2004. "Adada: Eine pisidische Kleinstadt in hellenistischer und römischer Zeit." *Historia* 55, pp. 385–413.

———. 2007. "Hellenization and Romanization in Pisidia? Two Case Studies: Adada and Pednelissos." Paper delivered before the AIA Narragansett Chapter, Providence RI, April 5.

Brandt, H., and F. Kolb. 2005. *Lycia and Pamphylia: Eine römische Provinz im Südwesten Kleinasiens*. Mainz am Rhein.

Brandt, J. R. 2012. "Content and Form: Some Considerations on Greek Festivals and Archaeology," in Brandt and Iddeng 2012, pp. 139–98.

Brandt, J. R., and J. W. Iddeng, eds. 2012. *Greek and Roman Festivals: Content, Meaning, and Practice*. Oxford.

Bremer, J. M. 1981. "Greek Hymns," in Versnel 1981, pp. 193–215.

Bremmer, J. 1992. "Walking, Standing, and Sitting in Ancient Greek Culture," in Bremmer and Roodenburg 1992, pp. 15–35.

———. 1998. "'Religion,' 'Ritual' and the Opposition 'Sacred vs. Profane': Notes towards a Terminological 'Genealogy,'" in *Ansichten griechischen Rituale*, ed. F. Graf. Leiden, pp. 9–33.

Bremmer, J., and H. Roodenburg, eds. 1992. *A Cultural History of Gesture*. Ithaca.

Bresson, A. 1988. "Richesse et pouvoir à Lindos à l'époque hellénistique," in Dietz and Papachristodoulou 1988, pp. 145–54.

Bresson, A., and R. Descat, eds. 2001. *Les cités d'Asie Mineure occidentale au IIe siècle*. Bordeaux.

Brewster, H. 1993. *Classical Anatolia: The Glory of Hellenism*. London.

Bringmann, K. 1993. "The King as Benefactor: Some Remarks on an Ideal Kingship in the Age of Hellenism," in Bulloch, Gruen, Long, and Stewart 1993, pp. 7–24.

Bringmann, K., H. von Steuben, W. Ameling, and B. Schmidt-Dounas. 1995–2000. *Schenkungen hellenistischer Herrscher an griechische Städte und Heiligtümer*. 3 vols. Berlin.

Brogan, T. M. 2003. "Liberation Honors: Athenian Monuments from Antigonid Victories in Their Immediate and Broader Contexts," in *The Macedonians in Athens 322–229 B.C.*, ed. O. Palagia and S. V. Tracy. Oxford, pp. 194–205.

Broneer, O. 1941. *The Lion Monument at Amphipolis*. Cambridge MA.

Brouskari, M. 1997. *The Monuments of the Acropolis*. Athens.

Brulé, P. 1987. *La fille d'Athènes: La religion des filles à Athènes à l'époque classique; Mythes, cultes et société*. Paris.

Brumfiel, E. 2004. "On the Archaeology of Choice: Agency Studies as a Research Stratagem," in Bintliff 2004, pp. 249–55.

Bruneau, P. 1969. "Prolongements de la technique des mosaïques de Galets en Grèce." *BCH* 93, pp. 308–32.

Brunet, M., A. Archondidou, J.-Y. Empereur, A. Muller, D. Mulliez, J.-Y. Perreault, and F. Blondé. 1987. "Thasos." *BCH* 111, pp. 619–27.

Brunet, M., J. des Courtils, J.-J. Maffre, A. Muller, D. Mulliez, A. Pariente, J.-Y. Perreault, and F. Blondé. 1986. "Thasos." *BCH* 110, pp. 790–812.

Bruns-Özgan, C. 1995. "Fries eines hellenistischen Altars in Knidos." *JdI* 110, pp. 239–73.

Bulloch, A., E. S. Gruen, A. A. Long, and A. Stewart, eds. 1993. *Images and Ideologies: Self-Definition in the Hellenistic World*. Berkeley, Los Angeles, and London.

Bundgaard, J. 1957. *Mnesicles: A Greek Architect at Work*. Copenhagen.

Bibliography

Bundrick, S. 2005. *Music and Image in Classical Athens.* Cambridge.

Buraselis, K. 2004. "Some Remarks on the Koan *Asylia* (242 BC) against Its International Background," in Höghammar 2004, pp. 15–20.

———. 2012. "Appended Festivals: The Coordination and Combination of Traditional Civic and Ruler Cult Festivals in the Hellenistic and Roman East," in Brandt and Iddeng 2012, pp. 247–65.

Burkert, W. 1983. *Homo Necans: The Anthropology of Ancient Greek Sacrificial Ritual and Myth.* Berkeley.

———. 1985. *Greek Religion.* Translated by J. Raffan. Cambridge MA.

———. 2012. "Ancient Views on Festivals: A Case of Near Eastern Mediterranean Koine," in Brandt and Iddeng 2012, pp. 39–51.

Buschor, E. 1957. "Altsamischer Bauschmuck." *AM* 72, pp. 1–34.

Buschor, E., and Schleif, H. 1933. "Heraion von Samos: Der Altarplatz der Frühzeit." *AM* 58, pp. 146–73.

Buxton, R. G. A., ed. 2000. *Oxford Readings in Greek Religion.* Oxford.

Büyükkolanci, M. 1998. *Adada: Pisidia'Da antik bir kent. Göltas Kültür Dizisi* 5. Ankara.

Cahill, N. 1988. "Taş Kule: A Persian-Period Tomb near Phokaia." *AJA* 92, pp. 481–501.

Camp, J. M. 1986. *The Athenian Agora: Excavations in the Heart of Classical Athens.* London.

———. 2001. *The Archaeology of Athens.* New Haven and London.

Campagna, L. 2011. "Exploring Social and Cultural Change in *Provincia Sicilia*: Reflections on the Study of Urban Landscapes," in Colivicchi 2011, pp. 161–83.

Capini, S. 1994. "Pietrabbondante." *EAA* Suppl. 2.4, pp. 371–75.

Carlsson, S. 2004. "Koan Democracy in Context," in Höghammar 2004, pp. 109–18.

———. 2010. *Hellenistic Democracies: Freedom, Independence and Political Procedure in Some East Greek City-States.* Stuttgart.

Carstens, A. M. 2009a. *Karia and the Hekatomnids: The Creation of a Dynasty. BAR International Series* 1943. Oxford.

———. 2009b. "Tomb Cult and Tomb Architecture in Karia," in Rumscheid 2009a, pp. 377–95.

———. 2011. "Achaemenids in Labraunda: A Case of Imperial Presence in a Rural Sanctuary in Karia," in Karlsson and Carlsson 2011, pp. 121–31.

———. 2013. "Karian Identity: Game of Opportunistic Politics or a Case of Creolisation?" in Henry 2013a, pp. 209–15.

Carter, J. C. 1983. *The Sculpture of the Sanctuary of Athena Polias at Priene.* London.

Casey, E. S. 1993. *Getting Back into Place: Toward a Renewed Understanding of the Place-World.* Bloomington and Indianapolis.

———. 1996. "How to Get from Space to Place in a Fairly Short Stretch of Time: Phenomenological Prolegomena," in Feld and Basso 1996, pp. 13–51.

Castagnoli, F. 1977. "Les sanctuaires du Latium archaïque." *CRAI,* pp. 460–76.

———. 1980. "Santuari e culti nel Lazio arcaico." *Archeologia Laziale* 3, pp. 164–67.

Catling, H. 1996–97. "Archaeology in Greece 1986–87, Amphipolis." *AR 1996–1997,* p. 43.

Cavalier, L., and P. Mora. 2011. "Présentation du modèle 3D d'Alazeytin." *Anatolia Antiqua* 19, pp. 377–84.

Cébeillac-Gervasoni, M. 2002. "Note relative aux élites du Latium et de a Campanie et à leurs rapports avec la Méditerranée orientale," in Müller and Hasenohr 2002, pp. 21–28.

Cébeillac-Gervasoni, M., and L. Lamoine, eds. 2003. *Les élites et leurs facettes: Les élites locales dans le monde hellénistique et romain.* Rome and Clermont-Ferrand.

Centre Jean Bérard. 1991. *La Romanisation du Samnium aux IIe et Ie siècles av. J.C.* Naples.

Chaniotis, A. 1995. "Sich selbst feiern? Städtische Feste des Hellenismus im Spannungsfeld von Religion und Politik," in Wörrle and Zanker 1995, pp. 147–68.

———. 1997. "Theatricality beyond the Theater. Staging Public Life in the Hellenistic World." *Pallas* 47, pp. 219–59.

———. 2006. "Rituals between Norms and Emotions: Rituals as Shared Experience and Memory," in Stavrianopoulou 2006c, pp. 211–38.

———. 2007. "Theatre Rituals," in P. Wilson 2007, pp. 48–66.

———. 2011. *Ritual Dynamics in the Ancient Mediterranean: Agency, Emotion, Gender, Representation. Heidelberger Althistorische Beiträge und Epigraphische Studien* 49. Stuttgart.

Chankowski, A. S. 2005. "Processions et cérémonies

d'accueil: Une image de la cité de la basse époque hellénistique," in *Citoyenneté et participation à la basse époque hellénistique*, ed. P. Fröhlich and C. Müller. Geneva, pp. 185–206.

Christopoulos, M. 1992. "ΟΡΓΙΑ ΑΠΟΡΡΗΤΑ: Quelques remarques sur les rites des Plyntéries." *Kernos* 5, pp. 27–39.

Cianfarani, V. 1960. *Santuari nel Sannio*. Chieti.

Clinton, K. 1993. "The Sanctuary of Demeter and Kore at Eleusis," in Marinatos and Hägg 1993, pp. 110–24.

——. 1994. "The Eleusinian Mysteries and Panhellenism in Democratic Athens," in Coulson et al. 1994, pp. 161–72.

Coarelli, F., ed. 1978. *Studi su Praeneste*. Perugia.

——. 1985. *Italia Centrale. Guide Archeologiche Laterza*. Rome.

——. 1987. *I santuari del Lazio in età repubblicana*. Rome.

——. 1993. *Lazio. Guide Archeologiche Laterza*. Rome.

Coarelli, F., and A. La Regina. 1984. *Abruzzo, Molise. Guide Archeologiche Laterza* 9. Rome and Bari.

Coarelli, F., D. Musti, and H. Solin. 1982. *Delo e l'Italia. OpFin* 2. Rome.

Coben, L. S. 2006. "Other Cuzcos: Replicated Theaters of Inka Power," in Inomata and Coben 2006a, pp. 223–59.

Cole, S. G. 2004. *Landscapes, Gender, and Ritual Space*. Berkeley and Los Angeles.

Colivicchi, F., ed. 2011. *Local Cultures of South Italy and Sicily in the Late Republican Period: Between Hellenism and Rome. JRA Suppl.* 83. Portsmouth RI.

Connelly, J. B. 2007. *Portrait of a Priestess: Women and Ritual in Ancient Greece*. Princeton and Oxford.

Connor, W. R. 1987. "Tribes, Festivals and Processions: Civic Ceremonial and Political Manipulation in Archaic Greece." *JHS* 107, pp. 40–50.

——. 1988. "'Sacred' and 'Secular': Ἱερὰ καὶ ὅσια and the Classical Athenian Concept of the State." *Ancient Society* 19, pp. 161–88.

Conze, A., and P. Schazmann. 1911. *Mamurt-Kaleh: Ein Tempel der Göttermutter unweit Pergamon*. Berlin.

Cook, J. M. 1975. Review of Tuchelt 1973. *JHS* 95, p. 274.

Corbet, R., R. Layton, and J. Tanner. 2004. "Archaeology and Art," in Bintliff 2004, pp. 357–79.

Coulson, W. D. E., O. Palagia, T. L. Shear, H. A. Shapiro, and F. J. Frost. 1994. *The Archaeology of Athens and Attica under the Democracy*. Oxford.

Coulson, W., and H. Kyrieleis, eds. 1992. Πρακτικά συμποσίου Ὀλυμπιακῶν Ἀγώνων: *Proceedings of an International Symposium on the Olympic Games, 1988*. Athens.

Coulton, J. J. 1964. "The Stoa by the Harbour at Perachora." *BSA* 59, pp. 100–131.

——. 1967. "The West Court at Perachora." *BSA* 62, pp. 353–71.

——. 1968. "The Stoa at the Amphiaraion, Oropos." *BSA* 63, pp. 147–83.

——. 1976. *The Architectural Development of the Greek Stoa*. Oxford.

——. 1982. *Greek Architects at Work: Problems of Structure and Design*. Ithaca.

Crampa, J. 1969. *Labraunda III.1: The Greek Inscriptions, Part I: 1–12 (Period of Olympichus)*. Lund.

——. 1972. *Labraunda III.2: The Greek Inscriptions, Part II: 13–133*. Stockholm.

Crawford, M. H. 1981. "Italy and Rome." *JRS* 71, pp. 153–60.

Cross, I., and Watson, A. 2006. "Acoustics and the Human Experience of Socially-Organized Sound," in Scarre and Lawson 2006, pp. 107–16.

Crowther, C. 2004. "The Dating of Koan Hellenistic Inscriptions," in Höghammar 2004, pp. 21–60.

Crumley, C. 1999. "Sacred Landscapes: Constructed and Conceptualized," in Ashmore and Knapp 1999, pp. 269–76.

Csapo, E. 2007. "The Men Who Built the Theatres: *Theatropolai, Theatronai* and *Arkhitektones*," in P. Wilson 2007, pp. 87–121.

Curti, E., E. Dench, and J. R. Patterson. 1996. "The Archaeology of Central and Southern Roman Italy: Recent Trends and Approaches." *JRS* 86, pp. 170–89.

Curtis, J. 2005a. "The Archaeology of the Achaemenid Period," in Curtis and Tallis 2005, pp. 30–49.

——. 2005b. "Greek Influence on Achaemenid Art and Architecture," in Villing 2005a, pp. 115–23.

Curtis, J., and N. Tallis, eds. 2005. *Forgotten Empire: The World of Ancient Persia*. Berkeley and Los Angeles.

Curtius, E., F. Adler, W. Dörpfeld, P. Graef, J. Partsch, and R. Weil. 1966. *Topographie und Geschichte von Olympia*, vols. 1–5. Amsterdam.

D'Alessio, A. 2011. "Spazio, funzioni e paesaggio nei santuari a terrazze italici di età tardo-repubblicana: Note per un *approcio sistemico* linguaggio di una grande architettura," in La Rocca and D'Alessio 2011, pp. 51–86.

Bibliography

Daly, L. 1939. "An Inscribed Doric Capital from the Argive Heraion." *Hesperia* 8, pp. 165–69.

Daniel, A. M. 1904. "Damophon." *JHS* 24, pp. 46–57.

Daux, G. 1967. *Guide de Thasos*. Paris.

Davison, J. A. 1958. "Notes on the Panathenaea." *JHS* 78, pp. 23–42.

De Angelis, F. 2003. *Megara Hyblaia and Selinous: The Development of Two Greek City-States in Archaic Sicily*. Oxford.

———. 2012. "Archaeology in Sicily 2006–2010." *AR 2011–2012*, pp. 123–93. Cambridge.

Debord, P. 1982. *Aspects sociaux et économiques de la vie religieuse dans l'Anatolie Gréco-Romaine*. Leiden.

DeCazenove, O. 2007. "Pre-Roman Italy, before and under the Romans," in Rüpke 2007, pp. 43–57.

de Certeau, M. 1984. "Walking in the City," in *The Practice of Everyday Life*. Translated by S. F. Rendall. Berkeley, Los Angeles, and London, pp. 91–110.

de Grummond, N., and B. S. Ridgway, eds. 2000. *From Pergamon to Sperlonga: Sculpture and Context*. Berkeley, Los Angeles, and London.

Demand, N. H. 1989. "Did Knidos Really Move? The Literary and Epigraphical Evidence." *ClAnt* 8.2, pp. 224–37.

———. 1990. *Urban Relocation in Archaic and Classical Greece*. Norman OK and London.

Demargne, P. 1901. "Les ruines de Goulas ou l'ancienne ville de Lato en Crète." *BCH* 25, pp. 282–307.

Demargne, P., and H. van Effenterre. 1937. "Recherches à Dréros." *BCH* 61, pp. 5–32, 333–48.

Dench, E. 1995. *From Barbarians to New Men: Greek, Roman, and Modern Perceptions of Peoples of the Central Apennines*. Oxford.

———. 2003. "Beyond Greeks and Barbarians: Italy and Sicily in the Hellenistic Age," in Erskine 2003, pp. 294–310.

Deniaux, E. 2002. "Les *gentes* de Délos et la mobilité sociale à Rome au Ier siècle av. J.-C.: L'exemple de Marcus Seius et des Seii," in Müller and Hasenohr 2002, pp. 29–39.

de Polignac, F. 1994. "Mediation, Competition, and Sovereignty: The Evolution of Rural Sanctuaries in Geometric Greece," in Alcock and Osborne 1994, pp. 3–18.

———. 1995. *Cults, Territory, and the Origins of the Greek City-State*. (Based on *La naissance de la cité grecque*, Paris 1984.) Translated by J. Lloyd. Chicago and London.

des Bouvrie, S. 2012. "Greek Festivals and the Ritual Process: An Inquiry into the Olympia-cum-Heraia and the Great Dionysia," in Brandt and Iddeng 2012, pp. 53–93.

des Courtils, J. 1992. "L'architecture et l'histoire d'Argos dans la première moitié du Ve siècle av. J.-C.," in Piérart 1992, pp. 241–51.

des Courtils, J., and J.-C. Moretti. 1993. *Les grands ateliers d'architecture dans le monde Égéen du VIe siècle av. J.-C.* Paris.

des Courtils, J., and A. Pariente. 1985. "Thasos: Herakleion." *BCH* 109, pp. 874–85.

———. 1986. "Thasos: Herakleion." *BCH* 110, pp. 790–812.

———. 1987. "Thasos: Herakleion." *BCH* 111, pp. 619–27.

———. 1988. "Excavations in the Heracles Sanctuary at Thasos," in Hägg, Marinatos, and Nordquist 1988, pp. 121–23.

———. 1991. "Problèmes topographiques et religieux à l'Hérakleion de Thasos," in Étienne and Le Dinahet 1991, pp. 67–73.

Deubner, L. 1932. *Attische Feste*. Berlin.

Deubner, O. 1990. "Eine Pergamenische Architekturordnung?" in *Echo: Beiträge zur Archäologie des Mediterranean und Alpinen Raumes*, ed. B. Otto and F. Ehrl. Innsbruck, pp. 89–98.

DeVries, K., ed. 1980. "Greeks and Phrygians in the Early Iron Age," in *From Athens to Gordion: The Papers of a Memorial Symposium for Rodney S. Young*, ed. K. DeVries. Philadelphia, pp. 33–49.

DeVries, K. 1990. "The Gordion Excavation Seasons of 1969–1973 and Subsequent Research." *AJA* 94, pp. 371–406.

———. 2003. "New Dates for Iron Age Gordion." *Antiquity* 77, p. 296. http://antiquity.ac.uk/ProjGall/devries/devries.html.

———. 2005. "Greek Pottery and Gordion Chronology," in Kealhofer 2005, pp. 36–55.

Dickenson, C. P., and van Nijf, O. M., eds. 2013. *Public Space in the Post-Classical City*. Leuven, Paris, and Walpole MA.

Dickins, G. 1905–6. "Damophon of Messene." *BSA* 12, pp. 109–36.

Dickins, G., and K. Kourouniotis. 1906–7. "Damophon of Messene II." *BSA* 13, pp. 357–404.

Dietz, S., and V. Papachristodoulou, eds. 1988. *Archaeology in the Dodecanese*. Copenhagen.

Dignas, B. 2002. *Economy of the Sacred in Hellenistic and Roman Asia Minor*. Oxford and New York.

Dilke, O. A. 1948. "The Greek Theatre Cavea." *BSA* 43, pp. 125–92.

———. 1950. "Details and Chronology of Greek Theater Caveas." *BSA* 45, pp. 20–62.

Dillon, M. 1997. *Pilgrims and Pilgrimage in Ancient Greece.* London and New York.

———. 2002. *Girls and Women in Classical Greek Religion.* London and New York.

Dinsmoor, W. B. 1941a. *Observations on the Hephaisteion.* Hesperia Suppl. 5. Princeton.

———. 1941b. "An Archaeological Earthquake at Olympia." *AJA* 45, pp. 399–427.

———. 1947. "The Hekatompedon on the Athenian Akropolis." *AJA* 51, pp. 109–51.

Dinsmoor, W. B., Jr. 1980. *The Propylaia to the Athenian Akropolis*, vol. 1: *The Predecessors.* Princeton.

Dinsmoor, W. B., Jr., and A. N. Dinsmoor. 2004. *The Propylaia to the Athenian Akropolis: The Classical Building.* Princeton.

DiVita, A. 1984. "Selinunte fra il 650 ed il 409: Un modello urbanistico coloniale." *ASAtene* 62 n.s. 36, pp. 7–68.

———. 1985. "L'urbanistica," in Pugliese Caratelli 1985, pp. 359–414.

———. 1986–87. "Atti della Scuola, 1986–1987." *ASAtene* 48–49, pp. 435–536.

———. 1990. "Camiro: Un esempio di urbanistica scenografica d'età ellenistica," in *Akten des XIII. Internationalen Kongresses für Klassische Archäologie, Berlin 1988.* Mainz am Rhein, pp. 482–83.

———. 1994. "Camiro." *EAA* Suppl. 2.1, pp. 829–31.

———. 1996. "Urban Planning in Ancient Sicily," in Pugliese Carratelli 1996, pp. 263–308.

Dobres, M.-A., and J. Robb, eds. 2000. *Agency in Archaeology.* London.

Donley-Reid, L. W. 1990. "A Structuring Structure: The Swahili House," in Kent 1990, pp. 114–26.

Donnay, G. 1967. "Damophon de Messène et les φαιδύνται d'Olympie." *BCH* 91, pp. 546–51.

Dörpfeld, W. 1890. "Metrologische Beiträge V. und VI." *AthMitt* 15, pp. 167–87, 234.

———. 1910. "Die Arbeiten zu Pergamon 1908–1909." *AM* 35, pp. 345–400.

———. 1912. "Die Arbeiten zu Pergamon 1909–1910." *AM* 37, pp. 233–76.

———. 1935. *Alt-Olympia: Untersuchungen und Ausgrabungen zur Geschichte des Ältesten Heiligtums von Olympia und der Älteren griechischen Kunst.* 2 vols. Berlin.

Dougherty, C., and L. Kurke, eds. 1993. *Cultural Poetics in Archaic Greece: Cult, Performance, Politics.* Cambridge.

———, eds. 2003. *The Cultures within Ancient Greek Culture: Contact, Conflict, Collaboration.* Cambridge and New York.

Dovey, K. 1999. *Framing Places: Mediating Power in Built Form.* London and New York.

———. 2010. *Becoming Places: Urbanism/Architecture/Identity/Power.* London and New York.

Doxiadis, C., 1972. *Architectural Space in Ancient Greece.* Translated and edited by J. Tyrwhitt (From *Raumordnung im griechischen Städtebau*, 1937). Cambridge MA.

Dreyfus, R., and E. Schraudolph. 1997. *Pergamon: The Telephos Frieze from the Great Altar*, vol. 2. San Francisco.

Ducrey, P., V. Hadjmichali, and O. Picard. 1970. "Latô." *BCH* 94, pp. 880–81.

Ducrey P., and O. Picard. 1969a. "Crète." *BCH* 93, pp. 1044–47.

———. 1969b. "Recherches à Latô, I: Trois fours archaïques." *BCH* 93, pp. 792–822.

———. 1970. "Recherches à Latô, II: Le Grand Temple." *BCH* 94, pp. 567–90.

———. 1971. "Recherches à Lato, IV: Le Théâtre." *BCH* 95, pp. 513–31.

———. 1972. "Recherches à Lato, V: Le Prytanée." *BCH* 96, pp. 567–92.

Dyer, L. 1905. "Olympian Treasuries and Treasuries in General." *JHS* 25, pp. 294–313.

———. 1906. "Details of the Olympian Treasuries." *JHS* 26, pp. 46–83.

———. 1908. "The Olympian Theatron and the Battle of Olympia." *JHS* 28, pp. 250–68.

Dygve, E., and V. Poulsen 1960. *Lindos fouilles de l'Acropole, 1902–1914*, vol. 3.2: *Le sanctuaire d'Athena Lindia et l'architecture lindienne.* Berlin and Copenhagen.

Ebert, J. 1982. "Zur Stiftungsurkunde der ΛΕΥΚΟΦΡΥΝΑ in Magnesia am Mäander." *Philologus* 126, pp. 198–216.

Edgü, A., F. Kuzucu, and M. Ural, eds. 2010. *Mylasa Labraunda: Archaeology and Rural Architecture in the Southern Aegean Region.* Istanbul.

Egelhaaf-Gaiser, U. 2007. "Roman Cult Sites: A Pragmatic Approach," in Rüpke 2007, pp. 205–21.

Bibliography

Ehrhardt, W. 2009. "Hellenistische Heiligtümer und Riten: Die westlichen Sakralbezirke in Knidos als Fallbeispiel," in Matthaei and Zimmerman 2009, pp. 93–115.

Eiteljorg, H., II. 1993. *The Entrance to the Athenian Acropolis before Mnesicles.* Dubuque.

Elderkin, G. W. 1941. "The Cults of the Erechtheion." *Hesperia* 10, pp. 113–24.

Elsner, J., and I. Rutherford. 2005. *Pilgrimage in Graeco-Roman and Early Christian Antiquity: Seeing the Gods.* Oxford.

Elton, H. and G. Reger, eds. 2007. *Regionalism in Hellenistic and Roman Asia Minor.* Paris.

Erskine, A., ed. 2003. *A Companion to the Hellenistic World.* Oxford.

Etienne, R. 1992. "Autels et sacrifices," in Schachter 1992, pp. 291–319.

———. 1996a. "Le sanctuaire de Poseidon et d'Amphitrite à Tenos," in Etienne 1996b, pp. 141–47.

———, ed. 1996b. *L'Espace grec: Cent cinquante ans de fouilles de l'École française d'Athènes.* Paris.

Etienne, R., and J.-P. Braun. 1986. *Tenos I: Le sanctuaire de Poseidon et d'Amphitrite.* Paris.

Etienne, R., and M.-T. Le Dinahet, eds. 1991. *L'espace sacrificiel dans les civilizations méditerranéennes de l'antiquité.* Lyon and Paris.

Fasolo, F., and G. Gullini. 1953. *Il santuario della Fortuna Primigenia a Palestrina.* Rome.

Fedak, J. 1990. *Monumental Tombs of the Hellenistic Age.* Toronto.

Feld, S., and K. H. Basso, eds. 1996. *Senses of Place.* Santa Fe NM.

Fiechter, E. 1930. *Antike griechische Theaterbauten*, vol. 1: *Das Theater in Oropos.* Stuttgart.

Fischer-Hansen, T., and B. Poulsen, eds. 2009. *From Artemis to Diana: The Goddess of Man and Beast.* Acta Hyperborea 12. Copenhagen.

Fisher, K. D. 2009. "Placing Social Interaction: An Integrative Approach to Analyzing Past Built Environments." *JAnthArch* 28, pp. 439–57.

Fitch, J. M., J. Templer, and P. Corcoran. 1974. "The Dimensions of Stairs." *Scientific American* 241.4, pp. 82–90.

Flensted-Jensen, P., and A.-M. Carstens. 2004. "Halikarnassos and the Lelegians," in Isager and Pedersen 2004, pp. 109–23.

Flower, H. I., ed. 2004. *The Cambridge Companion to the Roman Republic.* Cambridge.

Foertmeyer, V. 1988. "The Dating of the Pompe of Ptolemy II Philadelphus." *Historia* 37, pp. 90–104.

Fontenrose, J. 1988. *Didyma: Apollo's Oracle, Cult and Companions.* Berkeley.

Foucault, M. 1977. *Discipline and Punish: The Birth of the Prison.* Translated by A. Sheridan. New York.

Fowler, H. N., and R. Stillwell. 1932. *Corinth 1: Introduction, Topography, Architecture.* Cambridge MA.

Fraser, P. M. 1972. *Ptolemaic Alexandria.* Oxford.

Fraser, P. M., and G. E. Bean. 1954. *The Rhodian Peraea and Islands.* Oxford.

Frederiksen, R. 2002. "The Greek Theatre: A Typical Building in the Urban Centre of the *Polis*?" in T. H. Nielsen 2002b, pp. 65–124.

———. 2003. Review of I. Nielsen 2002. *Acta Hyperborea* 10, pp. 546–51.

French, D. 1994. *Studies in the History and Topography of Lycia and Pisidia: In Memoriam A. S. Hall.* London.

Fuchs, W. 1964. "Archäologische Forschungen und Funde in Sizilien 1955 bis 1964." *AA*, pp. 704–9.

Furley, W. D. 1995. "Praise and Persuasion in Greek Hymns." *JHS* 115, pp. 29–46.

———. 2007. "Prayers and Hymns," in Ogden 2007, pp. 117–31.

Gabrici, E. 1929. "Acropoli di Selinunte: Scavi e topografie." *MonAnt* 33, pp. 61–112.

Gabrielsen, V. 1997. *The Naval Aristocracy of Hellenistic Rhodes.* Studies in Hellenistic Civilization 6. Aarhus.

———. 2000. "The Synoikized *Polis* of Rhodes," in *Polis and Politics: Studies in Ancient Greek History*, ed. P. Flensted-Jensen, T. H. Nielsen, and L. Rubenstein. Copenhagen, pp. 177–205.

Gabrielsen, V., P. Bilde, T. Engberg-Pedersen, L. Hannested, and J. Zahle. 1999. *Hellenistic Rhodes: Politics, Culture and Society.* Studies in Hellenistic Civilization 9. Aarhus.

Gardiner, E. N. 1925. *Olympia: Its History and Remains.* Oxford.

Garwood, P. 1991. "Ritual Tradition and the Reconstitution of Society," in *Sacred and Profane: Proceedings of a Conference on Archaeology, Ritual and Religion*, ed. P. Garwood, D. Jennings, R. Skeates, and J. Toms. Oxford, pp. 10–32.

Gates, C., J. Morin, and T. Zimmerman. 2009. *Sacred Landscapes in Anatolia and Neighboring Regions.* BAR International Series 2034. London.

Gates, M.-H. 1994. "Archaeology in Turkey." *AJA* 98, pp. 249–78.

———. 1995. "Archaeology in Turkey." *AJA* 99, pp. 207–55.

———. 1996. "Archaeology in Turkey." *AJA* 100, pp. 277–335.

———. 1997. "Archaeology in Turkey." *AJA* 101, pp. 241–305.

Gauthier, P. 1985. *Les cités grecques er leurs bienfaiteurs*. BCH Suppl. 12. Paris.

Gebhard, E. 1974. "The Form of the Orchestra in the Early Greek Theater." *Hesperia* 43, pp. 428–40.

Gell, A. 1998. *Art and Agency: An Anthropological Theory*. Oxford.

Gerbino, A. 2002. *François Blondel (1618–1686): Architecture, Erudition, and Early Modern Science (France)*. Ph.D. dissertation, Columbia University.

Gero, J. M. 2000. "Troubled Travels in Agency and Feminism," in Dobres and Robb 2000, pp. 34–39.

Giddens, A. 1984. *Constitution of Society: Outline of the Theory of Structuration*. Berkeley and Los Angeles.

Ginouvès, R. 1972. *Le théâtron à gradins droits et l'Odéon d'Argos*. Études Péloponnésiennes 6. Paris.

Giuliani, C. F. 1970. *Tibur: Pars prima*. Forma Italiae I.7. Rome.

———. 2009. *Tivoli: Il Santuario di Ercole Vincitore*. Tivoli.

Glaser, F. 1981–82. "Lousoi." *ÖJh* 53, p. 24.

———. 1983. *Antike Brunnenbauten in Griechenland*. Vienna.

Goette, H. R. 1998. "Sanctuary of Zeus Hellanios." *AR 1997–1998*, pp.18–19.

———. 1999. "Mt. Oros: Sanctuary of Zeus Hellanios." *AR 1998–1999*, pp. 19–20.

———. 2001a. *Athens, Attica and the Megarid: An Archaeological Guide*. Revised English ed. London and New York.

———. 2001b. "Jahresbericht 2000." *AA*, pp. 642–43.

———. 2002. "Sanctuaryof Zeus Hellanios." *AR 2000–2001*, pp. 18–19.

Goffman, E. 1974. *Frame Analysis: An Essay on the Organization of Experience*. Cambridge MA.

Goldhill, S. 1999. "Programme Notes," in Goldhill and Osborne 1999, pp. 1–29.

Goldhill, S., and R. Osborne, eds. 1999. *Performance Culture and Athenian Democracy*. Cambridge.

Graf, F. 1996. "*Pompai* in Greece: Some Considerations about Space and Ritual in the Greek *Polis*," in Hägg 1996, pp. 56–65.

———, ed. 1998. *Ansichten griechischen Rituale*. Leiden.

Gros, P. 1973. "Hermodoros et Vitruve." *MEFRA* 85, pp. 137–61.

———. 1976. "Les premières générations d'architectes hellénistiques à Rome," in *L'Italie préromaine et la Rome républicaine: Mélanges offerts à Jacques Heurgon*. CÉFR 27. Rome, pp. 387–409.

———. 1978. *Architecture et société à Rome et en Italie centroméridionale aux deux derniers siècles de la République*. CollLatomus 156. Brussels.

———, ed. 1983a. *Architecture et société de l'archaïsme grec à la fin de la République romaine*. CÉFR 66. Paris and Rome.

———. 1983b. "Statut social et rôle culturel des architectes (période hellénistique et augustéenne)," in Gros 1983a, pp. 425–52.

———. 1987. *Architetture e società nell'Italia romana*. Rome.

———. 1996. *L'architecture romaine du début du IIIe siècle av. J.-C. à la fin du Haut-Empire*, vol. 1: *Les monuments publics*. Paris.

———. 2006. *Vitruve et la tradition des traits d'architecture: Fabrica et ratiocinatio, recueil d'études*. CÉFR 366. Rome.

Gruben, G. 1969. "Untersuchungen am Dipylon." *AA*, pp. 31–40.

———. 1980. *Die Tempel der Griechen*. 3rd ed. Munich.

Gruber, J. 2007. Review of Brandt and Kolb 2005. *Plekos* 9, pp. 93–98.

Gruen, E. S. 1975. "Rome and Rhodes in the 2nd Century BC: A Historiographical Inquiry." *CQ* 25, pp. 58–81.

———.1989. *The Hellenistic World and the Coming of Rome*. Berkeley.

———. 1993. "The Polis in the Hellenistic World," in Rosen and Farrell 1993, pp. 339–54.

———. 2000. "Culture as Policy: The Attalids of Pergamon," in de Grummond and Ridgway 2000, pp. 17–31.

———. 2004. "Rome and the Greek World," in Flower 2004, pp. 242–69.

Guaitoli, M. 1981. "Gabii." *PP* 36, pp. 152–73.

Guldager Bilde, P., I. Nielsen, and M. Nielsen. 1993. *Aspects of Hellenism in Italy: Towards a Cultural Unity? Acta Hyperborea* 5. Copenhagen.

Gunter, A. C. 1985. "Looking at Hecatomnid Patronage from Labraunda." *REA* 78, pp. 113–24.

Günther, W. 1971. *Das Orakel von Didyma in hellenistischer Zeit: Eine Interpretation von Stein-Urkunden*. IstMitt Suppl. 4. Tübingen.

Bibliography

Habermann, K. J. 2002. *Staircases: Design and Construction.* Basel, Boston, and Berlin.

Hadjimichali, V. 1971. "Recherches à Latô, III: Maisons." *BCH* 95, pp. 167–222.

Hägg, R., ed. 1992. *The Iconography of Greek Cult in the Archaic and Classical Periods.* Kernos Suppl. 1. Athens and Liège.

———, ed. 1994. *Ancient Greek Cult Practice from the Epigraphical Evidence.* Stockholm.

———, ed. 1996. *The Role of Religion in the Early Greek Polis.* Stockholm.

———, ed. 1998. *Ancient Greek Cult Practice from the Archaeological Evidence.* Stockholm.

———, ed. 2002. *Peloponnesian Sanctuaries and Cults.* Stockholm.

Hägg, R., N. Marinatos, and G. C. Nordquist, eds. 1988. *Early Greek Cult Practice.* Stockholm.

Haldane, J. A. 1966. "Musical Instruments in Greek Worship." *GaR* 13, pp. 98–107.

Hall, E. T. 1966. *The Hidden Dimension.* New York.

———. 1968. "Proxemics." *Current Anthropology* 9.2, pp. 83–95.

Hall, J. M. 1995. "How Argive Was the 'Argive Heraion'? The Political and Cultic Geography of the Argive Plain, 900–400 B.C." *AJA* 99, pp. 577–613.

———. 1997. "Alternative Responses within Polis Formation: Argos, Mykenai and Tiryns." *Acta Hyperborea* 7, pp. 85–110.

Hallof, L., and K. Hallof. 2004. "Geschichte des Corpus Inscriptionum Coarum (IG XII 4)," in Höghammar 2004, pp. 83–87.

Handelman, D. 2004. "Re-Framing Ritual," in Kreinath, Hartung, and Deschner 2004, pp. 9–20.

———. 2006. "Framing," in Kreinath, Snoek, and Stausberg 2006, pp. 571–82.

Hanfmann, G. 1972. *Letters from Sardis.* Cambridge MA.

Hansen, M.-H. 1983a. *The Athenian Ecclesia: A Collection of Articles 1976–1983.* Copenhagen.

———. 1983b. "The Athenian *Ecclesia* and the Swiss *Landsgemeinde*," in M.-H. Hansen 1983a, pp. 207–29.

Hansen, M.-H., and T. Fischer-Hansen. 1994. "Monumental Political Architecture in Archaic and Classical Greek *Poleis*: Evidence and Historical Significance," in *From Political Architecture to Stephanus Byzantius: Sources for the Ancient Greek Polis*, ed. D. Whitehead. Stuttgart, pp. 23–90.

Hansen, M.-H., and T. H. Nielsen. 2004. *An Inventory of Archaic and Classical Poleis.* Oxford.

Hanson, J. A. 1959. *Roman Theater-Temples.* Princeton.

Harris, E. M., and L. Rubenstein, eds. 2004. *The Law and the Courts in Ancient Greece.* London.

Haselberger, L. 1996. "Eine 'Krepis von 200 Fuss Gestreckter Länge': Bauarbeiten am Jüngeren Apollontempel von Didyma nach der Urkunde Nr. 42." *IstMitt* 46, pp. 153–78.

———, ed. 1999. *Appearance and Essence—Refinements of Classical Architecture: Curvature.* Philadelphia.

———. 2005. "Bending the Truth: Curvature and Other Refinements of the Parthenon," in Neils 2005, pp. 101–58.

Haspels, C. H. E. 1971. *The Highlands of Phrygia: Sites and Monuments.* Princeton.

Hatzfeld, J. 1912. "Les Italiens residents à Delos." *BCH* 36, pp. 1–218.

———. 1919. *Les trafiquants Italiens dans l'Orient Héllenique.* Paris.

Heilmeyer, W.-D. 1980. Review of Voigtländer 1975. *Gnomon* 52, pp. 736–44.

———. 1999. "ΘΕΟΙΣ ΠΑΣΙ—Rhodos, Pergamon und Rom," in Kypraiou and Zapheiropoulou 1999, pp. 83–88.

Hellman, M.-C. 2002. *L'architecture grecque,* vol. 1: *Les principes de la construction.* Paris.

Hellström, P. 1985. "Dessin d'architecture hécatomnide à Labraunda," in *Le dessin d'architecture dans les sociétés antiques.* Leiden, pp. 153–65.

———. 1988. "Labraunda: Mixed Orders in Hecatomnid Architecture," in Πρακτικὰ τοῦ XII διεθνούς συνεδρίου κλασικής ἀρχαιολογίας Ἀθῆνα, 4–10 Σεπτεμβρίου 1983. Athens, pp. 70–74.

———. 1990. "Hellenistic Architecture in Light of Late Classical Labraunda," in *Akten des XIII. Internationalen Kongress für Klassische Archäologie Berlin 1988.* Berlin, pp. 243–52.

———. 1991. "The Architectural Layout of Hecatomnid Labraunda." *RA*, pp. 297–308.

———. 1996a. "The Andrones at Labraynda: Dining Halls for Protohellenistic Kings," in Hoepfner and Brands 1996. Mainz, pp. 164–69.

———. 1996b. "Hecatomnid Display of Power at the Labraynda Sanctuary," in Hellström and Alroth 1996, pp. 133–38.

———. 2009. "Sacred Architecture and Karian Identity," in Rumscheid 2009a, pp. 267–90.

———. 2011. "Feasting at Labraunda and the Chronology of the *Andrones*," in Karlsson and Carlsson 2011, pp. 149–57.

Hellström, P., and B. Alroth, eds. 1996. *Religion and Power in the Ancient Greek World*. Uppsala.

Hellström, P., and T. Thieme. 1982. *Labraunda I.3: The Temple of Zeus*. Stockholm.

Henry, O. 2006. "Réflexions sur le propriétaire de la tombe monumentale de Labraunda." *REA* 108, pp. 415–32.

———. 2009. *Tombes de Carie: Architecture funéraire et culture carienne, VIe–IIe s. av. J.-C.* Rennes.

———. 2010a. "Hekatomnos, Persian Satrap or Greek Dynast? A Study on Funerary Architecture," in van Bremen and Carbon 2010, pp. 103–21.

———. 2010b. "The Necropolis of Labraunda," in Edgü, Kuzucu, and Ural 2010, pp. 93–105.

———. 2011. "Hellenistic Monumental Tombs: The Π-shaped Tomb from Labraunda and Karian Parallels," in Karlsson and Carlsson 2011, pp. 159–75.

———, ed. 2013a. *4th Century Karia: Defining a Karian Identity under the Hekatomnids*. Varia Anatolica 28. Istanbul.

———. 2013b. "A Tribute to the Ionian Renaissance," in Henry 2013a, pp. 81–91.

Hepding, H. 1910. "Die Arbeiten zu Pergamon 1908–1909, II: Die Inschriften." *AM* 35, pp. 439–42.

Herrmann, K. 1976. "Beobachtungen zur Schatzhaus-Architektur Olympias," in Jantzen 1976, pp. 321–50.

———. 1992. "Die Schatzhauser in Olympia," in Coulson and Kyrieleis 1992, pp. 25–32.

———. 1999. "Die Stützmauer am Kronoshügel." *OlBer* 11, ed. A. Mallwitz. Berlin, pp. 367–90.

Herzog, R. 1899. *Koische Forschungen und Funde*. Leipzig.

———. 1903a. "Vorläufiger Bericht über die archäologische Expedition auf der Insel Kos im Jahre 1902." *AA*, pp. 1–13.

———. 1903b. "Vorläufiger Bericht über die archäologische Expedition auf der Insel Kos im Jahre 1903." *AA*, pp. 186–99.

———. 1906. "Vorläufiger Bericht über die archäologische Expedition auf der Insel Kos im Jahre 1905." *AA*, pp. 1–15.

———. 1928. *Heilige Gesetze von Kos*. Berlin.

Herzog, R., and G. Klaffenbach. 1952. *Asylienurkunden aus Kos*. Berlin.

Herzog, R., and P. Schazmann. 1932. *Kos: Ergebnisse der deutschen Ausgrabungen und Forschungen*, vol. 1: *Asklepieion*. Berlin.

Higbie, C. 2003. *The Lindian Chronicle and the Greek Creation of Their Past*. Oxford.

Hillier, J., and E. Rooksby, eds. 2002. *Habitus: A Sense of Place*. Aldershot UK and Burlington VT.

Hitchcock, L. 2004. Review of Dobres and Robb 2000. *AJA* 108, pp. 112–13.

Hobsbawm, E., and T. Ranger, eds. 1983. *The Invention of Tradition*. Cambridge.

Hodder, I., and S. Hutson. 2003. *Reading the Past: Current Approaches to Interpretation in Archaeology*. 3rd ed. Cambridge.

Hodder, I., M. Shanks, A. Alexandri, V. Buchli, J. Carman, J. Last, and G. Lucas, eds. 1995. *Interpreting Archaeology: Finding Meaning in the Past*. London.

Hoepfner, W. 1984. "ΦΙΛΑΔΕΛΦΕΙΑ: Ein Beitrag zur frühen hellenistischen Architektur." *AM* 99, pp. 353–64.

———. 1988. "Der Stadtplan von Rhodos," in Dietz and Papachristodoulou 1988, pp. 96–97.

———. 1989. "Zu den grossen Altären von Magnesia und Pergamon." *AA*, pp. 603–18.

———. 1991. "Bauliche Details am Pergamonaltar." *AA*, pp. 189–202.

———. 1996. "Der vollendete Pergamonaltar." *AA*, pp. 115–34.

———, ed. 1997a. *Kult und Kultbauten auf der Akropolis*. Berlin.

———. 1997b. "Model of the Pergamon Altar (1:20)," in Dreyfus and Schraudolph 1997, pp. 59–67.

———. 1997c. "Planänderungen am Tempel von Bassai," in Hoepfner 1997a, pp. 178–83.

———. 1999. "Zur Gründung und zur Architektur von Rhodos," in Kypraiou and Zapheiropoulou 1999, pp. 51–58.

———. 2003. *Der Kolossos von Rhodos und die Bauten des Helios: Neue Forschungen zu einem der Sieben Weltwunder*. Mainz.

Hoepfner, W., and G. Brands, eds. 1996. *Basileia: Die Paläste der hellenistischen Könige*. Mainz am Rhein.

Hoepfner, W., and E.-L. Schwandner, eds. 1990. *Hermogenes und die hochhellenistische Architektur*. Mainz am Rhein.

Hoepfner, W., and Schwandner, E.-L. 1994. *Haus und Stadt im klassischen Griechenland*. Munich.

Hoffman, H. 1953. "Foreign Influence and Native Invention in Archaic Greek Altars." *AJA* 57, pp. 189–95.

Bibliography

Höghammar, K. 1993. *Sculpture and Society: A Study of the Connection between the Free-Standing Sculpture and Society on Kos in the Hellenistic and Augustan Periods*. Boreas 23. Uppsala.

———, ed. 2004. *The Hellenistic Polis of Kos: State, Economy and Culture*. Boreas 28. Uppsala.

Hölbe, G. 1984. "Ägyptischer Einfluss in der griechischen Architektur." *ÖJh* 55, pp. 1–18.

Holland, L. B. 1924a. "Erechtheum Papers III: The Post-Persian Revision." *AJA* 28, pp. 402–25.

———. 1924b. "Erechtheum Papers IV: 'The Building Called the Erechtheum.'" *AJA* 28, pp. 425–34.

Hollinshead, M. B. 1985. "Against Iphigeneia's Adyton in Three Mainland Temples." *AJA* 89, pp. 419–40.

———. 1992. "Steps to Grandeur: Monumental Staircases and Hellenistic Architectural Complexes," in *The Age of Pyrrhus*, ed. T. Hackens, N. D. Holloway, R. R. Holloway, and G. Moucharte. *Archaeologia Transatlantica* 11. Louvain-La-Neuve and Providence, pp. 83–96.

———. 1999. "Adyton, Opisthodomos, and the Inner Room of the Greek Temple." *Hesperia* 68, pp. 189–219.

———. 2012a. "Monumental Steps and the Shaping of Ceremony," in Wescoat and Ousterhout 2012, pp. 27–65.

———. 2012b. "The North Court of the Erechtheion and the Ritual of the *Plynteria*." *Archaeological Institute of America Abstracts of the 113th Annual Meetings*. Philadelphia, January, p. 260.

———. Forthcoming (2015). "The North Court of the Erechtheion and the Ritual of the Plynteria." *AJA* 119.

Holloway, R. R. 2000. *The Archaeology of Ancient Sicily*. 2nd ed. London.

Hölscher, T. 2002. "Rituelle Räume und politische Denkmäler im Heiligtum von Olympia," in *Olympia 1875–2000: 125 Jahre deutsche Ausgrabungen*, ed. H. Kyrieleis. Mainz am Rhein, pp. 331–46.

Hornblower, S. 1982. *Mausolus*. Oxford.

———. 1990. "A Reaction to Gunter's Look at Hekatomnid Patronage from Labraunda." *REA* 92, pp. 137–39.

Humann, C., J. Kohte, and C. Watzinger. 1904. *Magnesia am Maeander: Bericht über die Ergebnisse der Ausgrabungen der Jahre 1891–1893*. Berlin.

Hurwit, J. 1999. *The Athenian Acropolis: History, Mythology, and Archaeology from the Neolithic Era to the Present*. Cambridge.

———. 2005. "Space and Theme: The Setting of the Parthenon," in Neils 2005, pp. 9–34.

Iddeng, J. W. 2012. "What Is a Graeco-Roman Festival? A Polythetic Approach," in Brandt and Iddeng 2012, pp. 11–37.

Inomata, T., and L. S. Coben, eds. 2006a. *Archaeology of Performance: Theaters of Power, Community, and Politics*. Lanham MD.

Inomata, T., and L. S. Coben. 2006b. "Overture: An Invitation to the Archaeological Theater," in Inomata and Coben 2006a, pp. 11–44.

Interdonato, E. 2013. *L'Asklepieion di Kos: Archeologia del Culto*. ArchCl Suppl. 12, n.s. 9. Rome.

Isager, S., and P. Pedersen, eds. 2004. *The Salmakis Inscription and Hellenistic Halikarnassos*. Halikarnassian Studies 4. Odense.

Jacopi, G. 1931. "Esplorazione archeologica di Camiro I: Scavi nelle necropoli camiresi 1929–1930." *Clara Rodos* 4.

———. 1932. "Esplorazione archeologica di Camiro II." *Clara Rodos* 6–7, pp. 369–439.

Jameson, M. H. 1998. "Religion in the Athenian Democracy," in Morris and Raaflaub 1998, pp. 171–95.

———. 1999. "The Spectacular and the Obscure in Athenian Religion," in Goldhill and Osborne 1999, pp. 321–40.

Jantzen, U., ed. 1976. *Neue Forschungen in griechischen Heiligtümer: Internationales Symposium in Olympia vom 10.–12. Oktober 1974, anläßlich der Hundertjahrfeier der Abteilung Athen und der deutschen Ausgrabungen in Olympia*. Tübingen.

Jeffery, L. H. 1990. *The Local Scripts of Archaic Greece: A Study of the Origin of the Greek Alphabet and Its Development from the Eighth to the Fifth Centuries B.C.* Revised ed. with a supplement by A. W. Johnston. Oxford.

Jenkins, I. 1994. *The Parthenon Frieze*. Austin.

———. 2006. "Return to Cnidus." *Anatolian Archaeology* 12, pp. 26–28.

———. 2007. "The Lion of Knidos." *Anatolian Archaeology* 13, pp. 23–24.

Jenkins, R. 1992. *Pierre Bourdieu*. London and New York.

Jensen, J. T., G. Hinge, P. Schultz, and B. Wickkiser. 2009. *Aspects of Ancient Greek Cult: Context, Ritual and Iconography*. Aarhus.

Jeppesen, K. 1955. *Labraunda I.1: The Propylaea*. Lund.

———. 1976. "Neue Ergebnisse zur Wiederherstellung des Maussolleions von Halikarnassos." *IstMitt* 26, pp. 47–99.

———. 1978. "The Reconstruction of the Mausoleum," in *The Proceedings of the Xth International Congress of Classical Archaeology*, ed. E. Akurgal. Ankara, pp. 535–42.

———. 1987. *The Theory of the Alternative Erechtheion: Premises, Definition, and Implications*. Aarhus.

———. 1989. "What Did the Maussolleion Look Like?" in Linders and Hellström 1989, pp. 15–22.

———. 2000. *The Maussolleion at Halikarnassos*, vol. 4: *The Quadrangle: The Foundations of the Maussolleion and Its Sepulchral Compartments*. Aarhus.

———. 2002. *The Maussolleion at Halikarnassos*, vol. 5: *The Superstructure: A Comparative Analysis of the Architectural, Sculptural, and Literary Evidence*. Aarhus.

Jeppesen, K., F. Hojlund, and K. Aaris-Sorensen. 1981. *The Maussolleion at Halikarnassos*, vol. 1: *The Sacrificial Deposit*. Aarhus.

Jeppesen, K., and A. Luttrell. 1986. *The Maussolleion at Halikarnassos*, vol. 2: *The Written Sources and Archaeological Background*. Aarhus.

Johnson, M. 1989. "Concepts of Agency in Archaeological Interpretation." *JAnthArch* 8, pp. 189–211.

———. 2000. "Self-Made Men and the Staging of Agency," in Dobres and Robb 2000, pp. 213–31.

Jordan, B., and J. Perlin. 1984. "On the Protection of Sacred Groves," in *Studies Presented to Sterling Dow on His Eightieth Birthday*, ed. A. L. Boegehold and K. Rigsby. *GRBS Suppl.* 10. Durham NC, pp.153–59.

Jordan, P., X. Valle, and G. Munsch. 2007. "Architectural Studies at Mt. Lykaion: Documentation and Discovery." Paper delivered at symposium "At the Altar of Zeus: The Mt. Lykaion Excavation and Survey Project," University of Pennsylvania Museum, Philadelphia, February 24.

Jost, M. 1973. "Pausanias à Megalopolitide." *REA* 75, pp. 245–67.

———. 1985. *Sanctuaires et cultes d'Arcadie. Études Peloponnésiennes* 9. Paris.

———. 1992. "Sanctuaires ruraux et urbains en Arcadie," in Schachter 1992, pp. 205–39.

———. 1994. "The Distribution of Sanctuaries in Civic Space in Arkadia," in Alcock and Osborne 1994, pp. 217–30.

———. 1996. "Arcadian Cults and Myths," in *OCD*³ p. 139.

———. 1999. "Les schémas de peuplement de l'Arcadie aux époques archaïque et classique," in Nielsen and Roy 1999, pp. 192–247.

———. 2002. "À propos des sacrifices humains dans le sanctuaire de Zeus du Mont Lycée," in Hägg 2002, pp. 183–86.

———. 2003. "Mystery Cults in Arcadia," in *Greek Mysteries: The Archaeology and Ritual of Ancient Greek Secret Cults*, ed. M. Cosmopoulos. London and New York, pp. 143–68.

———. 2007. "The Cults of Mt. Lykaion." Paper delivered at symposium "At the Altar of Zeus: The Mt. Lykaion Excavation and Survey Project," University of Pennsylvania Museum, February 24.

Kähler, H. 1958a. "Das Fortunaheiligtum von Palestrina-Praeneste." *Annales Universitatis Saraviensis* 7, pp. 221–72. Reprinted in Coarelli 1978, pp. 189–240.

———. 1958b. Review of Fasolo and Gullini 1953. *Gnomon* 30, pp. 366–83.

———. 1962. Review of Hanson 1959. *Gnomon* 34, pp. 512–15.

Kaltsas, N. 2003. *Sculpture in the National Archaeological Museum, Athens*. Translated by D. Hardy. Los Angeles.

Kaltsas, N., and H. A. Shapiro, eds. 2008. *Worshipping Women: Ritual and Reality in Classical Athens*. Athens and New York.

Kane, S., and White, D. 2007. "Recent Developments in Cyrene's Chora South of the Wadi bel Gadir." *LibSt* 38, pp. 39–52.

Karlsson, L. 2010. "Labraunda: The Sanctuary of the Weather God of Heaven," in Edgü, Kuzucu, and Ural 2010, pp. 10–61.

———. 2011. "The Forts and Fortifications of Labraunda," in Karlsson and Carlsson 2011, pp. 217–51.

———. 2013. "Combining Architectural Orders at Labraunda: A Political Statement," in Henry 2013a, pp. 65–80.

Karlsson, L., and S. Carlsson, eds. 2011. *Labraunda and Karia. Boreas* 32. Uppsala.

Karouzos, Ch. 1926. Τὸ Ἀμφιάρειο τοῦ Ὠρωποῦ. Athens.

Kästner, V. 1998. "The Architecture of the Great Altar of Pergamon," in Koester 1998, pp. 137–61.

Kavoulaki, A. 1999. "Processional Performance and the Democratic Polis," in Goldhill and Osborne 1999, pp. 293–320.

Kealhofer, L., ed. 2005. *The Archaeology of Midas and the Phrygians: Recent Work at Gordion*. Philadelphia.

Keaveney, A. 1987. *Rome and the Unification of Italy*. London and Sydney.

Bibliography

Kelly, N. 1995. "The Archaic Temple of Apollo at Bassai: Correspondences to the Classical Temple." *Hesperia* 64, pp. 227–77.

Kent, S., ed. 1990. *Domestic Architecture and the Use of Space.* Cambridge.

Kern, O. 1900. *Die Inschriften von Magnesia am Maeander.* Berlin.

Kienast, H. 1991. "Neue Beobachtungen zum sog. Rhoikosaltar im Heraion von Samos," in Etienne and Le Dinahet 1991, pp. 99–102.

Kindt, J. 2009. "Polis Religion: A Critical Appreciation." *Kernos* 22, pp. 9–34.

———. 2012. *Rethinking Greek Religion.* Cambridge.

Kirsten, E. 1940a. "Amnisos." *RE Suppl.* 7, cols. 33–35.

———. 1940b. "Lato." *RE Suppl.* 4, cols. 342–65.

Kleiss, W. 1996. "Bemerkungen zum 'Pyramid Tomb' in Sardes." *IstMitt* 46, pp. 135–40.

Kluiver, J. 1996. "The Five Later 'Tyrrhenian' Painters." *BABesch* 71, pp. 1–58.

Knackfuss, H. 1941a. *Didyma I.1: Die Baubeschreibung.* Berlin.

Knackfuss, H. 1941b. *Didyma I.2: Die Baubeschreibung.* Berlin.

Knackfuss, H. 1941c. *Didyma I.3: Die Baubeschreibung.* Berlin.

Knell, H. 1971. "Eine Beobachtung am Asklepiostempel in Epidauros." *AA*, pp. 206–10.

Knigge, U. 1991. *The Athenian Kerameikos: History—Monuments—Excavations.* Athens.

Koenigs, W. 1981. "Stadion III und Echohalle." *OlBer* 10, ed. A. Mallwitz. Berlin, pp. 353–69.

Koester, H., ed. 1998. *Pergamon: Citadel of the Gods.* Harrisburg PA.

Köhler, J. 1996. *Pompai: Untersuchungen zur hellenistischen Festkultur.* Frankfurt am Main.

Kolb, F. 1975. "Agora und Theater in Morgantina." *Kokalos* 21, pp. 226–30.

———. 1976. "Politische versammlungslokale und Institutionen im kretischen Lato." *Gymnasium* 83, pp. 294–302.

———. 1978. "Ο ΔΗΜΟΣ ΚΑΘΗΜΕΝΟΣ: Zur Notiz des Etymologicum Magnum über die Diobelie." *Historia* 27, pp. 219–21.

———. 1981. *Agora und Theater: Volks- und Festversammlung.* AF 9. Berlin.

Kollias, E. 1980. *Rhodes: Ialyssos, Kamiros, Lindos, Museums and the Villages of Rhodes.* Athens.

———. 1988. *The City of Rhodes and the Palace of the Grand Master: From the Early Christian Period to the Conquest by the Turks (1522).* Athens.

———. 1999. "Ἡ παλαιοχριστιανική καὶ βυζαντινή Ῥόδος: Ἡ ἀντίσταση μίας ἑλληνιστικῆς πόλης," in Kypraiou and Zapheiropoulou 1999, pp. 299–308.

Kollias, M. M. 2000. "Μνημειώδες στωικὸ οἰκοδόμημα στις υπώρειες τῆς Ῥοδιακῆς ἀκροπόλης τὸ τέμενος τοῦ Ἡλίου ἢ δημοσίο κτίριο," in Kypraiou and Zapheiropoulou 1999, pp. 73–74.

Kondis, I. D. 1952. "Ἀνασκαφικαὶ ἔρευναι εἰς τὴν πόλιν τῆς Ῥόδου (ΙΙ)." *Prakt*, pp. 547–91.

———. 1953. "Ἀνασκαφικαὶ ἔρευναι εἰς τὴν πόλιν τῆς Ῥόδου (ΙΙΙ)." *Prakt*, pp. 275–87.

———. 1956. *Αἱ ἑλληνιστικαὶ διαμορφώσεις τοῦ Ἀσκληπιείου τῆς Κῶ.* Rhodes.

Kondis, I. D. 1963. Review of Dygve and Poulsen 1960. *Gnomon* 35, pp. 392–404.

Konstantinopoulos, G. 1968. "Rhodes: New Finds and Old Problems." *Archaeology* 21, pp. 115–23.

———. 1971. *Philermo-Ialysos-Kamiros.* Athens.

———. 1972. *Ὁ Ῥοδιακός Κόσμος Ι, Λίνδος: συμβολή εἰς τὴν μελέτην τῆς πρό τοῦ Ῥοδιακοῦ συνοικισμοῦ ἱστορίας τῆς Λίνδου.* Athens.

———. 1973. "Ἀνασκαφαὶ εἰς Ῥόδον." *Prakt*, pp. 127–36.

———. 1974. *Rhodes, City and Island.* Munich.

———. 1986. *Ἀρχαία Ῥόδος: ἐπισκόπηση τῆς ἱστορίας καί τῆς τέχνης.* Athens.

———. 1988. "Hippodamischer Stadtplan von Rhodos Forschungsgeschichte," in Dietz and Papachristodoulou 1988, pp. 88–95.

Korres, M. 1994. "Recent Discoveries on the Acropolis," in *Acropolis Restoration: The CCAM Interventions*, ed. R. Economakis. London, pp. 174–79.

———. 1995. *From Pentelicon to the Parthenon.* Athens.

———. 2002. "On the North Acropolis Wall," in *Excavating Classical Culture: Recent Discoveries in Greece*, ed. M. Stamatopoulou and M. Yeroulanou. BAR International Series 1031. Oxford, pp. 179–86.

Kosmetatou, E. 1997. "Pisidia and the Hellenistic Kings from 323 to 133 B.C." *Ancient Society* 28, pp. 5–37.

———. 2003. "The Attalids of Pergamon," in Erskine 2003, pp. 158–74.
Kostomitsopoulos, P. 1988. "Lindian Sacrifice: An Evaluation of the Evidence Based on New Inscriptions," in Dietz and Papachristodoulou 1988, pp. 121–28.
Kourouniotis, K. 1903. "Ἀνασκαφὴ Λυκαίου." *Prakt*, pp. 50–52.
———. 1904a. "Ἀνασκαφὴ Λυκαίου." *Prakt*, pp. 32–34.
———. 1904b. "Ἀνασκαφὴ Λυκαίου."*ArchEph*, pp. 153–214.
———. 1905. "Κατάλογοι Λυκαινικῶν." *ArchEph*, pp. 161–78.
———. 1906. "Αἱ ἐν Λυκοσούρᾳ ἐργασίαι." *Prakt*, pp. 120–23.
———. 1907. "Ἀνασκαφαὶ ἐν Λυκοσούρᾳ." *Prakt*, pp. 112–13.
———. 1909. "Ἀνασκαφὴ Λυκαίου." *Prakt*, pp. 185–200.
———. 1912. "Τὸ ἐν Λυκοσούρᾳ μέγαρον τῆς Δεσποίνης." *ArchEph*, pp. 142–61.
Kourouniotes [sic], K. 1936. *Eleusis: A Guide to the Excavations and the Museum*. Translated by O. Broneer. Athens.
Kourouniotis, K. 1938. "Παράρτεμα." *Deltion* 15 (1933–35), pp. 34–41.
Kowalzig, B. 2005. "Mapping Out *Communitas*: Performance of *Theoria* in Their Sacred and Political Context," in Elsner and Rutherford 2005, pp. 41–72.
Kreinath, J. 2004. "Theoretical Afterthoughts," in Kreinath, Hartung, and Deschner 2004, pp. 267–82.
Kreinath, J., C. Hartung, and A. Deschner, eds. 2004. *The Dynamics of Changing Rituals: The Transformation of Religious Rituals within Their Social and Cultural Context*. New York.
Kreinath, J., J. A. M. Snoek, and M. Stausberg, eds. 2006. *Theorizing Rituals*, vol. 1: *Issues, Topics, Approaches, Concepts*. Studies in the History of Religions 114.1. Leiden and Boston.
———. 2007. *Theorizing Rituals*, vol. 2: *Annotated Bibliography of Ritual Theory 1966–2005*. Studies in the History of Religions 114.2. Leiden and Boston.
Krinzinger, F. 1980. "Das Θέατρον von Olympia," in *Forschungen und Funde: Festschrift Bernard Neutsch*, ed. F. Krinzinger, B. Otto, and E. Walde-Psenner. Innsbruck, pp. 249–60.
Kritzas, Ch. 1992. "Aspects de la vie politique et économique d'Argos au Ve siècle avant J.-C.," in Piérart 1992, pp. 231–40.
———. 2003-4. "Literacy and Society: The Case of Argos." *KODAI* 13/14, pp. 53–60.
———. 2006. "Nouvelles inscriptions d'Argos: Les archives des comptes du trésor sacré (IVe siècle av. J.-C.)." *CRAI*, pp. 397–434.
Kron, U. 1996. "Priesthoods, Dedications and Euergetism: What Part Did Religion Play in the Political and Social Status of Greek Women?" in Hellström and Alroth 1996, pp. 139–82.
Kruft, H.-W. 1994. *A History of Architectural Theory from Vitruvius to the Present*. Translated by R. Taylor, E. Callander, and A. Wood. London and New York.
Kuhn, G. 1985. "Untersuchungen zur Funktion der Säulenhalle in archaischer und klassischer Zeit." *JdI* 100, pp. 169–317.
Kunze, E., and H. Schleif. 1938. *II. Bericht über die Ausgrabungen in Olympia* "Die Schatzhaus-Terrassenmauer." *JdI* 53, pp. 42–44.
Kunze, E., and H. Weber. 1948. "The Olympian Stadium, the Echo Colonnade and an 'Archaeological Earthquake.'" *AJA* 52, pp. 490–96.
Kunze, M. 1991. "Neue Forschungen zum Pergamonaltar," in Etienne and Le Dinahet 1991, pp. 135–40.
Kuttner, A. 1995. "Republican Rome Looks at Pergamon." *HSCP* 97, pp. 156–78.
Kyle, D. G. 1992. "The Panathenaic Games: Sacred and Civic Athletics," in Neils 1992a, pp. 77–101.
Kypraiou, E., and D. Zapheiropoulou, eds. 1999. Ῥόδος 2.400 Χρονιά: ἡ πόλη τῆς Ῥόδου ἀπὸ τὴν ἴδρυσή της μέχρι τὴν κατάληψη ἀπὸ τοὺς Τούρκους (1523). Athens.
Kyriakides, E., ed. 2007. *The Archaeology of Ritual*. Cotsen Advanced Seminars 3. Los Angeles.
LaFollette, L. 1986. "The Chalkotheke on the Athenian Akropolis." *Hesperia* 55, pp. 75–87.
Lajtar, A. 2006. *Deir el-Bahari in the Hellenistic and Roman Periods: A Study of an Egyptian Temple Based on Greek Sources*. JJurP Suppl. 4. Warsaw.
Lancaster, L. 2007. *Concrete Vaulted Construction in Imperial Rome: Innovations in Context*. Cambridge and New York.
Landels, J. G. 1999. *Music in Ancient Greece and Rome*. London.
Langer, R., D. Lüddeckens, K. Radde, and J. Snoek. 2006. "Transfer of Ritual." *Journal of Ritual Studies* 20.1, pp. 1–10.
La Regina, A. 1965. "Pietrabbondante," in *EAA* 6, pp. 160–62.
———. 1966a. "Le iscrizioni osche di Pietrabbondante e la questione di Bovianum Vetus." *RhMus* 109, pp. 260–86.

Bibliography

———. 1966b. "Sulmona," in *EAA* 7, pp. 555–57.

———. 1976. "Il Sannio," in Zanker 1976, pp. 219–54.

———, ed. 1980. *Sannio: Pentri e Frentani dal VI al I sec. A.C. Isernia, Museo Nazionale, Ottobre–Dicembre 1980.* Rome.

La Rocca, E. 2011. "La forza della tradizione: L'architettura sacra a Roma tra II e I secolo A.C.," in La Rocca and D'Alessio 2011, pp. 1–24.

La Rocca, E., and D'Alessio, A., eds. 2011. *Tradizione e innovazione: L'elaborazione del linguaggio ellenistico nell'architettura romana e italica di età tardo-repubblicana.* StMisc 35. Rome.

Laskowska-Kusztal, E. 1984. *Deir el-Bahari III: Le sanctuaire ptolémaïque de Deir el-Bahari.* Warsaw.

La Torre, G. F. 1989. "Il santuario di Ercole Curino," in *Dalla villa di Ovidio al santuario di Ercole*, ed. E. Mattiocco. Teramo, pp. 115–50.

Laumonier, A. 1958. *Les cultes indigène en Carie.* Paris.

Launey, M. 1944. *Le sanctuaire et le culte d'Héraklès à Thasos.* Études Thasiennes 1. Paris.

Launey, M., ed. 1979. *Thasiaca.* BCH Suppl. 5. Paris.

Lauter, H. 1968. "Ein Tempelgarten?" *AA*, pp. 628–31.

———. 1970. "Die hellenistische Agora von Aspendos." *BJb* 170, pp. 77–101.

———. 1972. "Kunst und Landschaft—ein Beitrag zum rhodischen Hellenismus." *AntK* 15, pp. 49–58.

———. 1975. "Zur frühklassischen Neuplanung des Heraions von Argos." *AM* 88, pp. 175–87.

———. 1976. "Die hellenistischen Theater der Samniten und Latiner in ihrer Beziehung zur Theaterarchitektur der Griechen," in Zanker 1976, pp. 413–30.

———. 1979. "Bemerkungen zur späthellenistischen Baukunst in Mittelitalien." *JdI* 94, pp. 390–459.

———. 1982. "Struktur statt Typus." *AA*, pp. 703–24.

———. 1986. *Die Architektur des Hellenismus.* Darmstadt.

Lawrence, D. L., and S. M. Low. 1990. "The Built Environment and Spatial Form." *Annual Review of Anthropology* 19, pp. 453–505.

Lawrence, R. J. 1990. "Public Collective and Private Space: A Study of Urban Housing in Switzerland," in Kent 1990, pp. 73–77.

Lazarides. D. 1980. "Ἀμφίπολις." *Ergon*, pp. 13–15.

———. 1982. "Ἀνασκαφές καὶ ἔρευνες τῆς Ἀμφίπολις." *Prakt*, pp. 43–51.

———. 1984. "Ἀμφίπολις." *Ergon*, pp. 21–25.

———. 1997. *Amphipolis.* Athens.

Lazarides, K. 1986. "Ἀμφίπολις." *Ergon*, pp. 57–61.

———. 1987. "Ἀνασκαφαὶ γυμνάσιου Ἀμφιπόλεως." *Ergon*, pp. 31–36.

Le Dinahet, M.-T. 2001. "Les Italiens de Délos: Complements onomastiques et prosopographiques." *REA* 103, pp. 103–23.

LeFebvre, H. 1991. *The Production of Space.* Translated by D. Nicholson-Smith. Oxford.

Lehmann, P. W. 1954. "The Setting of Hellenistic Temples." *JSAH* 13.4, pp. 15–20.

Lehmann-Hartleben, K. 1927. Review of Gardiner 1925. *Gnomon* 7, p. 385.

———. 1931. "Wesen und Gestalt griechischer Heiligtümer." *Die Antike* 7, pp. 29–31.

Leonardos, B. 1896a. "Ἀνασκαφαὶ τοῦ ἐν Λυκοσούρα ἱερὸν τῆς Δεσποίνης." *Prakt*, pp. 93–126.

———. 1896b. "Λυκοσούρας ἐπιγραφαί ἐκ τῶν ἐν τῷ ἱερῷ τῆς Δεσποίνης ἀνασκαφῶν." *ArchEph*, pp. 100–130.

———. 1925. "Ἀνασκαφαὶ Ἀμφιαρείου." *Prakt*, pp. 33–35.

———. 1926. "Ἀμφιαρείου ἀνασκαφαί." *Prakt*, pp. 103–106.

———. 1927. "Ἀμφιαρείου σκάφαι." *Prakt*, pp. 27–32.

———. 1928. "Ἀμφιαρείου ἀνασκαφαί." *Prakt*, pp. 27–32.

———. 1929. "Ἀμφιαρείου ἀνασκαφαί." *Prakt*, pp. 57–60.

Letesson, Q., and K. Vansteenhuyse. 2006. "Towards an Archaeology of Perception: 'Looking' at the Minoan Palaces." *JMA* 19, pp. 91–119.

Lévy, E. 1967. "Sondages à Lykosoura et date de Damophon." *BCH* 91, pp. 518–45.

Lévy, E., and Marcadé, J. 1972. "Au Musée de Lycosoura." *BCH* 96, pp. 967–1004.

Lind, T. T. 2009. "Music and Cult in Ancient Greece: Ethnomusicological Perspectives," in Jensen, Hinge, Schultz, and Wickkiser 2009, pp. 195–214.

Linders, T., and P. Hellström. 1989. *Architecture and Society in Hecatomnid Caria.* Boreas 17. Uppsala and Stockholm.

Linders, T., and G. Nordquist, eds. 1987. *Gifts to the Gods: Proceedings of the Uppsala Symposium 1985.* Uppsala.

Linfert, A. 1976. *Kunstzentren hellenistischer Zeit: Studien an weiblichen Gewandfiguren.* Wiesbaden.

———. 1995. "Prunkaltäre," in Wörrle and Zanker 1995, pp. 131–46.

Lippolis, E. 1988–89. "Il santuario di Athana a Lindo." *ASAtene* 48–49, pp. 97–157.

Lock, M. 1993. "Cultivating the Body: Anthropology and

Epistemologies of Bodily Practice and Knowledge." *Annual Review of Anthropology* 22, pp. 133–55.

Lolos, Y. 2003. "Greek Roads: A Commentary on the Ancient Terms." *Glotta* 79, pp. 137–74.

Lomas, K. 1996. *Roman Italy, 338 BC–AD 200*. New York.

———. 2004. "Italy during the Roman Republic 338–31 B.C.," in Flower 2004, pp. 199–224.

Loucas, I., and E. Loucas. 1988. "The Megaron of Lykosoura and Some Prehistoric Telesteria." *JPR* 2, pp. 25–34.

Loucas-Durie, É. 1992. "L'élément orgiastique dans la religion arcadienne." *Kernos* 5, pp. 87–96.

Love, I. C. 1968a. "A Preliminary Report of the Excavations at Knidos, 1967." *AJA* 72, pp. 137–39.

———. 1968b. "Recent Archaeological Research in Turkey." *AnatSt* 18, pp. 37–39.

———. 1968c. "Knidos Excavations in 1967." *TürkArkDerg* 16.2, pp. 133–59.

———. 1969a. "A Preliminary Report of the Excavations at Knidos, 1968." *AJA* 73, pp. 216–19.

———. 1969b. "Recent Archaeological Research in Turkey." *AnatSt* 19, pp. 16–18.

———. 1971. "A Preliminary Report of the Excavations at Knidos, 1969." *AJA* 74, pp. 149–55.

———. 1972a. "A Preliminary Report of the Excavations at Knidos, 1970." *AJA* 76, pp. 61–76.

———. 1972b. "A Preliminary Report of the Excavations at Knidos, 1971." *AJA* 76, pp. 393–405.

———. 1973a. "A Preliminary Report of the Excavations at Knidos, 1972." *AJA* 77, pp. 413–24.

———. 1973b. "Knidos Excavations in 1972." *TürkArkDerg* 20.2, pp. 97–142.

———. 1978. "A Brief Summary of Excavations at Knidos 1967–1973," in *The Proceedings of the 10th International Congress of Classical Archaeology, Ankara-Izmir (1973)*, ed. E. Akurgal. Ankara, pp. 1111–33.

Low, S. M., and D. Lawrence-Zúñiga, eds. 2003. *The Anthropology of Space and Place: Locating Culture*. Malden MA and Oxford.

Ma, J. 1999. *Antiochus III and the Cities of Western Asia Minor*. Oxford.

———. 2000. "The Epigraphy of Hellenistic Asia Minor: A Survey of Recent Research (1992–1999)." *AJA* 104, pp. 95–121.

———. 2003. "Peer Polity Interaction in the Hellenistic Age." *PastPres* 180.1, pp. 9–39.

———. 2013. "The Attalids: A Military History." in Thoneman 2013a, pp. 49–82.

MacDonald, W. A. 1943. *The Political Meeting Places of the Greeks*. Baltimore.

MacDonald, W. L. 1986. *The Architecture of the Roman Empire*, vol. 2: *An Urban Appraisal*. New Haven and London.

MacKay, A. G. 2004. "Samnites at Cumae," in *Samnium: Settlement and Cultural Change*, ed. H. Jones. Archaeologia Transatlantica 22. Providence, pp. 85–101.

Mackil, E. 2004. "Wandering Cities: Alternatives to Catastrophe in the Greek Polis." *AJA* 108, pp. 493–516.

Maiuri, A. 1928. "La topografia monumentale di Rodi." *Clara Rodos* 1, pp. 44–55.

Mallwitz, A. 1972. *Olympia and seine Bauten*. Munich.

———. 1981a. "Neue Forschungen in Olympia: Theater und Hestiaheiligtum in der Altis." *Gymnasium* 88, pp. 97–122.

———, ed. 1981b. *OlBer* 10. Berlin.

———. 1988. "Cult and Competition Locations at Olympia," in *The Archaeology of the Olympics: The Olympics and Other Festivals in Antiquity*, ed. W. J. Raschke. Madison, pp. 79–109.

———, ed. 1999a. *OlBer* 11. Berlin.

———. 1999b. "Ergebnisse und Folgerung: Brunnen und frühe Bauten," in Mallwitz 1999a, pp. 181–282.

Mallwitz, A., and W. Schiering. 1964. *Die Werkstatt des Phidias in Olympia*. OlForsch 5. Berlin.

Mallwitz, A., and H. van de Löcht. 1980. "Restaurierungsarbeiten in Olympia: Schatzhaus-Terrassenmauer." *AA*, pp. 361–67.

Mansfield, J. M. 1985. *The Robe of Athena and the Panathenaic Peplos*. Ph.D. dissertation, University of California, Berkeley.

Maran, J. 2006. "Architecture, Power and Social Practice—an Introduction," in Maran, Juwig, Schwengel, and Thaler 2006, pp. 9–14.

Maran, J., C. Juwig, H. Schwengel, and U. Thaler, eds. 2006. *Constructing Power: Architecture, Ideology and Social Practice / Konstruktion der Macht: Architektur, Ideologie und soziales Handeln*. Heidelberg.

Marangou, E.-L. I., et al. 1995. *Ancient Greek Art from the Collection of Stavros S. Niarchos*. Athens.

Marchese, R. 1989. *The Historical Archaeology of Northern*

Bibliography

Caria: A Study in Cultural Adaptations. BAR International Series 536. Oxford.

Marconi, C. 2007. *Temple Decoration and Cultural Identity in the Archaic Greek World: The Metopes of Selinus.* Cambridge.

———. 2010. "The Institute of Fine Arts, NYU Excavations on the Akropolis of Selinunte, 2006–2009." Paper delivered at the Annual Meeting of the Archaeological Institute of America, Anaheim CA, January 8.

Marconi, P. 2008. "Il santuario di Ercole Vincitore a Tivoli: Un concorso di progettazione recente," in *Ricerche di storia dell'arte 95: Architetti e archeologi costruttori d'identità.* Rome, pp. 69–78.

Marcus, J. 2003. "Monumentality in Archaic States: Lessons Learned from Large-Scale Excavations of the Past," in *Theory and Practice in Mediterranean Archaeology: Old World and New World Perspectives*, ed. J. K. Papadopoulos and R. M. Leventhal. Los Angeles, pp. 115–34.

Maré, E.A. 2013. "Conspicuous Display: Stairs Historical and Modern, Part I: A Theoretical Introduction and Examples of Historical Stairs in Stone." *South African Journal of Art History* 28.2, pp. 156–82.

Marinatos, N. 1996. "Cult by the Seashore: What Happened at Amnisos," in Hägg 1996, pp. 135–39.

Marinatos, N., and R. Hägg, eds. 1993. *Greek Sanctuaries: New Approaches.* London.

Marinatos, S. 1935. "Ἀνασκαφὴ Ἀμνισοῦ (Κρήτης)." *Prakt*, pp. 196–99.

———. 1936. "Le temple géométrique de Dréros." *BCH* 60, pp. 228–29.

———. 1938. "Ἀνασκαφὴ Ἀμνισοῦ (Κρήτης)." *Prakt*, pp. 130–38.

Martiensen, R. 1956. *The Idea of Space in Greek Architecture.* Johannesburg.

Martin, R. 1951. *Recherches sur l'agora grecque.* Paris.

———. 1957. "Sur deux expressions techniques de l'architecture grecque." *RPhil* 31, pp. 66–81.

———. 1970. Review of Orlandos 1967–68. *RA*, pp. 343–45.

———. 1973. "Architecture," in *Hellenistic Art (330–50 B.C.)*, ed. J. Charbonneaux, R. Martin, and F. Villard. Translated by P. Green. New York, pp. 3–94.

———. 1978. "Thasos, quelques problèmes de structure urbaine." *CRAI*, pp. 182–97.

Martin, R. P. 2003. "The Pipes Are Brawling: Conceptualizing Musical Performance in Athens," in Dougherty and Kurke 2003, pp. 153–80.

Massineo, G., and A. Pellegrino. 1995. *Sulmona e dintorni.* Rome.

Matthaei, A., and M. Zimmerman, eds. 2009. *Stadtbilder im Hellenismus.* Berlin.

Matthaiou, A. P., and Y. A. Pikoulas. 1986. "A Sacred Law from Lykosoura." *Horos* 4, pp. 75–78.

Matthews, R., ed. 1998. *Ancient Anatolia: Fifty Years' Work by the British Institute of Archaeology at Ankara.* London.

Mattiocco, E. 1997. *Sulmona: Guida storica artistica della città e dintorni.* Pescara.

Matz, F. 1953–54. "Archaische Gebäudegruppe." *ArchEph* part 2, pp. 84–100.

Mauss, M. 1934. "La technique du corps." *Journal de Psychologie* 32, nos. 3–4 (March 15–April 15, 1936). Reprinted in *Sociologie et anthropologie* (Paris 1950), pp. 365–86; *Sociology and Anthropology* (London 1979), pp. 97–123; available online at http://classiques.uqac.ca/classiques/mauss_marcel/socio_et_anthropo/6_Techniques_corps/Techniques_corps.html.

McGowan, E. P. 1995. "Tomb Marker and Turning Post: Funerary Columns in the Archaic Period." *AJA* 99, pp. 615–32.

McGuire, R. H., and Schiffer, M. B. 1983. "A Theory of Architectural Design." *JAnthArch* 2, pp. 277–303.

McMahon, A. 2013. "Space, Sound, and Light: Towards a Sensory Experience of Ancient Monumental Architecture." *AJA* 117, pp. 163–79.

Meiggs, R., and D. Lewis. 1988. *A Selection of Greek Historical Inscriptions to the End of the Fifth Century B.C.* 2nd revised ed. Oxford.

Melas, E. 1973. *Temples and Sanctuaries of Ancient Greece.* London.

Menadier, B. 1995. *The Sixth Century B.C. Temple and the Sanctuary and Cult of Hera Akraia, Perachora.* Ph.D. dissertation, University of Cincinnati.

———. 2002. "The Sanctuary of Hera Akraia and Its Religious Connections with Corinth," in Hägg 2002, pp. 85–91.

Mengoli, M. 2007. "Caratteri architettonici dei templi prostili di Pergamo: Tempio del teatro, tempio R." *Nuova Archeologia* Jan.–Feb., pp. 1–4.

Meritt, B. D., T. H. Wade-Gery, and M. F. McGregor. 1939. *The Athenian Tribute Lists,* vol. 1. Cambridge MA.

Merker, G. S. 2000. *Corinth 18.4: The Sanctuary of Demeter and Kore; Terracotta Figurines of the Classical, Hellenistic, and Roman Periods.* Princeton.

Merleau-Ponty, M. 1962. *Phenomenology of Perception.* Translated by C. Smith. London.

Mersich, N. 1986. "Einige Festungen im pisidisch-pamphylischen Grenzgebiet." *JÖBG* 36, pp. 191–200.

Mertens, D. 1989. "Die Mauern von Selinunt: Vorbericht der Arbeiten des Deutschen Archäologischen Instituts Rom 1971–75 und 1985–87." *RM* 96, pp. 87–154.

———.1984. *Der Tempel von Segesta und die dorische Tempelbaukunst des griechischen Westens in klassischer Zeit.* Mainz.

Mertens, D., and A. de Siena. 1982. "Metaponto: Il Teatro—Ekklesiasterion." *BdA* series VI.16, pp. 1–60.

Mertens-Horn, M. 1986. "Studien zu griechischen Löwenbildern." *RM* 93, pp. 1–61.

Merz, J. M. 2001. *Das Heiligtum der Fortuna in Palestrina und die Architektur der Neuzeit.* Munich.

Meskell, L., and R. W. Preucel. 2004a. *A Companion to Social Archaeology.* Oxford.

———. 2004b. "Places," in Meskell and Preucel 2004a, pp. 215–29.

Michl, J. 2002. "Form Follows What? The Modernist Notion of Function as a *Carte Blanche*." Available online at http://www.geocities.com/Athens/2360/jm-eng.fff-hai.html. Also in *Magazine of the Faculty of Architecture and Town Planning, Israel Institute of Technology* 10 (1995), pp. 20–31.

Migeotte, L. 1992. *Les souscriptions publiques dans les cités grecques.* Geneva and Quebec.

———. 1995. "Finances et constructions publiques," in Wörrle and Zanker 1995, pp. 79–86.

Mikalson, J. D. 1975a. "ΗΜΕΡΑ ἈΠΟΦΡΑΣ." *AJP* 96, pp. 19–27.

———. 1975b. *The Sacred and Civil Calendar of the Athenian Year.* Princeton.

Miller, D., and C. Tilley. 1984. *Ideology, Power and Prehistory.* Cambridge.

Miller, M. C. 1997. *Athens and Persia in the 5th Century B.C.: A Study in Cultural Receptivity.* Cambridge.

Miller, S. G. 1978. *The Prytaneion: Its function and Architectural Form.* Berkeley.

———. 1995. "Old Metroon and Old Bouleuterion in the Classical Agora of Athens," in *Studies in the Ancient Greek Polis,* ed. M.-H. Hansen and K. L. Raaflaub. *Historia Suppl.* 95. Stuttgart, pp. 133–56.

———. 2004. *Ancient Greek Athletics.* New Haven and London.

Mitchell, S. 1991. "The Hellenization of Pisidia." *MeditArch* 4, pp. 119–45.

———. 1992. "Hellenismus in Pisidia," in Schwertheim 1992, pp. 1–27.

———. 1994a. "Termessos, King Amyntas, and the War with the Sandaliôtai: A New Inscription from Pisidia," in D. French 1994, pp. 93–105.

———. 1994b. "Three Cities in Pisidia." *AnatSt* 44, pp. 129–48.

———. 1998. "The Pisidian Survey," in Matthews 1998, pp. 237–53.

———. 1999. "Archaeology in Asia Minor 1990–1998." *AR* 1998–1999, pp. 125–91.

———. 2003. "Recent Archaeology and the Development of Cities in Hellenistic and Roman Asia Minor," in Schwertheim and Winter 2003, pp. 21–34.

Mitchell, S., and M. Waelkens. 1987. "Sagalassus and Cremna 1986." *AnatSt* 37, pp. 37–47.

Mitens, K. 1993. "Theatre Architecture in Central Italy: Reception and Resistence," in Guldager Bilde, I. Nielsen, and M. Nielsen 1993, pp. 91–107.

Mitsopoulos-Leon, V. 1992. "Artémis de Lousoi: Les fouilles autrichennes." *Kernos* 5, pp. 97–108.

Moggi, M. 1976. *I sinecismi interstatali greci.* Pisa.

Momigliano, A. 1936. "Note sulla storia di Rodi." *RivFil* 14, pp. 49–63.

Montegu, J. C. 1976. "A Note on the Labyrinths of Didyma." *AJA* 80, pp. 304–5.

Moore, H. 1999a. "Anthropological Theory at the Turn of the Century," in Moore 1999a, pp. 1–23.

———, ed. 1999b. *Anthropological Theory Today.* Oxford and Malden MA.

Mooren, L., ed. 2000. *Politics, Administration and Society in the Hellenistic and Roman World. Studia Hellenistica.* Louvain.

Morgan, C. 1994. "The Evolution of a Sacral 'Landscape': Isthmia, Perachora and the Early Corinthia," in Alcock and Osborne 1994, pp. 105–42.

Morgan, C. 2007. *Debating Patronage: The Cases of Argos and Corinth.* Oxford and New York.

Bibliography

Montero-Herreros, S. 1983. Review of Almagro-Gorbea 1982. *ArchEspArq*, pp. 303–4.

Morris, I. 2000. *Archaeology as Cultural History*. Oxford.

Morris, I., and K. Raaflaub, eds. 1998. *Democracy 2500? Questions and Challenges*. Dubuque.

Moser, C., and Feldman, C. 2014a. "Introduction," in Moser and Feldman 2014b, pp. 1–12.

———, eds. 2014b. *Locating the Sacred: Theoretical Approaches to the Emplacement of Religion*. Oxford and Oakville CT.

Moustaka, A. 2002. "On the Cult of Hera at Olympia," in Hägg 2002, pp. 199–205.

Mouzelis, N. 1995. *Sociological Theory: What Went Wrong?* London.

Muller, A., D. Mulliez, and F. Blondé. 1988. "Les abords nord-est de l'agora de Thasos." *BCH* 112, pp. 247–48.

Müller, C., and C. Hasenohr. 2002. *Les Italiens dans le monde grec*. BCH Suppl. 41. Paris.

Murray, O., ed. 1990. *Sympotica: A Symposium on the Symposion*. Oxford.

Murray, P., and P. Wilson. 2004. *Music and the Muses: The Culture of "Mousike" in the Classical Athenian City*. Oxford.

Musti, D., et al. 1991. *La transizione dal Miceneo all'alto Arcaismo: Dal palazzo alla città*. Rome.

Myers, J. W., E. E. Myers, and G. Cadogan. 1992. *The Aerial Atlas of Ancient Crete*. Berkeley and Los Angeles.

Mylonas, G. E. 1961. *Eleusis and the Eleusinian Mysteries*. Princeton.

Mylonopoulos, J. 2006. "Greek Sanctuaries as Places of Communication through Rituals: An Archaeological Perspective," in Stavrianopoulou 2006c, pp. 69–110.

———. 2008. "The Dynamics of Ritual Space in the Hellenistic and Roman East." *Kernos* 21, pp. 49–79.

Nagy, B. 1991. "The Procession to Phaleron." *Historia* 40, pp. 288–306.

———. 1994. "Alcibiades' Second 'Profanation.'" *Historia* 43, pp. 275–85.

Naiden, F. S. 2013. *Smoke Signals for the Gods*. Oxford.

Naumann, R. 1973. *Didyma Führer*. Istanbul.

Neils, J., ed. 1992a. *Goddess and Polis: The Panathenaic Festival in Ancient Athens*. Hanover NH and Princeton.

Neils, J. 1992b. "The Panathenaia: An Introduction," in Neils 1992a, pp. 13–27.

———. 1994. "The Panathenaia and Kleisthenic Ideology," in Coulson et al. 1994, pp. 151–60.

———. 1996a. "Pride, Pomp and Circumstance: The Iconography of Procession," in Neils 1996b, pp. 177–97.

———, ed. 1996b. *Worshipping Athena: Panathenaia and Parthenon*. Madison.

———. 2001. *The Parthenon Frieze*. Cambridge.

———, ed. 2005. *The Parthenon: From Antiquity to the Present*. Cambridge.

———. 2007. "Replicating Tradition: The First Celebrations of the Greater Panathenaia," in Palagia and Choremis-Spetsieri 2007, pp. 41–51.

———. 2012. "The Political Process in the Public Festival: The Panathenaic Festival of Athens," in Brandt and Iddeng 2012, pp. 199–215.

Nielsen, A. E. 1995. "Architectural Performance and the Reproduction of Social Power," in Skibo, Walker, and Nielsen 1995, pp. 47–66.

Nielsen, I. 2000. "Cultic Theaters and Ritual Drama in Ancient Greece." *Proceedings of the Danish Institute at Athens* 3, pp. 107–33.

———. 2002. *Cultic Theaters and Ritual Drama*. Aarhus.

———. 2009. "The Sanctuary of Artemis Brauronia: Can Architecture and Iconography Help to Locate the Settings of the Rituals?" in Fischer-Hansen and Poulsen 2009, pp. 83–117.

Nielsen, T. H. 2002a. *Arkadia and Its Poleis in the Archaic and Classical Periods*. Hypomnemata 140. Göttingen.

Nielsen, T. H., ed. 2002b. *Even More Studies in the Ancient Greek Polis*. Historia Einzelschriften 162. Stuttgart.

Nielsen, T. H., and J. Roy, eds. 1999. *Defining Ancient Arkadia. Acts of the Copenhagen Polis Center* 6. Copenhagen.

Nilsson, M. P. 1916. "Die Prozessionstypen im griechischen Kult." *JdI* 31, pp. 309–39.

Noack, F. 1927. *Eleusis: Die baugeschichtliche Entwicklung des Heiligtums*. Berlin and Leipzig.

Nordquist, G. C. 1992. "Instrumental Music in Representations of Greek Cult," in Hägg 1992, pp. 143–68.

———. 1994. "Some Notes on Musicians in Greek Cult," in Hägg 1994, pp. 81–93.

Nylander, C. 1970. *Ionians at Pasargadae*. Uppsala.

Ogden, D., ed. 2007. *A Companion to Greek Religion*. Oxford.

Ohlemutz, E. 1940. *Die Kulte und Heiligtümer der Götter in Pergamon*. Reprint ed. 1968. Darmstadt.

Ohly, D. 1965. "Kerameikos-Grabung: Tätigkeitbericht 1956–1961." *AA*, cols. 309–13.

Ohnesorg, A. 2005. *Ionische Altäre: Formen und Varianten einer Architekturgattung aus Insel- und Ostionien*. AF 21. Berlin.

Olmsted, F. L. 1910. "Notes upon the Sizes of Steps Required for Comfort." *Landscape Architecture* 1, pp. 84–90.

Önen, Ü. 1989. *Caria*. Istanbul.

Orlandini, G. A. 1969–70. "Considerazioni sul Mégaron di Despoina a Licosura." *ASAtene* 31–32, pp. 343–57.

Orlandos, A. 1911. "Ἡ κρήνη τῆς Λυκοσούρας." *ArchEph*, pp. 200–206.

Orlandos, A. K. 1967–68. Ἡ Ἀρκαδικὴ Ἀλίφειρα καὶ τὰ μνημεῖα τῆς. Athens, pp. 9, 29, 43–45.

Osborne, R. 1987. "The Viewing and Obscuring of the Parthenon Frieze." *JHS* 107, pp. 98–105.

Osborne, R., and J. Tanner, eds. 2007a. *Art's Agency and Art History*. Oxford and Malden MA.

Osborne, R., and J. Tanner. 2007b. "Introduction: *Art and Agency* and Art History," in Osborne and Tanner 2007a, pp. 1–27.

Østby, E. 1994. "Recent Excavations in the Sanctuary of Athena Alea at Tegea (1990–93)," in *Archaeology in the Peloponnese: New Excavations and Research*, ed. K. A. Sheedy. Oxford, pp. 39–63.

———. 1995. "Chronological Problems of Ancient Selinus," in *Ancient Sicily. Acta Hyperborea* 6. Copenhagen, pp. 83–101.

Østby, E., J. M. Luce, G. C. Nordquist, C. Tarditi, and M. E. Voyatzis. 1994. "The Sanctuary of Athena Alea at Tegea: First Preliminary Report (1990–1992)." *OpAth* 20, pp. 89–141.

Özgan, R. 1982. "Zur Datierung des Artemisaltars in Magnesia am Maeander." *IstMitt* 32, pp. 196–209.

Pace, B. 1938. *Arte e civiltà della Sicilia antica*, vol. 2. Milan, Genoa, Rome, Naples.

Packard, R. T., ed. 1981. *Architectural Graphic Standards*. 7th ed. New York.

Paga, J. 2010. "Deme Theaters in Attica and the Trittys System." *Hesperia* 79, pp. 351–84.

Pakkanen, J. 1998. "The Column Shafts of the Propylaia and Stoa in the Sanctuary of Athena at Lindos," in *Proceedings of the Danish Institute at Athens*, vol. 2, ed. S. Dietz and S. Isager. Aarhus, pp. 147–59.

Palagia, O., and A. Choremis-Spetsieri. 2007. *The Panathenaic Games*. Oxford.

Palinkas, J. 2008. "Circling the Sanctuary of Demeter and Kore at Eleusis during the Archaic Period." *Abstracts of the 109th Meeting of the Archaeological Institute of America, Chicago 2008*, p. 91.

Palyvou, C. 2003. "Architecture and Archaeology: The Minoan Palaces in the Twenty-First Century," in Papadopoulos and Leventhal 2003, pp. 205–33.

Papachatzis, N. D. 1967. Παυσανίου Ἑλλάδος Περιήγησις, vol. 4: Ἀχαϊκά, Ἀρκαδικά. Athens.

Papadimitriou, J. 1948. "Ἀνασκαφαὶ ἐν Βραυρῶνι τῆς Ἀττικῆς." *Prakt*, pp. 81–89.

———. 1949. "Ἀνασκαφαὶ ἐν Βραυρῶνι τῆς Ἀττικῆς." *Prakt*, pp. 75–90.

———. 1950. "Ἀνασκαφαὶ ἐν Βραυρῶνι." *Prakt*, pp. 173–87.

———. 1963. "The Sanctuary of Artemis at Brauron." *Scientific American* 208.6, pp. 111–20.

Papadimitriou, V. 1988. "The Anastylosis of the Ancient Monuments on the Acropolis of Lindos: Past and Present Attempts," in Dietz and Papachristodoulou 1988, pp. 169–72.

Papadopoulos, J. K., and R. M. Leventhal. 2003. *Theory and Practice in Mediterranean Archaeology: Old World and New World Perspectives*. Los Angeles.

Papanikolaou, A. 2012. Ἡ Ἀποκατάσταση τοῦ Ἐρεχθείου (1979–1987), ed. F. Mallouchou-Tufano and Ch. Bouras. 2 vols. Athens.

Pariente, A., and G. Touchais, eds. 1992. *Argos kai Argolida: Topographia kai poleodomia / Argos et l'Argolide: Topographie et urbanisme*. BCH Suppl. 22. Paris.

Parke, H. W. 1977. *Festivals of the Athenians*. Ithaca.

———. 1985. *The Oracles of Apollo in Asia Minor*. Dover.

———. 1986. "The Temple of Apollo at Didyma: The Building and Its Function." *JHS* 106, pp. 121–31.

Parker, R. 1996. *Athenian Religion: A History*. Oxford.

———. 2004. "What Are Sacred Laws?" in Harris and Rubenstein 2004, pp. 57–70.

———. 2005. *Polytheism and Society at Athens*. New York and Oxford.

Parker Pearson, M., and C. Richards. 1994. *Architecture and Order: Approaches to Social Space*. London and New York.

Bibliography

Parsons, A. 1943. "Klepsydra and the Paved Court of the Pythion." *Hesperia* 12, pp. 191–267.

Patera, I. 2012. *Offrir en Grèce ancienne: Gestes et contexts.* Stuttgart.

Paton, J. M., G. P. Stevens, L. Caskey, H. Fowler, and T. Heermance. 1927. *The Erechtheum.* Cambridge MA.

Payne, H., et al. 1940. *Perachora: The Sanctuaries of Hera Akraia and Limenia,* vol. 1. Oxford.

Pedersen, P. 1988a. "The Maussolleion-Terrace at Halicarnassus and 4th Century B.C. Planning in South-Western Asia Minor," in Πρακτικὰ τοῦ XII διεθνούς συνεδρίου κλασικής ἀρχαιολογίας Ἀθῆνα, 4–10 Σεπτεμβρίου 1983. Athens, pp. 155–59.

———. 1988b. "Town-Planning in Halicarnassus and Rhodes," in Dietz and Papachristodoulou 1988, pp. 98–103.

———. 1989. "Some General Trends in Architectural Layout of 4th Century Caria," in Linders and Hellström 1989, pp. 9–14.

———. 1991. *The Maussolleion of Halikarnassos,* vol. 3.1: *The Maussolleion Terrace and Accessory Structures: Text and Appendices.* Aarhus.

———. 2004. "Pergamon and the Ionian Renaissance." *IstMitt* 54, pp. 409–33.

Peirce, S. M. 1984. *The Representation of Animal Sacrifice in Attic Vase-painting.* Ph.D. dissertation, Bryn Mawr College.

Pemberton, E. G. 1989. *Corinth 18.1: The Sanctuary of Demeter and Kore; The Greek Pottery.* Princeton.

Perreault, J.-Y., J.-Y. Empereur, A. Simossi, Y. Grandjean, H. Koukouli-Chryssanthaki, T. Koželj, F. Salviat, and M. Brunet. 1988. "Thasos." *BCH* 112, pp. 732–46.

Perrin, B. 1917 (1968). *Plutarch's Lives,* vol. 5. Cambridge MA.

Perrin-Saminadayar, E. 2011. Review of Bosnakis, Hallof, and Rigsby 2010. *BMCR* 2011.04.37.

Perrot, G., and C. Chipiez. 1892. *History of Art in Phrygia, Lydia, Caria, and Lycia.* London.

Peschlow-Bindokat, A. 1977. "Herakleia am Latmos: Vorläufiger Bericht über die Arbeiten in den Jahren 1974 und 1975." *AA,* pp. 90–104.

———. 1989. "Die Umgestaltung von Latmos in der ersten Hälfte des 4. Jhs. v. Chr.," in Linders and Hellstrom 1989, pp. 69–76.

———. 1996. *Der Latmos: Eine unbekannte Gebirgslandschaft an der türkische Westküste.* Mainz.

———. 2005. *Feldforschungen im Latmos: Die karische Stadt Latmos. Milet* 3.6. Berlin and New York.

Petrakos, B. Ch. 1967. "Τὸ Ἀμφιάρειον τοῦ Ὠρωποῦ." *ArchEph,* pp. 1–13.

———. 1968a. Ὁ Ὠρωπὸς καὶ τὸ ἱερὸν τοῦ Ἀμφιαράου. Athens.

———. 1968b. "Inscriptions from Oropos." *AAA* 33, p. 73.

———. 1974. *The Amphiaraion of Oropos.* Athens.

Petsa-Tzounakou, V. 1996. *Art and History of Rhodes: Lindos, Kamiros, Ialyssos, Embonas.* Florence.

Pfaff, C. A. 1992. *The Argive Heraion: The Architecture of the Classical Temple of Hera.* Ph.D. dissertation, New York University.

———. 1999. "The Early Iron Age Pottery from the Sanctuary of Demeter and Kore at Corinth." *Hesperia* 68, pp. 55–134.

———. 2002. *The Argive Heraion,* vol.1: *The Architecture of the Classical Temple of Hera.* Princeton.

Pfuhl, E. 1923. *Malerei und Zeichnung der Griechen.* Munich.

Picard, C. 1962. *Les murailles: Les portes sculptée à images divines. Études Thasiennes* 8. Paris.

Picard, O. 1992. "Lato," in *Aerial Atlas of Ancient Crete,* ed. J. W. Myers, E. E. Myers, and G. Cadogan. Berkeley, pp. 154–59.

Piérart, M., ed. 1992. *Polydipsion Argos: Argos de la fin des palais mycéniens à la constitution de l'état classique. BCH Suppl.* 22. Rome, Freiburg, and Paris.

Piérart, M., and G. Touchais. 1996. *Argos: Une ville grecque de 6000 Ans. Patrimonie de la Méditerranée.* Paris.

Pinkwart, D. 1984. Review of Bohtz 1981. *BJb* 184, pp. 768–72.

Piok Zanon, C. 2006. *The Sanctuary of Demeter at Pergamon: The Third-Century Attalids and the Creation of a Hellenistic Capital.* Ph.D. dissertation, University of Pittsburgh.

———. 2007. "Dank an Demeter." *IstMitt* 57, pp. 323–64.

Plommer, H. 1956. Review of Martiensen 1956. *JHS* 77, pp. 347–48.

Plommer, W. H., and F. Salviat. 1966. "The Altar of Hera Akraia at Perachora." *BSA* 61, pp. 207–15.

Polinskaya, I. 2006. "Lack of Boundaries, Absence of Oppositions: The City-Countryside Continuum of a Greek Pantheon," in Rosen and Sluiter 2006, pp. 61–92.

Pompeo, L. 1999. *Il complesso architettonico del Tempio M di Selinunte: Analisi tecnica e storia del monumento.* Turin.

Pottier, E. 1931. *CVA France 10, Bibliothèque Nationale, Cabinet des Médailles 2.* Paris.

Pouilloux, J. 1954. *Recherches sur l'histoire et les cultes de Thasos. Études Thasiennes 3.* Paris.

——. 1958. "Travaux de réfection au sanctuaire d'Apollon Pythéen sur une inscription d'Argos." *REA* 60, pp. 50–66.

Pounder, R. L. 1983. "A Hellenistic Arsenal in Athens." *Hesperia* 52, pp. 233–56.

Pred, A. 1984. "Place as Historically Contingent Process: Structuration and the Time-Geography of Becoming Place." *Annals of the Association of American Geographers* 74, pp. 279–97.

——. 1990. *Making Histories and Constructing Human Geographies.* Boulder, San Francisco, and Oxford.

Prent, M. 2005. *Cretan Sanctuaries and Cults: Continuity and Change from Late Minoan IIIC to the Archaic Period.* Leiden and Boston.

Price, S. 1999. *Religions of the Ancient Greeks.* Cambridge.

Pugliese Caratelli, G., ed. 1985. *Sikanie: Storia e civiltà della Sicilia greca.* Milan.

——, ed. 1985–90. *Magna Graecia.* 4 vols. Milan.

——, ed. 1996. *The Western Greeks.* Milan.

Purchiaroni, G. 1959–60. "Considerazione sull'Hephaisteion d'Atene." *ASAtene* 21–22, pp. 293–307.

Queyrel, A., J. des Courtils, Y. Garlan, J.-J. Maffre, A. Muller, D. Mulliez, and F. Blondé. 1984. "Thasos." *BCH* 108, pp. 869–80.

Radt, W. 1970. *Siedlungen und Bauten auf der Halbinsel von Halikarnassos. IstMitt Beiheft 3.* Tübingen.

——. 1978. "Die Leleger auf der Halbinsel von Halikarnassos," in *Proceedings of the Xth International Congress of Classical Archaeology,* vol. 1. Ankara, pp. 329–47.

——. 1988. *Pergamon: Geschichte und Bauten, Funde und Erforschung einen Antiken Metropole.* Cologne.

——. 1998. "Recent Research in and about Pergamon: A Survey (ca. 1987–1997)," in Koester 1998, pp. 1–40.

Raeck, W. 1983. Review of Bohtz 1981. *Gnomon* 55, pp. 525–30.

Rakob, F. 1976. "Hellenismus in Mittelitalien: Bautypen und Bautechnik," in Zanker 1976, pp. 366–86.

Rapoport, A., ed. 1976. *The Mutual Interaction of People and Their Built Environment: A Cross-Cultural Perspective.* The Hague and Paris.

Rapoport, A. 1990. "Systems of Activities and Systems of Settings," in Kent 1990, pp. 9–20.

Ratté, C. 1992. "The 'Pyramid Tomb' at Sardis." *IstMitt* 42, pp. 135–61.

——. 1993. "Lydian Contributions to Archaic East Greek Architecture," in des Courtils and Moretti 1993, pp. 1–12.

——. 2011. *Lydian Architecture.* Cambridge.

Reed, N. 1987. "The Euandria Competition at the Panathenaia Reconsidered." *AncW* 15, pp. 59–64.

Reger, G. 1999. "The Relations between Rhodes and Caria from 246 to 167 B.C.," in Gabrielsen et al. 1999, pp. 76–97.

——. 2001. "The Mykonian Synoikismos." *REA* 103, pp. 157–81.

Reggiani, A. M. 1998. *Tivoli: Il Santuario di Ercole Vincitore.* Milan.

Rehm, A., T. Wiegand, and R. Harder. 1958. *Didyma II: Die Inschriften.* Berlin.

Reichel, W., and A. Wilhelm. 1901. "Das Heiligtum der Artemis zu Lusoi." *ÖJh* 4, pp. 1–89.

Relph, E. 1985. "Geographical Experiences and Being-in-the-World: The Phenomenological Origins of Geography," in Seamon and Mugerauer 1985, pp. 15–31.

Rheidt, K. 1992. "Die Obere Agora: Zur Entwicklung des hellenistischen Stadtzentrums von Pergamon." *IstMitt* 42, pp. 235–85.

——. 1996. "Pergamenische Ordnungen—Der Zeustempel und seine Bedeutung für die Architektur der Attaliden," in Schwandner 1996, pp. 162–80.

Rhodes, P. J., and R. Osborne, eds. 2003. *Greek Historical Inscriptions 404–323 B.C.* Oxford.

Rice, E. E. 1983. *The Grand Procession of Ptolemy Philadelphus.* Oxford.

——. 1995. "Grottoes on the Acropolis of Hellenistic Rhodes." *BSA* 90, pp. 383–404.

Ridgway, B. S. 1992. "Images of Athena on the Akropolis," in Neils 1992a, pp. 119–42.

——. 2000. *Hellenistic Sculpture II.* Madison.

——. 2004. Review of Hoepfner 2003. *BMCR* 2004.01.25.

Rigsby, K. J. 1996. *Asylia: Territorial Inviolability in the Hellenistic World.* Berkeley and Los Angeles.

——. 2004. "Theoroi for the Koan Asklepieia," in Höghammar 2004, pp. 9–14.

Robert, J., and L. Robert. 1983. *Fouilles d'Amyzon en Carie,* vol. 1: *Exploration, histoire, monnaies et inscriptions.* Paris.

Bibliography

Robert, L. 1953. "Le sanctuaire d'Artémis in Amyzon." *CRAI*, pp. 403–15. Reprinted in *Opera minora selecta* 3 (Amsterdam 1969), pp. 3–15.

Robertson, N. 1983. "The Riddle of the Arrephoria at Athens." *HSCP* 87, pp. 214–88.

———. 1996. "Athena's Shrines and Festivals," in Neils 1996b, pp. 27–77.

———. 2004. "The Praxiergidae Decree (*IG* I^3 7) and the Dressing of Athena's Statue with the *Peplos*." *GRBS* 44, pp. 111–61.

Robinson, H. S. 1976a. "Excavations at Corinth: Temple Hill, 1968–1972." *Hesperia* 45, pp. 203–39.

———. 1976b. "Temple Hill, Corinth," in Jantzen 1976, pp. 239–60.

Rocconi, E. 2006. "Theatres and Theatre Design in the Graeco-Roman World: Theoretical and Empirical Approaches," in Scarre and Lawson 2006, pp. 71–76.

Roesch, P. 1984. "L'Amphiaraion d'Oropos," in *Temples et sanctuaires*, ed. G. Roux. Lyon, pp. 173–84.

Rogers, B. B. 1924. *Aristophanes*, vol. 3. London and New York.

Romano, D. G. 1997. "Topographical and Architectural Survey of the Sanctuary of Zeus on Mt. Lykaion, Arcadia." *AJA* 101, p. 374.

———. 2005. "A New Topographical and Architectural Survey of the Sanctuary of Zeus at Mt. Lykaion," in *Ancient Arcadia*, ed. E. Østby. *Papers from the Norwegian Institute at Athens* 8. Athens, pp. 381–96.

Romano, D. G., and B. C. Schoenbrun. 1993. "A Computerized Architectural and Topographical Survey of Ancient Corinth." *JFA* 20, pp. 177–90.

Roos, P. 2011. "The Stadion at Labraunda," in Karlsson and Carlsson 2011, pp. 257–65.

Roosevelt, C. 2009. *The Archaeology of Lydia, from Gyges to Alexander*. Cambridge.

Rose, C. B., and G. Darbyshire, eds. 2011. *The New Chronology of Iron Age Gordion. Gordion Special Studies* 6. Philadelphia.

Rosen, R. M., and J. Farrell. 1993. *Nomodeiktes: Greek Studies in Honor of Martin Ostwald*. Ann Arbor.

Rosen, R. M., and I. Sluiter, eds. 2006. *City, Countryside, and the Spatial Organization of Value in Classical Antiquity*. Mnemosyne Suppl. 279. Leiden and Boston.

Rossetto, P. C., and G. P. Sartorio, eds. 1994. *Teatri greci e romani: Alle origini del linguaggio rappresentato*, vols. 1–3. Rome.

Rotroff, S. I. 1982. *The Athenian Agora*, vol. 22: *Hellenistic Pottery: Athenian and Imported Moldmade Bowls*. Princeton.

———. 1983. "Three Cistern Systems on the Kolonos Agoraios." *Hesperia* 52, pp. 257–97.

Roux, G. 1954. "Chroniques des fouilles en 1953: Argos." *BCH* 78, pp. 170–73.

———. 1957. "Le sanctuaire argien d'Apollon Pythéen." *REG* 70, pp. 474–87.

———. 1961. *L'architecture de l'Argolide aux IVe et IIIe siècles avant J.-C.* Paris.

———. 1979. "L'Héracleion thasien: Problèmes de chronologie et d'architecture," in Launey 1979, pp. 191–211.

Rowland, I. 1994. "Raphael, Angelo Colocci, and the Genesis of the Architectural Orders." *ArtB* 76.1, pp. 81–104.

Rowland, I., and T. N. Howe. 1999. *Vitruvius: Ten Books on Architecture*. Cambridge.

Rumscheid, F. 1994. *Untersuchungen zur kleinasiatische Bauornamentik des Hellenismus*. Mainz.

———, ed. 2009a. *Die Karer und die Anderen*. Bonn.

———. 2009b. "Die Leleger: Karer oder Andere?" in Rumscheid 2009a, pp. 173–91.

Rüpke, J., ed. 2007. *A Companion to Roman Religion*. Oxford and Malden MA.

Rupp, D. W. 1974. *Greek Altars of the Northeastern Peloponnese c. 750/725 BC to c. 300/275 BC*. Ph.D. dissertation, Bryn Mawr College.

Rups, M. 1986. *Thesauroi: A Study of the Treasury Building as Found in Greek Sanctuaries*. Ph.D. dissertation, Johns Hopkins University.

Rutherford, I. 2013. *State Pilgrims and Sacred Observers in Ancient Greece*. Cambridge.

Şahin, S. 1972. *Die Entwicklung der griechischen Monumentalaltäre*. Bonn.

Şahin, S., E. Schwertheim, and J. Wagner, eds. 1978. *Studien zur Religion und Kultur Kleinasiens I: Festschrift für Karl Dorner zum 65. Geburtstag am 28. Februar 1976*. Leiden.

Salmon, E. T. 1967. *Samnium and the Samnites*. Cambridge.

Sams, G. K. 1994. "Aspects of Early Phrygian Architecture at Gordion," in *Anatolia Iron Ages 3: Proceedings of the Third Anatolian Iron Age Colloquium Held at Van, 6–12 August 1990*, ed. A. Çilingiroglu and D. H. French. Ankara, pp. 211–14.

Sams, G. K., and M. M. Voigt. 2011. "In Conclusion," in Rose and Darbyshire 2011, pp. 154–68.

Sanders, D. 1990. "Behavioral Convention and Archaeology: Methods for the Analysis of Ancient Architecture," in Kent 1990, pp. 43–72.

Savalli-Lestrade, I. 2001. "Les Attalides et les cites grecques d'Asie Mineure au IIe siècle," in Bresson and Descat 2001, pp. 77–106.

Scarre, C. 2006. "Sound, Place and Space: Towards an Archaeology of Acoustics," in Scarre and Lawson 2006, pp. 1–10.

Scarre, C., and G. Lawson, eds. 2006. *Archaeoacoustics*. Cambridge.

Schachter, A. 1981. "Amphiaros (Oropos)," in *The Cults of Boiotia. BICS Suppl.* 38.1. London, pp. 19–26.

———, ed. 1992. *Le sanctuaire grec. Entretiens sur l'Antiquité Classique* 37. Geneva.

Schäfer, J. 1991. "Amnisos 1984–1988: Das Problem der Kultkontinuität im Falle des Heiligtum des Zeus Thenatas," in Musti et al. 1991, pp. 349–58.

Schäfer, J., S. Alexiou, P. Brize, A. Chaniotis, W. Helck, S. Hiller, P. Knoblauch, W.-D. Niemeier, E. Stefanaki, and V. Stürmer. 1992. *Amnisos: Nach den archäologischen, historischen und epigraphischen Zeugnissen des Altertums und der Neuzeit.* Berlin.

Schafer, R. M. 1985. "Acoustic Space," in Seamon and Mugerauer 1985, pp. 87–98.

Schalles, H.-J. 1985. *Untersuchungen zur Kulturpolitik der pergamenischen Herrscher im dritten Jahrhundert vor Christus. IstForsch* 36. Tübingen.

Schepartz, L. A., S. C. Fox, and Ch. Bourbou. 2009. *New Directions in the Skeletal Biology of Greece. Hesperia Suppl.* 43. Princeton.

Schiffer, M. B., ed. 2000. *Social Theory in Archaeology*. Salt Lake City.

Schiffer, M. B., and J. M. Skibo. 1987. "Theory and Experiment in the Study of Technological Change." *Current Anthropology* 28, pp. 595–622.

Schilbach, J. 1984. "Untersuchungen der Schatzhausterasse Südlich des Schatzhauses der Sikyoner in Olympia." *AA*, pp. 225–36.

———. 1992. "Olympia, die Entwicklungsphases des Stadions," in Coulson and Kyrieleis 1992, pp. 33–37.

Schleif, H. 1933. "Der grosse Altar der Hera von Samos." *AthMitt* 58, pp. 174–210.

Schrammen, J. 1906. *Altertümer von Pergamon 3.1: Der grosse Altar: Der obere Markt.* Berlin.

Schultz, P. 2007. "The Iconography of the Athenian Apobates Race: Origins, Meanings, Transformation," in Palagia and Choremi-Spetsieri 2007, pp. 59–72.

Schwandner, E.-L. 1990. "Beobachtungen zur hellenistischen Tempelarchitektur von Pergamon," in Hoepfner and Schwandner 1990, pp. 85–103.

Schwandner, E.-L., and K. Rheidt. 2004. *Macht der Architektur, Architektur der Macht.* Berlin.

Schwertheim, E. ed. 1992. *Forschungen in Pisidia. Asia Minor Studien* 6. Bonn.

Schwertheim, E., and E. Winter. 2003. *Stadt und Stadtentwicklung in Kleinasien. Asia Minor Studien* 50. Bonn.

———, eds. 2005. *Neue Forschungen zu Ionien: Fahri Işik zum 60. Geburtstag gewidmet. Asia Minor Studien* 54. Bonn.

Scott, M. 2010. *Delphi and Olympia: The Spatial Politics of Panhellenism in the Archaic and Classical Periods.* Cambridge.

———. 2013. *Space and Society in the Greek and Roman Worlds.* Cambridge.

Scranton, R. 1949. "Group Design in Greek Architecture." *ArtB* 31, pp. 247–68.

Scullion, S. 2005. "'Pilgrimage' and Greek Religion: Sacred and Secular in the Pagan Polis," in Elsner and Rutherford 2005, pp. 111–30.

Scully, V. 1979. *The Earth, the Temple and the Gods: Greek Sacred Architecture*. 3rd ed. London and New Haven.

Seamon, D., and R. Mugerauer, eds. 1985. *Dwelling, Place and Environment: Towards a Phenomenology of Person and World.* Dordrecht.

Sear, F. 2006. *Roman Theatres.* Oxford.

Segré, M. 1949. "L'oracolo di Apollo Pythaeus a Rodi." *PP* 4, pp. 72–82.

Sekunda, N. V. 1997. "Nearchus the Cretan and the Foundation of Cretopolis." *AnatSt* 47, pp. 217–23.

Senseney, J. R. 2007. "Idea and Visuality in Hellenistic Architecture: A Geometric Analysis of Temple A of the Asklepieion at Kos." *Hesperia* 76, pp. 555–95.

———. 2011. *The Art of Building in the Classical World: Vi-*

Bibliography

sion, Craftsmanship, and Linear Perspective in Greek and Roman Architecture. Cambridge.

Shanks, M., and I. Hodder, eds. 1995a. *Interpreting Archaeology: Finding Meaning in the Past.* New York.

Shanks, M., and I. Hodder. 1995b. "Processual, Postprocessual and Interpretive Archaeologies," in Hodder et al. 1995, pp. 3–29.

Shanks, M., and C. Tilley. 1987. *Social Theory and Archaeology.* Cambridge.

Shapiro, H. A. 1989. *Art and Cult under the Tyrants in Athens.* Mainz.

———. 1992. "Mousike Agones: Music and Poetry at the Panathenaia," in Neils 1992a, pp. 53–75.

Shear, I. M. 1999. "The Western Approach to the Athenian Akropolis." *JHS* 119, pp. 86–127.

Shear, T. L. 1938. "Excavations in the Athenian Agora: The Campaign of 1937." *Hesperia* 7, pp. 311–62.

———. 1940. "Excavations in the Athenian Agora: The Campaign of 1939." *Hesperia* 9, pp. 261–307.

Shear, T. L., Jr. 1982. "The Demolished Temple at Eleusis." *Hesperia Suppl.* 20, pp. 128–40.

Sheedy, K. A., ed. 1994. *Archaeology in the Peloponnese: New Excavations and Research.* Oxford.

Sherwin-White, S. M. 1978. *Ancient Cos: An Historical Study from the Dorian Settlement to the Imperial Period.* Hypomnemata 51. Göttingen.

Shoe, L. T. 1936. *Profiles of Greek Mouldings.* Cambridge MA.

———. 1950. "Greek Mouldings of Kos and Rhodes." *Hesperia* 19, pp. 338–69.

Simon, E. 1983. *Festivals of Attica: An Archaeological Commentary.* Madison.

Sinn, U. 1990. "Das Heraion von Perachora: Eine sakrale Schutzzone in der korinthischen Peraia." *AM* 105, pp. 53–116.

Sinn, U. 2002. *Olympia: Kult, Sport und Feste in der Antike.* Munich.

Sion-Jenkis, K. 2001. "La disparation du mercenariat en Asie Mineure occidentale au IIe siècle a. C.: Elements de réflexion," in Bresson and Descat 2001, pp. 19–35.

Sjögren, L. 2003. *Cretan Locations: Discerning Site Variations in Iron Age and Archaic Crete (800–500 B.C.).* Oxford.

Sjövqvist, E. 1964. "Excavations at Morgantina 1963." *AJA* 68, pp. 137–47.

Skibo, J., and M. B. Schiffer. 1995. "The Clay Cooking Pot: An Exploration of Women's Technology," in Skibo, Walker, and Nielsen 1995, pp. 80–91.

Skibo, J. M., W. H. Walker, and A. E. Nielsen, eds. 1995. *Expanding Archaeology.* Salt Lake City.

Slater, W. 2007. "Deconstructing Festivals," in P. Wilson 2007, pp. 21–47.

Smith, M. E. 2011. "Empirical Urban Theory for Archaeologists." *Journal of Archaeological Method and Theory* 18, pp. 167–92.

Smithson, P. 1958. "Space and Greek Architecture." *The Listener,* October 16, pp. 599–601.

Snead, J. E., C. Erickson, and J. A. Darling. 2009. "Making Human Space: The Archaeology of Trails, Paths, and Roads," in *Landscapes of Movement: Trails, Paths, and Roads in Anthropological Perspective,* ed. J. E. Snead, C. Erickson, and J. A. Darling. Philadelphia, pp. 1–19.

Sokolowski, F. 1955. *Lois sacrées de l'Asie Mineure.* Paris.

———. 1969. *Lois sacrées des cités grecques.* Paris.

Solin, H. 1982. "Appunti sull'onomastica romana a Delo," in Coarelli, Musti, and Solin 1982, pp. 101–17.

Sourvinou-Inwood, C. 1988. "Further Aspects of Polis Religion." *AION* 10, pp. 259–74. Reprinted in Buxton 2000, pp. 38–55.

———. 1990. "What Is *Polis* Religion?" in *The Greek City from Homer to Alexander,* ed. O. Murray and S. Price. Oxford, pp. 295–322. Reprinted in Buxton 2000, pp.13–37.

———. 1994. "Something to Do with Athens: Tragedy and Ritual," in *Ritual, Finance, Politics: Athenian Democratic Accounts Presented to David Lewis,* ed. R. Osborne and S. Hornblower. Oxford, pp. 269–90.

Sourvinou-Inwood, C., with R. Parker, ed. 2011. *Athenian Myths and Festivals: Aglauros, Erechtheus, Plynteria, Panathenaia, Dionysia.* Oxford.

Sporn, K. 2002. *Heiligtümer und Kulte Kretas in klassischer und hellenistischer Zeit.* Heidelberg.

Stampolidis, N. Ch. 1984. "Der 'Nymphenaltar' in Knidos und der Bildhauer Theon aus Antiochia." *AA,* pp. 113–27.

Stansbury-O'Donnell, M. 2006. *Vase-Painting, Gender, and Social Identity in Archaic Athens.* Cambridge.

Stavrianopoulou, E. 2006a. "Introduction," in Stavrianopoulou 2006c, pp. 7–22.

———. 2006b. "Normative Interventions in Greek Rituals:

Strategies for Justification and Legitimation," in Stavrianopoulou 2006c, pp. 131–49.

———, ed. 2006c. *Ritual and Communication in the Graeco-Roman World*. Kernos Suppl. 16. Liège.

Stek, T. D. 2009. *Cult Places and Cultural Change in Republican Italy*. Amsterdam.

Stevens, G. P. 1936. "The Periclean Entrance Court of the Acropolis of Athens." *Hesperia* 5, pp. 442–520.

———. 1940. *The Setting of the Periclean Parthenon*. Hesperia Suppl. 3. Princeton.

———. 1946. "Architectural Studies Concerning the Acropolis of Athens." *Hesperia* 15, pp. 73–106.

Stewart, A. 1990. *Greek Sculpture: An Exploration*. New Haven and London.

———. 1993. *Faces of Power: Alexander's Image and Hellenistic Politics*. Berkeley.

———. 2000. "*Pergamo Ara Marmorea Magna*: On the Date, Reconstruction, and Functions of the Great Altar of Pergamon," in de Grummond and Ridgway 2000, pp. 32–57.

Stillwell, R. 1932. *Corinth 1.1: Architecture*. Cambridge MA.

———. 1957. Review of Martiensen 1956. *JSAH* 16.4, p. 33.

Stillwell, R., R. Scranton, and E. Freeman. 1941. *Corinth 1.2: Architecture*. Cambridge MA.

Stillwell, R., and E. Sjöqvist. 1957. "Excavations at Serra Orlando (Morgantina): Preliminary Report." *AJA* 61, pp. 151–59.

———. 1958. "Excavations at Serra Orlando (Morgantina): Preliminary Report II." *AJA* 62, pp. 155–69.

Strazzulla, M. J., and B. di Marco. 1972. *Il santuario sannitico di Pietrabbondante*. Rome.

Strøm, I. 1988. "The Sanctuary of the Argive Heraion and Its External Relations (8th–Early 6th cent. BC): The Monumental Architecture." *ActaArch* 59, pp. 173–203.

Stronach, D. 1978. *Pasargadae*. Oxford.

Stroud, R. S. 1968. "The Sanctuary of Demeter and Kore on Acrocorinth." *Hesperia* 41, pp. 299–330.

Strudwick, N. 2003. "Some Aspects of the Archaeology of the Theban Necropolis in the Ptolemaic and Roman Periods," in Strudwick and Taylor 2003, pp. 167–85.

Strudwick, N., and J. H. Taylor, eds. 2003. *The Theban Necropolis: Past, Present and Future*. London.

Sumi, G. 2004. "Civic Self-Representation in the Hellenistic World," in Bell and Davies 2004, pp. 79–92.

Szafranski, Z. E. 2001. "Deir el-Bahari: The Temple of Hatshepsut, Season 1999–2000." *Polish Archaeology in the Mediterranean* 12. Warsaw, pp. 185–205.

Tanoulas, T. 1987. "The Propylaea of the Acropolis at Athens since the Seventeenth Century." *JdI* 102, pp. 413–83.

———. 1991. "Greek Concepts of Space as Reflected in Ancient Greek Architecture," in *Concepts of Space: Ancient and Modern*, ed. K. Vatsyayan. New Delhi, pp. 157–72.

Tataki, A. B. 1997. *Lindos—Kameiros—Filerimos*. Athens.

Tavano, G. ed., 2001. "Pietrabbondante," in *Musei e siti archeologici d'Abruzzo e Molise*. Ascoli Piceno, pp. 144–49.

Templer, J. 1992a. *The Staircase: History and Theories*. Cambridge MA.

———. 1992b. *The Staircase: Studies of Hazards, Falls, and Safer Design*. Cambridge MA.

Thallon, I. C. 1906. "The Date of the Damophon of Messene." *AJA* 10, pp. 302–29.

Themelis, P. 1993. "Ὁ Δαμοφῶν καὶ ἡ δραστηριότητά του στὴν Ἀρκαδία," in *Sculpture from Arcadia and Laconia*, ed. O. Palagia and W. E. Coulson. Oxford, pp. 99–109.

———. 1994. "Artemis Ortheia at Messene: The Epigraphical and Archaeological Evidence," in Hägg 1994, pp. 101–22.

———. 1996. "Damophon," in *Personal Styles in Greek Sculpture*, ed. O. Palagia and J. J. Pollitt. YCS 30. Cambridge, pp. 154–85.

Theuer, M. 1979. *Das Mausoleum von Belevi*. Ephesos 6. Vienna.

Thieme, T. 1989. "Metrology and Planning in Hekatomnid Labraunda," in Linders and Hellström 1989, pp. 77–90.

———. 1993. "The Architectural Remains of Archaic Labraynda," in des Courtils and Moretti 1993, pp. 47–55.

Thiersch, H. 1899. *Tyrrhenische Amphoren*. Leipzig.

Thomas, C. M. 1998. "The Sanctuary of Demeter at Pergamon: Cultic Space for Women and Its Eclipse," in Koester 1998, pp. 277–98.

Thomas, E. 1984. "Zu den Schautreppen in griechischen Städten auf Kreta und ihren Vorbildern." *RdA* 8, pp. 37–42.

Thomas, J. 2000. "Reconfiguring the Social, Reconfiguring the Material," in Schiffer 2000, pp. 143–55.

Thomas, K. 1992. "Introduction," in Bremmer and Roodenburg 1992, pp. 1–14.

Thompson, D. B. 1937. "The Garden of Hephaistos." *Hesperia* 6, pp. 396–425.

———. 1937–39. Agora Excavation daybooks, Sections ΛΛ

Bibliography

VII, IX, X, and Section MM IV, VI, VII. Agora Excavation Office, Stoa of Attalos, Athens.

———. 1963. *Garden Lore of Ancient Athens*. Princeton.

Thompson, D. J. 2000. "Philadelphus' Procession: Dynastic Power in a Mediterranean Context," in Mooren 2000, pp. 365–88.

Thompson, H. A. 1937. "Buildings on the West Side of the Agora." *Hesperia* 6, pp. 1–226.

Thompson, H. A., and R. E. Wycherley. 1972. *The Athenian Agora*, vol. 14: *The Agora of Athens: The History, Shape, and Uses of an Ancient City Center*. Princeton.

Thoneman, P. ed., 2013a. *Attalid Asia Minor: Money, International Relations, and the State*. Oxford.

Thoneman, P. 2013b. "The Attalid State, 188–133 B.C." in Thoneman 2013a, pp. 1–47.

Tilley, C. 1994. *A Phenomenology of Landscape: Places, Paths and Monuments*. Oxford and Providence.

Tilton, E. L. 1902. "Architecture," in *The Argive Heraeum*, vol. 1, ed. C. Waldstein. Boston.

Tomlinson, R. A. 1972. *Argos and the Argolid: From the End of the Bronze Age to the Roman Occupation*. Ithaca.

———. 1977. "The Upper Terraces at Perachora." *BSA* 72, pp. 197–202.

———. 1982. Review of W. B. Dinsmoor Jr. 1980. *JHS* 102, pp. 280–81.

———. 1990. "The Chronology of the Perachora Hestiatorion and Its Significance," in Murray 1990, pp. 95–101.

———. 1992. "Perachora," in Schachter 1992, pp. 321–51.

Torelli, M. 1995. *Studies in the Romanization of Italy*. Edmonton.

———. 1999. *Tota Italia: Essays in the Cultural Formation of Roman Italy*. Oxford.

Travlos, J. 1971. *Pictorial Dictionary of Ancient Athens*. London.

———. 1988. *Bildlexikon zur Topographie des antiken Attika*. Tübingen.

Tsakirgis, B. 1995. "Morgantina: A Greek Town in Central Sicily." *Acta Hyperborea* 6, pp. 123–47.

Tuchelt, K. 1973. *Vorarbeiten zu einer Topographie von Didyma*. IstMitt Suppl. 9. Tübingen.

———. 1984. "Didyma 1980–1983." *IstMitt* 34, pp. 193–240.

———. 1986. "Fragen zum Naiskos von Didyma." *AA*, pp. 33–50.

Tuna, N., N. Atici, I. Sakarya, and E. Koparal. 2009. "The Preliminary Results of Burgaz Excavations within the Context of Locating Old Knidos," in Rumscheid 2009a, pp. 517–32.

Turner, V. W. 1977. *The Ritual Process: Structure and Anti-structure*. Ithaca.

Tusa, V. 1981–82. "L'attività della Soprintendenza alle Antichità della Sicilia Occidentale nel quadriennio maggio 1976–aprile 1980." *Kokalos* 26–27, vol. 2, pp. 809–52.

Umholtz, G. 2002. "Architraval Arrogance? Dedication Inscriptions in Greek Architecture of the Classical Period." *Hesperia* 71, pp. 261–93.

Vaag, L. E., V. Nørskov, J. Lund, K. Jeppesen, and A. Luttrell. 2002. *The Maussolleion of Halikarnassos*, vol. 7: *The Pottery*. Aarhus.

Valavanis, P. 2004. *Games and Sanctuaries in Ancient Greece: Olympia, Delphi, Isthmia, Nemea, Athens*. Translated by D. Hardy. Los Angeles.

van Bremen, R. 1996. *The Limits of Participation: Women and Civic Life in the Greek East in the Hellenistic and Roman Periods*. Amsterdam.

van Bremen, R., and J.-M. Carbon. 2010. *Hellenistic Karia: Proceedings of the First International Conference on Hellenistic Karia, Oxford, 29 June–2 July 2006. Études*. Paris and Bordeaux.

Vandeput, L. 1997. *The Architectural Decoration in Roman Asia Minor: Sagalassos, a Case Study*. Leuven.

Vanderpool, E. 1974. "The Date of the Pre-Persian City-Wall of Athens," in Bradeen and McGregor 1974, pp. 156–60.

van Dommeln, P., and N. Terrenato. 2007a. *Articulating Local Cultures: Power and Identity under the Expanding Roman Republic*. Portsmouth RI.

———. 2007b. "Introduction: Local Cultures and the Expanding Roman Republic," in van Dommeln and Terrenato 2007a, pp. 7–12.

van Effenterre, H. 1992. "Dreros," in Myers, Myers, and Cadogan 1992, pp. 86–90.

Vanhaverbeke, H., and M. Waelkens. 2005. "If You Can't Beat Them, Join Them? The Hellenization of Pisidia." *MeditArch* 18, pp. 49–65.

Vanhaverbeke, H., M. Waelkens, K. Vyncke, et al. 2010. "'Pisidian' Culture? The Classical-Hellenistic Site at Düzen Tepe near Sagalassus (Southwest Turkey)." *AnatSt* 60, pp. 105–28.

van Straten, F. 1981. "Gifts for the Gods," in Versnel 1981, pp. 65–150.

———. 1995. *Hiera Kala: Images of Animal Sacrifice in Archaic and Classical Greece.* Religions in the Graeco-Roman World 127. Leiden.

van Wonterghem, F. 1973. "Le culte d'Hercule chez les Paeligni." *AntCl* 42, pp. 36–48.

———. 1976. "Archäologische Zeugnisse spätrepublikanischer Zeit aus dem Gebiet der Peligner," in Zanker 1976, pp. 144–55.

———. 1984. *Forma Italiae Regio IV.1: Superaequum, Corfinium, Sulmo.* Florence.

———. 1994. "Sulmona," in *EAA Suppl.* 2.5, p. 490.

Versnel, H. S., ed. 1981. *Faith, Hope and Worship: Aspects of Religious Mentality in the Ancient World.* Leiden.

Veyne, P. 1990. *Bread and Circuses: Historical Sociology and Political Pluralism.* Translated and abridged version of *Le Pain et le cirque* (Paris 1976). Translated by B. Pearce. London.

Villing, A. 2005a. *The Greeks in the East.* London.

———. 2005b. "Persia and Greece," in Curtis and Tallis 2005, pp. 236–44.

Virgilio, B. 2008. "Sur quelques concessions attalides à des communautés sujettes," in *Pergame: Histoire et archéologie d'un centre urbain depuis ses origines jusqu'à la fin d'antiquité*, ed. M. Kohl. Lille, pp. 205–22.

Vischer, W. 1873. "Sitzend oder Stehen in den griechischen Volksversammlungen." *RhM* 28, pp. 380–90.

Voigt, M. 2005. "Old Problems and New Solutions: Recent Excavations at Gordion," in Kealhofer 2005, pp. 22–35.

Voigt, M., and R. C. Henrickson. 2000. "Formation of the Phrygian State: The Early Iron Age at Gordion." *AnatSt* 50, pp. 37–54.

Voigtländer, W. 1975. *Der jüngste Apollontempel von Didyma.* IstMitt Suppl. 14. Tübingen.

———. 1986. *Antike Aktuell: Didyma und Milet im Modell.* Frankfurt am Main.

Vollgraff, W. 1956. *Le sanctuaire d'Apollon Pythéen à Argos.* Paris.

von Bothmer, D. 1961. *Ancient Art from New York Private Collections.* New York.

von Gerkan, A. 1915. *Milet 1.4: Der Poseidonaltar bei Kap Monodendri.* Berlin.

———. 1924. "Der Altar des Athenatempels in Priene." *BJb* 129, pp. 15–35.

———. 1929. *Der Altar des Artemis-Tempels in Magnesia am Mäander.* Berlin.

———. 1938. Review of Doxiadis, *Raumordnung im griechischen Städtebau.* (Translated as *Architectural Space in Ancient Greece*, Cambridge MA 1972). *Gnomon* 14, pp. 529–34.

von Hesberg, H. 1994. *Formen privater Repräsentation in der Baukunst des 2. und 1. Jahrhunderts v. Chr.* Cologne, Weimar, and Vienna.

Voyatzis, M. E. 1990. *The Sanctuary of Athena Alea at Tegea and Other Archaic Sanctuaries in Arcadia.* Göteborg.

———. 1999. "The Role of Temple Building in Consolidating Arkadian Communities," in Nielsen and Roy 1999, pp.130–68.

Waelkens, M. 1989. "Hellenistc and Roman Influence in the Imperial Architecture of Roman Asia Minor," in *The Greek Renaissance in the Roman Empire*, ed. S. Walker and A. Cameron. BICS 55. London, pp. 77–88.

———. 1992. "Die neue Forschungen (1985–1989) und die belgischen Ausgrabungen (1990–1991) in Sagalassos," in Schwertheim 1992, pp. 43–60.

Waelkens, M. 1993a. "The 1992 Excavation Season. A Preliminary Report," in Waelkens and Poblome 1993, pp. 9–19.

———, ed. 1993b. *Sagalassos I.* ActaArchLov. Monographiae 5. Leuven.

———. 1998. "The 1996 Excavations at Sagalassos." *Kazi Sonuclari Toplantisi* 19, pp. 249–300.

———. 2002. "Romanization in the East: A Case-Study, Sagalassos and Pisidia (SW Turkey)." *IstMitt* 52, pp. 311–71.

———. 2004. "Ein Blick von der Ferne: Seleukiden und Attaliden in Pisidien." *IstMitt* 54, pp. 435–71.

Waelkens, M., et al. 1997. "The 1994 and 1995 Surveys on the Territory of Sagalassos," in Waelkens and Poblome 1997, pp. 11–102.

Waelkens, M., and L. Loots, eds. 2000. *Sagalassos V: Report on the Survey and Excavation Campaigns of 1996 and 1997.* ActaArchLov. Monographiae 11/A. Leuven.

Waelkens, M., and J. Poblome, eds. 1993. *Sagalassos II: Report on the Third Excavation Campaign of 1992.* ActaArchLov Monographiae 6. Leuven.

———, eds. 1997. *Sagalassos IV: Report on the Survey and Excavation Campaigns of 1994 and 1995.* ActaArchLov Monographiae 9. Leuven.

Waelkens, M., and L. Vandeput. 2007. "Regionalism in Hellenistic and Roman Pisidia," in Elton and Reger 2007, pp. 97–105.

Bibliography

Waldstein, C., H. S. Washington, E. L.Tilton, R. B. Richardson, J. R. Wheeler, G. H. Chase, J. C. Hoppin, T. W. Heermance, H. F. De Cou, R. Norton, and A. M. Lythgoe. 1902 and 1905. *The Argive Heraeum*. 2 vols. Boston.

Walker, S., and A. Cameron, eds. 1989. *The Greek Renaissance in the Roman Empire: Papers from the Tenth British Museum Classical Colloquium*. BICS 55. London.

Wallace-Hadrill, A. 2008. *Rome's Cultural Revolution*. Cambridge.

Walter, H. 1976. *Das Heraion von Samos: Ursprung und Wandel eines griechischen Heiligtums*. Athens.

Waywell, G. B. 1988. "The Mausoleum at Halicarnassus," in *The Seven Wonders of the Ancient World*, ed. P. A. Clayton and M. J. Price. New York, pp. 100–123.

Weber, G. 1885. "Trois tombeaux archaïques de Phocée." *RA* ser. 3.5, pp. 129–38.

Weller, C. H. 1921. "Original Plan of the Erechtheum." *AJA*, pp. 130–41.

Welter, G. 1938a. "Aeginetiaca I–XII." *AA*, cols. 1–33.

———. 1938b. *Aigina*. Berlin.

Wescoat, B., and R. Ousterhout, eds. 2012. *Architecture of the Sacred: Space, Ritual, and Experience from Classical Greece to Byzantium*. Cambridge.

West, M. L. 1992. *Ancient Greek Music*. Oxford.

Westholm, A. 1963. *Labraunda I.2: The Architecture of the Hieron*. Stockholm.

———. 1978. "Labraunda," in *The 10th International Congress of Classical Archaeology, Ankara-Izmir 23–30/IX/1973*, ed. E. Akurgal. Ankara, pp. 543–47.

White, D., ed. 1984. *The Extramural Sanctuary of Demeter and Persephone at Cyrene, Libya, Final Reports*, vol. 1: *Backround and Introduction to the Excavations*. Philadelphia, pp. 14–17, 46–47.

White, D. 1985. "Cyrene's Suburban Expansion South of Its Ramparts," in *Cyrenaica in Antiquity*, ed. G. Barker, J. Lloyd, and J. Reynolds. *BAR International Series* 236. London, pp. 105–17.

Whitney, D. L. 1994. *The Pergamene Style of Doric Temple Architecture: A Study of the Doric Temples at Pergamon, Mamurt Kale, and Aigai*. Ph.D. dissertation, University of North Carolina at Chapel Hill.

Wiegand, T., and H. Schrader. 1904. *Priene: Ergebnisse der Ausgrabungen und Untersuchungen in den Jahren 1895–1898*. Berlin.

Wikander, C. 1992. "Pomp and Circumstance: The Procession of Ptolemaios II." *OpAth* 19, pp. 143–50.

Will, E. 1985. *Exploration archéologique de Délos: Le sanctuaire de la déesse Syrienne*. Paris.

Willetts, R. F. 1965. *Ancient Crete: A Social History*. London.

Williams, C. K., II. 1969. "Excavations at Corinth, 1968." *Hesperia* 38, pp. 36–63.

———. 1970. "Corinth, 1969: Forum Area." *Hesperia* 39, pp. 1–39.

———. 1978. *Pre-Roman Cults in the Area of the Forum of Ancient Corinth*. Ph.D. dissertation, University of Pennsylvania.

———. 1993. "Roman Corinth as a Commercial Center," in *The Corinthia in the Roman Period*, ed. T. E. Gregory. *JRA Suppl.* 8. Ann Arbor, pp. 31–46.

Williams, C. K., II, and N. Bookidis, eds. 2003. *Corinth, the Centenary, 1896–1996*. Princeton.

Williams, C.K., II, and J. E. Fisher. 1971. "Corinth, 1970: Forum Area." *Hesperia* 40, pp. 1–51.

Williamson, C. 2013. "Public Space beyond the City: The Sanctuaries of Labraunda and Sinuri in the Chora of Mylasa," in Dickenson and van Nijf 2013, pp. 1–36.

———. 2014. "Power of Place: Ruler, Landscape and Ritual at the Sanctuaries of Labraunda and Mamurt Kale in Asia Minor," in Moser and Feldman 2014b, pp. 87–110.

Wilson, A. J. N. 1966. *Emigration from Italy in the Republican Age of Rome*. Manchester.

Wilson, P. 1999. "The *aulos* in Athens," in Goldhill and Osborne 1999, pp. 58–95.

———, ed. 2007. *The Greek Theatre and Festivals: Documentary Studies*. Oxford.

Wörrle, M., and P. Zanker, eds. 1995. *Stadtbild und Bürgerbild im Hellenismus*. Munich.

Wright, J. C. 1982. "The Old Temple Terrace at the Argive Heraeum and the Early Cult of Hera in the Argolid." *JHS* 102, pp. 186–201.

———. 2006. "The Social Production of Space and the Architectural Reproduction of Society in the Bronze Age Aegean during the 2nd Millennium B.C.E.," in Maran, Juwig, Schwengel, and Thaler 2006, pp. 49–73.

Würster, W. W. 1973. "Dorische Peripteraltempel mit gedrungenem Grundriss." *AA*, pp. 200–11.

Wycherley, R. E. 1957. *The Athenian Agora*, vol. 3: *Literary and Epigraphical Testimonia*. Princeton.

———. 1978. *The Stones of Athens*. Princeton.
Yavis, C. G. 1949. *Greek Altars*. St. Louis.
Yildirim, B., and M.-H. Gates. 1997. "Archaeology in Turkey." *AJA* 101, pp. 253–54.
Zahle, J. 1978. "The Mausoleum-Site before the Mausoleum," in *The Proceedings of the Xth International Congress of Classical Archaeology*, ed. E. Akurgal. Ankara, pp. 529–34.
Zahle, J., and Kjeldsen, K. 2004. *The Maussolleion at Halikarnassos*, vol. 6: *Subterranean and Pre-Maussollan Structures on the Site of the Maussolleion*. Aarhus.

Zanker, P., ed. 1976. *Hellenismus in Mittelitalien: Kolloquium in Göttingen vom 5. bis 9. Juni 1974*. Göttingen.
Zedeño, M. N. 2000. "On What People Make of Places: A Behavioral Cartography," in Schiffer 2000, pp. 97–111.
Ziegenaus, O. 1959. "Zur Altarneuerung des samischen Heraions." *AM* 74, pp. 4–5.
Zscheitzschmann, W. 1936. Review of Herzog and Schazmann 1932. *Gnomon* 12, pp. 86–90.
Zuesse, E. M. 1975. "Meditation on Ritual." *Journal of the American Academy of Religion* 43, pp. 517–30.

Index

Note: Page numbers in italics refer to entries in the "Catalogue of Sites."

abaton (Kos), 73–74
acropolis: Athenian (*see* Athens, Acropolis); creation of, 50
Adada, 78–80, *97*
Aegina, Sanctuary of Zeus Hellanios, 38–40, 82, *97*
Aelian (Claudius Aelianus), *De natura animalium 12.30*, 185n54
agency, 27–28, 85–86, 177n19
agora, 78, 84–85; at Adada, 78; at Alazeytin, 36; at Athens, 9, 41, 47, 49–50, 99, 183n81; at Dreros, 37; at Kameiros, 65; at Latmos, 42, *102*; at Lato, 23, 26, 52; at Morgantina, 66–67, *103*
Alazeytin, 36
Alberti, Leon Battista, 19–20
Alcock, S., 6
Alexander the Great, 59, 63, 192n76
Alexandria, 29
alignment, 8; at Alipheira, 42; at Argive Heraion, 43–44; at Athenian Acropolis, 48; at Athenian Agora, 49–50; at Athenian Erechtheion, 49; at Athenian Kolonos Agoraios, 66; in central Italy, 81, 84, 94; at Corinth, 45–46; at Gabii, 92–93; at Kameiros, 65; at Kos, 23, 74, 76; at Labraunda, 23; at Lato, 52; at Morgantina, 66; at Mount Lykaion, 54; at Olympia, 53–54; at Oropos, 42; at Pergamon, 70; at Pietrabbondante, 93; at Rhodes City, 62, 187n5; at Selinus, 39, 82; at Sulmo, 91; at Thasos, 68; at Tivoli, 94
Alinda, 58, 78
Alipheira, Sanctuary of Athena, 41–42, 44, *97*, 180n5
altar: at Aegina, 39; at Argive Heraion, 43; at Aspis of Argos, 67–68; at Athenian Erechtheion, 49; at Corinth, 45; at Eleusis, 38; framed by stepped structures, 31; at Gabii, 92–93, 194n26; at Kameiros, 65; at Knidos, 77; at Kos, 74, 76–77; at Lato, 52; at Lindos, 63–64; at Lykosoura, 55–56; at Mount Lykaion, 54; at Oropos, 42; at Pergamon, 8, 70; at Rhodes, 62; at Selinus, 41; at Thasos, 68–69
Amandry, P., 43, 181n18, 181n26, 181n27
Amnisos, 35, *97*
Amphipolis, 61, 71; Gymnasium, 66, *98*; Lion Tomb, 179n14
Amyzon, 51, 56, 85, *98*; Sanctuary of Artemis, 59
andron (banqueting hall), 4, 57–60, 75, 83
animal, sacrificial, 21, 29, 84
Apollo: Deiradiotes, 74, 188n50; Karneios, 77–78; Kyparissios, 73; Triopian, 78
Apollonis, Queen (Pergamon), 70–72, 84, 189n79
appropriation, 27, 86, 89–90. *See also* emulation; hellenization
Archaic, use of term, 5, 82
Architectural Graphic Standards, 20, 23
Argive Heraion, 32, 41–45, 50, 60, 67, 82, *98*, 180n7
Argos, 32, 41–45, 54, 56, 61, 71, 85, 181n29; sanctuary of Hera (*see* Argive Heraion)
Argos Aspis, 67–78, *98*; Sanctuary of Pythian Apollo, 67–68
Ariassos, 78
Aristophanes, *Thesmophorizusai*, 9
Artemis, 55–56, 191n30
ascent/descent, 20, 52–54, 65, 69, 77–78, 82, 190n24
Asia Minor, 4, 7–8, 21, 27–28, 35–37, 42, 56, 72, 75, 78, 80, 193n15. *See also* Karia; Pisidia; *names of specific sites*
Asklepieia, 75, 190n9
Asklepieion, 68. *See also* Kos
Asklepios, 73
Assos, 78
Athena, 29, 48–49, 77, 187n8; as Alseia, 73; Athena Oxyderkes, 68
Athenaeus, 9; *Deipnosophistai 4.167*, 29, 174n47; *Deipnosophistai 197C–203B*, 177n5

Athens, 6, 21, 28, 38, 40–41, 47–49, 54, 62–63, 71, 82, 182n59, 182n65; Kerameikos, 9, 65; Klepsydra spring house, 183n77; Panathenaia, 29, 38, 47, 50, 182n65; *pompe* of City Dionysia, 31
Athens, Acropolis: Erechtheion, 26, 47–49, 60, 83, 183n79; Erechtheion North Court, 48–49, 82–83, 99; Panathenaic procession, 29, 38, 47; Parthenon, 19, 47–48, 50, 69; predecessor to Propylaia, 47, 98–99; Propylaia, 47, 63, 83; ramp to Acropolis, 37, 47, 98; steps west of Parthenon, 47–48, 99; temenos of Pandrosos, 49
Athens, Agora, 9, 41, 47; benches on west side, 49–50, 99, 183n81; Hephaisteion, 50, 65; Kolonos Agoraios, 49–50, 61, 65–66, 99, 188n32; Metroon, 50, 66; Old Bouleutereion, 49; Panathenaic Way, 38; Stoa of Zeus, 49, 63; temple of Apollo Patroos, 50, 66
Attaleia, 76
Attalos I, 70–71, 76
Attalos II, 76
aulos, 31, 178n6, 178n12
authority: and monumentality, 4–5, 7, 41, 61, 65; and shared experience, 29, 32
axiality, 63–64, 76, 81–82, 84, 89, 92, 94

Bankel, H., 77, 192n51
banqueting, 39, 46, 50–51, 59, 63, 68, 74, 185n52
Bassai, 55, 185n41
Basso, K., 26
bathing, 49, 58
Becker, T., 5, 7, 56, 64, 73, 178n1, 179n18, 180n1, 180n6, 183n4, 184n17, 184n19, 184n20, 187n24, 188n40, 191n24, 191n25, 191n35, 191n36
behavior, human: architecture and, 26, 46, 81; of worshippers at Kos, 76. *See also* shared experience
behavioral archaeology, 176n13

Index

Bell, C., 28, 31, 67
bema, 67, 83
benches, 49–50, 66
Bergquist, B., 6, 189n66, 189n70
Billot, M.-F., 43, 181n22
biomechanics, 19–24, 81
bleachers. See *ikria*
Blinkenberg, C., 63, 187n9
Blondel, François, 20
body, human: and use of steps, 19–24, 81. See also biomechanics; sitting; standing; walking
Boegehold, A. L., 50, 183n81
Bookidis, N., 70
bouleuterion, 8, 51–53, 184n12
Bourdieu, Pierre, 25–26
Brandt, H., 79
Brauron, 63; Temple of Artemis, 21, 182n65
building codes, modern, 20, 175n6
buildings incorporating steps, 7–9

Cahill, N., 36
Capua, 93
Carstens, M.-P., 58, 179n10, 185n54, 186n72
Cartesian approach, 25, 81, 94
Casey, E., 26
cavea, 9, 23, 92, 94, 194n19
Chaniotis, A., 6
chariot racing scenes, 10–11
Cicero, M. Tullius, 23; *De divinatione 2.41*, 93; *De divinatione 2.87*, 94; *Pro Flacco 16*, 176n28
cistern, 49, 52, 62, 188n30
Classical, use of term, 5, 82
Cole, S. G., 6
concrete: Roman use of, 91, 93–94, 194n27; used for reconstruction, 61–62, 64, 73, 187n10, 191n37
Connor, W. R., 6
contests, 29, 75, 78, 191n28; athletic, 29, 44, 53–54, 59, 66, 69, 181n29, 189n72
control: of access, 4, 59, 70, 92, 186n68; of behavior, 26–27, 81, 176n15; political, 44, 61, 75; of topography, 44, 50–51, 53–54, 71, 74, 81, 83, 86, 94, 188n43
Corinth, 40, 41, 44, 61, 68, 71, 82; *ikria*, 10; Northwest Shops, 38; Sanctuary of Demeter and Kore, 27–28, 41, 45–47, 50, 70–71, 83, *100*; stepped ramp to temenos of Apollo, 37–38, 42, 47, *99*; steps by Sacred Spring, 45–46, *99–100*
Cremna, 78
Crete, 37, 52, 75, 192n76. See also Dreros; Lato
crowds, 3–4, 21, 26–27, 61, 84–85. See also seating capacity; shared experience
cultural practices, Greek, adoption of, 27, 60, 78–80, 90
Cuzco (Peru), Inka sanctuary, 186n74

Cyrene, 174n27; sanctuary of Demeter and Kore, 7
Cyrus the Great, 36, 179n12

Damophon of Messene, 55
De Certeau, Michel, 31, 178n9
Deir el-Bahri (Egypt), funerary complex of Hatshepsut, 28, 76
Delos, 75, 90, 92, 94, 194n6; sanctuary of the Syrian Gods, 195n39
Delphi, 43–44, 54, 56, 186n74; Sacred Way, 83
Demeter, 55, 70
democracy, 45, 78–79
De Polignac, F., 6, 31, 173n24
Descartes, René, 25, 81, 94, 176n2
Despoina, 55
destruction, 70, 92; by fire, 36, 43, 62, 188n39
Dickenson, C. P., 6
Didyma, 61, 63, 71; grandstand beside temple, 69, *100*; temple of Apollo, 8
Dilke, O. A., 5
dimensions, change in, 48, 52, 191n37
dining rooms, 46, 51, 57, 62–63, 68–71, 73–74, 83, 185n60. See also banqueting
Diodorus Siculus: *15.18.1–3*, 58; *26.8.1*, 186n1
display, 21, 26–27, 29, 31–32, 36, 48, 57, 61, 173n8, 175n19; architectural, 4, 21, 31, 38, 48, 60, 67–69, 71–72, 82, 85, 89, 95, 182n65; political, 5, 59, 61, 173; religious, 29, 47, 55–56, 59, 77, 90
donors. See euergetism; patronage
doublet shrines, 32, 54–56, 85
Doxiadis, C., 6
drains and drainage, 51, 53, 66, 188n39
Dreros, 37, 40, *100*, 179n18
Dygve, E., 63–64, 71, 187n23, 189n85

earthquake (227/6 B.C.), 61–62, 64–65
Egypt, 179n14. See also Deir el-Bahri
ekklesia, 24
ekklesiasterion, 8–10, 51–52, 67
Eleusis, 37, 82; sixth-century grandstand, 38, *100*; Telesterion, 7–8
emulation, 7, 27, 86, 89, 179n12, 179n13, 186n74; competitive, 84, 95
emulation of Greek architectural forms, 72, 78, 83; in Italy, 28, 84, 90; in Pisidia, 80, 84
ephebic law, 66, 188n41
Ephesos, 63
Epidauros: Temple of Asklepios, 75; tholos, 185n46
Erechtheion. See under Athens, Acropolis
Eretria, 31
erosion control, 50–51, 66
Euclid, 25, 176n2
euergetai, 86–87, 193n11

euergetism, 3, 27, 72, 86, 90. See also patronage
Eumenes, 70–71, 84
Eumenes II (Eumenes Soter), 76
exedra, 52, 54, 74, 93, 182n54
expansion, architectural, 7, 94–95; at Argive Heraion, 32, 50, 56; at Kos, 75–76; at Labraunda, 56–59, 85; at Pergamon, 70, 189n79; at Selinus, 41, 50; at Sulmo, 90–91

Feldman, C., 6
Ferentino, 93
festivals, 28–29; Asklepieia, 75, 190n9; Attaleia, 76; Panathenaia, 29, 38, 47, 50, 182n65. See also contests; processions
Fischer-Hansen, T., 6, 8, 51, 174n39, 183n82, 184n12
fortifications, 58, 78–79
Fortuna, 94
Foucault, Michel, 26, 176n15
fountain houses, 49, 54, 57–58, 65, 183n77
framing spaces, 4, 49–50, 61, 69, 71, 83
Frederiksen, R., 5

Gabii, 81–82, 84, 89–90, 93–94; sacred grove, 92; Sanctuary of Juno, 92–93, *105*
gait, for ascending/descending steps, 20
Giddens, A., 26
Ginouvès, R., 5, 178n1
Goette, H. R., 39
Gordion, 35–36
Gournia, theatral area, 35
Graf, F., 6
grandstand, 3–4, 7, 9, 26–27, 29, 31, 35–38, 53, 71, 81–83, 85, 91; at Argive Heraion, 43–44, 50; at Didyma, 69; at Dreros, 37; at Gordion, 36–37; at Olympia, 23, 53; at Perachora, 37–38; in vase paintings, 9–10, 13, 15, 23. See also *ikria*
Gruben, G., 74
gymnasium: at Amphipolis, 66, *98*; at Pergamon, 76, 80

habitus, 25–27, 85–86
Halikarnassos, 32, 56, 58–60, 75, 85; Maussolleion steps, *100–101*, 179n14
Hall, J. M., 44–45, 52
Hannibal, 92
Hansen, M.-H., 6, 8, 51, 174n39, 174n42, 176n25, 183n82, 184n12, 185n50
Hanson, J. A., 91
Hatshepsut, 28, 76
healing, 75, 190n9
Heilmeyer, W.-D., 65
Hekataion, 47
Hekate, 73
Hekatomboia, 44, 181n30

Index

Hekatomnids (satrapal family, Karia), 51, 56–60. *See also* Idrieus; Mausolos
Helios, 62
Hellenistic, use of term, 5, 7, 61, 82
hellenization, self-, 78–80, 84, 89–90. *See also* emulation, competitive
hellenization, use of term, 80
Hellström, P., 59, 75, 83, 185n52, 185n58, 186n64, 186n71, 186n74, 186n83
Hera Argeia, games of, 44
Herakleia, 42
Herakles, 68–69, 188n41
Hermodorus of Salamis in Cyprus (architect), 90, 194n18
Hermogenes (architect), 90
Herodas, Fourth Mime, 190n14
Herodotus: *1.31*, 43; *1.144*, 78; *3.140*, 193n11; *5.119*, 57; *8.85*, 193n11
Herrmann, K., 54
hestiatorion, 68–69
Hesychius, 9
Hieron II, 5, 66–67
hippodrome, 44, 54
Hoepfner, W., 62, 75, 187n3, 187n5
Hölscher, T., 6
Homer, 23; *Iliad 23*, 10; *Odyssey 2.239*, 176n28

Ialysos, 61
Idrieus (Hekatomnid satrap), 57–59, 80, 186n67
ikria, 9–15
inscribing, of ruler's name on building façade, 58
inscriptions, 3, 44–45, 90, 179n20, 186n68, 187n28, 188n41, 190n2, 192n75, 193n11, 194n6; from Amphiaraion at Oropos, 23; from Amphipolis, 66; Argive, 45; from Aspis of Argos, 67; concerning Mausolos and Idrieus, 58–59; from Delos, 94; from Delphi, 44; from Dreros, 37; from Eretria, 31; from Kos, 31, 72–73, 75–76; from Lato, 52; from Lindos, 61–62; from Magnesia, 29–31; from Mount Lykaion, 54; from Pergamon, 70, 84; from Pietrabbondante, 92; from Pisidia, 79; Roman, 186n75; from Termessos, 78
interanimation, between structures and human conduct, 26, 87
Interdonato, E., 73–74, 76, 190n2, 190n19, 190n21, 191n24, 191n35, 191n37
Italy, 4, 7, 9, 21, 28, 81, 84, 86, 89–95, 194n8, 194n10. *See also* names of specific sites

Jost, M., 6, 55–56, 185n46

Kakasbos, 80
Kallynteria, 49
Kameiros, 61, 64–65, 71, *101*
Kapikaya (Kapilitaş), 78–80, *101*
Karia, 6, 32, 36–37, 39, 42, 51, 56–60, 80, 85, 186n72. *See also* Hekatomnids
kithara, 31, 178n6, 178n12
Knidos, 27, 72, 77–78, *101*; Lion Tomb, 179n14
Knossos, theatral area, 35
Koenigs, W., 54
Kolb, F., 5, 52, 67, 184n12, 188n48
Kondis, I. D., 64
Kos, 5, 21–23, 27, 64, 94–95, 180n29, 190n2, 190n4; Sanctuary of Asklepios (Asklepieion), 28, 72–77, 81–86, 90, 95, *101–2*, 187n10
Kritzas, Ch., 45

Labraunda, 27–28, 31–32; Sanctuary of Zeus, 4, 21–23, 51, 56–60, 71, 75, 83, 85–86, *102*, 185n52, 185n57, 186n67. *See also* Sacred Way, from Mylasa to Labraunda
landings, 46, 51, 75, 182n46, 191n24, 191n35
Latmos, agora steps, 42, *102*
Lato, 51–53, 78, *102–3*, 179n18, 184n10, 184n12; agora, 23, 26, 52; prytaneion, 52, 188n48
Launey, M., 69
Lauter, H., 43, 181n27
Lehmann, P. W., 6
Leleges, 36
Limyra, heroon, 36–37
Lindian Chronicle, 62–63
Lindos, 5, 37, 40, 61, 71–72, 82, 86, 94–95, *103*; Sanctuary of Athena, 27–28, 38, 62–64, 83–84, 86, 95
linking spaces and/or structures, 4, 6–7, 23, 46, 50, 64–65, 67, 72, 82–84, 89, 93, 95
Lippolis, E., 62, 187n9
Lousoi, 55
ludi scaenici, 90
Lydian culture, 35–37, 39, 179n12
Lykaian games, 54
Lykosoura, 28, 32, 51, 60, *103*, 185n49; Sanctuary of Despoina, 55, 85

MacDonald, W. A., 5
Macedonia, 54
Machaon (son of Asklepios), 73
Magnesia, 8, 31, 178n6, 191n30; inscription, 29–30; sanctuary of Artemis Leukophryne, 29–30
Mamurt Kale, 80, 193n84
market building, 78–79
Martiensen, R., 6
Martin, R., 69, 186n83
Mausolos (Hekatomnid satrap), 32, 57–60, 80, 83, 85, 190n4
Mauss, Marcel, 20
McMahon, A., 6
measurements, ideal, 19–20, 42
Megalopolis, 32, 54, 56, 85, 185n49
Metapontum, 9–10
metoikesis, 3, 31–32, 87
Mitchell, S., 78
Mnesikles (architect), 47, 63
monumentality, 3, 31, 39, 50, 63, 82, 89, 173n1
Morgantina, 5, 27, 61, 71–72, 83–84, 191n30; Agora, 66–67, *103*
Moser, C., 6
Mount Lykaion, 32, 51; Sanctuary of Zeus, 54–56, *103–4*
movement, associated with steps, 26, 39, 60, 82, 175n19. *See also* ascent/descent; biomechanics; walking
music, 31, 178n6, 178n12, 178n15
Mycenae, 32, 44, 82, 85
Mylasa, 31–32, 58, 85, 185n54
Mylonopoulos, J., 6

Nauplion, 32
Neils, J., 15, 175n57
Nielsen, I., 5, 7, 37, 184n12, 194n19
Nielsen, T. H., 56, 185n49

observing, 23, 27, 29, 31, 35, 37, 39, 42–49, 51–53, 55, 67–68, 71, 77–78, 81, 87. *See also* spectators; viewing
odeion, 61
oikoi, 39, 46, 57–58, 68–69, 185n57, 185n60, 189n69
Olmsted, Frederick Law, 20, 175n11
Olympia, 6, 23, 51, 60, 83, 185n46; Sanctuary of Zeus, 53–54, *104*, 184n27
Orlandini, G. A., 55
Orlandos, A., 42
Oropos, Amphiaraion, 42, *104*
Osborne, R., 6
Ousterhout, R., 6

Paian (healing god), 73
palaistra, at Amphipolis, 66, 188n39
Palladio, Andrea, 19, 175n5
Panathenaia, 29, 38, 47, 50, 182n65
Panhellenism: Kos and, 75, 86; Magnesia and, 191n30
Parthenon frieze, 29
Pasargade, tomb of Cyrus, 36, 179n12, 179n13
patronage, 51, 57, 59, 62, 70–72, 75–76, 80, 84–85, 90, 92, 95, 173n8, 183n84, 187n9; and agency, 27; for large-scale projects, 76–77. *See also* Hekatomnids
Pausanias, 53–54, 68; *2.24.1*, 67–68, 188n50; *5.21.2–5*, 54; *8.27.1*, 56; *8.27.3–6*, 54; *8.27.6*, 56; *8.37.1–6*, 55–56; *8.37.8*, 55
paving, 39, 48–49, 58, 68, 76, 91, 178n6, 182n71, 183n72, 183n73, 183n77, 189n58
Peace of Apamea, 79

Index

Pedersen, P., 59
Pednilessos, 78
Perachora, 37–38, 40, 51, 68, 82; Sanctuary of Hera Akraia, 51–52, *104*
performance: characteristics, 26, 176n13, 177n15; festival as, 28; and *ikria*, 9
Pergamon, 72, 80, 83, 90; ceded to Rome (133 B.C.), 72; Great Altar of Zeus, 8, 95; gymnasium, 76, 191n27; Sanctuary of Demeter, 23, 61, 69–71, 78, 84–85, *104*; temple of Dionysos, 80; temple of Hera Basileia, 80; temple above Upper Gymnasium, 80
Persian culture, 35–37, 39, 179n13, 179n14
Phaistos, theatral area, 35
phenomenological approach, 25, 81
Philetairos, 70–71, 84, 189n79, 193n84
Phrygian culture, 35–37, 39, 178n7
Pietrabbondante, 82, 84, 89–90, 92–94, *106*, 194n6
Pindar: *Olympian 39.71*, 63–64; *Tenth Nemean Ode*, 45
Piok Zanon, C., 70, 189n75, 189n79
Pisidia, 7, 27, 72, 78–80, 84, 89, 192n76. *See also* names of specific sites
pitch, 19–21, 38, 42, 47, 175n15, 180n29, 182n59, 190n24; change in, 43–44
platforms, 7–9, 19, 36, 41, 46–48, 63, 65, 67–69, 75, 93. *See also ikria*
Pliny: *Historia naturalis 34.41*, 186n1; *Historia naturalis 34.60*, 187n3; *Historia naturalis 36.4.31*, 179n14
Plutarch, *Pompey 42.4*, 90
Plynteria, 48–49, 83
podium, stepped, 36, 38, 80
podium temple, 80, 84, 92–94, 193n85
political dominance, 3, 173n1, 177n16; Argos and, 44–45, 50; association of monumental steps with, 5, 51, 95. *See also* synoikism
Pollux, Iulius, *Onomasticon 7.125*, 9, 174n47
pompe, 26, 29–32, 63–64, 71, 77, 82, 86; criteria for, 30; participation in, 48, 77
Pompeo, L., 39
portico, 43, 48, 62–63, 74–75, 83–84, 89–95, 179n9, 181n19, 191n43, 195n39
post-holes. *See ikria*
power: individual, 5, 41; symbolic, 27, 82
power relations, 26, 60–61. *See also* political dominance
practice theory, 25–26
Praeneste (Palestrina), 81–82, 84, 89–91, 93–95, 194n6; Sanctuary of Fortuna Primigenia, 93–94, *106*
processional routes, 31, 39, 58–59, 82, 84, 86, 185n54; Panathenaic Way, 65; Sacred Way, from Mylasa to Labraunda, 31–32, 57–59, 85. *See also pompe*

processions, 9, 26, 29–32, 38–39, 42–43, 46–47, 52, 63, 65, 68, 71, 73, 75–78, 83, 86, 90, 94, 190n9. *See also pompe*
proportions, for steps, 11, 42; change in, 43–44
propylaia, 57–59, 62, 188n39, 189n75
propylon, 69–71, 74, 76
prytaneion, 52, 185n60
Ptolemy II Philadelphos, 29, 75–76
public assembly, 5–6, 8–9, 36, 67, 71, 79, 91–92
public buildings, 51, 79, 174n39

quarrying, 38, 62, 179n7, 185n54

Radt, W., 36
railings, 39, 69
ramp, 20–21, 35–39, 42–44, 47–49, 66, 76, 82, 93–94, 175n15, 180n27, 180n29, 182n59; stepped, 21, 41
reconfiguration, of agora at Morgantina, 66–67
reconstruction, ancient. *See* renovation
reconstruction, modern: at Delos, 94; at Kameiros, 64–65; at Knidos, 77; at Kos, 73–74, 191n37; at Lindos, 62–64; at Perachora, 51–52; at Rhodes, 61–63; at Selinus, 39
renovation, 27, 76–77, 82–83, 89, 187n10, 188n39, 189n79, 189n84, 190n24; at Argive Heraion, 42–45, 85; at Athens, Kolonos Agoraios, 65–66; at Corinth, 70–71; at Eleusis, 8; at Kameiros, 65; at Kos, 74–76, 191n37; at Labraunda, 58; at Lindos, 31, 62–63, 71; at Lykosoura, 55–56; at Morgantina, 71; at Olympia, 54; at Oropos, 42; at Perachora, 51–52; at Pergamon, 70; at Rhodes, 61–62; at Selinus, 41; at Thasos, 69
restoration. *See* renovation
retaining wall, 7, 21, 37, 39, 82; at Alipheira, 41–42; at Argos, 41, 43–44, 68, 184n17, 184n28, 189n84; at Athens, 47–48, 60; at Corinth, 45, 180n29; at Didyma, 8, 69; at Dreros, 37, 40; at Knidos, 77–78; at Kos, 74; at Labraunda, 57; at Lykosoura, 55, 60; at Morgantina, 67; at Olympia, 23, 53–54, 60, 83; at Perachora, 40; at Selinus, 39–41, 82, 180n1, 180n3, 189n84; at Sulmo, 91; at Thasos, 68
reuse, of existing elements, 35, 42, 47–48, 58, 66
Rhodes City, 54, 61–65, 71, 90; Precinct of Apollo Pythios, 61–62, *104*–5, 187n10
riser (vertical face), 19
risk of falling, 48, 175n21
ritual, 43, 75; and change, 28; as cultural performance, 29

Ritual Dynamics, 6, 177n23
Romanization, 89–90, 193n1, 194n26
Romano, D. G., 54, 184n32
Rome: new construction in, 90; Theater of Pompey, 194n16
roof, 45, 49, 79, 179n14; stepped, 36, 179n14
routes of access, 38, 50–52, 58, 60–61, 66–68, 76, 78, 82, 181n27; changing, 27, 63, 77
Roux, G., 68–69, 189n58, 189n66

sacred and secular, distinction between, 23–24
sacred grove, 59, 92; at Gabii, 92; at Kos, 73–76, 84
Sacred Way, from Mylasa to Labraunda, 31–32, 57–59, 85
sacrifice, 29–31, 45–46, 50, 63–64, 75, 77, 84; human, 54
Sagalassos, 78; Temple of Zeus (Kakasbos), 80, *105*
sanctuaries, 28; as locus for monumental steps, 3, 51, 84–85; and synoikism, 56–59, 85. *See also* names of specific sites
Sardis: conquest of, 179n13; Pyramid Tomb, 36, 179n13
Scamozzi, Vincent, 19, 175n5
Schäfer, J., 35
Schazmann, P., 73, 190n19, 191n27
Schwandner, E.-L., 76
Scott, M., 6, 174n27
Scranton, R., 6
seating, theatral, 46, 176n25
seating capacity, 4, 26–27, 38, 46, 70, 77–79, 81, 183n74, 183n81, 194n19, 194n24; at Erechtheion, 49; at Kolonos Agoraios, 50; at Labraunda, 60; at Lato, 52. *See also* sitting; standing; standing room
Selinus, 37, 40, 50, 60, 67–68; Acropolis, 38–39, *105*; temple at Triolo North, 39; Temple C, 21, 41; Temple M, 39, 82, *105*, 194n21; Temple of Malophoros, 39; Temple of Zeus Meilichios, 39
shared experience, 45, 59, 84–85, 181n26. *See also* observing; processions; spectators; viewing
Sia, 7, 79
Sicily, 4, 7, 37, 41, 66, 75, 194n8, 194n10. *See also* Morgantina; Selinus
side doorways, in temples, 55
sitting, 37, 42, 45–47, 52, 55, 66–70, 77–79, 179n23, 183n74, 184n37. *See also* standing; walking
slope. *See* pitch
Social War, 89–90
Sourvinou-Inwood, C., 6, 31
space: existential, 30–31; and place, 25
spatial segmentation, 26–27

Index

spectators, 9–15, 23, 27, 37, 43–44, 46, 50, 53, 55, 69–70, 185n42, 192n56, 194n19
spring houses, 57, 74
stabilization of terrain, 67, 70, 74, 78
stadium, 54, 58, 61
Staii family, 92
stairway: at Argive Heraion, 43, 50; at Athens, 48, 50, 65–66; at Corinth, 45–46, 71, 83; at Cyrene, 7; at Didyma, 8; at Gordion, 35–36; at Halikarnassos, 59; at Kameiros, 64–65; at Kos, 74–77, 86, 95; at Labraunda (Great Stairway), 57, 60, 71, 83; at Lato, 23; at Lindos, 62–64, 83; at Perachora, 51; at Pergamon, 70; at Praeneste, 84, 93–94; at Sagalassos, 80; at Tivoli, 94
standing, 37, 45–47, 52, 65–69, 79, 183n74, 184n37
standing room, 46, 49, 52–53, 183n74
statuary: sculptural group of Demeter and Despoina with Anytos and Artemis (Lykosoura), 55–56; statue of Athena (Lindos), 187n8; statue of Helios by Lysippos, 187n3; statue of Helios in his quadriga (Rhodes), 62; Zanes (Olympia), 53–54
statue bases: at Kameiros, 65; at Kos, 74; at Lykosoura, 55; at Mount Lykaion, 54; for Zanes, 53
Stevens, G. P., 48, 182n65
stoa: at Aegina, 39; at Argos, 43–44, 67–68, 181n19; at Athens, 49; at Corinth, 71; at Kameiros, 64–65, 191n27; at Kos, 74–76; at Labraunda, 57–58, 186n64; at Lato, 52; at Lindos, 28, 38, 62–64, 83, 86, 95, 187n13, 187n24; at Lykosoura, 55–56; at Mount Lykaion, 54, 184n32; at Perachora, 51, 183n4; at Pergamon, 70; at Sulmo, 91; at Thasos, 68
Strabo, 185n54; *14.2.5*, 186n1; *14.2.23*, 57; *659*, 58
Stronach, D., 36, 179n12
Stroud, R., 70
structuration, 26
Sulmo (Sulmona), 90–93, 194n27; Sanctuary of Hercules, 90–92, *106*

Sumi, G., 75
symmetry, 4, 39, 44, 63–64, 71, 76, 81, 83–85, 89, 92–93
synhedrion (meeting place), 50
synoikism, 31–32, 44–45, 54–56, 58, 61–65, 72–73, 85, 185n50, 190n4
syrinx, 31, 178n6

Taş Kule, tomb at, 36
Telesterion, 38
temple. *See* sanctuaries; *names of specific sites*
Templer, J., 20, 175n11
Termessos, 78–79
terms for steps, German: *Schautreppen*, 175n19; *Sitzstufen*, 175n19, 181n10; *Stufenmauer*, 53; *Stutzmauer*, 175n19
terraces, connected, 42–47, 50, 72
Terracina, 91, 93
terracing, 42–45, 50, 57, 59, 61, 64–65, 67, 74, 77, 84, 91, 93, 181n19
Thasos, Sanctuary of Herakles (Herakleion), 61, 68–69, 71, 105
theater, 8–9, 23–24, 53, 59, 89–90; cultic, 5, 184n12; Greek, 42, 78, 92, 176n15, 176n25; Roman, 78, 92–94
theater temple, 91–94
theatral area, 27, 35, 46–47, 49, 70, 93, 182n54
theatral court, 48–49, 82–83
theatral steps, 7, 9, 23, 26, 36, 42, 45–46, 49, 55, 60, 70, 77–78, 84, 87, 94
theatron, 37, 42, 53
Themelis, P., 56
theoroi, 75
Thesmophoria, 70
Thucydides, 23; *1.67*, 176n28; *1.87.3*, 176n28; *1.129.3*, 193n11; *6.13.1*, 176n28; *8.76*, 176n28
Tilley, C., 30
Tiryns, 32, 44, 82, 85
Tivoli, 81–82, 89–91, 194n6; Sanctuary of Hercules Victor, 93–94, *106*
tomb, 36–37, 58; of Mausolos, 59–60
Tomlinson, R. A., 68, 182n55, 183n8
transporting, of stone blocks, 57, 182n59
tread (horizontal surface), 19

treasury, 53–54, 57, 77
treaty, between Termessos and Adada, 78–79
Treaty of Apamaea (189 B.C.), 72
Triopion, 78

Umholtz, G., 58
urban relocation, 31–32, 42. *See also metoikesis*; synoikism

Vandeput, L., 80
Vanhaverbeke, H., 80
Van Nijf, O. M., 6
vase paintings, 9–15, 23, 29–30, 40, 177n4, 178n12; Athens NM 15499, 10–11, 174n51; Berlin 1711, 174n53; Florence 3773, 11, 174n53; London British Museum (GR1879.10–4.1, vase B80), 177n4; Paris Cabinet des Médailles 243, 11–15, 175n56; Private Collection, 29–30; Tampa ex Noble, 15; Vatican Astarita 565, 11, 175n55
vaulting, Roman use of, 93
viewing, 7–9, 21, 23, 26, 37–39, 47–51, 53–55, 60, 65, 70, 75, 77–78, 82. *See also* spectators
Vitruvius, 19; *2.8.10–11*, 58
votive offerings, 46–47, 50–51, 70, 180n3, 189n84

Waelkens, M., 80, 192n65, 193n82, 193n85
walking, 31, 57, 66–67, 75, 178n9
Wescoat, B., 6
wheeled vehicles, and ramps, 21
Williamson, C., 6
Wilson, P., 6
wood, lost stepped structures of, 3. *See also ikria*

xenon, 54
Xenophon, 23; *Anabasis 7.1.33*, 176n28; *Cyropaedia 7.4.5*, 179n13; *Hellenica 7.4.28*, 53

Zanes (Olympia), 53–54
Zedeño, M. N., 5, 176n13
Zeus: as Alseios, 73; Sosipolis, 29–30; Thenatas, 35

Wisconsin Studies in Classics

Patricia A. Rosenmeyer, Laura McClure, and Mark Stansbury-O'Donnell, Series Editors

E. A. Thompson
Romans and Barbarians: The Decline of the Western Empire

H. I. Marrou
A History of Education in Antiquity
Histoire de l'Education dans l'Antiquité, translated by George Lamb

Jennifer Tolbert Roberts
Accountability in Athenian Government

Erika Simon
Festivals of Attica: An Archaeological Commentary

Warren G. Moon, editor
Ancient Greek Art and Iconography

G. Michael Woloch
Roman Cities: Les villes romaines by Pierre Grimal, translated and edited by G. Michael Woloch, together with A Descriptive Catalogue of Roman Cities by G. Michael Woloch

Katherine Dohan Morrow
Greek Footwear and the Dating of Sculpture

John Kevin Newman
The Classical Epic Tradition

Jeanny Vorys Canby, Edith Porada, Brunilde Sismondo Ridgway, and Tamara Stech, editors
Ancient Anatolia: Aspects of Change and Cultural Development

Ann Norris Michelini
Euripides and the Tragic Tradition

Wendy J. Raschke, editor
The Archaeology of the Olympics: The Olympics and Other Festivals in Antiquity

Paul Plass
Wit and the Writing of History: The Rhetoric of Historiography in Imperial Rome

Barbara Hughes Fowler
The Hellenistic Aesthetic

F. M. Clover and R. S. Humphreys, editors
Tradition and Innovation in Late Antiquity

Brunilde Sismondo Ridgway
Hellenistic Sculpture I: The Styles of ca. 331–200 B.C.

Barbara Hughes Fowler, editor and translator
Hellenistic Poetry: An Anthology

Kathryn J. Gutzwiller
Theocritus' Pastoral Analogies: The Formation of a Genre

Vimala Begley and Richard Daniel De Puma, editors
Rome and India: The Ancient Sea Trade

Rudolf Blum
Hans H. Wellisch, translator
Kallimachos: The Alexandrian Library and the Origins of Bibliography

David Castriota
Myth, Ethos, and Actuality: Official Art in Fifth Century B.C. Athens

Barbara Hughes Fowler, editor and translator
Archaic Greek Poetry: An Anthology

John H. Oakley and Rebecca H. Sinos
The Wedding in Ancient Athens

Richard Daniel De Puma and Jocelyn Penny Small, editors
Murlo and the Etruscans: Art and Society in Ancient Etruria

Judith Lynn Sebesta and Larissa Bonfante, editors
The World of Roman Costume

Jennifer Larson
Greek Heroine Cults

Warren G. Moon, editor
Polykleitos, the Doryphoros, and Tradition

Paul Plass
The Game of Death in Ancient Rome: Arena Sport and Political Suicide

Margaret S. Drower
Flinders Petrie: A Life in Archaeology

Susan B. Matheson
Polygnotos and Vase Painting in Classical Athens

Jenifer Neils, editor
Worshipping Athena: Panathenaia and Parthenon

Pamela A. Webb
Hellenistic Architectural Sculpture: Figural Motifs in Western Anatolia and the Aegean Islands

Brunilde Sismondo Ridgway
Fourth-Century Styles in Greek Sculpture

Lucy Goodison and Christine Morris, editors
Ancient Goddesses: The Myths and the Evidence

Jo-Marie Claassen
Displaced Persons: The Literature of Exile from Cicero to Boethius

Brunilde Sismondo Ridgway
Hellenistic Sculpture II: The Styles of ca. 200–100 B.C.

Pat Getz-Gentle
Personal Styles in Early Cycladic Sculpture

Catullus
David Mulroy, translator and commentator
The Complete Poetry of Catullus

Brunilde Sismondo Ridgway
Hellenistic Sculpture III: The Styles of ca. 100–31 B.C.

Angeliki Kosmopoulou
The Iconography of Sculptured Statue Bases in the Archaic and Classical Periods

Sara H. Lindheim
Mail and Female: Epistolary Narrative and Desire in Ovid's "Heroides"

Graham Zanker
Modes of Viewing in Hellenistic Poetry and Art

Alexandra Ann Carpino
Discs of Splendor: The Relief Mirrors of the Etruscans

Timothy S. Johnson
A Symposion of Praise: Horace Returns to Lyric in "Odes" IV

Jean-René Jannot
Religion in Ancient Etruria
Devins, Dieux et Démons: Regards sur la religion de l'Etrurie antique, translated by Jane K. Whitehead

Catherine Schlegel
Satire and the Threat of Speech: Horace's "Satires," Book 1

Christopher A. Faraone and Laura K. McClure, editors
Prostitutes and Courtesans in the Ancient World

Plautus
John Henderson, translator and commentator
Asinaria: The One about the Asses

Patrice D. Rankine
Ulysses in Black: Ralph Ellison, Classicism, and African American Literature

Paul Rehak
John G. Younger, editor
Imperium and Cosmos: Augustus and the Northern Campus Martius

Patricia J. Johnson
Ovid before Exile: Art and Punishment in the "Metamorphoses"

Vered Lev Kenaan
Pandora's Senses: The Feminine Character of the Ancient Text

Erik Gunderson
Nox Philologiae: Aulus Gellius and the Fantasy of the Roman Library

Sinclair Bell and Helen Nagy, editors
New Perspectives on Etruria and Early Rome

Barbara Pavlock
The Image of the Poet in Ovid's "Metamorphoses"

Paul Cartledge and Fiona Rose Greenland, editors
Responses to Oliver Stone's "Alexander": Film, History, and Cultural Studies

Amalia Avramidou
The Codrus Painter: Iconography and Reception of Athenian Vases in the Age of Pericles

Shane Butler
The Matter of the Page: Essays in Search of Ancient and Medieval Authors

Allison Glazebrook and Madeleine Henry, editors
Greek Prostitutes in the Ancient Mediterranean, 800 BCE–200 CE

Norman Austin
Sophocles' "Philoctetes" and the Great Soul Robbery

Sophocles
A verse translation by David Mulroy, with introduction and notes
Oedipus Rex

John Andreau and Raymond Descat
The Slave in Greece and Rome
Esclave en Grèce et à Rome, translated by Marion Leopold

Amanda Wilcox
The Gift of Correspondence in Classical Rome: Friendship in Cicero's "Ad Familiares" and Seneca's "Moral Epistles"

Mark Buchan
Perfidy and Passion: Reintroducing the "Iliad"

Sophocles
A verse translation by David Mulroy, with introduction and notes
Antigone

Geoffrey W. Bakewell
Aeschylus's "Suppliant Women": The Tragedy of Immigration

Elizabeth Paulette Baughan
Couched in Death: "Klinai" and Identity in Anatolia and Beyond

Benjamin Eldon Stevens
Silence in Catullus

Horace
Translated with commentary by David R. Slavitt
Odes

Mary B. Hollinshead
Shaping Ceremony: Monumental Steps and Greek Architecture

Martial
Translated with notes by Susan McLean
Selected Epigrams

Ovid
A verse translation by Julia Dyson Hejduk, with introduction and notes
The Offense of Love: "Ars Amatoria," "Remedia Amoris," and "Tristia" 2

Sophocles
A verse translation by David Mulroy, with introduction and notes
Oedipus at Colonus

www.ingramcontent.com/pod-product-compliance
Lightning Source LLC
Chambersburg PA
CBHW081152290426
44108CB00018B/2520